THE GREATER PARIS GUIDE

THE GREATER PARIS GUIDE

The Publisher

Magasins Généraux is a cultural space founded by BETC in 2017 on the banks of the Canal de l'Ourcq in Pantin. A laboratory where different creative fields meet with a year-round programme of exhibitions and events open to all, Magasins Généraux believes that the future is being invented in Greater Paris.
magasinsgeneraux.com

The Translator

Marc Feustel is a writer, editor and translator specialized in photography, contemporary art, design, architecture and urban issues.
marcfeustel.com

The Authors

The journalists from Enlarge your Paris, an independent local media platform, have been exploring Greater Paris since 2013, with a special focus on culture and what goes on beyond the périphérique. Every week, they send their newsletter of weekend outings in Greater Paris to over 80,000 subscribers. They also regularly organize events or hikes to discover the landscapes and cultural treasures beyond the Paris walls.
enlargeyourparis.fr

DISCLAIMER

The entries that appear in *The Greater Paris Guide* were chosen by journalists from the editorial staff of Enlarge your Paris and the Magasins Généraux team. This subjective selection aims to show the diversity of Greater Paris on both sides of the *périphérique*. Each location was visited at least once by the authors. However, it is possible that some of the information in this guide may no longer be up-to-date. An updated edition of this guide will be published in 2026.

GREATER PARIS, A 12,000-KM² SPORTS FIELD

What if Greater Paris were the largest low-carbon sports ground in the world? It may come as a surprise, but once you get to know it better, the Greater Paris region is tailor-made for sport.

With its 390 train stations outside Paris itself, it forms a gigantic stadium covering 12,000 km^2 that connects natural areas larger than inner Paris and world-class facilities that are accessible to all.

Thanks to the R line of the Transilien network, you can go climbing in the Fontainebleau forest and visit its château on the same outing. Because that's what Greater Paris is all about too: a cultural heritage and scene that's unrivalled anywhere else in the world. Sport, nature and culture are the keywords in this guide to experiencing and exploring Greater Paris in a different way.

Proof that tourism is good for you!

THE TEN MAJOR DISTRICTS OF GREATER PARIS

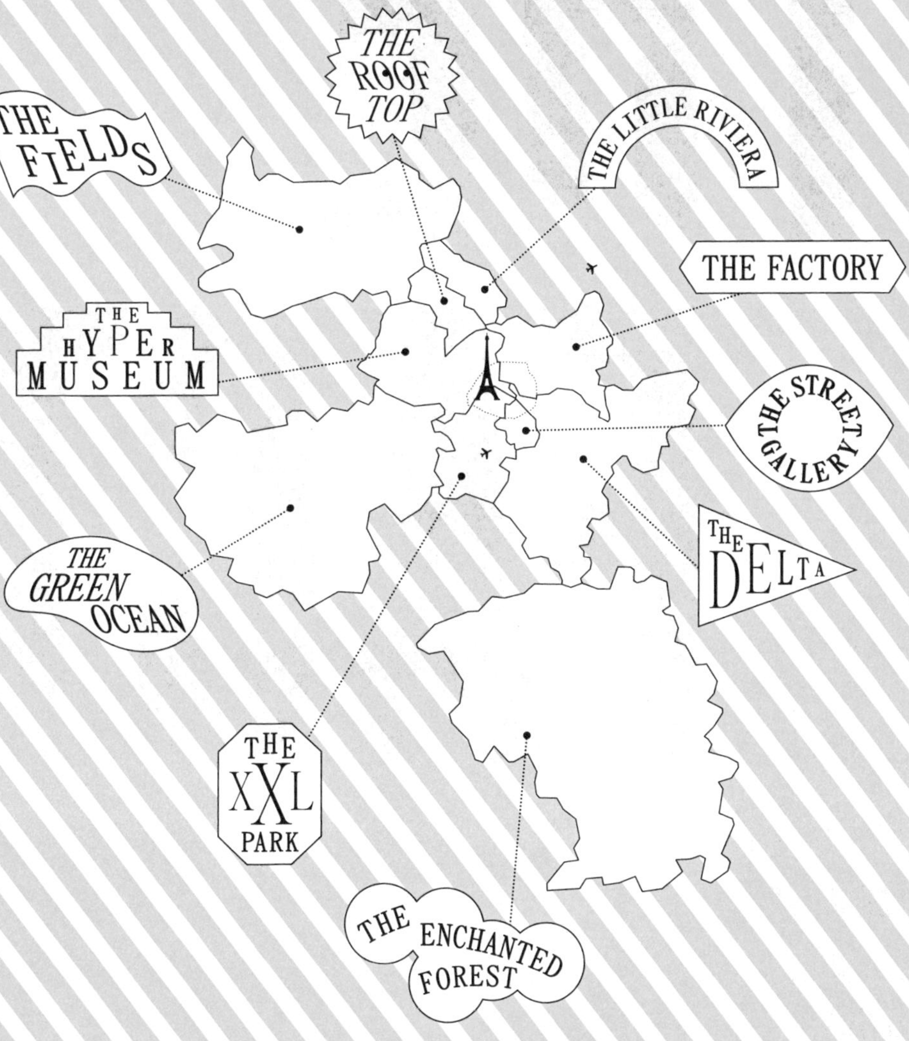
THE ROOF TOP
THE FIELDS
THE LITTLE RIVIERA
THE FACTORY
THE HYPER MUSEUM
THE STREET GALLERY
THE DELTA
THE GREEN OCEAN
THE XXL PARK
THE ENCHANTED FOREST

THE FACT

AUBERVILLIERS
BAGNOLET
BOBIGNY
BONDY

CLICHY-SOUS-BOIS
DRANCY
LA COURNEUVE
LA PLAINE SAINT-DENIS

MONTREUIL
NEUILLY-PLAISANCE
NEUILLY-SUR-MARNE

LE BOURGET
LIVRY-GARGAN

ORY

PANTIN
PARIS
ROISSY-EN-FRANCE
ROMAINVILLE
SAINT-DENIS
SAINT-OUEN

While the Île de la Cité could be considered the cradle of Paris, the incubator of Greater Paris might well be located in Seine-Saint-Denis in the northeast of Paris. From the Canal Saint-Martin to the working class *cités* of Seine-Saint-Denis, a new approach to the city is emerging in these diverse and inventive districts where fortune favours the bold. Urban farmers, artists, makers, architects and local citizens have made the industrial wastelands of this vast area their land of opportunity in the hope of creating the conditions for a more sustainable city. A work in progress that is as promising as it is inspiring.

THE FACTORY

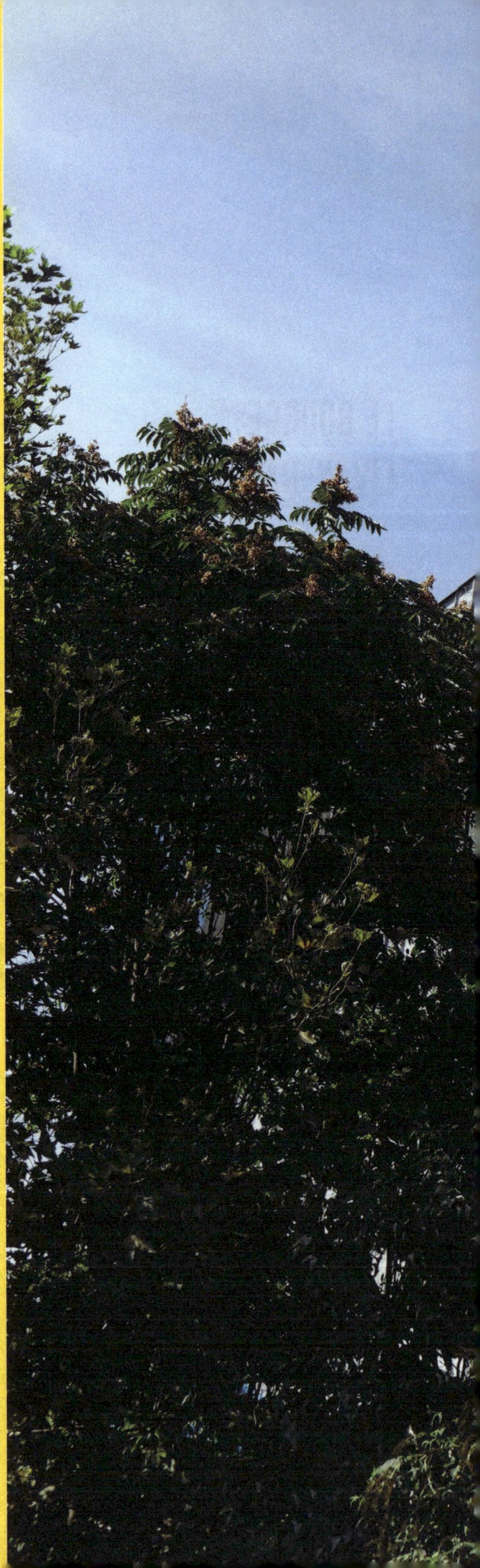

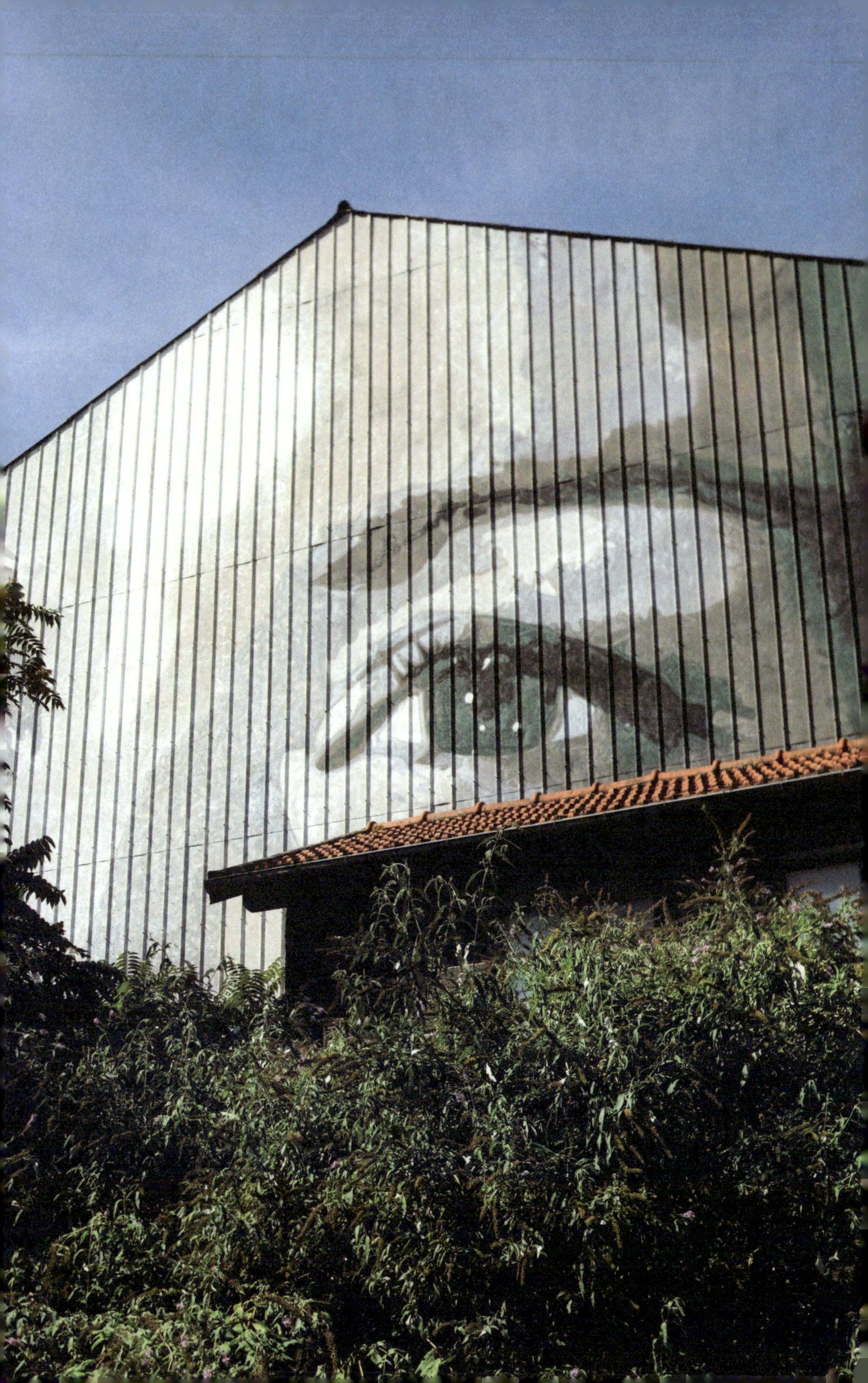

THE FACTORY

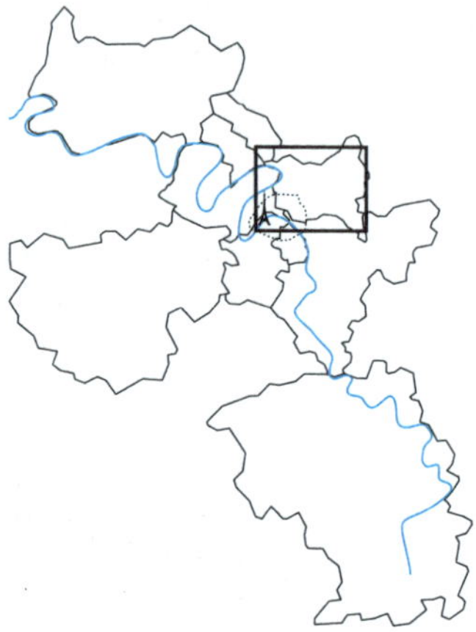

SPORT

01 HOOPS FACTORY
02 CLIMB UP CLIMBING GYM
03 GOLF DÉPARTEMENTAL DE LA POUDRERIE
04 PISCINE ALICE-MILLIAT
05 SAND FABRIK

CULTURE

06 THÉATRE DE LA COMMUNE
07 THÉATRE ÉQUESTRE ZINGARO
08 CANAL 93
09 MC 93
10 ATELIERS MÉDICIS
11 MÉMORIAL DE LA SHOAH
12 ACADÉMIE FRATELLINI
13 CENTRE NATIONAL DE LA DANSE
14 GALERIE THADDAEUS ROPAC
15 MAGASINS GÉNÉRAUX
16 CIRQUE ÉLECTRIQUE
17 PHILHARMONIE DE PARIS
18 KOMUNUMA
19 BASILIQUE CATHÉDRALE SAINT-DENIS

LIFESTYLE

20 LE SAMPLE
21 LE CHINOIS
22 LA MARBRERIE
23 LES TATAS FLINGUEUSES
24 DOCK B
25 CENTQUATRE
26 LA GARE - LE GORE
27 LE HASARD LUDIQUE
28 KILOMÈTRE25
29 PAVILLON DES CANAUX
30 LA RECYCLERIE
31 LA STATION - GARE DES MINES
32 PARIS-CHARLES DE GAULLE AIRPORT
33 6B
34 SAINT-DENIS MARKET
35 FERME URBAINE DE SAINT-DENIS
36 LA FABRIQUE DU MÉTRO
37 SAINT-OUEN FLEA MARKET

OUTDOORS

38 PARC JEAN MOULIN - LES GUILANDS
39 PARC GEORGES-VALBON
40 PARC DE LA HAUTE-ÎLE
41 BASSIN DE LA VILLETTE
42 BUTTES-CHAUMONT
43 PETITE CEINTURE

WHERE TO EAT

44 FLEUR D'ORIENT
45 KEBAB EV'ET BY SAMY
46 LE BISTROT DES PIANOS
47 GYPSE
48 ISOLÉ
49 LES PANTINS
50 CAFÉ LE 19M
51 CAFÉ-FLEURISTE DÉSIRÉE
52 CANTINE DU JARDIN21
53 LE RIPAILLEUR

FAMILY

54 MUSÉE DE L'AIR ET DE L'ESPACE
55 LA VILLETTE

WHERE TO SLEEP

56 CAMPING LES RIVES DE PARIS
57 MOB HÔTEL

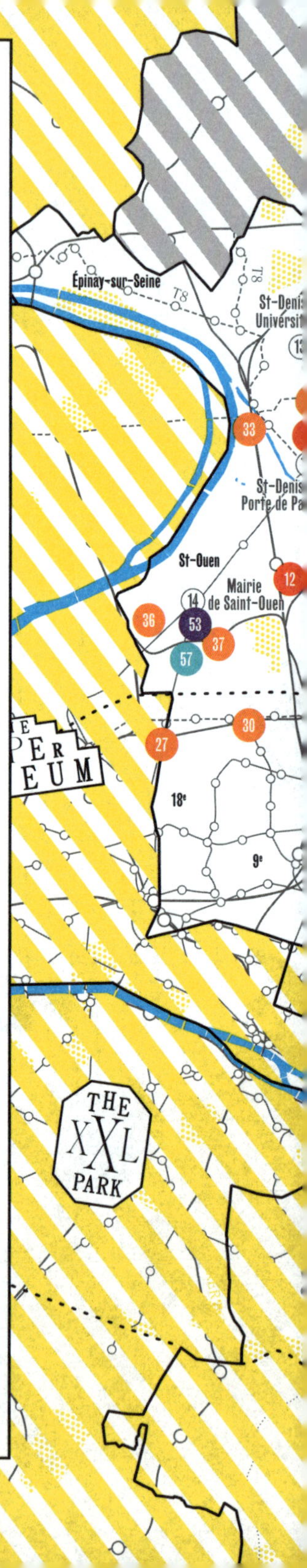

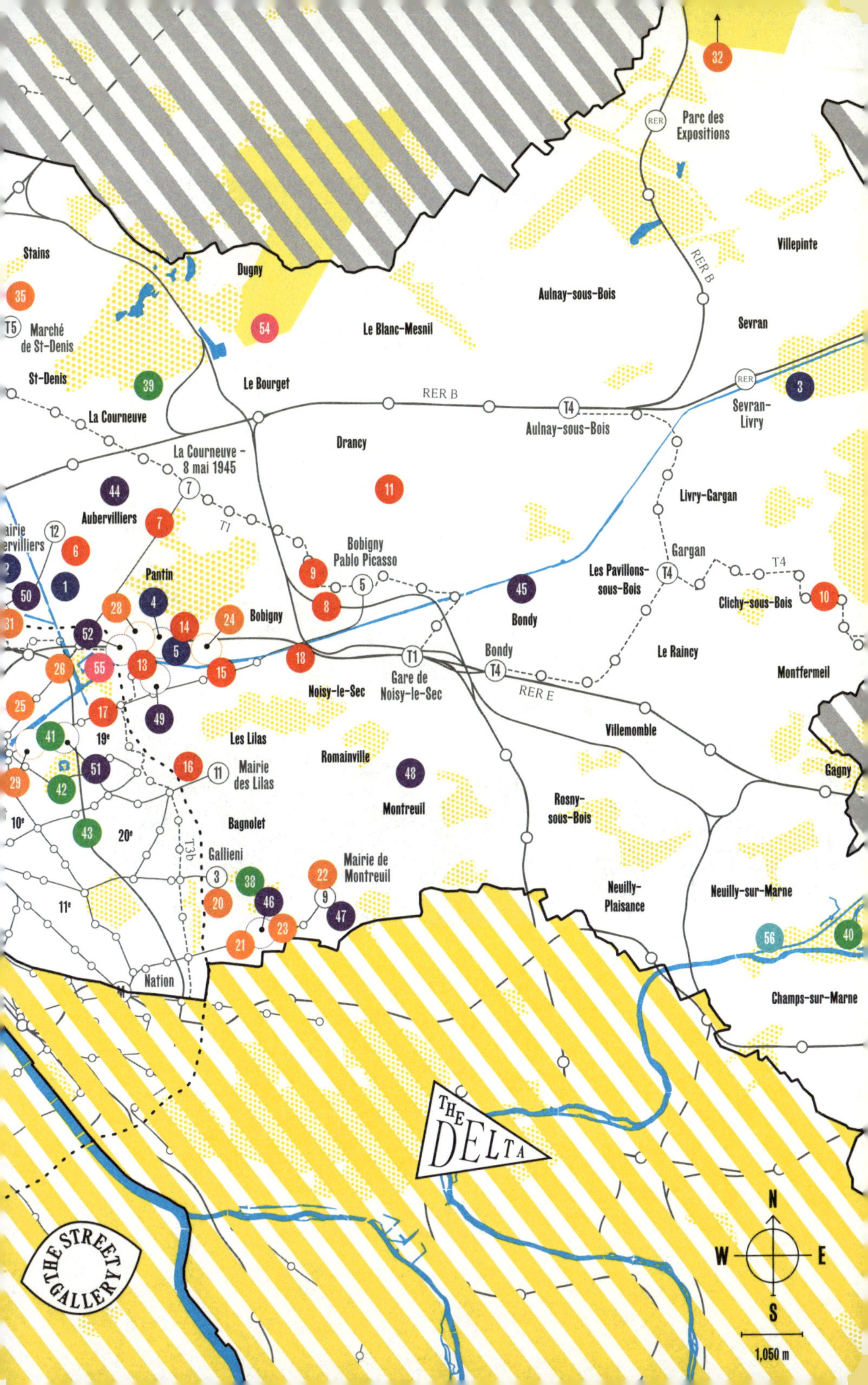

Parc des Expositions
RER
RER B
Villepinte
Aulnay-sous-Bois
Sevran
Stains
Dugny
Le Blanc-Mesnil
T5
Marché de St-Denis
St-Denis
Le Bourget
La Courneuve
RER B
T4
Aulnay-sous-Bois
Sevran-Livry
Drancy
La Courneuve - 8 mai 1945
Aubervilliers
T1
Livry-Gargan
Bobigny Pablo Picasso
Gargan
T4
Les Pavillons-sous-Bois
Clichy-sous-Bois
Pantin
Bobigny
Bondy
Le Rainçy
Bondy
Montfermeil
Gare de Noisy-le-Sec
RER E
Noisy-le-Sec
Villemomble
19e
Les Lilas
Romainville
Mairie des Lilas
Gagny
Rosny-sous-Bois
10e
20e
Bagnolet
Montreuil
T3b
Gallieni
Mairie de Montreuil
Neuilly-Plaisance
Neuilly-sur-Marne
11e
Nation
Champs-sur-Marne
THE DELTA
THE STREET GALLERY
N
W
E
S
1,050 m

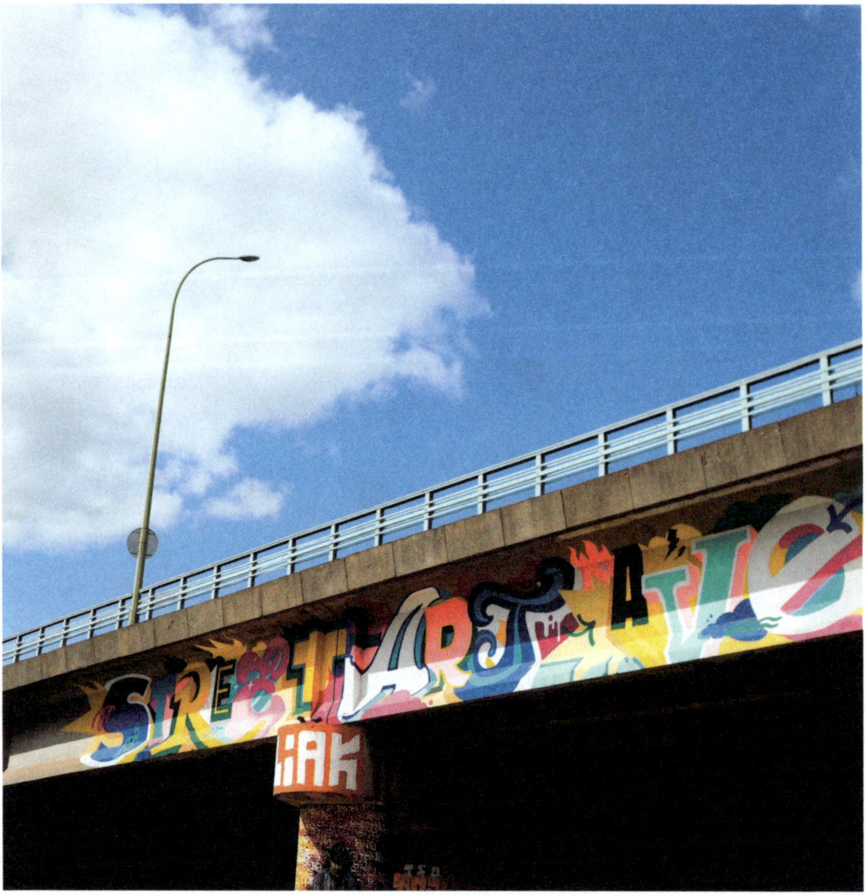

Street art is on the up | *Quai de l'Allier, Paris.*

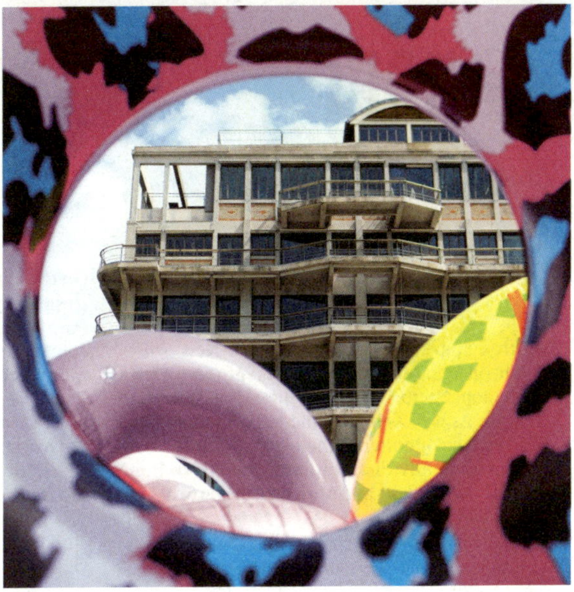

Squaring the circle | *Magasins Généraux, Pantin.*

5-point basket | *Pigalle Basketball, Paris.*

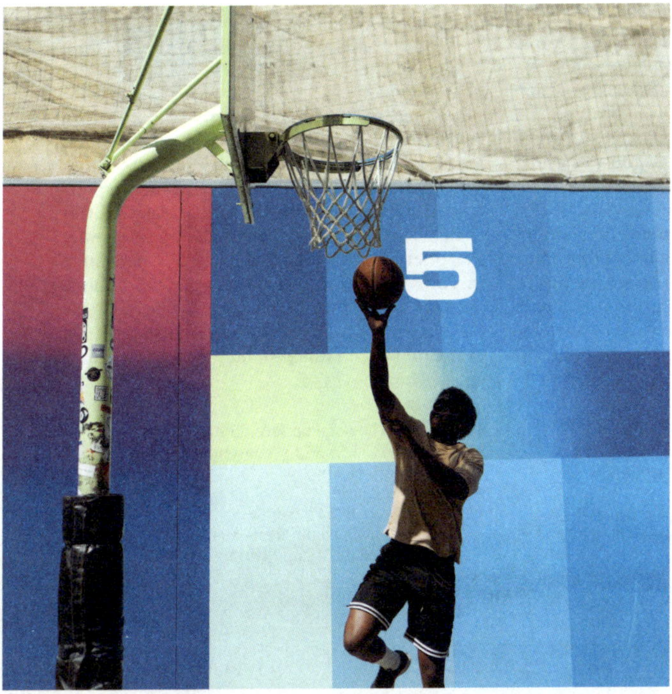

sport

AUBERVILLIERS

01 HOOPS FACTORY

#BASKETBALL #NBASTYLE
#NOTHINGBUTNET

With a sparkling court worthy of New York's Madison Square Garden or LA's Crypto.com Arena, the Hoops Factory in Aubervilliers is a basketball temple. As well as being able to book courts and find worthy opponents, the Hoops Factory offers group and individual training sessions to hone your shooting skills and work on your vertical leap.

Price: from €5.
Open daily.

3, rue Pierre Larousse, 93300 Aubervilliers
Tel: +33 (0)1 72 59 88 99 / hoopsfactory.com

- M — Line 7: Aubervilliers – Pantin – Quatre Chemins, M — Line 12: Aimé Césaire
- Bus — 139: Karman-Félix Faure
- Vélib' — Boulevard Félix Faure, Aubervilliers

02 CLIMB UP CLIMBING GYM

#REACHFORTHESKY
#OPENTOALL #CAFE

Opened in 2022, the Climb Up climbing gym is one of the largest indoor climbing complexes in the world. With 7,000 m² of floor space, of which 5,000 m² is devoted exclusively to climbing, the space is huge, with routes that reach right up to the ceiling. In total, there are over 500 routes – which get updated every three months –and 170 metres of bouldering, which changes every six weeks. Novices can try out the fun climbing area, where they can (among other things) climb a reproduction of the Tetris game, or take private lessons to learn the basics of climbing (climbing as a pair, belaying, etc.). And as a reward for your exertions, the Climb Kitchen has a great menu to help you recharge your batteries.

Price: from €10.
Open daily.

111, avenue Victor Hugo, 93300 Aubervilliers
Tel: +33 (0)1 77 37 37 87 / aubervilliers.climb-up.fr

- M — Line 12: Aimé Césaire
- Bus — 45, 139: Quai Lucien Lefranc, Aubervilliers
- Vélib' — Boulevard Félix-Faure, Aubervilliers

LIVRY-GARGAN

03 GOLF DÉPARTEMENTAL DE LA POUDRERIE

#GOLFFORALL #CANALSIDE
#FREETRYOUT

On the banks of the Canal de l'Ourcq, a 1-km walk from Livry-Gargan RER station and next to the Parc Forestier de la Poudrerie, the Poudrerie golf course, designed by the Seine-Saint-Denis departmental council and managed by UCPA, has set itself the aim of making the sport accessible. In practical terms, this means affordable prices: from €14 for adults to play the 9-hole course, and €11.85 for children. On Sundays, you can even take part in a free introductory session between 1.30pm and 3.30pm (booking required on 01 41 52 19 30). The club house is open to everyone for a drink with a view of the greens.

Price: from €14 for a 9-hole round / €11.85 for children.
Open daily.

Allée Paul Vieille, 93190 Livry-Gargan
Tel: +33 (0)1 41 52 19 30
ucpa.com/centres-sportifs/golf-poudrerie

- RER — B: Sevran-Livry
- Bus — 623: Square Henri Legrand

PANTIN

04 PISCINE ALICE-MILLIAT

#HERITAGE #ARTDECO
#GLASSROOF

Reopened in 2022 after extensive renovation work, the Alice-Milliat swimming pool (named after a swimmer from the early twentieth century who made a great contribution to women's sport) is an Art Deco jewel from the inter-war period. Get changed in the first floor cabins along passageways that offer a bird's-eye view of the pool. Once you're in your swimming costume, you can choose between the historic 33-metre pool (the right size for competitions in the 1930s) with its glass roof, or the more fun, family-friendly 25-metre pool.

Price: from €2.20 to €5.50.
Open daily.

49, avenue du Général Leclerc, 93500 Pantin
Tel: +33 (0)1 83 74 56 60 / est-ensemble.fr/piscine-pantin

- M — Line 5: Hoche
- RER — E: Pantin
- Tram — T3b: Ella Fitzgerald
- Bus — 151, 249: Pantin RER – Mairie
- Vélib' — Quai de l'Aisne, Pantin

05 SAND FABRIK

#BEACHSPORTS #FEETINTHESAND #ENDLESSSUMMER

You don't need the sea to enjoy beach sports. With the Sand Fabrik, located in a 1,000 m² former warehouse in Pantin, you can play beach volleyball, beach tennis, beach soccer, beach rugby, beach handball and beachminton all year round on sand imported from Fontainebleau. And because you're sure to work up an appetite, the Sand Fabrik saves you the hassle of bringing your cooler, by serving up poke bowls, burgers and cocktails. Tie to hit the beach!

Price: €10 per person. Open daily. Bookings on sandfabrik.com or by phone on +33 (0)1 88 12 00 04

45, rue Delizy, 93500 Pantin

- RER — E: Pantin
- Vélib' — Rue Delizy, Pantin

culture

AUBERVILLIERS

06 THÉÂTRE DE LA COMMUNE

#THEATREOFIDEAS #SOCIALENGAGEMENT #THEATREFORALL

What role can theatre play in one of the poorest cities in France? Marie-José Malis asked herself this question upon arriving at the head of the Théâtre de La Commune in Aubervilliers in January 2014. One of her answers was to launch a cycle entitled *Pièces d'actualité*, which aims to depict local inhabitants' reality. She has also supported the creation of the École des actes, a truly committed initiative which brings together people from different backgrounds. The bar-restaurant overlooking Parc Stalingrad is a great place to have lunch or relax and work over a cup of coffee.

2, rue Édouard Poisson, 93300 Aubervilliers
Tel: +33 (0)1 48 33 16 16 / lacommune-aubervilliers.fr

- M — Line 7: Aubervilliers-Pantin-Quatre Chemins, then bus 150 or 170: André Karman
- Vélib' — Rue André Karman, Aubervilliers
- Free return shuttles to Paris from Tuesday to Friday stopping at Porte de la Villette, Stalingrad, Gare de l'Est, Châtelet

07 THÉÂTRE ÉQUESTRE ZINGARO

#EQUESTRIANBALLET #VIRTUOSITY #BARTABAS

The Zingaro venue alone is worth a visit. Created by the architect Patrick Bouchain, this wooden building next to the fort of Aubervilliers, a former military enclosure that is about to be transformed into an eco-neighbourhood, serves as the setting for the troupe of the horseman and director Bartabas. Designed so as to fully immerse spectators, the Zingaro Equestrian Theatre creates its own universe with its stables and caravans. Since 1989, shows combining equestrian art, theatre, dance and music have set the stage alight. On performance evenings, a restaurant with a magical atmosphere can cater for up to 500 people.

176, avenue Jean-Jaurès, 93300 Aubervilliers
Tel: +33 (0)1 48 39 18 03 / bartabas.fr

- M — Line 7: Fort d'Aubervilliers
- Bus — 250, 330: Fort d'Aubervilliers / 134, 234: Fort d'Aubervilliers-Métro
- Vélib' — Avenue Jean Jaurès, Aubervilliers

BOBIGNY

08 CANAL 93

#CONCERTS #SCHOOLOFURBANARTS #FROMROCKTOHIPHOP

In its twenty years of existence, Canal 93 has built a solid reputation. This little jewel of a concert hall vibrates to the sound of rock and hip-hop and makes its equipment (rehearsal studios, recording studio) available to amateurs and professionals alike. Canal 93 also hosts the École des arts urbains (School of Urban Arts) which specializes in music, dance, comedy, theatre and film and is open to all from the age of 12.

63, avenue Jean Jaurès, 93300 Bobigny
Tel: +33 (0)1 49 91 10 50 / canal93.net

- M — Line 5: Bobigny-Pablo Picasso
- Bus — 301: Louise Michel

09 MC 93

#THEATRE#SHARING
#UNLIMITEDACCESS

In the cultural mosaic of Greater Paris, the MC93 public theatre is a key player that promotes access to culture for all. In addition to its pioneering programming including theatre, dance and live music, it launched the Fabrique d'expériences, which aims to bring people from diverse backgrounds together by allowing the public to participate in pre-shows, workshops and adult education sessions. The venue has three performance spaces, a café-restaurant and a bookshop. It's also a great place to have lunch or to grab some food on show nights, thanks to its large, bright café.

Price: Unlimited annual pass at €14 per month (full price).

9, boulevard Lénine, 93300 Bobigny
Tel: +33 (0)1 41 60 72 60 / mc93.com

- M — Line 5: Bobigny - Pablo Picasso
- Tram — T1: Hôtel de Ville
- Bus — 134, 234, 251, 301: Conservatoire Jean Wiener

CLICHY-SOUS-BOIS

10 ATELIERS MÉDICIS

#CULTUREFORALL #ARTISTSTUDIOS
#PERFORMANCES

Major cultural institutions should not be limited to inner Paris. Launched in 2016 in Clichy-Montfermeil, the Ateliers Médicis were created to establish a prestigious venue inspired by the villa Medici in Rome. While the official opening is planned for 2025, a temporary venue opened in 2018, including a performance hall and artist residencies.

4, allée François N'Guyen, 93390 Clichy-sous-Bois
Tel: +33 (0)1 58 31 11 00 / ateliersmedicis.fr

- M — Line 16 (planned 2025/2026): Clichy - Montfermeil
- RER — E: Le Raincy - Villemomble - Montfermeil, then bus 601: Administrateur or Émile Zola
- Tram — T4: Clichy - Montfermeil

DRANCY

11 MÉMORIAL DE LA SHOAH

#HISTORY #NEVERFORGET
#EXHIBITIONS

While it is not as well-known as its Parisian counterpart, the Drancy Shoah Memorial is a historical necessity. Inaugurated in 2012, it faces the Cité de la Muette, which became a place of internment in 1941 and then, in 1942, the assembly camp for Jews in France with a view to their deportation to the extermination camps. Beneath its fortress-like exterior covered with mirrors, the building houses exhibition and conference spaces as well as an information centre. Visits to the former Bobigny deportation station are also organized on a regular basis. More information can be found on the website garedeportation.bobigny.fr. This visit should be combined with a trip to the Bobigny deportation station memorial, which opened in July 2023.

Free entry.
Closed Monday, Tuesday and Wednesday.

110–112, avenue Jean-Jaurès, 93700 Drancy
Tel: +33 (0)1 42 77 44 72 / memorialdelashoah.org
and garedeportation.bobigny.fr

- M — Line 5: Bobigny - Pablo Picasso, then bus 251: Place du 19 mars 1962

LA PLAINE SAINT-DENIS

12 ACADÉMIE FRATELLINI

#NEWCIRCUS #SHOWS
#WORKSHOPS

If you want to leave all the clichés associated with the circus behind, then a trip to the Académie Fratellini is required. Here, you can choose how to redefine your circus experience. First of all, take a seat in the big top and experience a show inspired by the new circus, mixing dance, acrobatics and juggling. Then you can experiment with a circus-aperitif during which performers entertain you while you have drinks. Finally, you can step through the looking-glass by participating in workshops for young and old alike. The circus won't ever look the same again.

1–9, rue des Cheminots, 93210 La Plaine Saint-Denis
Tel: +33 (0)1 49 46 00 00 / academie-fratellini.com

- M — Lines 14, 16, 17 (planned 2024/2026): Saint-Denis Pleyel
- RER — D: Stade de France - Saint-Denis
- Bus — 139, 173: Landy - Cheminots
- Vélib' — Rue André Campra, Saint-Denis

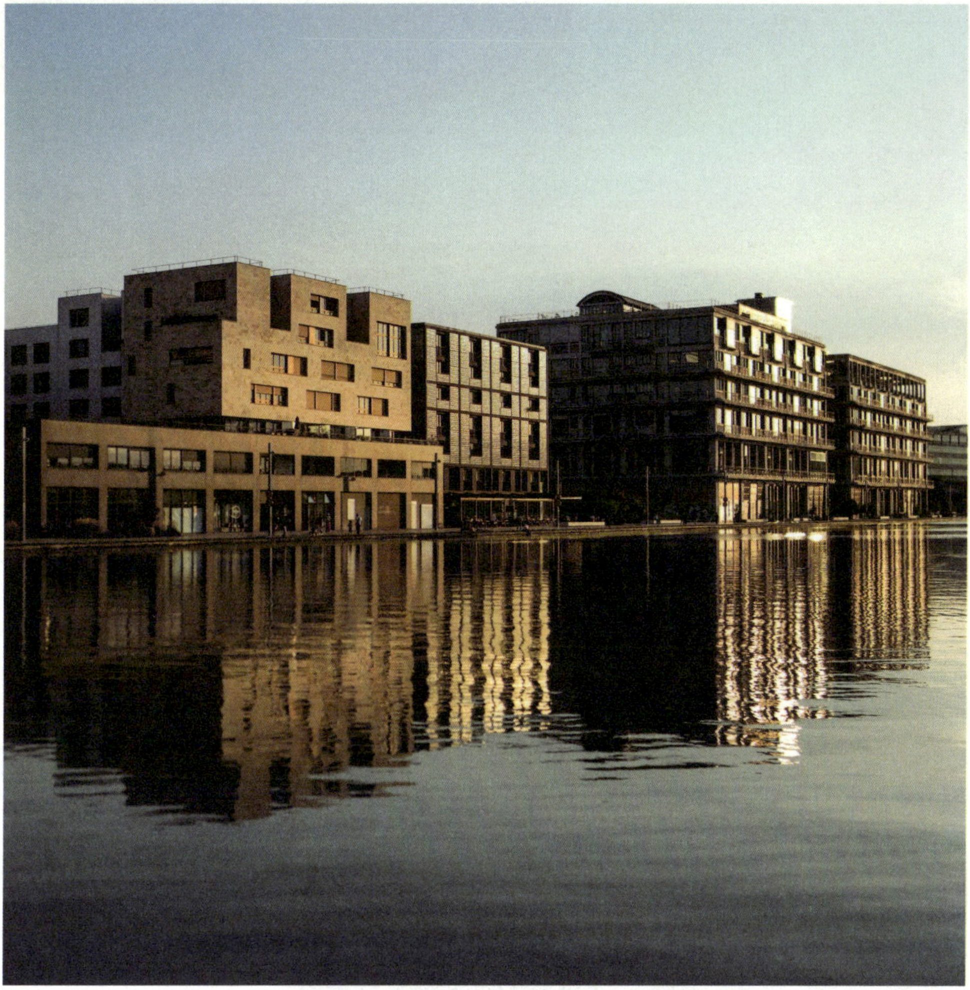

Golden hour on Ourcq | *Rue de l'Ancien Canal, Pantin.*

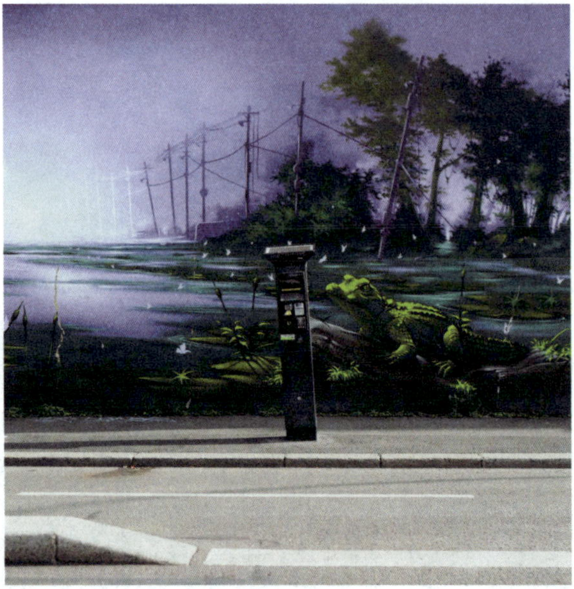

Bayou parking | *Rue Étienne Marcel, Montreuil.*

The neighbours | *Rue du Capitaine Dreyfus, Montreuil.*

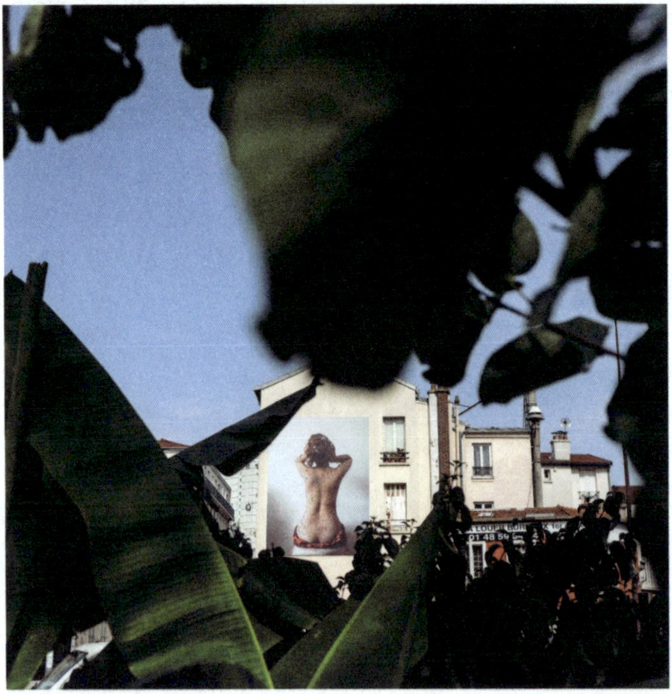

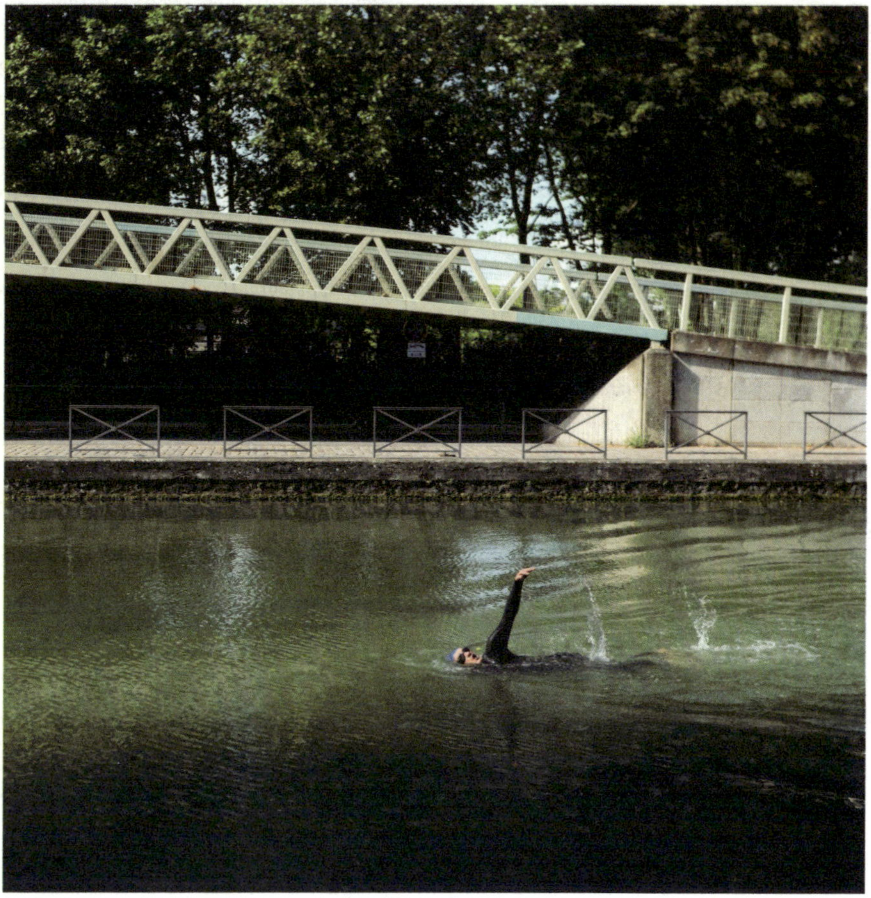

Freestyle canal | *Canal de l'Ourcq, Pantin.*

PANTIN

13 CENTRE NATIONAL DE LA DANSE

#CONTEMPORARYDANCE #RAWCONCRETE #COMMUNITYKITCHEN

Despite its facade of heavy concrete cubes, the Centre national de la danse (CN D) is full of grace. Originally designed to house Pantin's administrative offices, the building has hosted the finest in contemporary dance since 2004. Alongside its artist residencies, the CN D also serves as a performance venue with several highlights throughout the year such as "Camping" and "Shared Dances", which allow encounters between professionals and amateurs. Dance enthusiasts can also access the media library (for free) and explore a collection that is unique in Europe.

Mingway restaurant-bar, 3-course menu for €16. Saturday brunch for €23. Open daily from 9.30am–7pm and until 9.30pm on Friday and Saturday. Closed Sunday.

1, rue Victor Hugo, 93500 Pantin
Tel: +33 (0)1 41 83 27 27 / cnd.fr

- M — Line 5: Hoche
- RER — E: Pantin
- Bus — 151, 170, 330: Centre National de la Danse
- Vélib' — Quai de l'Aisne, Pantin

14 GALERIE THADDAEUS ROPAC

#CONTEMPORARYART #IRONWORKS #CAFE

With its three 10-metre-high exhibition "naves" bathed in natural light, the Galerie Thaddaeus Ropac in Pantin is a genuine cathedral of contemporary art. Formerly an ironworks factory, it has presented the works of leading contemporary artists from the collaborative British art duo Gilbert and George to the German painter Georg Baselitz. After visiting the exhibitions, take a break at the Café Bleu in front of the gallery entrance to reflect on the place of art in society.

Free entry. Closed Sunday.

69, avenue du Général Leclerc, 93500 Pantin
Tel: +33 (0)1 55 89 01 10 / ropac.net

- M — Line 5: Église de Pantin
- RER — E: Pantin
- Transilien — Line P: Pantin
- Bus — 151: Diderot
- Vélib' — Quai de l'Aisne, Pantin

15 MAGASINS GÉNÉRAUX

#COLOSSUSOFRHODES #FREE #CULTURALMELTINGPOT

With the Grands Moulins de Pantin, Magasins Généraux is the other Colossus of Rhodes of the Canal de l'Ourcq. In 2016 these former warehouses were transformed into a creative hub under the impetus of the advertising agency BETC, which made the buildings its headquarters. The agency decided to open the site up by making the vast ground floor a venue for a high-quality and accessible cultural programme. To reach the broadest possible audience, the venue puts together a year-long eclectic programme including cultural seasons which spotlight current social issues and the emerging artistic scenes. The gigantic cultural bar-restaurant, Dock B (see p. 26), opened by the creators of the Bellevilloise is the latest to come on board.

Free entry.

1, rue de l'Ancien Canal, 93500 Pantin
magasinsgeneraux.com

- M — Line 5: Église de Pantin
- Bus — 61: Église de Pantin
- Vélib' — Avenue Jean Lolive, Pantin

PARIS

16 CIRQUE ÉLECTRIQUE

#PUNK #BIGTOP #CIRCUSSCHOOL

Entering this big-top is like stepping into a parallel universe. The Cirque Électrique breaks the mould of the circus ring: everything is more punk, more destructive, more gothic, more erotic. Don't be surprised if you are greeted by a friendship shot at an evening performance before you are taken on a wild ride. You may also find the performers bartending at the Nouveau Tigre, the local dance hall. Finally, the Cirque Électrique also runs a school dedicated to circus arts that is open to children from the age of 2.

Place du Maquis du Vercors, 75020 Paris
Tel: +33 (0)9 54 54 47 24 / cirque-electrique.fr

- M — Lines 3bis, 11: Porte des Lilas
- Tram — T3b: Porte des Lilas
- Bus — 105, 115, 129, 249: Porte des Lilas
- Vélib' — Place du Marquis du Vercors, Paris 19th

17 PHILHARMONIE DE PARIS

#CONCERTS #EXHIBITIONS
#SILVERDRAGON

Its metallic scales give it a reptilian appearance, making it look like a silver dragon. Let yourself be drawn into the coils of the Philharmonie and you will be dazzled by the design and acoustics of the Pierre Boulez hall, a giant cocoon in which you are enveloped by music. In addition to concerts, the venue's exhibition space has put on a number of blockbuster shows. And if you are feeling brave, try climbing this music-loving dragon's back to gain free access to a rooftop from Wednesday to Sunday from which you can enjoy a panoramic view across Paris and beyond.

221, avenue Jean Jaurès, 75019 Paris
Tel: +33 (0)1 44 84 44 84 / philharmoniedeparis.fr

- M — Line 5: Porte de Pantin
- Tram — T3b: Porte de Pantin / Parc de la Villette
- Vélib' — Avenue Jean Jaurès, Paris 19th

ROMAINVILLE

18 KOMUNUMA

#OLDFACTORY #REDBRICK
#CONTEMPORARYART

A symbol of the industrial heritage of Seine-Saint-Denis, the former Roussel-Uclaf pharmaceutical labs in Romainville began their transformation in spring 2019 to become Komunuma (commune in esperanto), a district open to the public and dedicated to artistic creation. Under the impetus of the Fondation Fiminco®, this complex of red brick buildings houses major contemporary galleries, artists in residence as well as the FRAC contemporary art collection. The project aims to put an end to the cultural centralism of inner Paris and contribute to a new metropolitan vision.

Komunuma includes Air de Paris, Fondation Fiminco, Fra Île-de-France, Galerie Sator, Galerie Jocelyn Wolff, In situ - fabienne leclerc, Laurel Parker Book, and 22,48 m².

43, rue de la Commune de Paris, 93230 Romainville
komunuma.com
More info on Facebook @fondationfiminco

- M — Line 5: Bobigny - Pantin - Raymond Queneau
- Bus — 147: Avenue de Metz
- Vélib' — Avenue Anatole France

SAINT-DENIS

19 BASILIQUE CATHÉDRALE DE SAINT-DENIS

#ROYALNECROPOLIS #RECUMBENTSTATUES
#HIDDENTREASURE

While Notre-Dame welcomed close to 20 million annual visitors before the tragic fire of April 2019, the Basilica of Saint-Denis only receives 130,000, despite the fact that it is one of the most powerful symbols in the history of France. No less than 42 kings and 32 queens were buried here before being thrown into a common grave by the revolutionaries. Even today, 70 monumental recumbent statues and tombs can still be seen, including those of Francis I, Catherine de' Medici, Louis XVI and Marie-Antoinette. Another particularity of the Basilica is that its spire, dismantled in 1847 after a violent tornado, is currently being rebuilt. A project you can follow thanks to the organization "Suivez la flèche!" (suivezlafleche.com).

Free entry. Entrance fee for the sculpted tombs: €9.50 (full price) / Combined ticket with the Panthéon: €16 (tickets can be used 3 days apart) / Free for under-25s. Open daily.

1, rue de la Légion d'Honneur, 93200 Saint-Denis
saint-denis-basilique.fr

- M — Line 13: Basilique de Saint-Denis
- Tram — T1: Basilique de Saint-Denis
- Bus — 153, 253: Basilique de Saint-Denis
- Vélib' — Rue Franciade, Saint-Denis

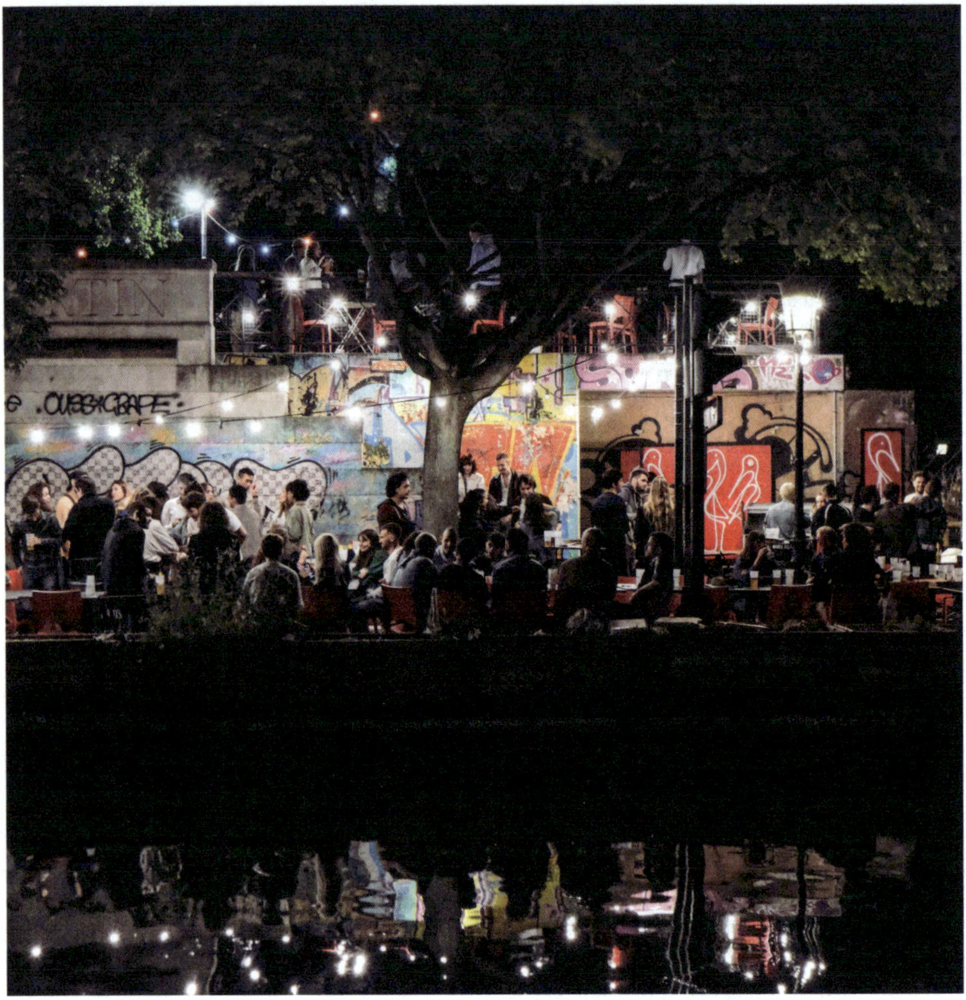

Canalside cocktails | *25°Est, Paris.*

lifestyle

BAGNOLET

20 LE SAMPLE

#THIRDSPACE #CUTTINGEDGESOUNDS #INTHEMIX

A stone's throw from the monumental Porte de Bagnolet, Le Sample is a third space that has made its home in former workshops. You enter via a concrete ramp lit by purple neon which leads to a charming courtyard. Overgrown vegetation, toilets in a breeze-block hut, mismatched garden furniture... the balance is just right: neither too underground nor too trendy. As well as cutting edge musical selections, Le Sample also hosts artists in residence and neighbourhood associations (yoga, theatre). A mix worth sampling.

18, avenue de la République, 93170 Bagnolet
lesample.fr / Facebook @lesamplebagnolet

- M — Line 3: Porte de Bagnolet or Galliéni
- Tram — T3b: Porte de Bagnolet
- Bus — 76: Général de Gaulle
- Vélib' — Rue du Château, Bagnolet

MONTREUIL

21 LE CHINOIS

#CONCERTS #CLUBBING #PARISINMONTREUIL

Right next to the Croix-de-Chavaux metro station, Le Chinois is one of those places that has succeeded in bringing Paris and the suburbs together. A former Chinese restaurant (hence the name), in 2012 the place was transformed into a fun club without any snobbery but with good music. Here, DJ sets and live bands take it in turns to set a joyous fire to the dancefloor.

6, place du Marché, 93100 Montreuil
Facebook @lechinoisdemontreuil

- M — Line 9: Croix de Chavaux
- Bus — 102: Marché de Montreuil
- Velib' — Rue de Paris, Montreuil

22 LA MARBRERIE

#MUSIC #NOFRILLS #ORGANICFOOD

Until 2006, this 1,500 m² venue was home to – you guessed it – a marble workshop, specialising in chimney repairs. Spotted by three accomplices who had set up a temporary Turkish café in the middle of the Tuileries Gardens in 2009, it soon became a festive space with a fine programme of concerts and evenings, as well as a café open for lunch during the week (€14 and €16 menus) and on concert nights as well as a vegetarian Sunday brunch (€20). La Marbrerie is undeniably a rare example of nightlife outside the *périphérique*.

2, rue Alexis Lepère, 93100 Montreuil
Tel: +33 (0)1 43 62 71 19 / lamarbrerie.fr

- M — Line 9: Mairie de Montreuil
- Bus — 322: Mairie de Montreuil
- Vélib' — Boulevard Paul Vaillant-Couturier, Montreuil

23 LES TATAS FLINGUEUSES

#CONCEPTSTORE #VINTAGE #MADEINMONTREUIL

The name of this café-boutique (a feminine version of the 1963 comedy-crime caper *Les Tontons flingeurs*) sums up its unique spirit perfectly – a mix of rock 'n' roll and cheeky-chic. Whether you need to buy someone a gift or just feel like treating yourself, Les Tatas Flingueuses is the ideal place for vintage finds, decorative gems and local products. There is even a lunch service to make the shopping experience even more pleasurable. A favourite.

Closed Sunday.

52, rue de Paris, 93100 Montreuil
Tel: +33 (0)9 84 43 65 65 / Facebook @lesflingueuses

- M — Line 9: Croix de Chavaux
- Bus — 102: Marché de Montreuil
- Vélib' — Rue de Paris, Montreuil

PANTIN

24 DOCK B

#ONESPACEFITSALL
#HUGETERRACE #CANALSIDE

Specialty coffee, modern bistro, concert venue, exhibition space, citizen forum and coworking space – Dock B is the perfect encapsulation of the new spirit taking hold in Pantin. Located on the ground floor of Magasins Généraux (see p. 22), a former customs warehouse that has been completely renovated, this hybrid site has one major advantage over the competition thanks to its huge terrace that allows you to fully enjoy the banks of the Canal de l'Ourcq.

Open from 4–10pm on weekdays and from 12–10pm on weekends.

1, place de la Pointe, 93500 Pantin
Tel: +33 (0)1 41 71 49 69 / dockbpantin.com
- M — Line 5: Église de Pantin
- Bus — 61: Église de Pantin
- Vélib' — Avenue Jean Lolive, Pantin

PARIS

25 CENTQUATRE

#ARTINMOTION #FREEDOM
#PERFORMANCE

Located in the former municipal funeral service building, the Centquatre is a unique cultural space. In this 200-metre-long covered hall, you can watch performers of all stripes and backgrounds rehearsing breakdance moves or ballet sequences. Have a drink at the café, check out the Emmaus Défi charity shop, take in a contemporary art exhibition, a concert, a dance performance or a play – the Centquatre is in constant motion. The perfect place to spend an hour or to while away a Sunday afternoon.

Free entry.
Closed Monday.

5, rue Curial, 75019 Paris
Tel: +33 (0)1 53 35 50 00 / 104.fr
- M — Line 7: Riquet
- Bus — 34, 45: Riquet
- Vélib' — Rue Riquet, Paris 19th

26 LA GARE – LE GORE

#OLDTRAINSTATION #JAZZ
#FREECONCERTS

Deprived of its raison d'être for more than 80 years, this former station of the abandoned Petite Ceinture train line (see p. 34) has found a new lease of life with free nightly jazz concerts. Even if jazz is not your thing, La Gare is worth the trip in and of itself. Perched on a hill, a paved path leads up to this venue lit by multicoloured string lights by night. Inside, even though this is a jazz club, the atmosphere is on the grungy side. Don't forget to go through the door at the back of the room to discover one of the best hidden terraces in Paris.

Open daily.

1, avenue Corentin-Cariou, 75020 Paris
Facebook @LaGareJazz
- M — Line 7: Corentin Cariou
- Bus — 239: Rosa Parks - Curial
- Vélib' — Avenue de Flandre, Paris 20th

27 LE HASARD LUDIQUE

#OLDTRAINSTATION #EVENTS
#BIGTERRACE

Once upon a time, there was a pretty little station that had long been the pride of the neighbourhood. Along the way, it was transformed into a cinema and then a supermarket before it was finally abandoned. Thankfully, this story has a happy ending as a handful of friends brought it back to life with a new identity as Le Hasard Ludique, combining music, good food and a range of activities for all ages (laughter yoga, recycling and gardening, improv, etc.). In addition, there is an outdoor space that runs along the platforms of the Petite Ceinture train line (see p. 34).

Closed Monday.

128, avenue de Saint-Ouen, 75018 Paris
Tel: +33 (0)1 42 28 35 91 / lehasardludique.paris
- M — Line 13: Porte de Saint-Ouen
- Bus — 81: Navier
- Vélib' — Rue Jacques-Kellner, Paris 18th

28 KILOMÈTRE25

#SUNDERTHEOVERPASS
#OPENAIR #ALLNIGHTER

Along with La Bretelle (see p. 181) and La Station-Gare des Mines (see p. 29), Kilomètre25 is the dancing proof that the Paris ring road now occupies a central place on the Paris night scene. This gigantic open-air venue of more than 2,000 m², run by teams from the Glazart concert hall and the Jardin21 third space (in the 19th arrondissement),

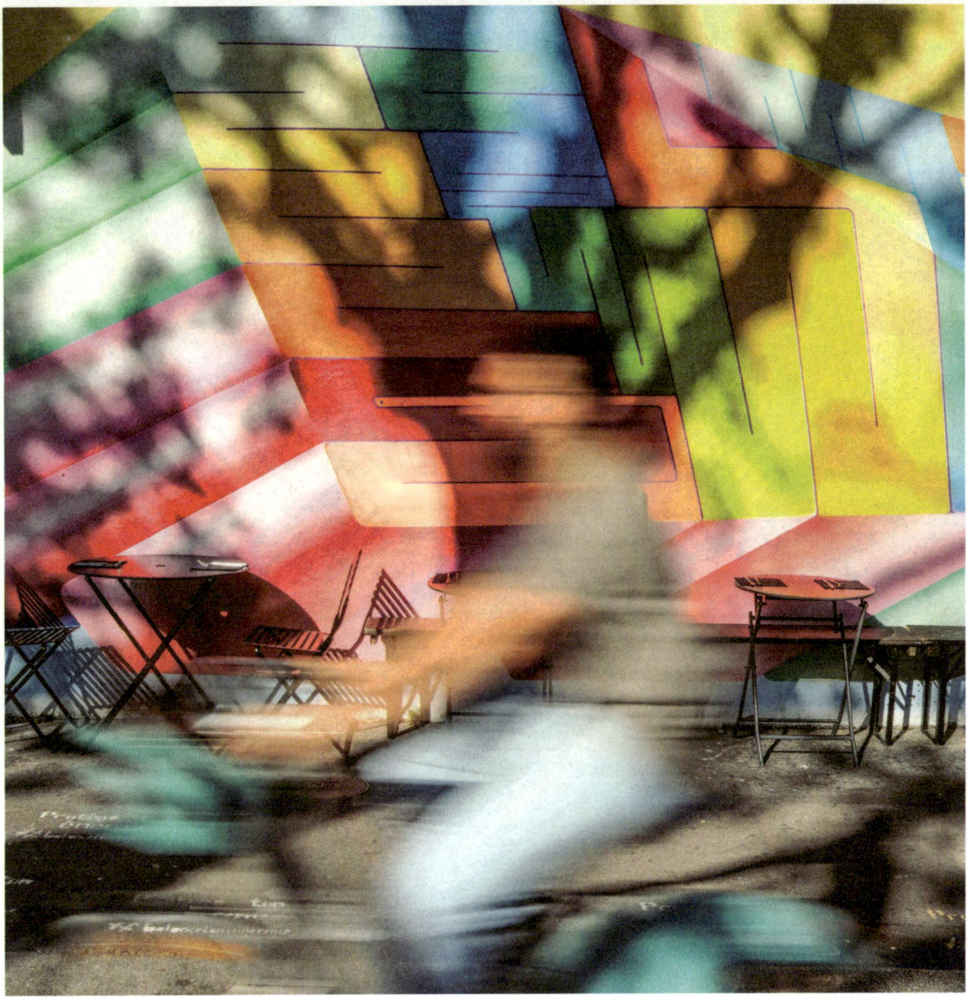

Deconstructed rainbow | *Quai de Jemmapes, Paris.*

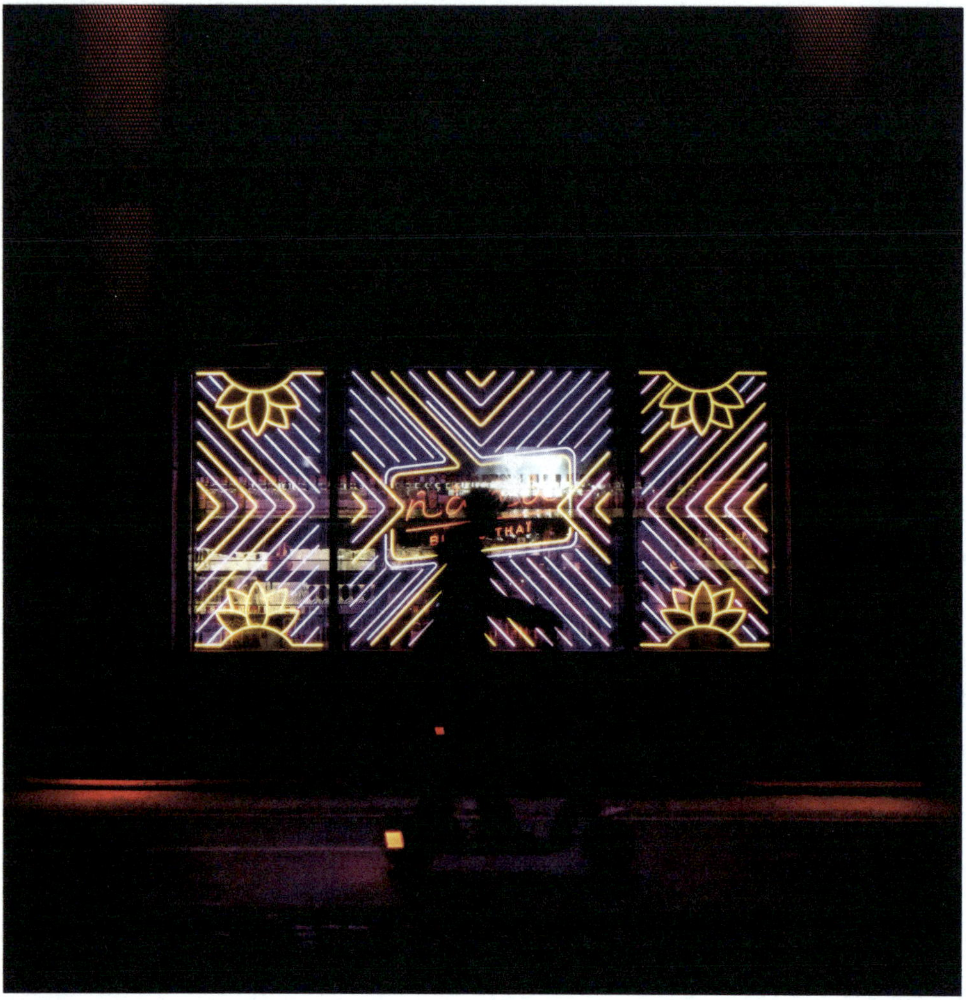

Neonderthal | *Quai de la Loire, Paris.*

opened in 2021 under the ring road, at the 25th kilometre (hence the name). Since then, it's been one electro all-nighter after another from spring to autumn. It just goes to show that you can set up under a road that goes all the way round Paris and still be at the heart of things.

Open from spring to autumn.

8, boulevard Macdonald, 75019 Paris
kilometre25.fr

- M — Line 7: Porte de la Villette,
  M — Line 5: Porte de Pantin
- Tram T3b — Ella Fitzgerald
- Bus 139, 150: Porte de la Villette
- Vélib' — Avenue Corentin Cariou, Paris

29 PAVILLON DES CANAUX

#COWORKING #RESTAURANT
#BRILLIANTDECOR

Are you familiar with the "coffice"? This contraction of "coffee" and "office" refers to a workspace which is open to everyone – even those who don't feel like working – and serves food. The Pavillon des canaux, on the banks of the Bassin de la Villette, applies this concept perfectly in a terrific setting. You can choose to sit in the guest room, around the dining table or in the bathtub propped up against large cushions. When the weather is good, take advantage of its big terrace with its deckchairs.

Open daily.

39, quai de la Loire, 75019 Paris
Tel: +33 (0)7 80 91 52 93/ pavillondescanaux.com

- M — Line 5: Stalingrad
- Bus — 60: Jean Jaurès - Lorraine
- Vélib' — Rue Euryale Dehaynin, Paris 19th

30 LA RECYCLERIE

#OLDTRAINSTATION #ECOPARADISE #COFFEE

Located in the former Boulevard Ornano station on the Petite Ceinture (see p. 34), the Recyclerie – as its name suggests – has made sustainability the core of its project. Here you'll find a 1,000 m² urban farm with chickens, bees and even ducks. It's also the ideal place to learn how to do-it-yourself or to have things repaired in René's workshop (watch out, it's closing soon!). Let's not forget the café where a cup only costs €1. And, of course, the debates and workshops that make this place such an essential Greater Paris destination.

Open daily.

83, boulevard Ornano, 75018 Paris
Tel: +33 (0)1 42 57 58 49 / larecyclerie.com

- M — Line 4: Porte de Clignancourt
- Tram — T3b: Porte de Clignancourt
- Bus — 85, 137, 341: Porte de Clignancourt
- Vélib' — Rue Belliard, Paris 18th

31 LA STATION – GARE DES MINES

#FORMERCOALSTATION
#ELECTRO #BERLINSTYLE

Like many of the former industrial sites in the 93 district, this former coal station has been converted into a temple of Parisian nightlife. But La Station isn't for everyone, with its cutting-edge and unashamedly electro line-up. The decor is a cross between Greater Paris and Berlin, with an old red brick building on one side and metal containers on the other. Parisian-Berlin nights are yours for the taking!

29, avenue de la Porte d'Aubervilliers, 75018 Paris
Tel: +33 (0)9 73 26 11 47 / lastation.paris

- RER — E: Rosa Parks
- Tram — T3b: Porte d'Aubervilliers
- Vélib' — Rue Madeleine Vionnet, Aubervilliers

ROISSY-EN-FRANCE

32 PARIS-CHARLES DE GAULLE AIRPORT

#TRAVELFORTRAVELSSAKE
#THESKYISTHELIMIT #FIRSTCLASSSEAT

In the words of Robert Louis Stevenson, "I travel not to go anywhere but to go. I travel for travel's sake." So even if you don't have a plane to catch, you can still head to Roissy and discover the landscapes along the RER B on the way, as the writer François Maspero did in *Les Passagers du Roissy-Express* some 30 years ago. On your way, you can visit the Musée de l'Air et de l'Espace (see p. 37), picnic in the Natura 2000-certified Sausset park in Villepinte (parcsinfo.seinesaintdenis.fr) and, once you arrive in Roissy, slip into a first-class seat in the "first" section of the Pathé-Gaumont® cinema in Aéroville (aeroville.com/store/pathe). The lucky ones with a plane ticket can explore the Espace Musées in Terminal 2E (espacemusees.com). In the words of Du Bellay, "Happy the man who, like Ulysses, has travelled well."

Avenue Charles de Gaulle, 95700 Roissy-en-France
parisaeroport.fr

- RER — B: Aéroport Ch. De Gaulle 1
  or Aéroport Ch. De Gaulle 2

SAINT-DENIS

33 6B

#CULTURALSPACE #EVENTS
#EXHIBITIONS

Seen from the street, the 6b doesn't look like much. This greyish office building was for many years the headquarters of Alstom®, one of France's largest industrial companies. Across this 7,000-m² maze spread over six floors, the meeting rooms were replaced by art galleries, the offices by artist studios and the dining room by a ballroom. Since 2010, there has always been something happening at the 6b: exhibitions, concerts, electro nights, and talks, while every summer a sandy beach opens to the delight of the Greater Parisians. In one of the prefab spaces in the courtyard, you can even buy delicious bread from Sébastien, the local baker. The 6b also has a café, Le Cerveau, open at lunchtime from Monday to Friday.

6–10, quai de Seine, 93200 Saint-Denis
Tel: +33 (0)1 42 43 23 34 / le6b.fr

- RER — D: Saint-Denis
- Transilien — Line H: Saint-Denis
- Tram — T1, T8: Saint-Denis
- Bus — 254: Rue du Port
- Vélib' — Quai du Port, Saint-Denis

34 SAINT-DENIS MARKET

#COVEREDMARKET #CROWDS
#WORLDFOOD

Under the glass roof of an old-fashioned market pavilion, a stone's throw from the basilica and necropolis of the kings and queens of France (see p. 23), the Saint-Denis market is a theatre: fishmongers go in for some verbal jousting, grocers' boast about the freshness of their tomatoes or prickly pears, while olive sellers stop passers-by to offer them a tasting. Outside, the same atmosphere prevails, but with a focus on textiles and knick-knacks (decorations, oriental teapots, etc.). Because you can find everything here. A real old-fashioned market, just the way we like it.

Open Tuesday from 8am–2pm, Friday from 8am–3pm and Sunday from 8am–2.30pm.

Place Victor Hugo, 93200 Saint-Denis

- M — Line 13: Basilique de Saint-Denis
- Tram — T1: Basilique de Saint-Denis
- Bus — 153, 253: Basilique Saint-Denis
- Vélib' — Place Victor-Hugo, Saint-Denis

35 FERME URBAINE DE SAINT-DENIS

#URBANFARM #PROOFOFCONCEPT
#AGRICULTUREMEETSCULTURE

In late 2017, after more than a century of existence, the last vegetable farm in Seine-Saint-Denis began a new life. Les Fermes de Gally (see p. 76) and the collective of beekeepers and artists known as the Parti Poétique came together to create the Ferme urbaine de Saint-Denis. The purpose of this place, which is open to the public, is twofold: to preserve agricultural production and to offer a rich cultural programme. An unusual pairing that deserves to be followed closely.

Closed Monday and Tuesday

112, avenue de Stalingrad, 93200 Saint-Denis
lesfermesdegally.com, Facebook @zonesensible

- M — Line 13: Saint-Denis - Université
- Bus — 356: Clos Hanot
- Vélib' — Rue Guynemer, Saint-Denis

SAINT-OUEN

36 LA FABRIQUE DU MÉTRO

#GRANDPARISEXPRESS
#SNEAKPEEK #FREE

The first metro line of the Grand Paris Express is scheduled to open in 2025. However, thanks to La Fabrique du métro in Saint-Ouen, you can already stroll along its platforms. In this huge 2,500-m² hall, a life-size replica of a station on line 15 has been set up, a way for travellers to get a glimpse of the future. The Fabrique also has architectural models, an immersive room with projections in 3D, and touch screens you can use to explore the stations of the future. Entry is free during open days and free visits can also be booked online.

Free entry.

50, rue Ardoin, 93400 Saint-Ouen
grandparisexpress.fr/fabrique-du-metro

- M — Line 13, 14: Mairie de Saint-Ouen
- Bus — 66, 173, 214: Capitaine Glarner
- Vélib' — Quai de Seine, Saint Ouen

37 SAINT-OUEN FLEA MARKET

#ANOTHERWORLD #GIANTFLEAMARKET #FLYINGSAUCER

Paris has the Eiffel Tower®, Versailles its château, and the Saint-Ouen flea market has a real flying saucer. This rare piece is on show in the Dauphine market, one of the 14 flea markets in Saint-Ouen, located at 132 rue des Rosiers. Designed by Finnish architect Matti Suuronen and named Maison Futuro, around a hundred units were built in total, most of which have disappeared from the face of the earth. This collector's item is one of the many fantastical oddities you will come across when you explore the alleys of the Saint-Ouen flea market, one of the largest antique and flea markets in the world. You won't be leaving empty-handed.

Closed from Tuesday to Thursday.

Rue des Rosiers, 93400 Saint-Ouen
pucesdeparissaintouen.com

- M — Line 13: Garibaldi
- Bus — 85: Marché aux Puces
- Vélib' — Rue René Binet, Paris 18th

Outdoors

BAGNOLET

38 PARC JEAN MOULIN – LES GUILANDS

#TWOPARKSFORTHEPRICEOFONE #LOOKOUTPOINT #FILMSET

Brought together by a long strip of impeccably manicured lawn, the Parc Jean Moulin and the Parc des Guilands in Bagnolet and Montreuil cover 26 hectares, almost the same area as the Montsouris (see p. 204), Monceau and Belleville parks combined. This great place for a hilly stroll, which provided the setting for several scenes of Romane Bohringer's film *L'Amour flou*, is one of the essential lookout points that surround Paris alongside the Butte d'Orgemont, the Butte des Châtaigniers in Argenteuil (see p. 94) and the Mont Valérien in Suresnes (see p. 61). And for those looking to climb even higher, it is also regularly used for yoga, taï chi and qigong.

Open daily.

Rue Robespierre, 93170 Bagnolet
parcsinfo.seinesaintdenis.fr

- M — Line 3: Gallieni
- Bus — 76, 102, 221: Gallieni
- Vélib' — Rue des Champeaux, Bagnolet

LA COURNEUVE

39 PARC GEORGES-VALBON

#BIGGERTHANCENTRALPARK #LANDSCAPING #SPRAWLINGLAWNS

With its 415 hectares, the Parc Georges-Valbon is 70 hectares bigger than Central Park. However, it is not just big – like its New York counterpart, it is also beautifully landscaped. A perfect place for walks and activities, with its three hectares of playgrounds for children, its equestrian centre and its pétanque pitch, the park has one of the most beautiful open-air sports centres in Greater Paris, on the shores of the main lake. Finally, its sprawling lawns deserve a special mention, maintained in part by the Clinamen urban shepherds' herd, whose sheepfold is located on this green plain.

Open daily (hours vary according to the season).

55, avenue Waldeck-Rochet, 93120 La Courneuve
parcsinfo.seinesaintdenis.fr

- RER — B: La Courneuve - Aubervilliers then bus 249: Cimetière de La Courneuve
- Vélib' — Avenue Romain-Rolland, Saint-Denis

NEUILLY-PLAISANCE

40 PARC DE LA HAUTE-ÎLE

#ISLAND #GREENPARADISE #RIVERSIDESTROLL

Just 10 km as the crow flies from the *périphérique*, you'll find a peaceful paradise on an island in the Marne: 65 hectares of greenery to delight walkers, birdwatchers (the site is teeming with birds), and the young ones (the castle-themed play area is well worth a visit). The Parc de la Haute-Île, as this paradise is known, is also a great place to take a stroll from Neuilly-Plaisance RER station along the left bank of the River Marne.

Open daily (opening times vary according to the season)

34, avenue Jean-Jaurès, 93360 Neuilly-Plaisance
parcsinfo.seinesaintdenis.fr

- RER — A: Neuilly-Plaisance
- Bus — 20, 213, 421: Église de Gournay

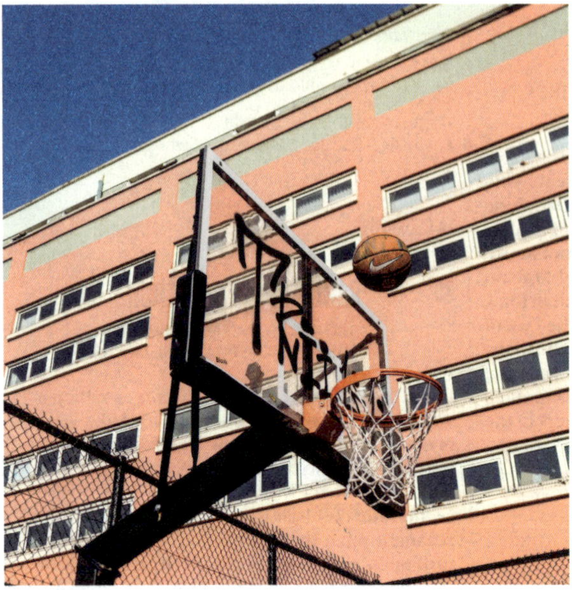

"I'm in over my head" | *Quai de Jemmapes, Paris.*

Tetris City | *Quai Kathrine Switzer, Pantin.*

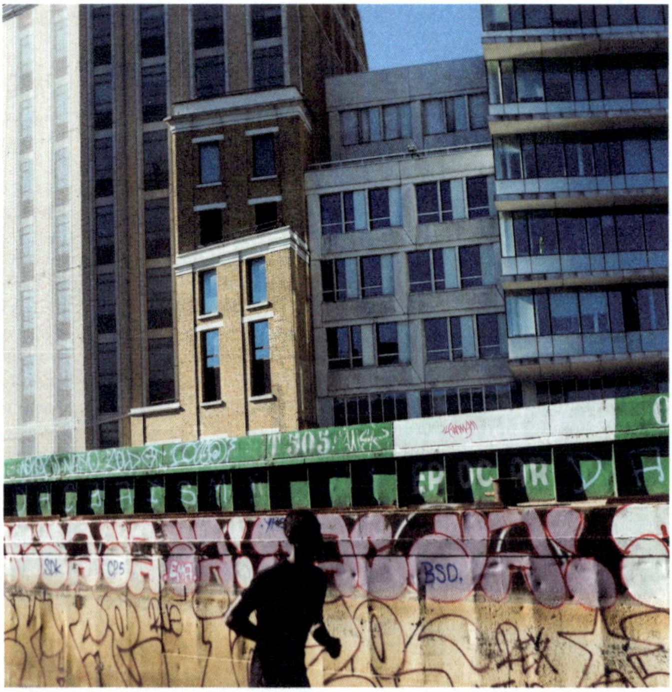

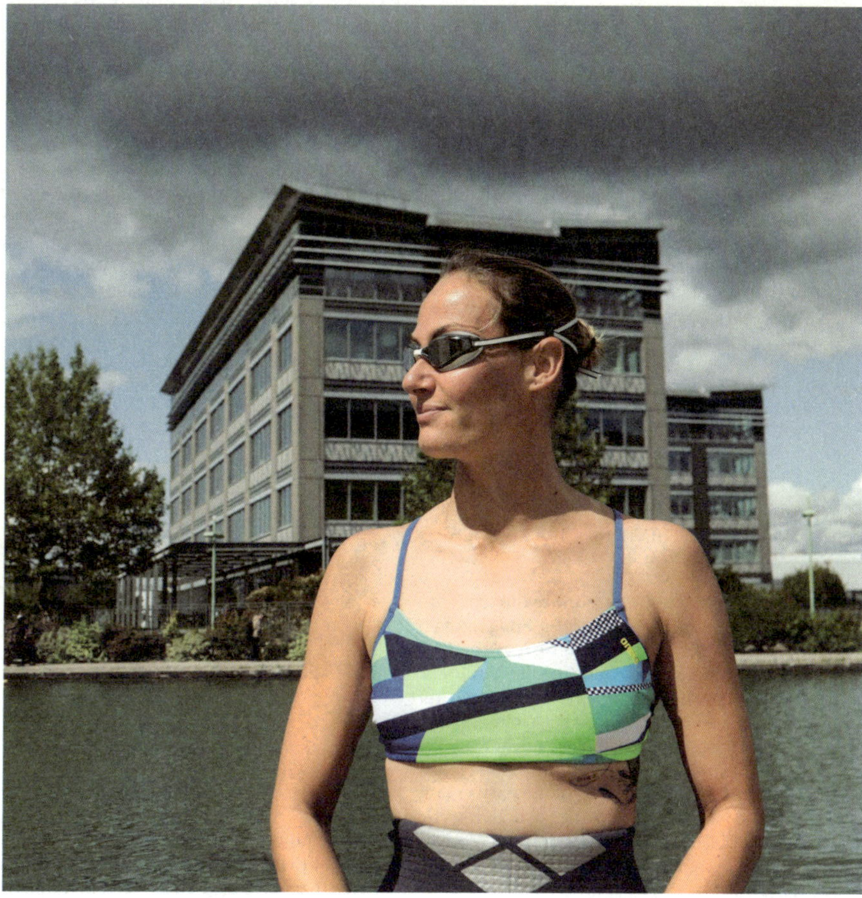

Taking the plunge | *Place de la Pointe, Pantin.*

41 BASSIN DE LA VILLETTE

#CANAL #OPENAIRSWIMMING
#CHOOSEYOURPOOL

Although it was banned for a long time, swimming has been open every summer on the Quai de la Loire side of the Bassin de la Villette. Three flowing water pools 40cm, 1.20m and 2m deep have been created by the city, which has strived to guarantee the water quality and swimmers' safety. A winning gagnante that attracts thousands of swimmers who are happy to enjoy the pleasure of floating on their backs while contemplating the Paris sky rather than a suspended ceiling.

Open daily from July to September, from 11am–9pm.

Quai de la Loire, 75019 Paris
paris.fr

- M — Line 5: Laumière
- Bus — 60: Jean Jaurès - Lorraine
- Vélib' — Quai de la Loire, Paris 19th

42 PARC DES BUTTES-CHAUMONT

#MOUNTAINSINTHECITY #PANORAMICVIEW
#EATDRINKANDPLAY

The Parc des Buttes-Chaumont avoids the formalism of the *jardin à la française*. The engineer Jean-Charles Alphand, to whom we owe the Bois de Vincennes (see p. 113) and Bois de Boulogne (see p. 60) in particular, created a landscape inspired by the mountains with rocks, cliffs, waterfalls, caves, lakes and gazebos. A former quarry, the Buttes-Chaumont has some impressive climbs, to the delight - or the dismay - of the park's many joggers. The park has no shortage of activities for children as well as a number of good places to eat and drink like the Rosa Bonheur *guinguette*.

Open daily (hours vary according to the season).

1, rue Botzaris, 75019 Paris
Tel: +33 (0)1 48 03 83 10 / paris.fr

- M — Line 7 bis: Buttes-Chaumont / Botzaris
- Bus — 26: Buttes-Chaumont,
  48, 60, 75: Armand Carrel - Mairie du 19e
- Vélib' — Rue Botzaris, Paris 19th

43 PETITE CEINTURE

#OLDRAILWAYTRACKS
#COMINGBACKTOLIFE #OASIS

A railway track built around Paris during the Second Empire (1852–70) and abandoned with the arrival of the metro, the Petite Ceinture is gradually waking up from its long sleep. Some of the line has been opened to the public, including the section located between rue de la Mare and rue de Ménilmontant. On this 400-metre stretch converted into a square, wooden deckchairs invite you to relax while surrounded by wild nature. A few hundred metres from this green oasis, another park, the Parc de Belleville, provides a breathtaking view of Paris and Greater Paris.

Open daily. Open sections can be found at paris.fr

79, rue de Ménilmontant, 75020 Paris

- M — Line 2: Ménilmontant
- Bus — 96: Henri Chevreau

where to eat

AUBERVILLIERS

44 FLEUR D'ORIENT

#CHABATTI #HOMEMADEHARISSA
#STREETFOOD

Matisse-blue walls, stacks of canned harissa, garlands of dried chillies: "colourful", in the words of *Elle* magazine. As well as the traditional fricassés and *chabatti*, Salem and his small team make delicious *kefteji* sandwiches at unbeatable prices. For €5, they'll fill half a baguette with crumbled tuna, two fried eggs cooked to perfection, homemade chips, raw red onions and cucumber, crunchy pickles, black and green olives, homemade carrot pickles, all spiced up with harissa (also homemade) and green and red chilli, and served by the kindest of staff. No inside tables, but two tables outdoors. This spot is also a great way to explore the Montfort area on foot, a nineteenth-century working-class heritage of small houses with gardens, sandwich in hand.

Kefteji: €5 / Chabatti: €4.50 / Fricassé: €2.50.
Open Tuesday to Saturday, 9am to 7pm,
Sunday 10am to 12.30pm. Closed Monday.

96, rue Charles Tillon, 93300 Aubervilliers
- M — Line 7: Fort d'Aubervilliers
- RER — B: La Courneuve - Aubervilliers
- Bus — 249, 250: Danielle Casanova - Pont Blanc
- Vélib' — Rue Charles-Tillon, Aubervilliers

BONDY

45 KEBAB EV'ET BY SAMY

#ARTISANALKEBAB #PETROLSTATION
#FILLUPTHETANK

It's not the most attractive of places: a petrol station on the side of the RN3 main road. But behind this rough exterior lies an excellent eatery run by Samy Kurt, who has taken up the Turkish tradition of setting up shop next to petrol pumps. He offers a top-of-the-range kebab where everything is homemade: the chips, the sauces, and the bread. As for the meat, it is marinated the previous day in herbs before being skewered. You can also try the well-seasoned lentil soup or *iskender*, pieces of bread fried in tomato with meat and yoghurt. A great way to fill up on goodness.

Open daily (except Tuesday) from 11.45am to 10.30pm.

108, avenue Gallieni, 93140 Bondy
Tel: +33 (0)1 88 50 26 27 / Instagram @evet_by_samy
- RER — E: Bondy then twenty-minute walk / Noisy-le-Sec then bus 105, Église de Bondy
- Vélib' — Rue Simone-Signoret, Noisy-le-Sec

MONTREUIL

46 LE BISTROT DES PIANOS

#FORMERSHOWROOM #CENTRALPERK
#CULINARYSYMPHONY

A long glass facade runs the length of rue Robespierre. Once upon a time, the pianos of the Klein factory were proudly displayed in this former showroom. Today, only one piano remains. But it doesn't go unnoticed. On certain evenings, it floods the vast space with its chords, while the guests of the Bistrot des pianos sit around in an atmosphere reminiscent of Central Perk from *Friends*. On the plate, everything is fresh (sustainable fish, meat sourced from small butchers), seasonal, and home-made. There's a salad of octopus, mirepoix of peppers, red onions, and Marchigiana olives, and a caramelised pork shank with honey and ginger, served with mashed potatoes with herbs and spinatta (Italian-style chorizo). Wash it all down with a craft beer (including the famous Deck & Donohue made in Bonneuil-sur-Marne in the Val-de-Marne département) or a glass of organic wine. A tune that you'll never get tired of.

Dishes from €7.
Open daily.

26, rue Robespierre, 93100 Montreuil
Tel: +33 (0)9 63 53 85 17 / lespianos.fr
- M — Line 9: Robespierre
- Bus — 318 Robespierre
- Vélib' — Rue de Paris, Montreuil

47 GYPSE

#GEM #TALKOFTHETOWN
#WORDOFMOUTH

When a dish delights the taste buds, the mouth feels the urge to spread the word. The more the word-of-mouth, the better the cuisine. This theory is borne out at the Gypse in Montreuil, which opened in 2019 and has been riding a word-of-mouth wave since then. With its large skylight and its decor mixing wood, concrete and bricks, the Gypse showcases its inventiveness when pairing deer with mango or fishcakes with lime mayonnaise. The Gypse truly is a gem.

Lunch menu Tuesday to Saturday: €18.50 (2 courses),
€22 (3 courses) / 5-course tasting menu: €48
Closed Sunday and Monday.

26, rue du Capitaine Dreyfus, 93100 Montreuil
Tel: +33 (0)1 88 49 47 53 / Facebook @GYPSE.RESTO
- M — Line 9: Croix de Chavaux
- Bus — 127: Croix de Chavaux Métro
- Vélib' — Rue de Vincennes, Montreuil

48 ISOLÉ

#SUBURBIA #SEASONAL
#YOULLNEVEREATALONE

The place looks like a suburban bungalow, tucked behind the Méliès cinema. But it's really a restaurant opened by chef Victor Gaillard who, with his partner Alice di Cagno, wanted to set up in an unusual venue. In fact, the terrace is not on the pavement but in a pretty little garden. Inside, several tastefully decorated rooms follow one another like so many rooms in a house. When it comes to the food, Isolé has it both ways: at lunchtime, the menu focuses on simple dishes offering unbeatable value for money. And on Thursday, Friday, and Saturday evenings, there is an à la carte menu, always with seasonal produce.

Set lunch menu for €19.
Closed Monday and Sunday.

7, rue de Rosny, 93100 Montreuil
Tel: +33 (0)1 48 51 65 04 / Facebook @Isolé

- M — Line 9: Mairie de Montreuil
- Bus — 102, 121, 122: Centre administratif
- Vélib' — Rue Franklin, Montreuil

PANTIN

49 LES PANTINS

#BAR #BISTRO #GOURMET

While it looks like a typical neighbourhood bistro with its zinc counter, its café curtains and its fake leather teal armchairs, Les Pantins has more up its sleeve. The egg mayo is served with herring eggs, the ribs are delicately spiced with satay and the peach soup is seasoned with Timut pepper. However, the bill is not at all spicy –three courses will only set you back €25. Les Pantins is one of Greater Paris's culinary up-and-comers. The team has also opened a cocktail bar, Le Pastoral, right next door as well as a wine shop and delicatessen, Les Pantins Cave & Epicerie.

Fixed-price menus €22 (2 courses) and €25 (3 courses).
Closed Sunday.

6, rue Victor Hugo, 93500 Pantin
Tel: +33 (0)1 57 14 38 74 / restaurantlespantins.fr

- M — Line 5: Hoche
- RER — E: Pantin
- Transilien — Line P: Pantin
- Bus — 151, 170, 330: Centre National de la Danse
- Vélib' — Quai de l'Aisne, Pantin

PARIS

50 CAFE LE 19M

#HAUTECOUTURE #RESIDENTCHEFS
#LOCALANDGLOBAL

At le19M, Chanel has chosen to bring together the 11 Maisons d'art (Lesage, Lemarié, Maison Michel...) that work for the brand under one roof with a gallery and a café-restaurant. Lunch is served in a vast space decorated by well-known designers and artists. The chefs in residence are mostly local, so the menu changes regularly. What doesn't change, however, is the quality of the dishes.

Lunch menu from €18.
Closed Saturday and Sunday.
Booking recommended on lecafe@le19m.fr

2, place Skanderbeg, 75019 Paris
le19m.fr

- M — Line 12: Front Populaire
- Tram — T3b: Porte d'Aubervilliers
- RER — E: Rosa Parks
- Bus — 45, 239: Parc du Millénaire
- Vélib' — Rue Madeleine Vionnet, Aubervilliers

51 CAFÉ-FLEURISTE DÉSIRÉE

#CONCEPTSTORE #LOCAL
#MATHILDEANDAUDREY

At Désirée you can treat yourself to simple produce from the kitchen of an environmentally friendly florist. Mathilde and Audrey have set up a little eatery next to their shop, which sells seasonal bouquets from local suppliers. On the menu are just two dishes, one of which is vegetarian, along with healthy juices. The little terrace is not bad for sunbathing, but the room is also full of charm, with its open kitchen, navy blue tiled counter, and little vases of dried flowers on the tables. Smell the roses!

Set lunch menu from €17.
Open daily.

96, rue de Meaux, 75019 Paris
Tel: +33 (0)1 71 21 95 20 / desireefleurs.fr

- M — Line 5: Laumière
- Bus — 60: Jean-Jaurès - Lorraine
- Vélib' — Rue Petit, Paris 19th

52 CANTINE DU JARDIN21

#THIRDSPACE #STREETFOOD #CANALSIDE

On the opposite bank, a huge barge delivers cement blocks. Behind you, the silhouette of the Moulins de Pantin rises up. It is in this industrial landscape along the Canal de l'Ourcq – on the border between Pantin and Paris – that Jardin21, a cultural and environmental third space, has been opening its gates from spring to early autumn since 2018. As well as the bar, you can sit down to sample dishes from the kitchen which serves up quality street food. On the menu: hot dogs, nachos, poke bowls, and even a vegetable-based chickpea effiloché with a pleasant smoky flavour. Afterwards, take a digestive stroll along the canal, which can lead you all the way to Parc de la Bergère in Bobigny, 5km away.

Open Wednesday to Sunday from spring to early autumn.

12A, rue Ella-Fitzgerald, 75019 Paris
jardin21.fr

- M — Line 5: Porte de Pantin
  M — Line 7: Porte de la Villette
- Tram — T3b: Ella Fitzgerald
- RER — E: Pantin
- Vélib' — Rue Ella-Fitzgerald, Paris 19th

SAINT-OUEN

53 LE RIPAILLEUR

#NEOBISTRO #WARMWELCOME #BAR

A warm, simple bistro where you can eat or just have a drink. Although it is not pretentious, the cuisine of chef Stanislas Borsik, who has also worked at the Tour d'Argent, is nonetheless superb, as confirmed by the mushroom and miso broth with ravioles de Royan and herbs, or the beef tataki with citrus kosho, redcurrants, and bitter cacao. Good to know: at Le Ripailleur, you can enjoy your meal at any time of day, even in the afternoon...

Starters €8 to €12 / Mains €18 to €26 /
Daily menus from €19–24.
Closed Sunday and Monday.

9, rue du Docteur Bauer, 93400 Saint-Ouen
Tel: +33 (0)9 83 04 68 50 / leripailleur.fr

- M — Line 13, 14: Mairie de Saint-Ouen
- Bus — 137, 237, 274: Mairie de Saint-Ouen – République
- Vélib: Rue Diderot, Saint-Ouen

Family

LE BOURGET

54 MUSÉE DE L'AIR ET DE L'ESPACE

#ARIANEROCKETS #ONTHECONCORDE #PLANETARIUM

It's not often you come face to face with a rocket. But that is exactly what is awaiting you at the Musée de l'Air et de l'Espace at Le Bourget, the largest aeronautical museum in France and one of the biggest in the world. In addition to the life-size replicas of the Ariane 1 and Ariane 5 rockets, there are no less than 350 flying machines housed here, including two replicas of the Concorde which you can board. The museum also has a planetarium, flight simulators and a dedicated space for children, Pilot Planet.

Price: from €6 / Free for under-4s.
Closed Monday.

Aéroport de Paris-Le Bourget, 93350 Le Bourget
Tel: +33 (0)1 49 92 70 00 / museeairespace.fr

- M — Line 7: La Courneuve
  then bus 152: Musée de l'Air et de l'Espace
- RER — B: Le Bourget
  then bus 152: Musée de l'Air et de l'Espace

PARIS

55 LA VILLETTE

#NONSTOPCULTURE #FORALLAGES #THEBIGGESTPARKINPARIS

La Villette is a cultural platform like few others. In a 55-hectare park, the largest one in inner Paris, you will find an exceptional concentration of cultural venues dedicated to music (Philharmonie de Paris (see p. 23), Cité de la Musique, Trabendo, Cabaret Sauvage, Zénith), science (Cité des Sciences et de l'Industrie), theatre (Théâtre Paris-Villette) and the circus (Espace chapiteaux). And since there is no age limit for culture, the Cité des Enfants, which is integrated into the Cité des Sciences, and Little Villette, a space for initiation and entertainment, welcome children from 2 years old. Proof that not every amusement park needs a roller coaster.

Place de la Fontaine aux Lions, 75019 Paris
Tel: +33 (0)1 40 03 75 75 / lavillette.com

- M — Line 5: Porte de Pantin
- Tram — T3b: Porte de Pantin
- Bus — 151: Porte de Pantin
- Vélib' — Avenue Jean Jaurès, Paris 19th

where to sleep

NEUILLY-SUR-MARNE

56 CAMPING LES RIVES DE PARIS

#ISLANDLIFE #NATURA2000 #BIRDSONG

Just 10 km beyond the *périphérique*, this fully renovated campsite is quite simply the only one of its kind in Seine-Saint-Denis. And not just in any old location: it has set up on an island in the Marne (France's longest river), in the midst of 68 hectares of nature that is part of the European Natura 2000 network. For once, wake up to the sounds of blackbirds, herons, and great crested grebes which nest in the neighbouring Parc de la Haute-Île.

From €15 for a pitch / €95 for a tiny house
Closed in January and February.

Chemin de l'Écluse, 93330 Neuilly-sur-Marne
Tel: +33 (0)1 43 08 21 21 / camping.lesrivesdeparis.fr

- RER — A: Neuilly – Plaisance
- Bus — 113, 127, 203, 303: Place de la Résistance

SAINT-OUEN

57 MOB HÔTEL

#CONCEPTHOTEL #BEDROOMSWITHNOTV #ORGANICRESTAURANT

Set up by the philosopher-businessman Cyril Aouizerate, the co-creator of the Mama Shelter hotels, MOB Hôtel is an avant-garde hotel a stone's throw from the Saint-Ouen flea market (see p. 31). Located in the former offices of General Electric®, the rooms are colourful and simple – so simple that they don't even have TV sets. Instead, you can enjoy a large courtyard, a gym, an organic restaurant, two rooftop bars, a self-service library and various activities (meditation, outdoor cinema, etc.). Every Friday, from 8pm to 10pm, the MOB will give your funny bones a workout with its line-up of guest comedians. Not just a place to rest your head.

Price: Hotel, from €79 night /
Restaurant: dishes from €13 to €25.

4–6, rue Gambetta, 93400 Saint-Ouen
Tel: +33 (0)1 47 00 70 70 / mobhotel.com

- M — Line 13: Garibaldi
- Bus — 85: Eugène Lumeau – les Écoles, 137: Kléber
- Vélib' — Avenue Gabriel-Péri, Saint-Ouen

TO GO EVEN FURTHER

DISCOVER THE "WELCOME TO SEINE-SAINT-DENIS" MAP

An illustrated painting that reveals the highlights of the Seine-Saint-Denis département. Food, fashion, culture and heritage, walks, parks, soft mobility, festivals... So many unusual places and venues that make the youngest département in France one of the most attractive and innovative.

BOOK YOUR VISITS ON EXPLOREPARIS.COM

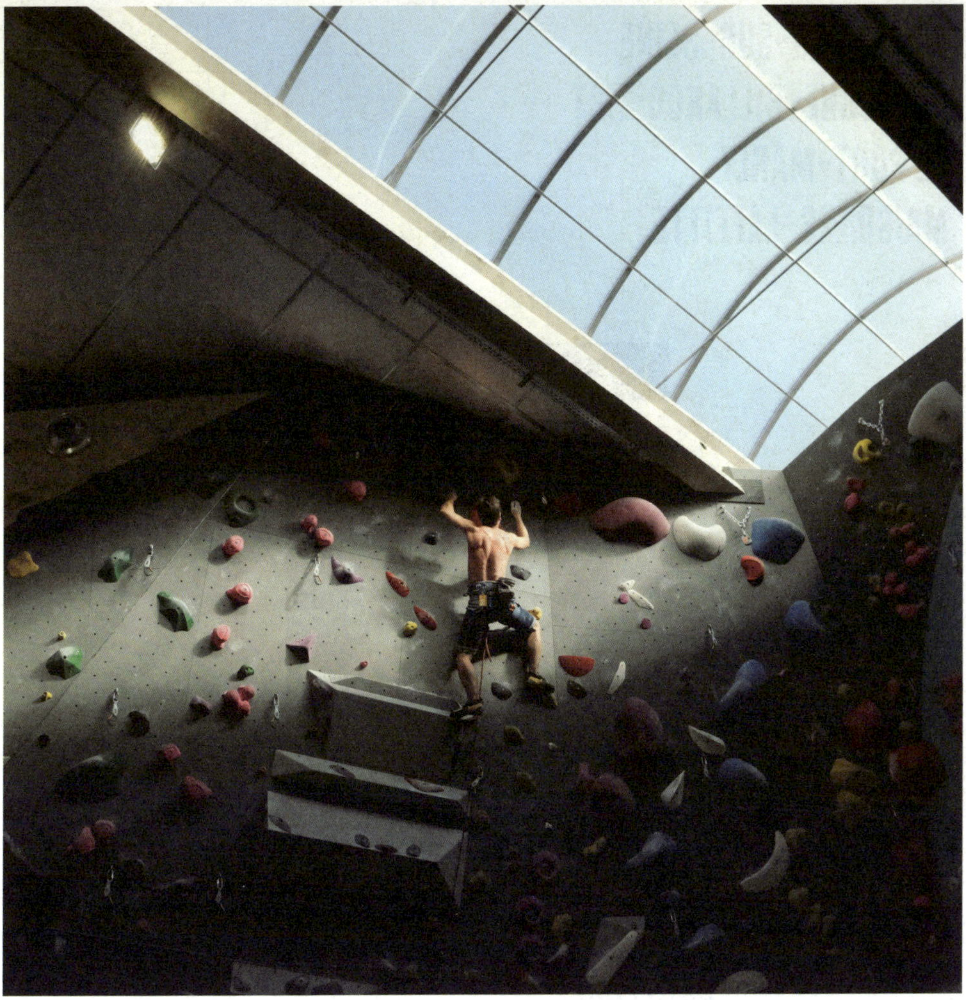

Don't look down | *Climb Up, Aubervilliers.*

ASNIÈRES-SUR-SEINE
BOULOGNE-BILLANCOURT
LE PORT-MARLY
MAISONS-LAFFITTE

THE

PARIS
PUTEAUX

MARLY-LE-ROI
NANTERRE

MUS

RUEIL-MALMAISON
SAINT-CLOUD
SAINT-GERMAIN-EN-LAYE

SURESNES
VILLENEUVE-LA-GARENNE

HYPER
EUM

A mere thirty kilometres separate the Centre Pompidou in Paris from the Château de Saint-Germain-en-Laye. This short stretch has become one of the most prestigious cultural showrooms in the world with an unrivalled concentration of works of art, museums, theatres and monuments. From the Renaissance to the present day, from Le Nôtre to Jean Nouvel, the area is a window into the universal artistic genius. In a single day you can go from a one-to-one with the Mona Lisa at the Louvre to contemplating Joan Miró's fantastic characters in the middle of the skyscrapers of La Défense. A cultural experience like no other.

THE HYPER MUSEUM

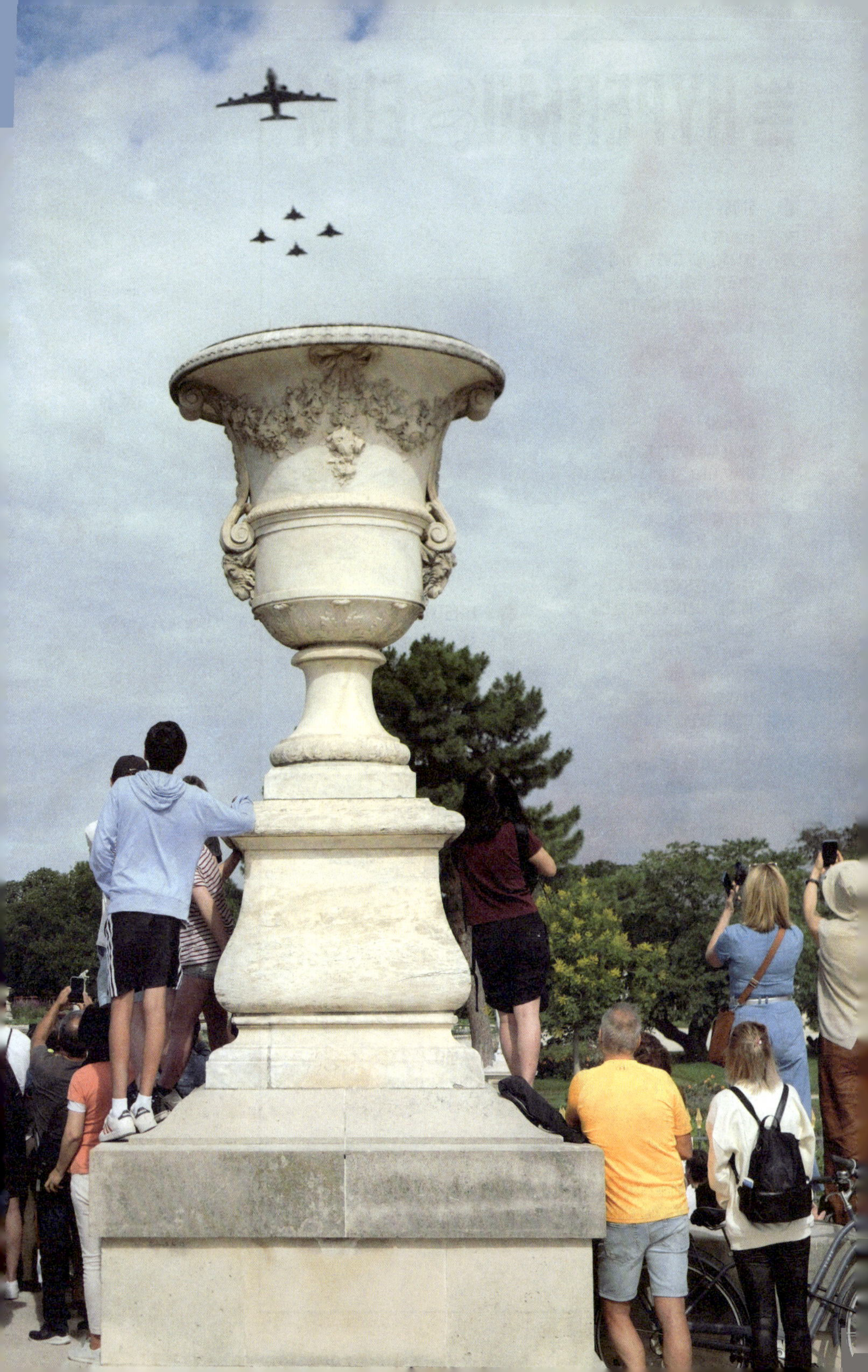

THE HYPERMUSEUM

SPORT

58 ANNETTE K.
59 SKI NAUTIQUE CLUB DE PARIS
60 SOCIÉTÉ SPORTIVE DU JEU DE PAUME ET DE RACQUETS
61 ACCROCAMP
62 AQUA HAUTS-DE-SEINE DIVING CENTRE

CULTURE

63 MUSÉE DES ANNÉES TRENTE
64 MUSÉE ALBERT-KAHN AND GARDENS
65 MUSÉE PAUL-BELMONDO
66 LA SEINE MUSICALE
67 CHÂTEAU DE MONTE-CRISTO
68 CHÂTEAU DE MAISONS
69 PARIS LA DÉFENSE ARENA ®
70 THÉÂTRE NANTERRE-AMANDIERS
71 BOURSE DE COMMERCE - PINAULT COLLECTION
72 CENTRE POMPIDOU
73 LA COMÉDIE-FRANÇAISE
74 FONDATION LOUIS-VUITTON
75 FORUM DES IMAGES
76 GRAND PALAIS AND GRAND PALAIS ÉPHÉMÈRE
77 LOUVRE
78 MAISON DE BALZAC
79 MEP - MAISON EUROPÉENNE DE LA PHOTOGRAPHIE
80 MUSÉE CERNUSCHI
81 MUSÉE D'ART MODERNE DE PARIS
82 MUSÉE D'ORSAY
83 MUSÉE DU QUAI BRANLY-JACQUES CHIRAC
84 MUSÉE MARMOTTAN MONET
85 MUSÉE NATIONAL DES ARTS ASIATIQUES GUIMET
86 PALAIS DE TOKYO
87 PETIT PALAIS
88 THÉÂTRE NATIONAL DE CHAILLOT
89 PARVIS DE LA DÉFENSE
90 CHÂTEAU DE MALMAISON AND PARC DE BOIS-PRÉAU
91 MUSÉE D'ARCHÉOLOGIE NATIONALE

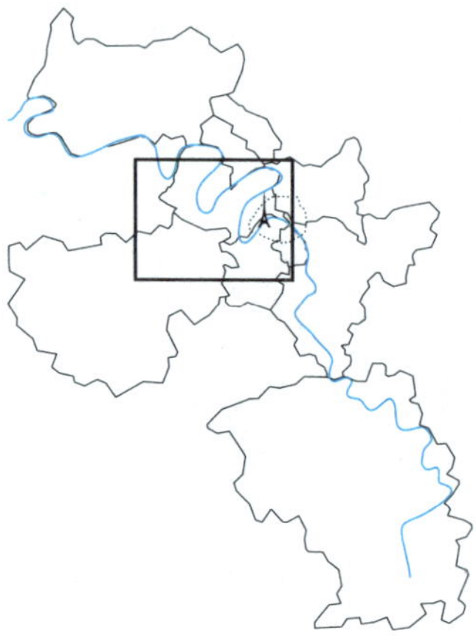

LIFESTYLE

92 ROSA BONHEUR À L'OUEST
93 VIVE LES GROUES

OUTDOORS

94 DOMAINE DE MARLY
95 BOIS DE BOULOGNE
96 DOMAINE NATIONAL DE SAINT-CLOUD
97 FORÊT DE SAINT-GERMAIN-EN-LAYE
98 MONT-VALÉRIEN TERRACE

WHERE TO EAT

99 OSABAK
100 LE VILLAGE TOMOHIRO
101 LES MARCHES
102 L'ESCARGOT 1903

FAMILY

103 JARDIN D'ACCLIMATATION

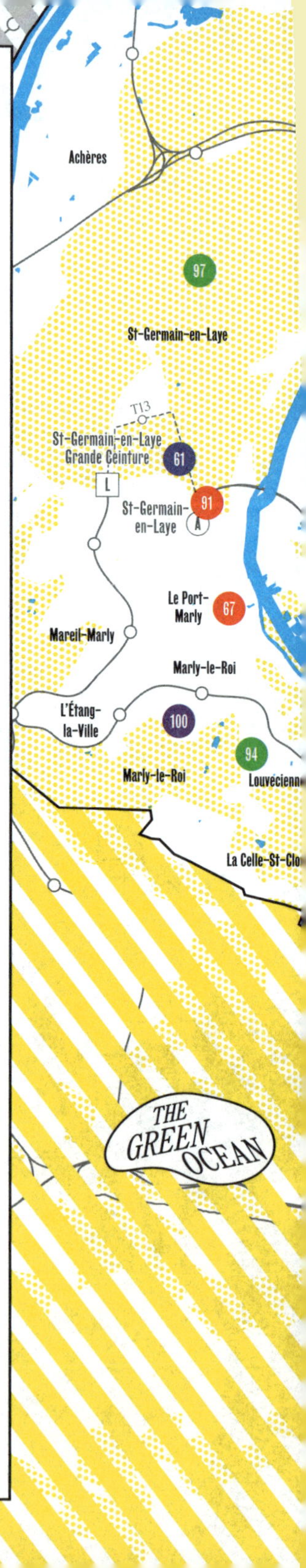

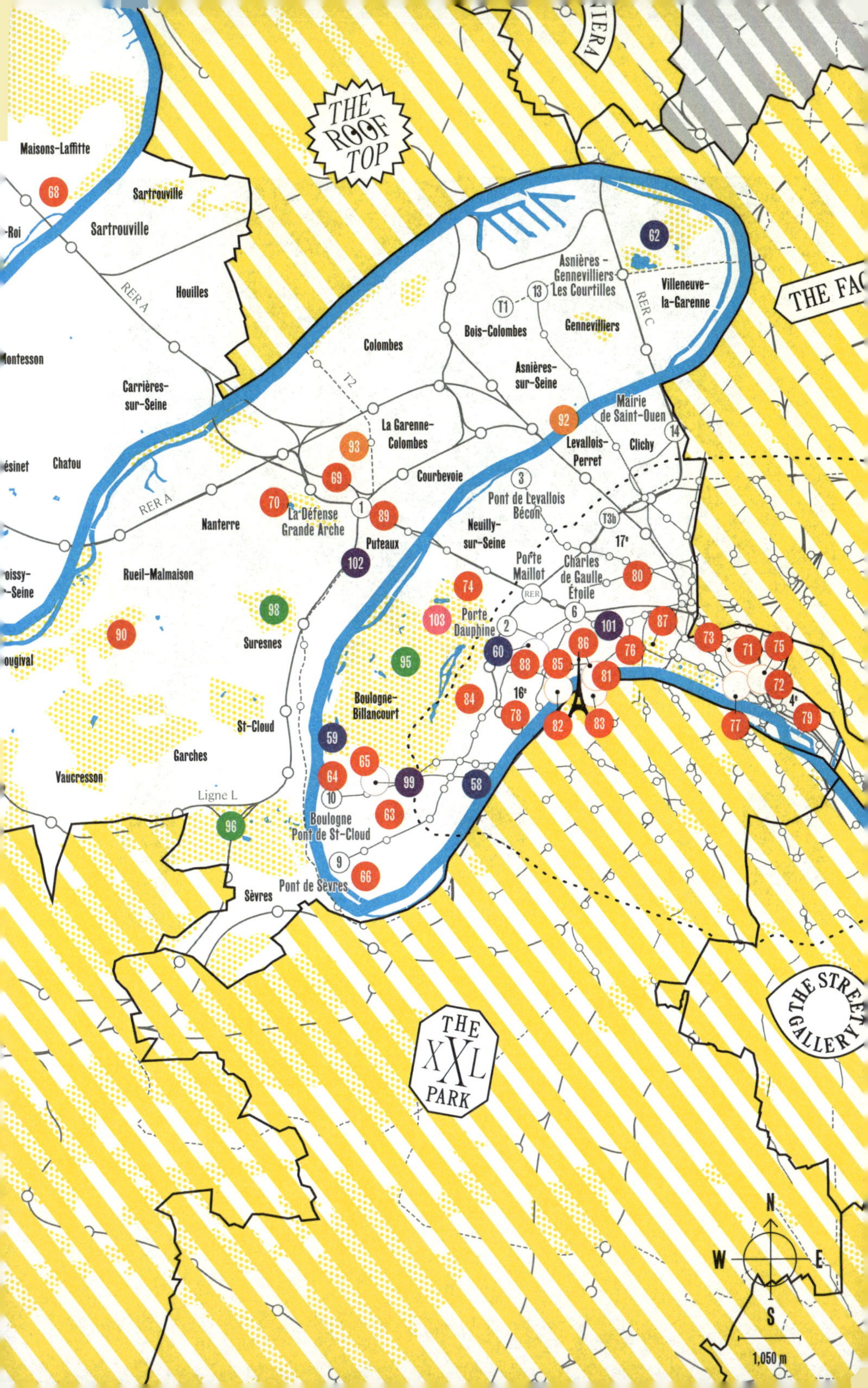

THE ROOF TOP
THE XXL PARK
THE STREET GALLERY
Maisons-Laffitte
Sartrouville
Houilles
Carrières-sur-Seine
Chatou
Nanterre
Rueil-Malmaison
Colombes
La Garenne-Colombes
Courbevoie
La Défense Grande Arche
Puteaux
Suresnes
St-Cloud
Garches
Vaucresson
Boulogne-Billancourt
Boulogne Pont de St-Cloud
Pont de Sèvres
Sèvres
Bois-Colombes
Asnières-sur-Seine
Asnières - Gennevilliers Les Courtilles
Gennevilliers
Villeneuve-la-Garenne
Mairie de Saint-Ouen
Clichy
Levallois-Perret
Pont de Levallois Bécon
Neuilly-sur-Seine
Porte Maillot
Charles de Gaulle Étoile
Porte Dauphine
RER A
RER C
T2
Ligne L
1,050 m
N
S
E
W

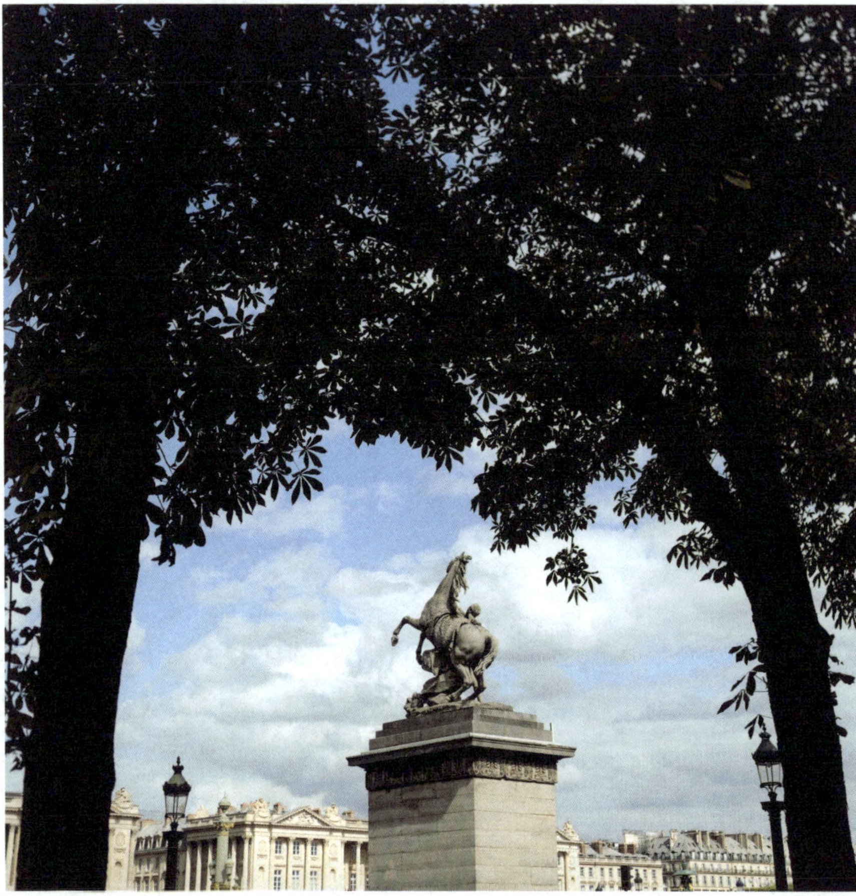

Get off your high horse | *Place de la Concorde, Paris.*

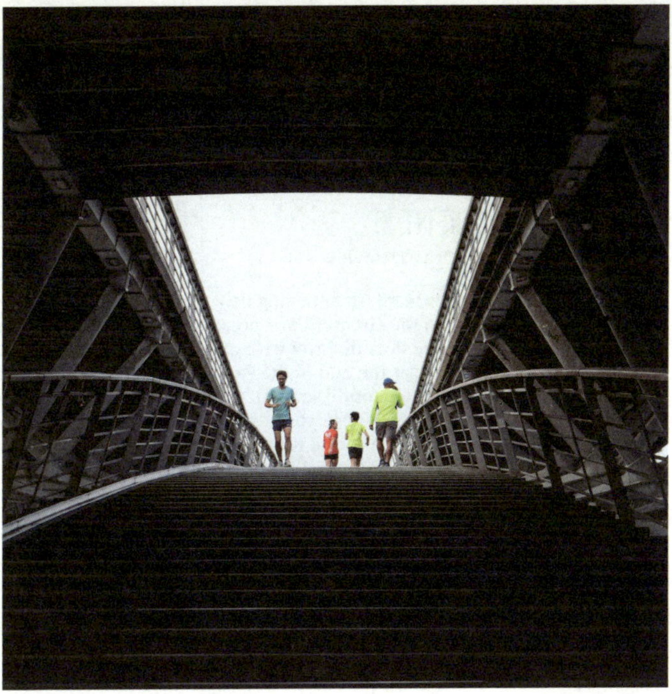

Colour run | *Passerelle Léopold-Sédar-Senghor, Paris.*

"Do you think anyone's actually going to buy us?" | *Quai de Montebello, Paris.*

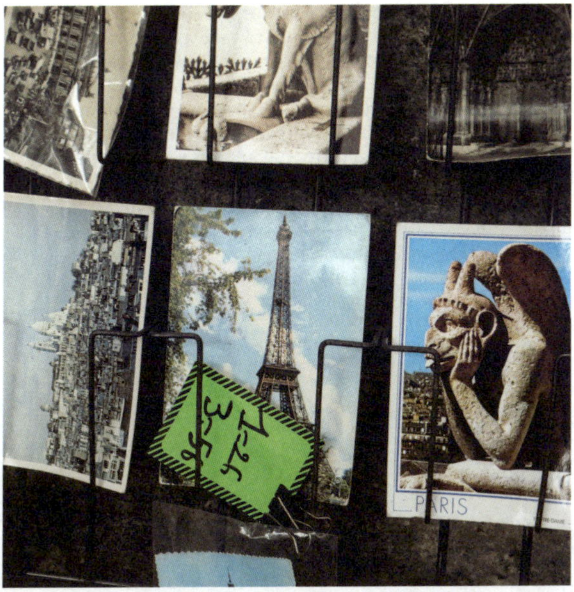

Sport

PARIS

58 ANNETTE K.

#FLOATINGGYM #POOLWITHAVIEW #DJSETS

When the Rosa Bonheur team isn't opening new *guinguettes* (see p. 59) in the Greater Paris area, its moored alongside the Port de Javel with an unusual floating complex at the end of the Parc André Citroën in the 15th arrondissement. On the menu: sport and wellness for everyone – with no membership required. At Annette K (named after Annette Kellermann, the Australian swimmer who popularized the swimming costume), you can swim in an Olympic-size pool on the roof of the barge (with a view of the Eiffel Tower), do yoga under a glass roof, work up a sweat on the weight machines, or just book an appointment with a physiotherapist, dietician or osteopath. The icing on the cake is that the coffee shop doubles up as a *guinguette*, with DJ sets in the evenings. AOK!

Open daily.

Port de Javel Bas, 75015 Paris
Tel: +33 (0)1 85 34 27 47 / annettek.fr

- M — Line 10: Javel-André Citroën
- RER — C: Pont du Garigliano - Hôpital européen Georges-Pompidou
- Tram — T3a: Pont du Garigliano
- Bus — 42, 54, 88: Pont du Garigliano
- Vélib' — Place du Moulin de Javel, Paris 15th

59 SKI NAUTIQUE CLUB DE PARIS

#WATERSKI #WAKEBOARD #STUNNINGVIEWS

On the banks of the Seine, just on the edge of the Bois de Boulogne, the Ski Nautique Club de Paris provides a picture-postcard landscape in which to practice your favourite sport. In the background, the skyline of La Défense rises up before your astonished eyes, while your hands hold the rudder and your feet rest on skis or a wakeboard. Once your session is over, you can continue to savour the spectacle with a drink on the pontoon.

Price: €60 for an introductory session.
Closed Tuesday and Thursday.

1, allée du Bord de l'eau, 75016 Paris
Tel: +33 (0)6 14 61 87 51 or +33 (0)6 09 49 78 84
skinautiqueclubdeparis.com

- M — Line 9: Boulogne - Pont de Saint-Cloud
- Bus — 241: Passerelle de l'Avre
- Vélib' — Transvaal - Charles de Gaulle, Boulogne-Billancourt

60 SOCIÉTÉ SPORTIVE DU JEU DE PAUME ET DE RACQUETS

#SPORTANDHISTORY #REALTENNIS #TIMEMACHINE

In Paris, the ancestor of tennis, aka the *jeu de paume*, has long since deserted the Jeu de paume gallery on Place de la Concorde, replaced by exhibitions devoted to photography and video. But its enthusiasts (and there still are some left) have found refuge in the 16th arrondissement. With the help of some generous investors from England where the sport is known as real tennis, they have created the Société sportive du jeu de paume et de racquets in elegant facilities (old stone and glass roof) where you can play the sport while travelling back in time.

Price: from €15.
Open Monday to Friday 8am to 10pm,
Saturday and Sunday 9am to 8pm.

74 ter, rue Lauriston, 75016 Paris
Tel. + 33 (0)1 47 27 46 86 / squashjeudepaume.com

- M — Line 6: Boissière
- Bus — 82: Lauriston
- Vélib' — Rue Lauriston, Paris 16th

SAINT-GERMAIN-EN-LAYE

61 ACCROCAMP

#BIGSWINGERS #TREETOPBAR #INTOTHEVOID

To be crowned king or queen of the Saint-Germain forest (see p. 61), head for AccroCamp in Saint-Germain-en-Laye where seven tree climbing courses await you. For the thrill seekers, a diving board invites you to take a leap into the void, attached to a fall-arresting system that will ensure a safe landing 15 metres below. For the little ones, there's a special course where you can walk through the air starting from the age of 3. Finally, a platform bar for up to 8 people lets you sip a drink from a treetop perch, comfortably seated on beanbags. Squirrel life has never been so much fun!

Price: from €10 to €35/person (online booking recommended).
Open from February to November.

Parc forestier de la Charmeraie, 48, rue Albert-Priolet, 78100 Saint-Germain-en-Laye
Tel: +33 (0)1 85 39 10 74 / accrocamp.com

- RER — A: Saint-Germain-en-Laye
- Tram — T13: Lisière - Pereire

VILLENEUVE-LA-GARENNE

62 AQUA HAUTS-DE-SEINE DIVING CENTRE

#FREEDIVING #THEBIGBLUE #BREATHLESS

There's more to freediving than plugging your nose and sticking your head underwater! In Villeneuve-la-Garenne, you can practise this sport, popularised by the 1988 film *The Big Blue*, in four pools with depths of 2.5, 5, 10 and 20 metres respectively. Experienced divers can dive on their own, but beginners can also discover the sport through activities supervised by qualified instructors. So pull on your mask and flippers (but not your snorkel!) and get in the water. Don't worry, the pools are heated, the deepest pit is illuminated and there's even a little background music to make the depths feel less lonely.

Price: one-hour introductory session €26 / 10-session pass €187. Open daily.

119, boulevard Charles de Gaulle,
92390 Villeneuve-la-Garenne
Tel: +33 (0)1 40 85 81 28
ucpa.com/centres-sportifs/aqua-hauts-de-seine

- M — Line 4: Porte de Clignancourt,
  M — Line 13: Mairie de Saint-Ouen, then bus 137, Villeneuve-la-Garenne Z.I. Nord stop
- Vélib' — Gare de Gennevilliers

culture

BOULOGNE-BILLANCOURT

63 MUSÉE DES ANNÉES TRENTE

#DESIGN #COLONIALART #INNOVATIONS

Hidden away in the gigantic Landowski cultural space, the Musée des Années Trente showcases the art of the inter-war period over no less than 3,000 m² spread over three floors. Immerse yourself in the splendour of lavish French apartments once filled with wonders. The first large space presents the bold design and architecture of the period. The collection then spans across the artistic trends of the early twentieth century, also providing a fine overview of orientalist and colonial art. A museum that is as rich as it is unexpected.

Price: €7 (full price) / Free for under-26s. Closed Monday.

Espace Landowski, 28, avenue André Morizet,
92100 Boulogne-Billancourt
Tel: +33 (0)1 55 18 46 42 / boulognebillancourt.com

- M — Line 9: Marcel Sembat
  M — Line 10: Boulogne Pont de Saint-Cloud
- Bus — 126, 175, 389: Hôtel de Ville de Boulogne-Billancourt
- Vélib' — Avenue André Morizet, Boulogne

64 MUSÉE ALBERT-KAHN AND GARDENS

#AROUNDTHEWORLDINAGARDEN #ARCHIVESOFTHEWORLD #WORLDPEACE

Entering the Albert Kahn museum and gardens is like entering the waking dream of a travelling humanist. This philanthropic banker created a global garden in Boulogne inspired by his travels. Afghan lavender, Japanese cherry trees, Oregon grapevine, Indian lilac, Welsh poppies... the list is long. Convinced that knowledge of foreign cultures is necessary to pacify the world, Albert Kahn (1860–1940) also commissioned filmmakers and photographers to undertake work in over 50 countries. This unique collection, assembled between 1909 and 1931, has been brought together in a redesigned museum since 2022.

Price: €8 (full price), free for under-26s. Closed Monday (gardens open daily).

1, rue des Abondances, 92100 Boulogne-Billancourt
Tel: +33 (0)1 55 19 28 00 / albert-kahn.hauts-de-seine.fr

- M — Line 10: Boulogne – Pont de Saint-Cloud
- Bus — 52, 126, 160, 175, 467: Pont de Saint-Cloud – Albert Kahn
- Vélib' — 15 rond-point Rhin-Danube, Boulogne

65 MUSÉE PAUL BELMONDO

#SCULPTURE #BELMONDOSENIOR #TACTILEGALLERY

In the Belmondo family, Paul, the father (1898–1982), was one of the last major figures in classical French sculpture. Entirely dedicated to his work, the museum is set up in a beautiful building surrounded by a garden with a few monumental sculptures, opening with a very realistic reconstruction of the sculptor's studio. Upstairs, a tactile gallery allows visually impaired visitors to discover through touch busts made by Belmondo. Under the roof, in the half-light, drawings, watercolours, charcoals, as well as a hundred medallion

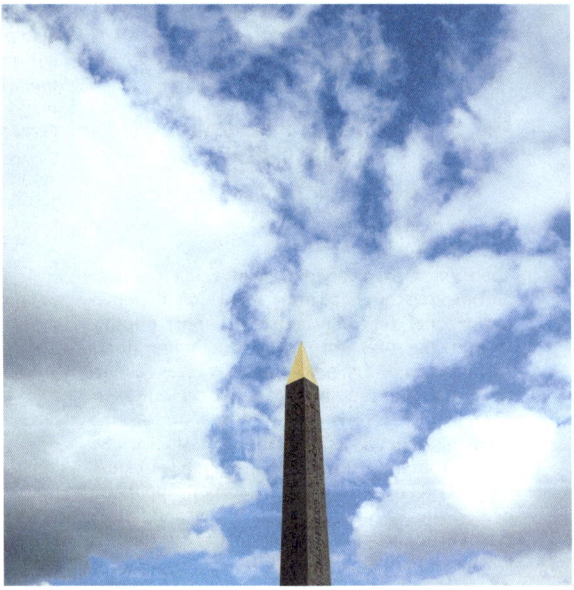

Asterix's best friend | *Place de la Concorde, Paris.*

To be gold, or not to be | *Pont Alexandre III, Paris.*

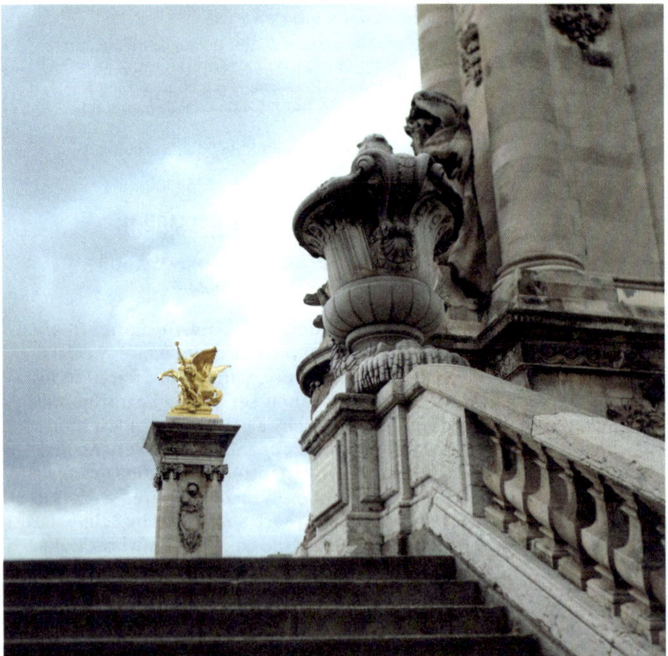

engravings made for the Monnaie de Paris® are preserved. You can explore the nooks and crannies and open the drawers to discover all the artist's works, as if you were sneaking into his home.

Price: €7 (full price) / Free for under-26s.
Closed Monday.

14, rue de l'Abreuvoir, 92100 Boulogne-Billancourt
Tel: +33 (0)1 55 18 69 01 / boulognebillancourt.com

- M — Line 10: Boulogne-Jean Jaurès
- Bus — 123, 260: Église de Boulogne-Billancourt
- Vélib' — Rue du Transvaal

66 LA SEINE MUSICALE

#MUSICALCRUISE #COCKTAILBAR #ROOFTOPGRADEN

In 2017, the Seine Musicale, a glass and concrete liner, docked on the Île Seguin, the former home of the legendary Renault® factories. This unique nautical venue hosts a splendid auditorium with more than 1,000 seats, as well as a large modular concert hall with 6,000 seats capable of hosting megastars such as Bob Dylan, symphonic concerts and musicals. To ensure that visitors have the perfect musical cruise, the New Rose cocktail bar has opened on the lower deck while the upper deck has been transformed into a rooftop garden.

Cours de l'Île Seguin, 92100 Boulogne-Billancourt
Tel: +33 (0)1 74 34 54 00 / laseinemusicale.com

- M — Line 9: Pont de Sèvres
- Bus — 42, 260, 389: Cours de l'Île Seguin
- Vélib' — Cours de l'Île Seguin, Boulogne

LE PORT-MARLY

67 CHÂTEAU DE MONTE-CRISTO

#ALEXANDREDUMAS #PARK #DREAMWORLD

Built at the request of Alexandre Dumas (1802–1870) who wanted a quiet place in which to write, the Château de Monte-Cristo offers a setting conducive to strolling. Children love to explore the large wooded garden, with its caves and hidden prison. In the grounds, Dumas' mini Bastille-like study heightens the romantic character of the site. In the château, with its old parquet floors which smell like wax, one room stands out: the Moorish salon that the writer had built on his return from a trip to Tunisia. Beyond its bourgeois lustre, the Château de Monte-Cristo is a truly imaginative place.

Price: €8 (full price) / €6 (under-25s)
Closed Monday from 1 April to 1 November / Open Saturday and Sunday afternoon from 2 November to 31 March.

Chemin du Haut des Ormes, 78560 Le Port-Marly
Tel: +33 (0)1 39 16 49 49 / chateau-monte-cristo.com

- RER — A: Saint-Germain-en-Laye
  then bus 259: L'Ermitage

MAISONS-LAFFITTE

68 CHÂTEAU DE MAISONS

#RENAISSANCE #ATTIC #LADEFENSE

From the windows of this Renaissance masterpiece, you can see the skyline of La Défense. A striking anachronism for this castle that inspired Versailles and continues to amaze its visitors. "The Château de Maisons is so beautiful that there is no stranger who does not go and see it as one of the most beautiful things we have in France," wrote Charles Perrault (1628–1703). All will become clear when you walk up the steps of the vestibule of honour, a sumptuous staircase topped by a dome. The château, which has been soberly but perfectly refurnished, also surprises with its paintings, including the spectacular *Eruption du Vésuve* by Pierre-Jacques Volaire (1729–1799).

Price: €8 (full price) / Free for under-18s.
Closed Tuesday.

2, avenue Carnot, 78600 Maisons-Laffitte
Tel: +33 (0)1 39 62 01 49 / chateau-maisons.fr

- RER — A: Maisons-Laffitte
- Transilien — Lines L, J: Maisons-Laffitte
- Bus — 262: Rue du Mesnill

NANTERRE

69 PARIS LA DÉFENSE ARENA®

#STADIUM #CONCERTHALL #FUTURISTIC

Until now, there were either concert halls like Bercy, which seats 20,000, or stadiums like the Parc des Princes. So rather than having to choose between the two, the Paris La Défense Arena® decided to be a stadium for shows. Designed to host the Racing 92® rugby club's matches, it is covered by a permanent roof. Its stands, inspired by English stadiums, ensure proximity to the pitch, which is adorned with custom-made artificial turf. With a capacity of 25,000 people on match days, this futuristic cocoon, with its 1,400 m² giant screen, can cater for 40,000 people for concerts or events such as Supercross® in Paris. On the ground floor, the Comptoirs Gourmands offer burgers, pizzas and grilled meats, all cooked live on site, just like the music.

99, Jardins de l'Arche, 92000 Nanterre
parisladefense-arena.com
- M — Line 1: La Défense - Grande Arche
- RER — A: La Défense - Grande Arche
- Transilien — Lines L, U: La Défense - Grande Arche
- Tram — T2: La Défense - Grande Arche
- Bus — 163: Les Terrasses
- Vélib' — Place Nelson Mandela, Nanterre

70 THÉÂTRE NANTERRE-AMANDIERS

#MYTH #THEATREFOREVERYONE #NATIONALSTAGE

The myth of Les Amandiers all began under a tent in 1965, at the Côte des Amandiers. In 1971, the adventure continued in a temporary building before the theatre opened in 1976 with the same philosophy of breaking theatre's elitist image. Since then, the programming has spanned from classical repertoire to delirious contemporary creations. As the theatre is undergoing renovations until 2025, the company is currently set up in a temporary space on the site of its set workshops. They are already thinking ahead and experimenting with what the future of the theatre might look like, in particular by opening outside of performance times. Don't miss out on one of Greater Paris's cult venues.

Price: €32 (full price), €10 (under-30s)

7, avenue Pablo Picasso, 92000 Nanterre
Tel: +33 (0)1 46 14 70 00 / nanterre-amandiers.com
- RER — A: Nanterre Préfecture
- Bus — 159, 259: Joliot-Curie
- Vélib' — Avenue Pablo Picasso, Nanterre
- Free shuttles between Nanterre Préfecture RER station (on the corner of rue Célestin Hébert and boulevard de Pesaro) and Nanterre Amandiers. Schedule on the theatre's website.

PARIS

71 BOURSE DE COMMERCE - PINAULT COLLECTION

#CONTEMPORARYART #NEWWITHTHEOLD #LESHALLES

The contemporary art collection of the Breton businessman François Pinault was already on display in Venice, in the sumptuous setting of Palazzo Grazzi and Punta della Dogana. In 2021, it has found a further space, the former commodities exchange, renovated by the Japanese architect Tadao Ando, in the rapidly changing district of Les Halles in the 1st arrondissement. In addition to exhibitions, there is also a full cultural programme on offer and a 300-seat auditorium for talks, screenings and concerts as well as the Halle aux grains café-restaurant opened by the Michelin-starred chefs Michel and Sébastien Bras.

Price: €14 (full price) / €10 (for 18–26 year-olds)

2, rue de Viarmes, 75001 Paris
Tel: +33 (0)1 55 04 60 60 / boursedecommerce.fr
- M — Line 4: Les Halles
- RER — A, B, D: Châtelet - Les Halles
- Vélib' — Rue Jean-Jacques Rousseau, Paris 1st

72 CENTRE POMPIDOU

#MODERNANDCONTEMPORARYART #PLANYOURVISIT #PANORAMICVIEW

The queues snaking out across the piazza of the Centre Pompidou can be daunting (e-tickets can be bought in advance), but once you have made it inside there are many different ways to explore the temple of modern and contemporary art. Start with the view across the Paris rooftops which gives the impression of floating above the city – a €5 ticket will grant you access. But it would be sacrilegious to make the trip without seeing any of the work on show, even if you stick to the exhaustive permanent collection which is a pleasure to explore. The museum's teams have concocted a journey through the history of twentieth-century art in a skilfully orchestrated, condensed form. As for the temporary exhibitions, they regularly cause a sensation. The Centre Pompidou will be closed for renovations from 2025 to 2030 but will be opening a new space in Massy (Square XXL) in 2026.

Price: €17 (full price) for access to the museum and temporary exhibitions / Free for under-18s. Closed Tuesday.

Place Georges-Pompidou, 75004 Paris
Tel: +33 (0)1 44 78 12 33 / centrepompidou.fr
- M — Line 11: Rambuteau,
  M — Line 1: Hôtel de Ville
- Bus — 38, 47, 75: Centre Georges Pompidou
- Vélib' — Rue Rambuteau, Paris 4th

73 LA COMÉDIE-FRANÇAISE

#THEATRE #CLASSICS #INSTITUTION

If you think of overacted period pieces when you think of the Comédie-Française, then it's time for you to pay this theatre another visit. Under the gold and velvet of the Salle Richelieu and in the most intimate Vieux-Colombier and Studio-Théâtre theatres, the company members of the Comédie-Française restage the classics from Shakespeare to Racine in often highly inventive, thrilling and exciting productions. The romantic

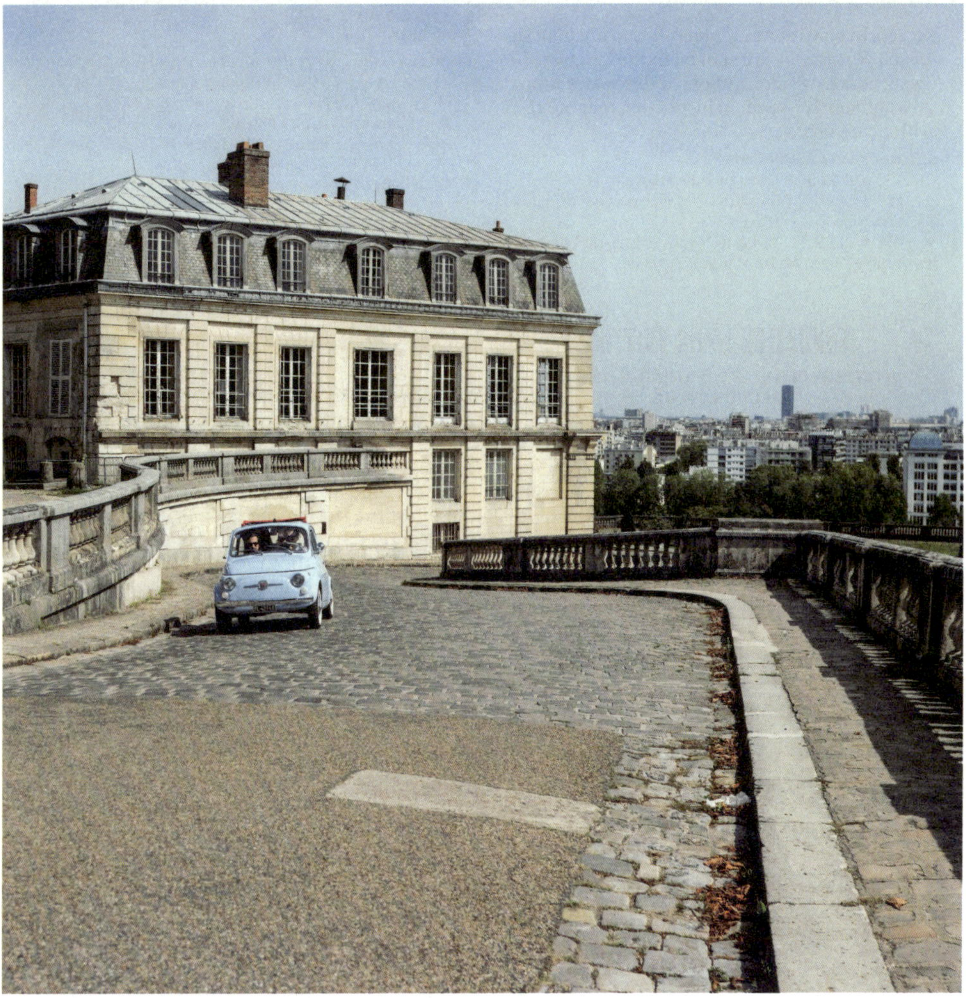

Parisian dolce vita | *Allée de la Carrière, Saint-Cloud.*

secrets in Marivaux's eighteenth-century play *La Double Inconstance* are spoken in the language of today. Contemporary authors or film adaptations also light up the stage. An institution that bristles with excitement.

1, place Colette, 75001 Paris
Tel: +33 (0)1 44 58 15 15 / comedie-francaise.fr

- M — Lines 1, 7: Palais Royal - Musée du Louvre,
  M — Line 14: Pyramides
- Bus — 21, 69, 72, 81: Palais Royal - Musée du Louvre
- Vélib' — Place André Malraux, Paris 1st

74 FONDATION LOUIS VUITTON

#CONTEMPORARYART #LATENIGHTEVENTS #ARCHITECTURE

A sailboat with curved glass sails designed by the renowned architect Frank Gehry, the Fondation Louis Vuitton impresses with its architecture, but also with its programming, which includes a number of blockbuster exhibitions like the presentation of the Morozov collection in 2021 or the two-man show by Jean-Michel Basquiat and Andy Warhol in 2023. However, the foundation also knows how to stray off the beaten track to seduce new visitors (and keep them coming back), especially during its late-night events organized on the first Friday of the month, which provide an opportunity to see and experience the building, the work and the exhibitions in a different way.

Price: €16 (full price). Tickets also give access to the Jardin d'Acclimatation (see p. 62).
Closed Tuesday except during school holidays.

8, avenue du Mahatma Gandhi, 75016 Paris
Tel: +33 (0)1 40 69 96 00 / fondationlouisvuitton.fr

- M — Line 1: Les Sablons
- Bus — 244: Fondation Louis Vuitton
- Vélib' — Avenue du Mahatma Gandhi, Paris 16th

75 FORUM DES IMAGES

#SILVERSCREEN #MASTERCLASS #VIRTUALREALITY

In the maze of Les Halles, the Forum des Images takes you into a world where the image is king. You can choose to view the archives of a bygone Paris or explore Greater Paris, enjoy the best that cinema has to offer, past and present, or devour documentaries and animated films. Every kind of moving image is available here, including virtual reality with the NewImages festival, which takes place each year in the spring. Look out for the master classes organized throughout the year with the legends of filmmaking.

Closed Monday.

Forum des Halles, 2, rue du Cinéma, 75001 Paris
Tel: +33 (0)1 44 76 63 00 / forumdesimages.fr

- M — Line 4: Les Halles,
  M — Lines 1, 4, 7, 11, 14: Châtelet
- RER — A, B, D: Châtelet - Les Halles
- Bus — 67, 74, 85: Coquillière - Les Halles
- Vélib' — Rue de la Cossonnerie, Paris 1st

76 GRAND PALAIS AND GRAND PALAIS ÉPHÉMÈRE

#EVENTS #EXHIBITIONS #GRANDSCALE

With a name like the Grand Palais, renovations were always going to be a major undertaking. A symbol of the 1900 Universal Exhibition, the building has been undergoing a facelift since 2021 with a view to reopening for the Paris Olympics, when it will host the fencing and taekwondo events. In the meantime, a temporary 10,000-m² building has been erected on the Champ de Mars, designed by the architect Jean-Michel Wilmotte, whose credits include the Nice stadium and Seoul airport. The Grand Palais Éphèmere, which serves as a showcase for the major events usually hosted in the nave of the Grand Palais, is also on the list of Olympic venues for judo, wrestling, wheelchair rugby and para-judo.

Place Joffre, 75007 Paris
Tel: +33 (0)1 44 13 17 17 / grandpalais.fr

- M — Line 8: École Militaire
- Bus — 80: École Militaire, Paris 7th

77 LOUVRE

#LARGESTMUSEUMINTHEWORLD #LATENIGHTOPENING #BEATTHECROWDS

With no less than 500,000 artworks, the Louvre is the largest museum in the world. It is also the most popular, with more than 10 million annual visitors. The secret to avoid the crowds? You have to come on Friday evenings. Emptied of the daytime crowd, the Louvre seems almost deserted and the atmosphere is full of mystery.

Price: €17 / Free for under-18s.
Open daily from 9am–6pm except Tuesday.
Late-night openings until 9.45pm on Friday.

Rue de Rivoli, 75001 Paris
Tel: +33 (0)1 40 20 53 17 / louvre.fr

- M — Lines 1, 7: Palais Royal - Musée du Louvre
- Bus — 21, 48, 67, 69, 72, 81: Palais Royal - Musée du Louvre,
  27: Musée du Louvre
- Vélib' — Rue Saint-Honoré, Paris 1st

78 MAISON DE BALZAC

#ONEOFAKIND #HUMANCOMEDY #COSYCAFE

Nestling on the slopes of Passy, the Maison de Balzac is the only remaining residence of the novelist in Paris. It was in this garden-level house that he wrote the whole of *The Human Comedy* between 1840 and 1847. Now transformed into a museum, it tells the story of his life, his work and his thousands of characters through an original display. Events are organized here throughout the year, including workshops, plays, readings and photo exhibitions. With its garden, sun loungers and unique view of the Eiffel Tower, the Maison de Balzac is one of the most popular spots in the area. It is now home to the Rose Bakery café, a cosy lounge with a library full of Balzac books, surrounded by picture windows displaying quotations from the writer, gourmand and bon vivant.

Free admission
Open Tuesday to Sunday, 10am to 6pm

47, rue Raynouard, 75016 Paris
Tel: +33 (0)1 55 74 41 80 / maisondebalzac.paris.fr

- M — Line 6: Passy
  M — Linz 9: La Muette
- RER — C: Avenue du Président Kennedy - Maison de Radio France
- Bus — 72: Lamballe - Ankara
- Vélib' — Rue du Ranelagh, Paris 16th

79 MEP - MAISON EUROPÉENNE DE LA PHOTOGRAPHIE

#FROMTHE50STOTODAY #LIBRARY #GOLDMINE

The Maison européenne de la photographie (MEP) has been building up a gold mine of contemporary photography since 1978. With its collection of 20,000 prints, it exhibits both leading figures and young talents from the 1950s to the present day. In addition to its museum, with its intimate architecture, the MEP also houses an auditorium, a library with 30,000 publications and a video library of 750 films.

Price: €13 (full price) / €8 (under-30s)
Closed Monday and Tuesday.

5–7, rue de Fourcy, 75004 Paris
Tel: +33 (0)1 44 78 75 00 / mep-fr.org

- M — Line 1: Saint-Paul,
  M — Line 7: Pont Marie
- Bus — 69, 76, 96: Rue du Pont Louis-Philippe
- Vélib' — Rue Saint-Antoine, Paris 4th

80 MUSÉE CERNUSCHI

#ASIANARTS #GIANTBUDDHA #JAPANESEGARDEN

Tucked away at the end of Parc Monceau, the Musée Cernuschi's jewels might be well hidden, but this is the second largest collection of Asian art in France. You can admire extraordinary gems such as the eighteenth-century Japanese Buddha, a four-metre-tall black bronze from a Tokyo temple. A museum worth revisiting as it was renovated in 2023. On your way out, don't hesitate to take a stroll through the romantic Anglo-Japanese park with its pool.

Price: for temporary exhibitions €10 (full price) / Free for under-18s.
Open from Tuesday to Sunday, 10am to 6 pm.

7, avenue Velasquez, 75008 Paris
Tel: +33 (0)1 53 96 21 50 / cernuschi.paris.fr

- M — Line 2: Villiers or Monceau,
  M — Line 3: Malesherbes
- Bus — 20, 93, 94: Malesherbes - Courcelles
- Vélib' — Rue de Monceau, Paris 8th

81 MUSÉE D'ART MODERNE DE PARIS

#MONUMENT #15000WORKS #FROMPICASSOTOBOLTANSKI

A legacy of the 1937 International Exhibition, the Palais de Tokyo is home to, on one side, the Palais de Tokyo (see p. 57) contemporay art centre, and on the other, the Musée d'Art Moderne de Paris. A striking combination for anyone interested in the artistic world of the 20th and 21st centuries. Within its marble walls, the Musée d'Art Moderne's collection includes 15,000 artworks from Picasso to Boltanski, Modigliani, Chagall and Picabia, and its temporary exhibitions are always of the highest standard. Recently renovated, it now has a bookshop-boutique on two levels as well as a restaurant open for lunch and dinner. A way of satisfying all appetites.

Price: €5 to €12 depending on the exhibition / Free for under-18s. Free access to the permanent collection.
Open from Tuesday to Sunday, 10am to 6pm

11, avenue du Président Wilson, 75016 Paris
mam.paris.fr

- M — Line 9: Iéna
- Bus — 63: Iéna
- Vélib' — Rue de Longchamp, Paris 16th

82 MUSÉE D'ORSAY

#IMPRESSIONISM #LATENIGHTEVENTS #OLDTRAINSTATION

If you think you know everything about the Musée d'Orsay, an old train station that became the haunt of impressionists such as Monet and Renoir, let yourself be surprised by "Les Curieuses Nocturnes". Organized four Thursdays a year, these evenings last until 11pm and include all kinds of activities: concerts in the nave, live performances, talks and guided tours in the permanent collection, and lunchtime or evening concerts. Look out for dates on the museum's Facebook page.

Price: €16 (full price) / Free for under-26s.
Closed Monday. Late-night opening until 9.45pm on Thursday.

Esplanade Valéry Giscard-d'Estaing, 75007 Paris
Tel: +33 (0)1 40 49 48 14 / musee-orsay.fr

- M — Line 12: Solférino
- RER — C: Musée d'Orsay
- Bus — 24, 68, 69, 73, 84, 87: Musée d'Orsay
- Vélib' — Rue de Lille, Paris 7th

83 MUSÉE DU QUAI BRANLY – JACQUES CHIRAC

#AROUNDTHEWORLD #CIVILIZATIONS #GARDEN

To reach the collections of the Quai Branly, the journey starts on the banks of the Seine, in front of the Debilly footbridge. You have to pass through a glass cocoon, cross a garden teeming with ferns and grasses and take the footbridge illuminated with the 16,000 names of the peoples of the world. In the half-light, on a single level without walls, you can navigate between 3,500 objects from Oceania to Asia, Africa and the Americas. Of course, no two journeys will be the same: some will hear the calls of Vanuatu's huge slit drums, while others will dream of wearing the diadems of the Ottoman era in Algiers. Still others will feel invincible thanks to the protective statuettes of Congo. In its own way, the Quai Branly invites visitors to leave the shores of Greater Paris and to set sail.

Price: from €12 (full price) / Free for under-18s.
Access to the panoramic terrace from June to September: €3. Free for museum ticket-holders.
Open from Tuesday to Sunday from 10.30am to 7pm.
Late-night opening on Thursday until 10pm.

37, quai Branly, 75007 Paris
Tel: +33 (0)1 56 61 70 00 / quaibranly.fr

- M — Line 9: Alma-Marceau or Iéna
- RER — C: Pont de l'Alma
- Bus — 42: Tour Eiffel
- Vélib' — Quai Branly, Paris 7th

84 MUSÉE MARMOTTAN MONET

#IMPRESSIONISM #IMPRESSIVE #FROMMONETTORENOIR

Tourist buses park at the borders of the 16th arrondissement just for a single painting, but *Impression, Sunrise* should not eclipse all the other masterpieces of the Marmottan Monet Museum. Starting with Monet's other paintings, his *Water Lilies* where the sky and water meet, or his *Rose Path, Giverny*. It's quite simple: the institution houses the world's largest collection of works by the artist. Bequeathed by Claude Monet's son, the collection required the creation of a special room beneath the museum. Above the pedestal tables or Empire candelabras of this private mansion also shine the pearls of other impressionists: Pierre-Auguste Renoir's *Julie Manet* staring into space, or the sparkling streets of Paris in the rain by Gustave Caillebotte. The first woman of the movement, Berthe Morisot, even has a room of her own. Her technique derived from watercolour creates extraordinary translucent effects. Get ready for a painting lesson.

Price: €14 (full price) / Free for under-7s.
Open from Tuesday to Sunday from 10am to 6pm.
Late-night opening on Thursday until 9pm.

2, rue Louis Boilly, 75016 Paris
Tel: +33 (0)1 44 96 50 33 / marmottan.fr

- M — Line 9: La Muette
- RER — C: Boulainvilliers
- Bus — 32: Louis Boilly
- Vélib' — Place de la Porte de Passy, Paris 16th

85 MUSÉE NATIONAL DES ARTS ASIATIQUES GUIMET

#ASIA #50000ARTWORKS #VESTIGEOFANGKOR

The industrialist, globetrotter and art collector, Émile Guimet decided to build his own museum in 1889 on Place d'Iéna. Fifty years later, the museum chose to exchange its Egyptian pieces for the entire Asian art department of the Louvre, thereby creating one of the most famous institutions in the world dedicated to the cultures of the Far East with some 50,000 works. Above all, do not miss the imposing *Giant's Way*, a fragment of the Angkor Wat temple that amazed visitors at the 1878 Universal Exhibition.

Price: €11.5 (full price) / Free for under-26s.
Open daily except Tuesday from 10am to 6pm.

6, place d'Iéna, 75016 Paris
Tel: +33 (0)1 56 52 53 00 / guimet.fr

- M — Lines 6, 9: Trocadéro, Iéna
- Bus — 63: Iéna
- Vélib' — Rue de Longchamp, Paris 16th

86 PALAIS DE TOKYO

#CONTEMPORARYART
#EATANDDRINK #CLUBBING

The Palais de Tokyo embraces the paradoxes of today's world, combining the radicality of contemporary expression while cultivating the art of conviviality. Lose yourself in the 22,000 m² of this cathedral of raw concrete, the largest contemporary art centre in Europe. Beyond its diverse exhibition programme, its colourful bookshop is full of beautiful publications – a place of discovery in and of itself. But the Palais de Tokyo also offers other pleasures. You can have a bite to eat in front of the Eiffel Tower® at Monsieur Bleu or Bambini, or take to the dancefloor at YOYO, in the Cinémathèque française's former space. All this until late, as the Palais de Tokyo is open from noon to 10pm.

Price: €12 (full price) / Free for under-18s.
Open daily except Tuesday from 12pm to 10pm.
Late-night opening on Thursday until midnight.

13, avenue du Président Wilson, 75016 Paris
Tel: +33 (0)1 81 97 35 88 / palaisdetokyo.com

- M — Line 9: Iéna
- Bus — 72: Musée d'Art Moderne - Palais de Tokyo
- Vélib' — Marceau - Président Wilson, Paris 8th

87 PETIT PALAIS

#MUSEUM #GARDENOFEDEN
#HIDDENTERRACE

The Petit Palais, built for the 1900 Universal Exhibition, like the Grand Palais, is a haven of tranquillity in the heart of the capital's madness, a stone's throw from the Champs-Elysées. Its interior garden, decorated with ponds, is particularly lush with its exotic plants and its palm and banana trees. Seated on the terrace of the museum café, you can contemplate this garden of Eden while nibbling on the salad or pasta of the day. The permanent collections are just as striking, from Rodin's *Amour et Psyché* kiss to Carpeaux's *Ugolin* with its deformed features distorted by despair.

Free access to the permanent collection.
Entry fee for temporary exhibitions.
Open from Tuesday to Sunday from 10am to 6pm.

Avenue Winston Churchill, 75008 Paris
Tel: +33 (0)1 53 43 40 00 / petitpalais.paris.fr

- M — Lines 1, 13: Champs-Élysées - Clémenceau
- Bus — 72, 83, 93: Grand Palais
- Vélib' — Avenue Dutuit, Paris 8th

88 THÉÂTRE NATIONAL DE CHAILLOT

#PALACE #ARTDECO
#CONTEMPORARYDANCE

"In these walls devoted to marvels..." Engraved on the facade, this quote by Paul Valéry (1871–1945) perfectly encapsulates the effect of the Palais de Chaillot. This art deco jewel may have been described as "totalitarian" for its monumental neo-classical architecture, but it has never ceased to amaze. What was, in the 1950s, the headquarters of Jean Vilar's national popular theatre was transformed, in the early 2000s, into a temple of contemporary dance. In addition to the performances, it is possible to attend many other events such as balls or group dance classes led by the greatest choreographers.

1, place du Trocadéro, 75016 Paris
Tel: +33 (0)1 53 65 31 00 / theatre-chaillot.fr

- M — Lines 6, 9: Trocadéro
- Bus — 32, 63: Trocadéro
- Vélib' — Avenue d'Eylau

PUTEAUX

89 PARVIS DE LA DÉFENSE

#OPENAIRMUSEUM
#OVER50WORKS #MIRÓ

Art is able to find a home in the most unexpected locations, even on the Parvis de La Défense where around fifty works of art are presented, spread out over a space equivalent to five football fields. A visit here takes on the form of a treasure hunt with some unforgettable discoveries such as *Les Personnages Fantastiques* by the Spanish artist Joan Miró, *Le Pouce* by the French sculptor César or *La Défense de Paris* by Louis-Ernest Barrias, inaugurated in 1883, giving the district its name. Despite the skyscrapers of this financial district, the area is surprisingly quiet, as cars are relegated underground. The other pleasant surprise is the change initiated by La Défense, Europe's leading business district, which has chosen to open up to culture and leisure with new venues such as the Paris La Défense Arena®, a futuristic entertainment stadium (see p. 51).

Free entry.

Parvis de la Défense, 92800 Puteaux
parisladefense.com/en/discover/artworks/

- M — Line 1: La Défense - Grande Arche
- RER — A: La Défense - Grande Arche
- Transilien — Lines L, U: La Défense - Grande Arche
- Tram — T2: La Défense - Grande Arche
- Bus — 144, 159, 178: La Défense - Grande Arche

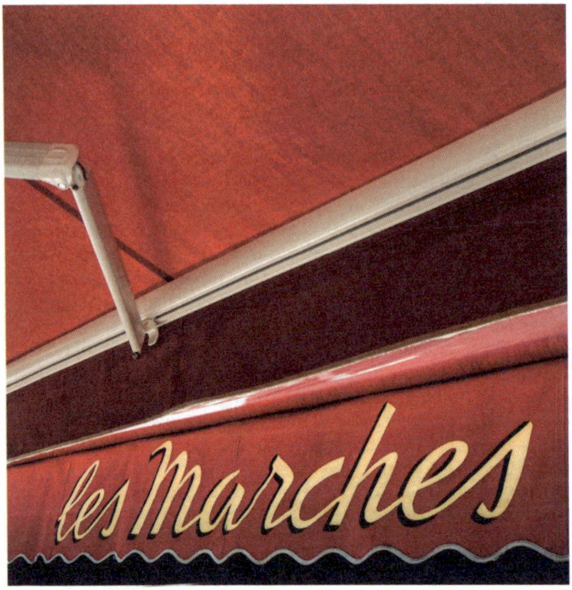

Mind the gap | *Rue de la Manutention, Paris.*

Rosa, rosa, rosam, rosae... | *Rosa Bonheur, Paris.*

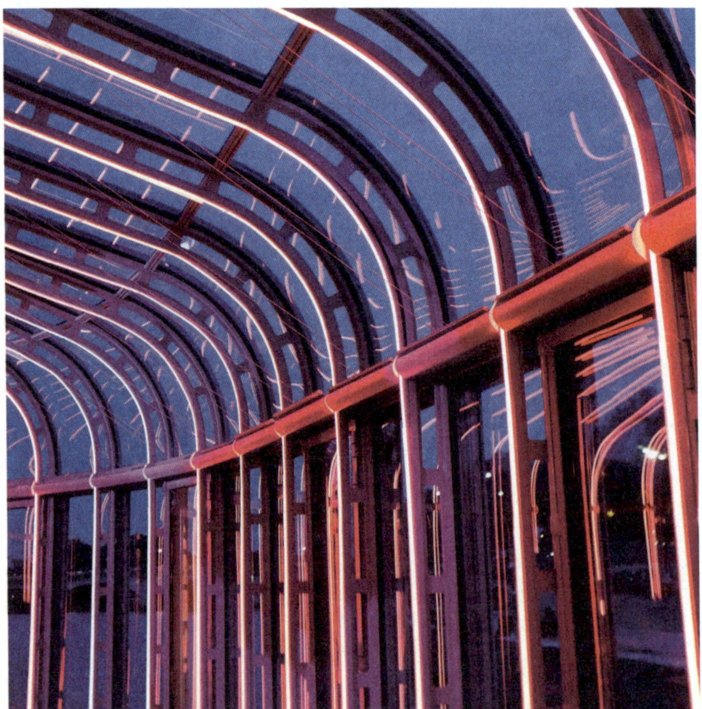

RUEIL-MALMAISON

90 CHÂTEAU DE MALMAISON AND PARC DE BOIS-PRÉAU

#NAPOLEONANDJOSEPHINE
#PARK #SPRAWLINGLAWNS

Pierre Fontaine (1762–1853), Napoleon's architect, described it as an "ugly house". Let's just say that its appearance is not the Château de Malmaison's main attribute. Acquired by Napoleon Bonaparte and Josephine de Beauharnais in 1799, it became the latter's exclusive residence in 1809, following the imperial couple's divorce. Transformed into a museum, this large white building has some beautiful rooms such as the library and the council chamber where Napoleon gathered his ministers. On the other side of the street, a stroll in the Parc de Bois-Préau is a must. This English-style garden offers vast lawns on which to catch the sun and some beautiful specimens such as a giant redwood.

Price: €6.5 (full price) / €5 (reduced price)
Closed Tuesday.

12, avenue du Château de Malmaison,
92500 Rueil-Malmaison

Tel: +33 (0)1 41 29 05 55
musees-nationaux-malmaison.fr/chateau-malmaison

- RER — A: Rueil-Malmaison
- Bus — 258, 259: Le Château
- Vélib' — Boulevard Marcel Pourtout, Rueil-Malmaison

SAINT-GERMAIN-EN-LAYE

91 MUSÉE D'ARCHÉOLOGIE NATIONALE

#CHATEAU #HISTORYOFFRANCE
#FORTHEWHOLEFAMILY

Did you know that the Musée d'Archéologie Nationale is located in a twelfth-century château in Saint-Germain-en-Laye? The royal residence of Louis VI the Fat, the castle of Saint-Germain-en-Laye is just as imposing as its first occupant's name. In 1862, Napoleon III, a passionate archaeologist, decided to create the museum of Celtic and Gallo-Roman antiquities here. From the Paleolithic period, about 2.6 million years ago, to the Early Middle Ages, the museum's collections reconstruct French history. The presentation of the museum is well-documented and the sublime view of the château's courtyard is every bit as good as that of the Louvre. So many reasons to stroll for hours through ancestral France.

Price: €6 (full price) / Free for under-26s.
Open daily except Tuesday from 10am to 5pm.

Place Charles de Gaulle, 78100 Saint-Germain-en-Laye
Tel: +33 (0)1 39 10 13 00
musee-archeologienationale.fr

- RER — A: Saint-Germain-en-Laye
- Bus — 259: Saint-Germain-en-Laye

lifestyle

ASNIÈRES-SUR-SEINE

92 ROSA BONHEUR À L'OUEST

#MODERNGUINGUETTE #SEINESIDE
#KIDFRIENDLY

After settling in the north at the Buttes Chaumont, in the centre at Invalides, and in the east in the bois de Vincennes (see p. 109), Rosa Bonheur has a new outpost in the west on the banks of the Seine in Asnières. The Rosa spirit is intact: sip on a glass of spritz before tucking into a pizza from the wood-fired oven while sitting at the long, wooden outdoor tables. On the water, a barge provides shelter when it is needed. To top it all off, the Rosa even has provided a small playground for children, so that parents can put the world to rights without being interrupted.

Closed Monday and Tuesday.

20, quai du docteur Dervaux, 92600 Asnières-sur-Seine
rosabonheur.fr

- Transilien — Lines L, J: Asnières-sur-Seine
- Bus — 238: Rue de la Station
- Vélib' — Rue Denis Papin, Asnières-sur-Seine

NANTERRE

93 VIVE LES GROUES

#ECOSPACE #FIESTAS
#CAMPING

After running the mythical third space, Les Grands Voisins, in Paris, until it closed in 2020, the prolific Parisian-Marseillais team of Yes We Camp has taken on a completely different challenge by opening a 9,000-m² third space in Nanterre. The objective this time is to grow a plant nursery through playful workshops, collective plantations and parties. Designed as a public square, the location offers a rich programme of events, artistic installations, a bar and – a Yes We Camp trademark – a campsite.

290, rue de la Garenne, 92000 Nanterre
vivelesgroues.org

- RER — A: Nanterre Préfecture
- Tram — T2: Les Fauvelles
- Bus — 163: Arras
- Vélib' — Place François Mitterand, Nanterre

Outdoors

MARLY-LE-ROI

94 DOMAINE DE MARLY

#PARKLAND #SPRAWLINGLAWNS #ROYALTY

Originally designed by the Sun King Louis XIV to receive hand-picked courtiers, the Domaine de Marly is now one of the most beautiful picnic areas in Greater Paris. While only the foundations of the castle remain, the park is still going strong. Its large pool with its pointed boxwood hedges evokes Versailles, while its gigantic lawns guarantee you plenty of space on which to spread out your picnic rug. For the history buffs, there is a museum where you can find out more about the Domaine.

Open daily.

78160 Marly-le-Roi
musee-promenade.fr

- Transilien — Line L: Marly-le-Roi

PARIS

95 BOIS DE BOULOGNE

#2.5TIMESBIGGERTHANCENTRALPARK #RIVERSANDLAKES #LANDSCAPEDGARDENS

With its 850 hectares, the Bois de Boulogne is 2.5 times the size of New York's Central Park. However, apart from its somewhat scandalous reputation, the Bois de Boulogne (like the Bois de Vincennes) is still largely unknown to the people of Greater Paris, as a study by the Atelier parisien d'urbanisme highlighted in 2020. Originally a royal hunting forest, it was given to Parisians by Napoleon III, who wanted to add greenery to the capital. He entrusted the engineer Adolphe Alphand – who also designed the Buttes-Chaumont (19th arrondissement) and the Bois de Vincennes (12th arrondissement) – with the task of remodelling it in the style of English landscaped gardens. The brief was to create a place of relaxation and entertainment for the residents of the new but already chic districts of western Paris. Rivers and lakes were intended to recreate mountain and countryside landscapes at a time when travel was still rare. Virginie Jannière, a journalist with Enlarge your Paris, went there for the first time in 2023. You can follow her steps on enlargeyourparis.fr.

Free entry.
Open daily (opening times are seasonal).

Allée de Longchamp, 75016 Paris

- M — 9: Ranelagh,
  M — 1: Porte Maillot,
  M — 2: Porte Dauphine
- RER — C: Avenue Foch
- Bus — 63: Route de Suresnes
- Vélib' — Chemin de ceinture du lac Inférieur

SAINT-CLOUD

96 DOMAINE NATIONAL DE SAINT-CLOUD

#SPRAWLINGLAWNS #PANORAMAS #FIREWORKS

Designed by one of the architects of the Château de Versailles, Jules Hardouin-Mansart, the Parc de Saint-Cloud boasts no less than 460 hectares of greenery at the gates of Paris. In addition to its beautiful lawns to relax on, the park offers unexpected views of Paris and also houses several restaurants.

Free entry for pedestrians, €3 for motorcycles, €5.50 for cars.

1, avenue de la Grille d'honneur, 92210 Saint-Cloud
domaine-saint-cloud.fr

- M — Line 9: Pont de Sèvres
- Transilien — Lines L, U: Sèvres - Ville-d'Avray
- Tram — T2: Musée de Sèvres
- Bus — 169, 171, 179, 426: Musée de Sèvres
- Vélib' — Place de la Manufacture Nationale, Sèvres

SAINT-GERMAIN-EN-LAYE

97 FORÊT DE SAINT-GERMAIN-EN-LAYE

#INTHEHEARTOFTHEFOREST #PATHS #FAIRGROUND

Thanks to the Achères - Grand Cormier station, you can take the RER straight into the heart of a forest 160 times larger than the Jardin du Luxembourg (see p. 204). From there, you can enjoy over 50 km of marked trails, 70 km of bridle paths, three bicycle paths and several hundred kilometres of roads and forest paths closed to traffic. From late June to mid-August, the Saint-Germain-en-Laye forest is home to one of the oldest fairgrounds in France, the Fête des Loges.

onf.fr

- RER — A: Achères - Grand Cormier
- Transilien — Line J: Achères - Grand Cormier

SURESNES

98 MONT-VALÉRIEN TERRACE

#ROOFTOP #BESTVIEW #FRENCHHISTORY

From this spacious promontory you can get an unobstructed view of Paris, the Bois de Boulogne and the towers of La Défense. The perfect place for a four-star picnic but also to immerse yourself in history, as the Mont Valérien is dedicated to the memory of France's soldiers. An impressive memorial is located at the foot of the fortress built in the 19th century, which was used by the German army as the main location for executions of resistance fighters and hostages during World War II. An American cemetery with perfectly aligned white crosses is also located on the slopes of the Mont Valérien. In addition, there is a park with large lawns, games for children, a riding school, tennis courts overlooking La Défense, a skate park and a 2.5-km trail - the Jacques-Baumel promenade.

Rue du Fécheray, 92150 Suresnes
Tel: +33 (0)1 47 32 35 75 / hauts-de-seine.fr

- Transilien — Lines L, U: Suresnes - Mont Valérien
- Bus — 160, 241, 360: Mont Valérien
- Vélib' — Rue Gardenat-Lapostol, Suresnes

where to eat

BOULOGNE-BILLANCOURT

99 OSABAK

#WINEBAR #THEBASQUEUNCLES #SMALLPLATES

It all started with two friends running a catering service, Les Tontons du Tartare, which specialized in revisiting this classic form of cuisine using products and combinations that were little known to the general public. Hit hard by the Covid crisis, the pair decided to reinvent themselves and, in 2023, opened their own place: Osabak, which means "the uncles" in Basque. The result is a wine bar for eating and drinking that's in perfect tune with the times.

Lunch: starter/main or main/dessert for €25, starter/main/dessert for €29. Evening: dishes from €9 to €24. Closed Monday and Sunday.

50, rue Escudier, 92100 Boulogne-Billancourt
Tel: +33(0)1 40 96 07 80 / osabak.fr

- M — 10: Boulogne Jean Jaurès
- Bus — 123: Escudier - Marché
- Vélib' — Place Denfert-Rochereau, Boulogne-Billancourt

MARLY-LE-ROI

100 LE VILLAGE TOMOHIRO

#ONEMICHELINSTAR #FRANCEJAPAN #REDWALLS

Walking up Marly-le-Roi's Grande Rue from the park (see p. 60) is already a change of scenery that feels more Provençal than Parisian. Inside, the journey continues towards even more distant horizons courtesy of the Michelin-starred chef Tomohiro Uido. In his intimate restaurant with its red walls, he brings together French and Japanese cuisine with dishes like blue lobster and foie gras

goï cuôn. A restaurant that is guaranteed to leave you with beautiful gastronomic memories. Don't forget to book ahead.

Price: 5 dishes for €72, 6 dishes for €87 or 10 dishes for €152. Closed Monday, Saturday lunchtime and Sunday evening.

3, Grande Rue, 78160 Marly-le-Roi
Tel: +33 (0)1 39 16 28 14 / restaurant-levillage.fr

- Transilien — Line L: Marly-le-Roi
- Bus — 10: Mairie

PARIS

101 LES MARCHES

#ROADSIDECAFE #VALUEFORMONEY #CHECKEREDTABLECLOTHS

A roadside café in the 16th arrondissement seems unlikely. And yet, in a little street next to the Palais de Tokyo (see p. 57), the restaurant Les Marches can lay claim to the famous label. In terms of value for money, you'll be hard-pressed to find anything better in the area, which is more familiar with tourist traps and trendy bistros. You won't regret the trip if you try the snails, the lamb kidneys in mustard sauce and the profiteroles.

Price: dishes from €6 to €30.
Open daily from noon to 2.30pm and from 7.30–10.30pm.

5, rue de la Manutention, 75016 Paris
Tel: +33 (0)1 47 23 52 80 / lesmarches-restaurant.com

- M — 9: Iéna
- RER — C: Pont de l'Alma
- Bus — 72: Musée d'Art Moderne - Palais de Tokyo
- Vélib' — Longchamp - Place d'Iéna, Paris 16th

PUTEAUX

102 L'ESCARGOT 1903

#2016PASTRYCHEFOFTHEYEAR #CULINARYSURPRISES #TAKEYOURTIME

Voted pastry chef of the year in 2016 by the Omnivore group, Yannick Tranchant doesn't only cater to those with a sweet tooth. In 2018 he took over the restaurant L'Escargot 1903, where he offers a surprise tasting menu every evening. He takes the same care with the presentation of his dishes as he does with his cakes, with a subtle interplay of flavours and textures. The décor is warm, the service relaxed and the pretty terrace is ideal for summer evenings.

Price: Tasting menu at €65.
Open Monday to Friday.

94, rue Sadi-Carnot, 92800 Puteaux
Tel: +33 (0)1 47 75 03 66 / lescargot1903.com
(booking recommended)

- Transilien — Line L and U: Puteaux
- Tram — T2: Puteaux
- Vélib' — Place du 8 mai 1945, Puteaux

Family

PARIS

103 JARDIN D'ACCLIMATATION

#FAIRGROUND #EDUCATIONALFARM #BOISDEBOULOGNE

After undergoing a serious facelift in 2018, the Jardin d'Acclimatation, in the heart of the Bois de Boulogne, now houses 40 rides including the "Speed Rockets": a 3-minute course with 400 metres of twists and turns. Inaugurated in 1860 by Napoleon III and Empress Eugénie, the garden's original vocation remains intact: to allow visitors to observe animals in a natural setting. Between the Norman farm and the large aviary, more than 500 boarders live here. There is plenty on offer to plan a busy day out with the family, with the added bonus of a choice of twelve different restaurants and five food trucks.

Open daily.

Carrefour des Sablons, 75016 Paris
Tel: +33 (0)1 40 67 90 85 / jardindacclimatation.fr

- M — Line 1: Les Sablons
- Bus — 244: Jardin d'acclimatation
- Vélib' — Avenue du Mahatma Gandhi, Paris 16th

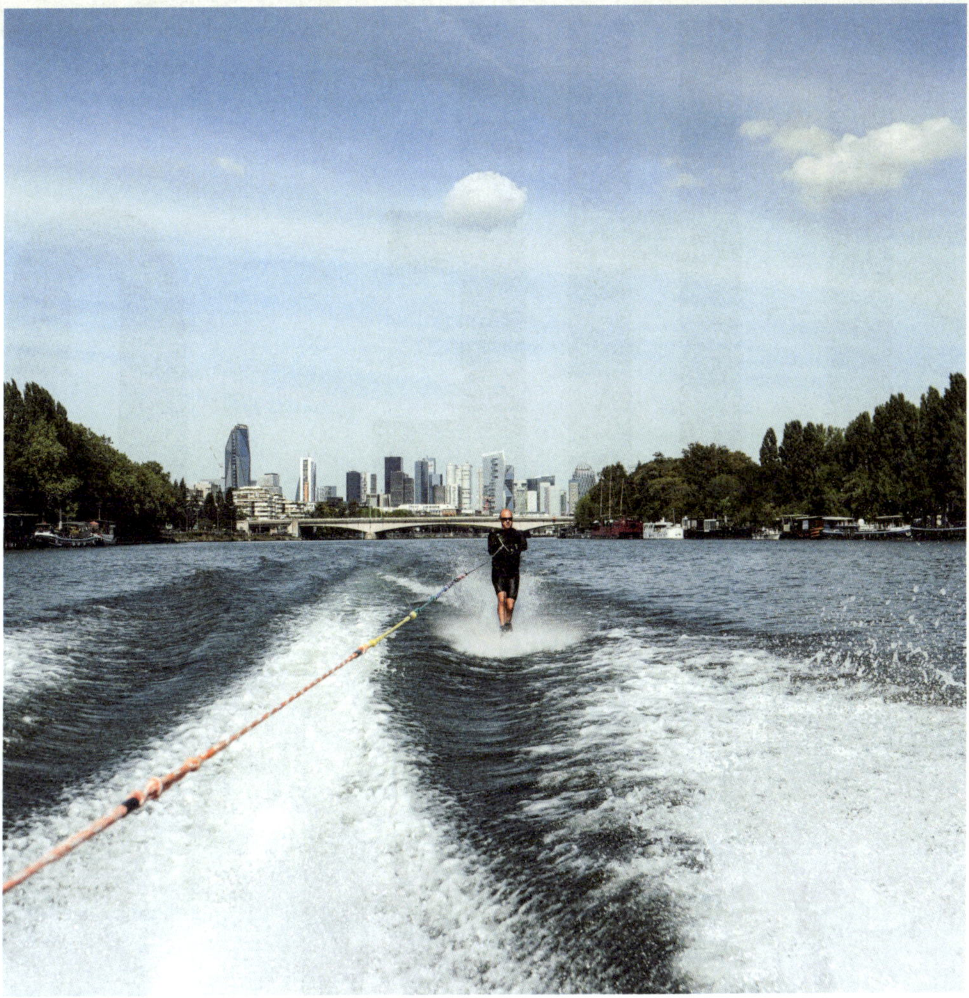

Not your average commute | *On the Seine, Paris.*

THE G

AUFFARGIS
CHEVREUSE
CLAIREFONTAINE-EN-YVELINES

CE

DAMPIERRE-EN-YVELINES
ÉLANCOURT
JOUY-EN-JOSAS

LA QUEUE-LEZ-YVELINES

LE CHESNAY-ROCQUENCOURT

ROEEN AN

LES ESSARTS-LE-ROI

MONTFORT L'AMAURY

MONTIGNY-LE-BRETONNEUX

RAMBOUILLET

ROCQUENCOURT

SAINT-CYR-L'ÉCOLE

SONCHAMP

VERSAILLES

VILLE-D'AVRAY

Trees as far as the eye can see, the charm of old stone and the soothing tranquility of one of France's most beautiful areas of countryside. Entering the extraordinary garden that is the Haute Vallée de Chevreuse is an endlessly surprising experience. A natural park like the Landes or the Luberon, it covers 630 km², six times the area of Paris, but with only 110,000 inhabitants. And on the edge of this earthly paradise sits Versailles, a town that everyone thinks they know, but which has so much more to offer for those who know how to explore it.

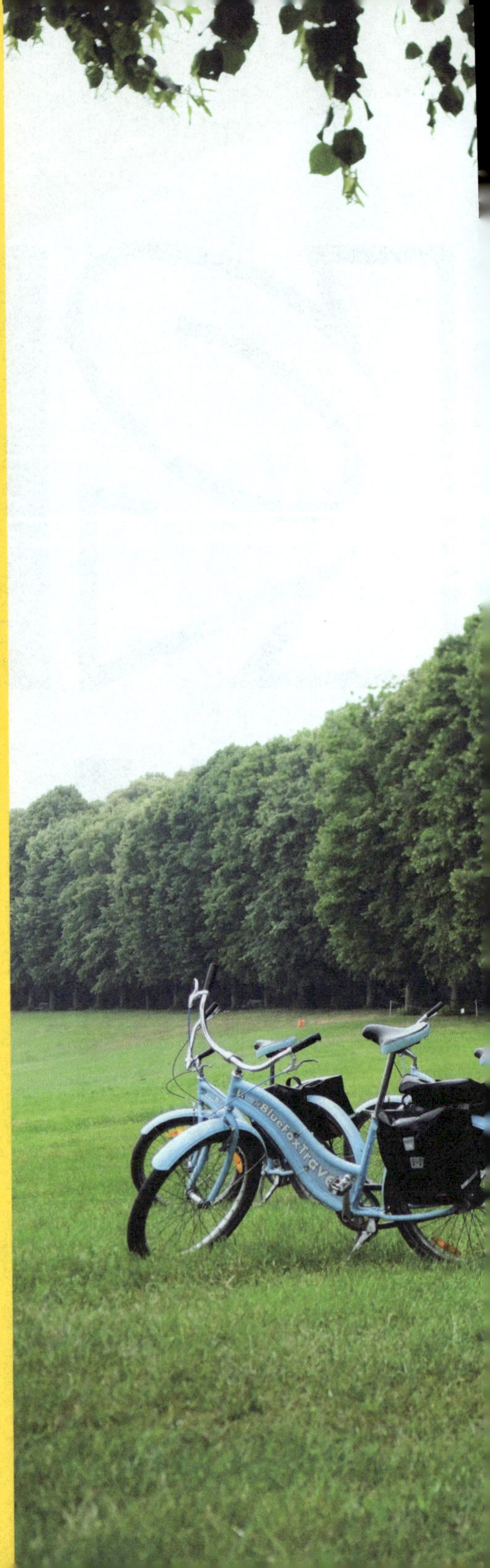

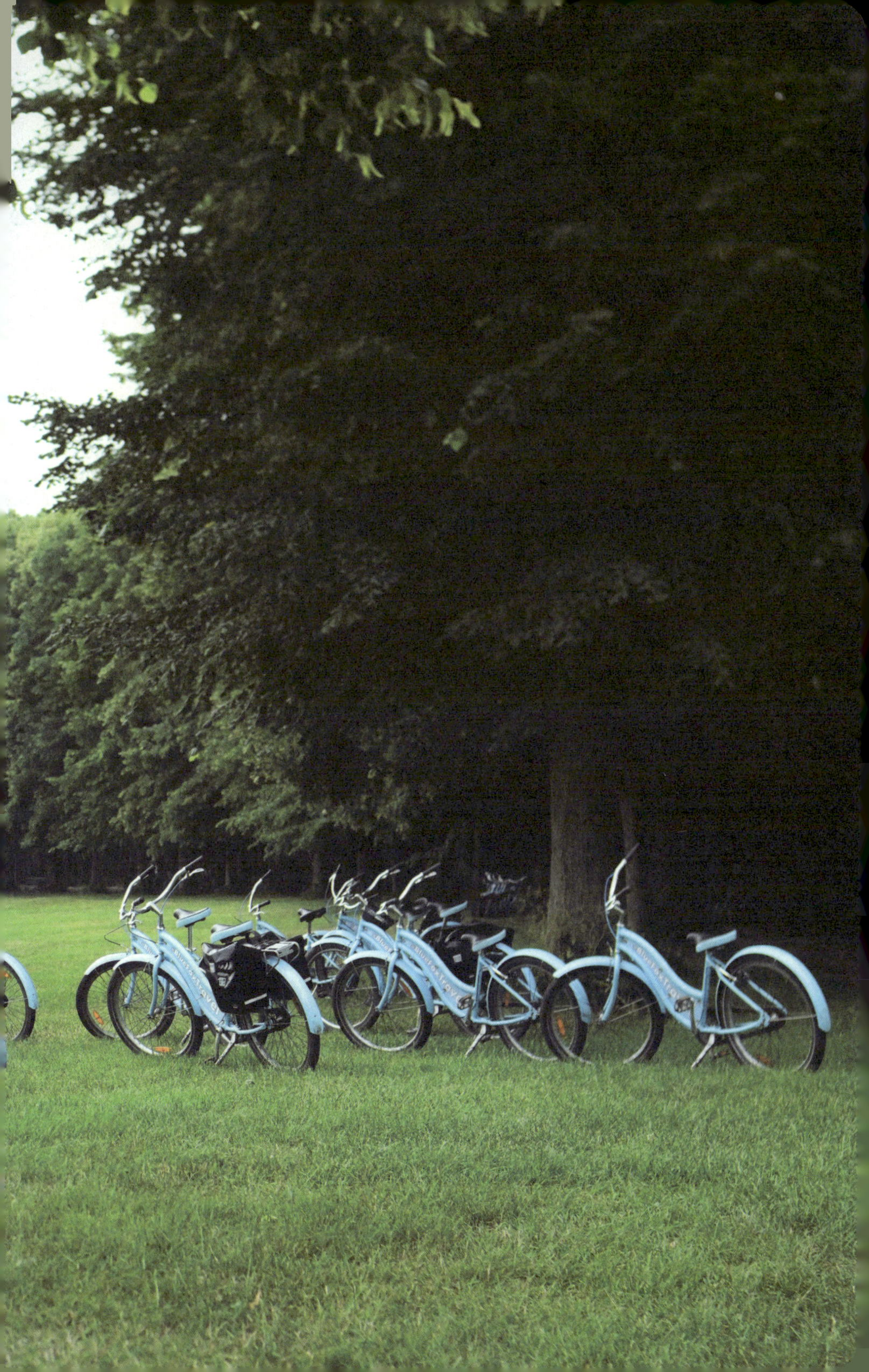

THE GREEN OCEAN

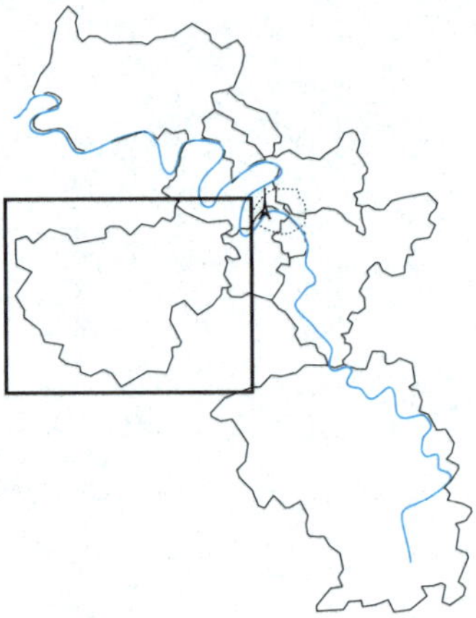

SPORT

104 MOUNTAIN BIKING ON ÉLANCOURT HILL
105 BOIS DES 500 ARPENTS
106 VÉLODROME NATIONAL

CULTURE

107 DOMAINE DE DAMPIERRE
108 MUSÉE DE LA TOILE DE JOUY
109 MAISON-MUSÉE MAURICE RAVEL
110 ACADÉMIE ÉQUESTRE DE VERSAILLES
111 CHÂTEAU DE VERSAILLES
112 JEU DE PAUME ROOM

LIFESTYLE

113 FERME AUX 4 ÉTOILES
114 L'ALCHIMISTE
115 BOULANGERIE LE HÉRISSON
116 LES FERMES DE GALLY
117 LES BADAUDS
118 LONG STORY

OUTDOORS

119 FORÊT DE RAMBOUILLET AND ÉTANGS DE HOLLANDE
120 THE CYCLING TRAILS OF THE RAMBOUILLET FOREST
121 ARBORETUM OF VERSAILLES - CHÈVRELOUP
122 FORÊT DE FAUSSES-REPOSES
123 PARC DU CHÂTEAU DE VERSAILLES
124 POTAGER DU ROI
125 PARC NATUREL DE LA HAUTE VALLÉE DE CHEVREUSE

WHERE TO EAT

126 LA CUILLER EN BOIS
127 FILOMENA
128 LA TABLE DU 11

FAMILY

129 FRANCE MINIATURE
130 FERME DE VILTAIN
131 LA SERRE AUX PAPILLONS
132 BERGERIE NATIONALE
133 MUSÉE RAMBOLITRAIN
134 ESPACE RAMBOUILLET

WHERE TO SLEEP

135 CAMPING HUTTOPIA
136 ÉTANGS DE COROT

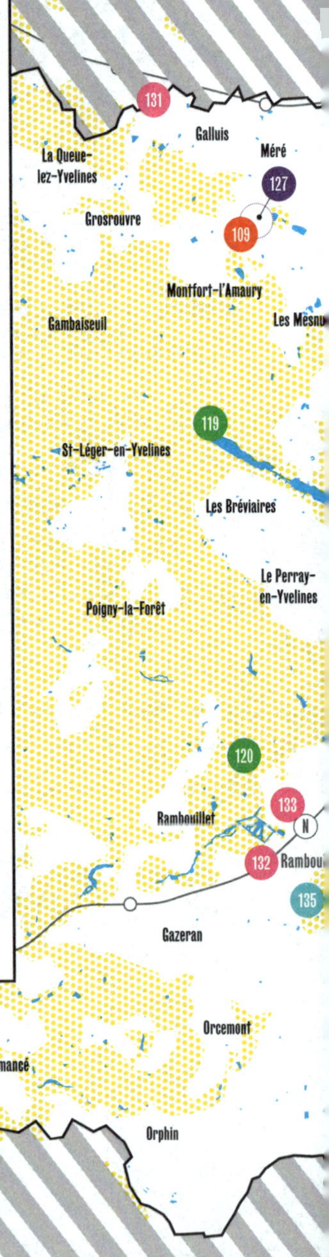

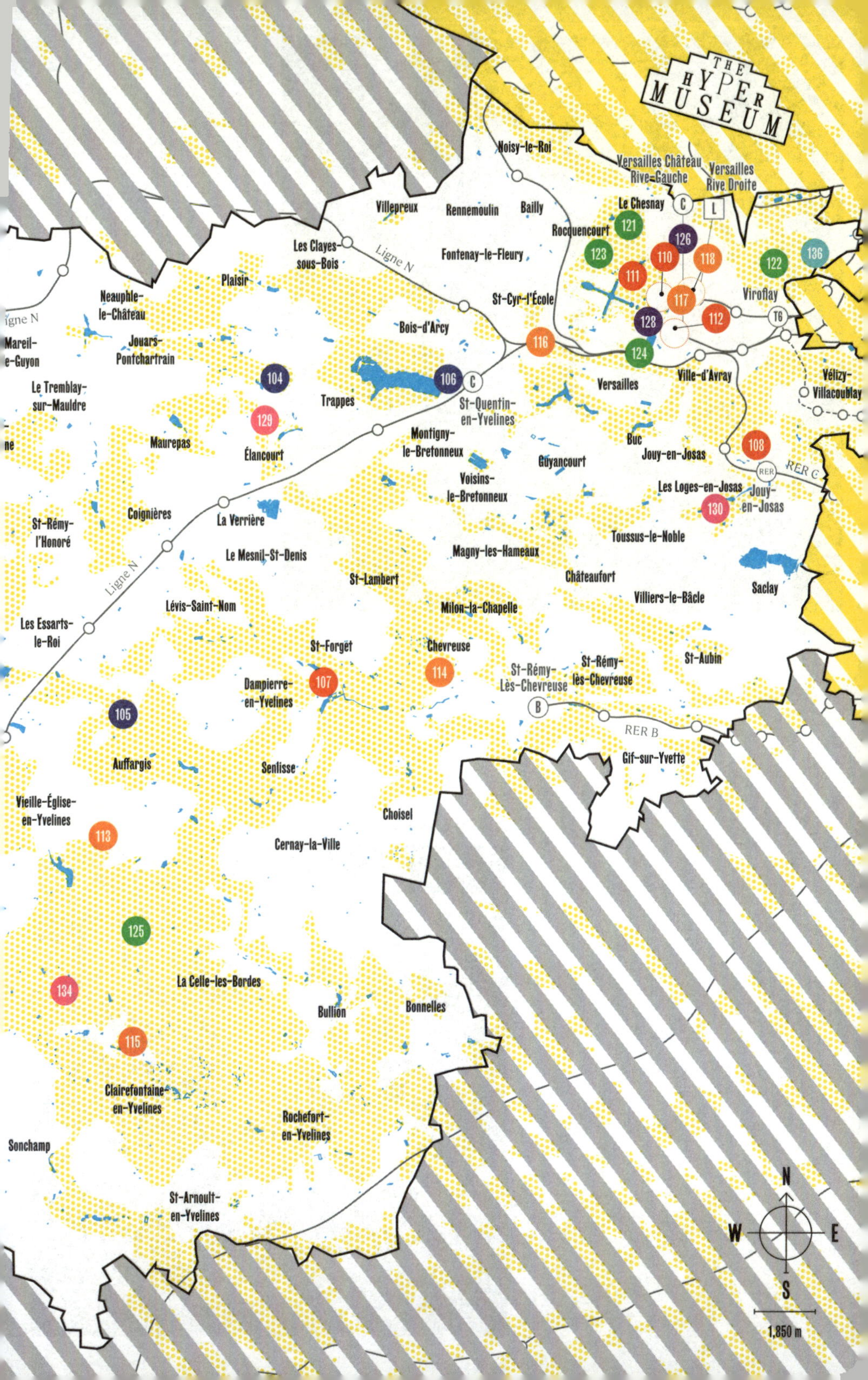
THE HYPER MUSEUM
Noisy-le-Roi
Versailles Château Rive-Gauche
Versailles Rive Droite
Le Chesnay
Villepreux
Rennemoulin
Bailly
Rocquencourt
Les Clayes-sous-Bois
Ligne N
Fontenay-le-Fleury
Plaisir
Neauphle-le-Château
St-Cyr-l'École
Viroflay
Bois-d'Arcy
Mareil-le-Guyon
Jouars-Pontchartrain
Le Tremblay-sur-Mauldre
Trappes
St-Quentin-en-Yvelines
Versailles
Ville-d'Avray
Vélizy-Villacoublay
Maurepas
Élancourt
Montigny-le-Bretonneux
Buc
Guyancourt
Jouy-en-Josas
RER C
Voisins-le-Bretonneux
Les Loges-en-Josas
Jouy-en-Josas
St-Rémy-l'Honoré
Coignières
La Verrière
Toussus-le-Noble
Le Mesnil-St-Denis
Magny-les-Hameaux
St-Lambert
Châteaufort
Saclay
Villiers-le-Bâcle
Lévis-Saint-Nom
Milon-la-Chapelle
Les Essarts-le-Roi
St-Forget
Chevreuse
St-Aubin
St-Rémy-lès-Chevreuse
St-Rémy-lès-Chevreuse
Dampierre-en-Yvelines
RER B
Gif-sur-Yvette
Auffargis
Senlisse
Vieille-Église-en-Yvelines
Choisel
Cernay-la-Ville
La Celle-les-Bordes
Bullion
Bonnelles
Clairefontaine-en-Yvelines
Rochefort-en-Yvelines
Sonchamp
St-Arnoult-en-Yvelines
N
W
E
S
1,850 m

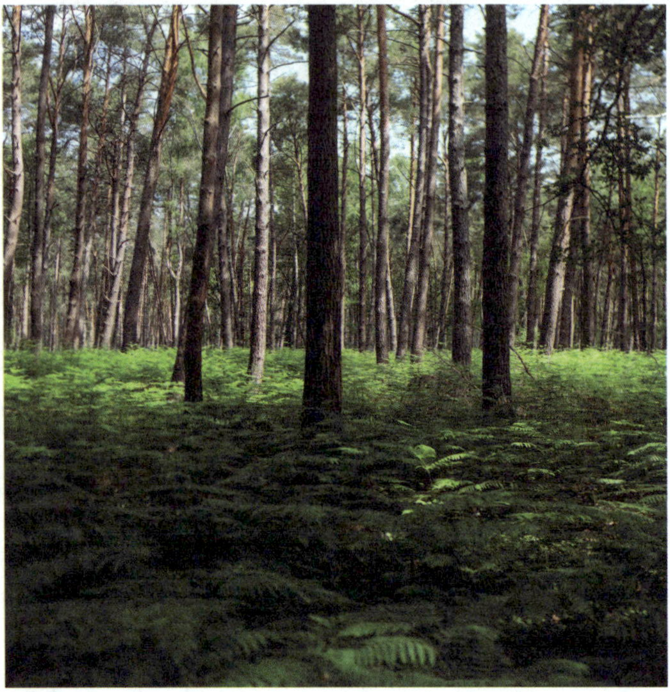

Ferntastic | *Forêt de Rambouillet.*

Future Tour de France winner | *Forêt de Rambouillet.*

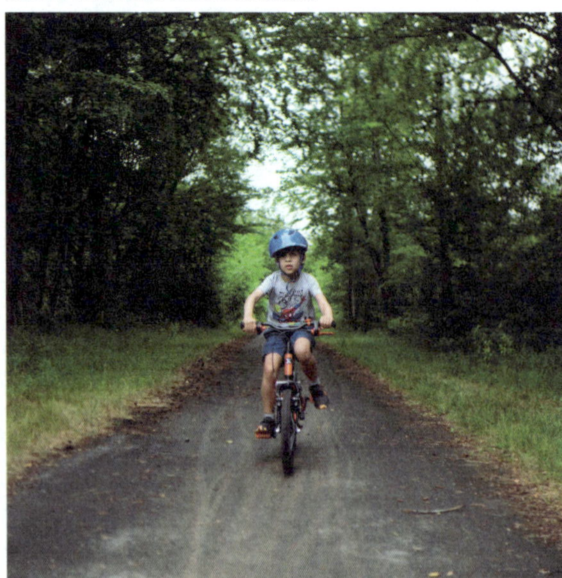

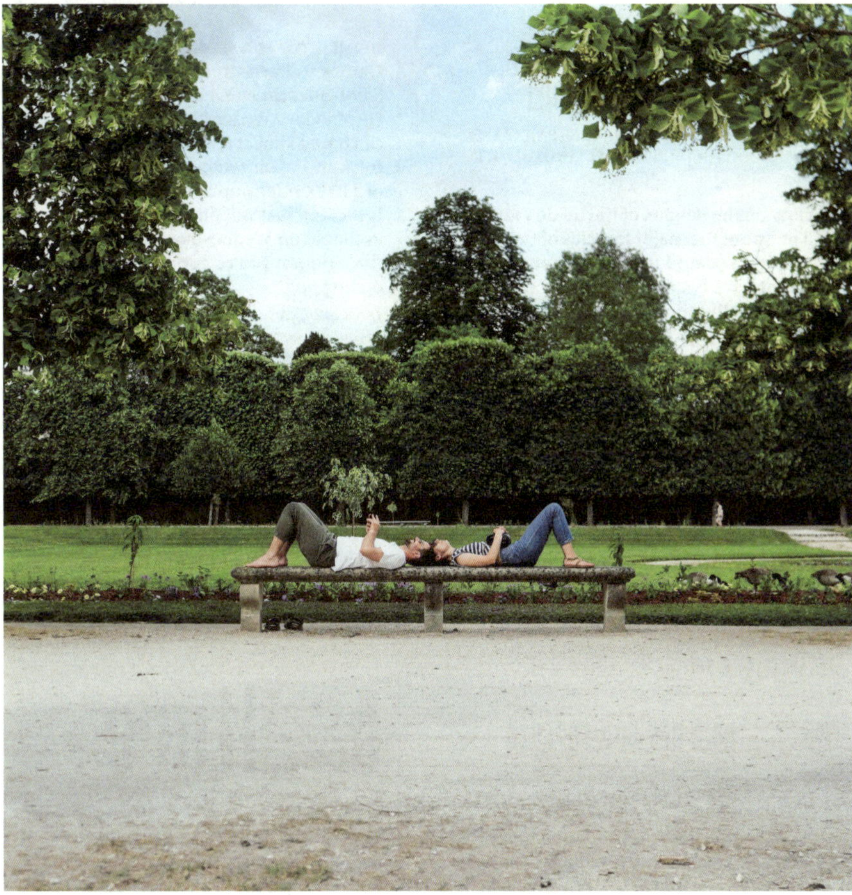

Tête-à-tête | *Château de Rambouillet, Rambouillet.*

sport

ÉLANCOURT

104 MOUNTAIN BIKING ON ÉLANCOURT HILL

#TALLERTHANTOURMONTPARNASSE
#2024OLYMPICS #CYCLINGSUMMIT

Cycling on the heights of the Île-de-France region will be one of the major legacies of the Paris 2024 Olympics. Located on former sandstone quarries that have been unused since the 1970s, the Élancourt hill, which stands at 231 metres high (20 metres higher than the Tour Montparnasse), has been transformed into a stadium to host the crème de la crème of cross-country mountain biking. After the Olympics, the site will be opened up to the people of Greater Paris, who will be able to hurtle down the mountain bike tracks and have a blast on the mogul courses for BMXs, scooters and rollerblades. A future cycling summit for Greater Paris.

Avenue Marcel Dassault, 78990 Élancourt
- Transilien — Line N: Trappes
- Bus — 418: Avenue Le Verrier

LES ESSARTS-LE-ROI

105 BOIS DES 500 ARPENTS

#STATIONTOSTATION
#ELEVATION #HIKING

Who said there were no mountains in Île-de-France? Just ask the regular visitors to the Haute Vallée de Chevreuse nature park! There's something of an Alpine feel to the Bois des 500 Arpents. Your thighs and buttocks will be (moderately) warmed up by the 400-metre elevation difference of the route between Les Essarts-le-Roi and Le Perray-en-Yvelines. It's a solid 22-km route from station to station, shaded by pines and oaks perched on cliffs or beside rivers. The perfect way to keep fit!

Bois domanial des 500 Arpents
helloways.com/hike/bois-des-500-arpents-les-essarts-le-roi
- Transilien — Line N / TER: Les Essarts-le-Roi

MONTIGNY-LE-BRETONNEUX

106 VÉLODROME NATIONAL

#OLYMPICS #BMX
#TRACKCYCLING

It will serve as a showcase for the 2024 Olympic Games in Paris. But the Vélodrome national in Saint-Quentin-en-Yvelines is not just for pro riders. On Mondays, Wednesdays and Saturdays, everyone can have a shot at testing themselves on this speed track and its dizzyingly steep bends. If you're more of a BMX rider, one of Europe's only indoor tracks is located just outside the Vélodrome with slots available on Wednesdays and Saturdays for first time riders. You're sure to come away with the cycling bug.

Track cycling lessons on Monday, Wednesday and Saturday: €39 for one hour (including equipment) /
BMX lessons on Wednesdays and Saturdays: €30 per hour (including equipment). Book online.
Open Monday to Friday 9am–10pm and weekends 9am–8pm.

Place de la Paix céleste, 78180 Montigny-le-Bretonneux
Tel: +33 (0)1 76 21 93 20 / velodrome-national.com
- RER — C: Saint-Quentin-en-Yvelines / Montigny-le-Bretonneux
- Transilien — Lines N, U: Saint-Quentin-en-Yvelines / Montigny-le-Bretonneux

culture

DAMPIERRE-EN-YVELINES

107 DOMAINE DE DAMPIERRE

#CHÂTEAU #WILDPARK
#PICNIC

Built in the 17th century by Jules Hardouin-Mansart, who was also the architect of the Château de Versailles, the Château de Dampierre is one of the jewels of the Haute Vallée de Chevreuse natural park. Bought in 2018 by Franky Mulliez, the founder of the Kiloutou® equipment rental company and one of the 500 richest people in France, the château plans to house a museum and is welcoming visitors to its gardens in the meantime. You can choose to enjoy the landscaped gardens with their natural playgrounds and picnic tables,

take a Segway ride through the forest, discover a forgotten garden in the Chimères grove, stop for a drink at the tea room or take a "photo safari" carriage ride in the 300-hectare wild park on the lookout for deer and wild boar.

Price: €8 (full price), free for under-18s.
Open daily from March to November, closed Monday.

2, Grande Rue, 78720 Dampierre-en-Yvelines
Tel: +33 (0)1 30 52 52 83 / domaine-dampierre.com

- RER — B: Saint-Rémy-lès-Chevreuse
- Transilien — Line U: La Verrière
- Baladobus: Domaine de Dampierre stop (on Sundays and public holidays in July and August)

JOUY-EN-JOSAS

108 MUSÉE DE LA TOILE DE JOUY

#FASHION #SUCCESSSTORY
#INDUSTRY

Nestled in a 19th-century castle, the Musée de la Toile de Jouy reveals everything about the history and activity of the eponymous manufactory of this quintessentially French fabric. The tour pays tribute to Christophe-Philippe Oberkampf, a German immigrant who became one of the greatest entrepreneurs of his time, and retraces this remarkable industrial adventure that has now been forgotten. From 1760 to 1843, more than 30,000 designs were created in Jouy-en-Josas for fashion and furniture, taking over Europe. To make sure you don't miss a thing, guided tours are organized one or two days a month, on Wednesdays or Sundays. A tea room and a shop await on the way out.

Price: €9 (full price) / €7 for under-16s and students.
Closed Monday. Open on Tuesday afternoons and from 11am to 6pm from Wednesday to Sunday.

54, rue Charles de Gaulle, 78350 Jouy-en-Josas
Tel: +33 (0)1 39 56 48 64 / museedelatoiledejouy.fr

- RER — C: Petit Jouy - Les Loges
- Bus — Z: Musée de Jouy, L: Trois Canards

MONTFORT-L'AMAURY

109 MAISON-MUSÉE MAURICE RAVEL

#DOLLHOUSE #GARDEN
#BOLERO

Entering the Belvédère, Maurice Ravel's last home, it feels like you might run into him, as the place has remained the same since the composer's death in 1937. It was here, away from Paris, that the virtuoso lived from 1921 onwards and conceived some of his major works, starting with *Boléro* and the *Piano Concerto for the Left Hand*. The house, which is full of various objects collected by Ravel (mechanical toys, clocks, etc.), offers a beautiful view of the surrounding countryside and a Japanese garden below.

Price: €11 (full price), €5 (12–18 years old) / Free for under-12s. Booking required through the tourist office of Montfort-l'Amaury at +33 (0)1 34 86 87 96. or by email tourisme@montfortlamaury.fr.

5, rue Maurice Ravel, 78490 Montfort-l'Amaury
fondationmauriceravel.com

VERSAILLES

110 ACADÉMIE ÉQUESTRE DE VERSAILLES

#DANCESWITHHORSES
#HERITAGE #ONEOFAKIND

While ballet is not usually a four-legged practice, in Versailles the horses are known for their grace. Founded in 2003 by the famous horseman and director Bartabas, the National Equestrian Academy is a unique place where dressage is taught alongside other disciplines such as fencing, dance and singing. The Academy is also a performance space: the weekend *Way of the Equerry* show makes you wonder if the star dancer Rudolf Nureyev has not been reincarnated as a horse. On Saturday and Sunday mornings you can also visit the riders and their mounts during equestrian working sessions.

The Way of the Equerry show on Saturday and Sunday (1h10) followed by an open tour of the stables.
Price: €16 to €28.
Guided tour organized by the Office du tourisme de Versailles once a month, outside school holidays.
Price: €12 to €17.

Grande Écurie Royale, avenue Rockefeller, 78000 Versailles
Tel: +33 (0)1 39 02 62 70
bartabas.fr/academie-equestre-de-versailles
c.desmet@acadequestre.fr (for group quotes)

- RER — C: Versailles Rive Gauche
- Bus — 171: Château de Versailles

111 CHÂTEAU DE VERSAILLES

#BEHINDTHESCENES
#VERSAILLESCONFIDENTIAL #GUIDEDTOUR

The Palace of Versailles has over 2,000 different rooms. However, many people only know the Hall of Mirrors and the King's State Apartments. Step off the beaten track and take a guided tour of the private apartments of Louis XV and Louis XVI. Because, unlike Louis XIV, the two monarchs aspired to a more secluded life, away from the protocol that required them to go to bed or wash in public, for example. Among their most intimate secrets, you will discover Louis XV's toilet, a small room with a red velvet chaise percée. You will also visit the games room and the dispatch room, where the two sovereigns were informed of world news. This all takes place away from the crowds which you will glimpse from time to time through the opening of a door.

Guided tour of the Kings' Private Apartments (duration 1h30). Price: €10 + €18 admission to the Château.
Bookings on chateauversailles.fr.

Place d'armes, 78000 Versailles

- RER — C: Versailles Rive Gauche
- Transilien — Lines N, U: Versailles - Chantiers
- Bus — 171: Château de Versailles

112 JEU DE PAUME ROOM

#HISTORY #JEUDEPAUMEOATH
#MONUMENTALPAINTING

On 20 June 1789, 578 representatives of the Estates General took an oath within the Jeu de Paume room and vowed not to leave until they had given France a constitution. Since then, over fifteen have been written. Entering the room is therefore a form of pilgrimage for today's French citizen. Reconverted into a museum since 1880, its collections are outshone by the room itself. An extraordinary mise en abyme awaits as soon as you set eyes on the monumental painting by Luc-Olivier Merson (1846–1920), inspired by the famous drawing by Jacques-Louis David (1748–1825), which immortalized this democratic dawn.

Free entry on weekends from 2–6.30pm.
Guided tours available on the Château de Versailles website.

Rue du Jeu de paume, 78000 Versailles
Tel: +33 (0)1 39 24 88 88 / versailles.fr

- RER — C: Versailles Rive Gauche
- Bus — 171: Château de Versailles

lifestyle

AUFFARGIS

113 FERME AUX 4 ÉTOILES

#LOCALPRODUCE #BRUNCH
#HOMEMADEMOZZARELLA

Once you discover the bar-boutique of the Ferme aux 4 étoiles (and its homemade mozzarella), it is difficult to shop anywhere else. Here, you can fill your basket with produce from the Greater Paris region. You can watch the cows grazing peacefully as you sit on the boutique's terrace and enjoy a plate of charcuterie and cheese or a homemade dish served with good wine. Such is the 4-star life on this farm.

Bar-boutique open from Wednesday to Sunday. Food served on Saturday and Sunday (reservations recommended).

La Petite Hogue, 78610 Auffargis
Tel: +33 (0)6 20 04 37 54 / les4etoiles.free.fr

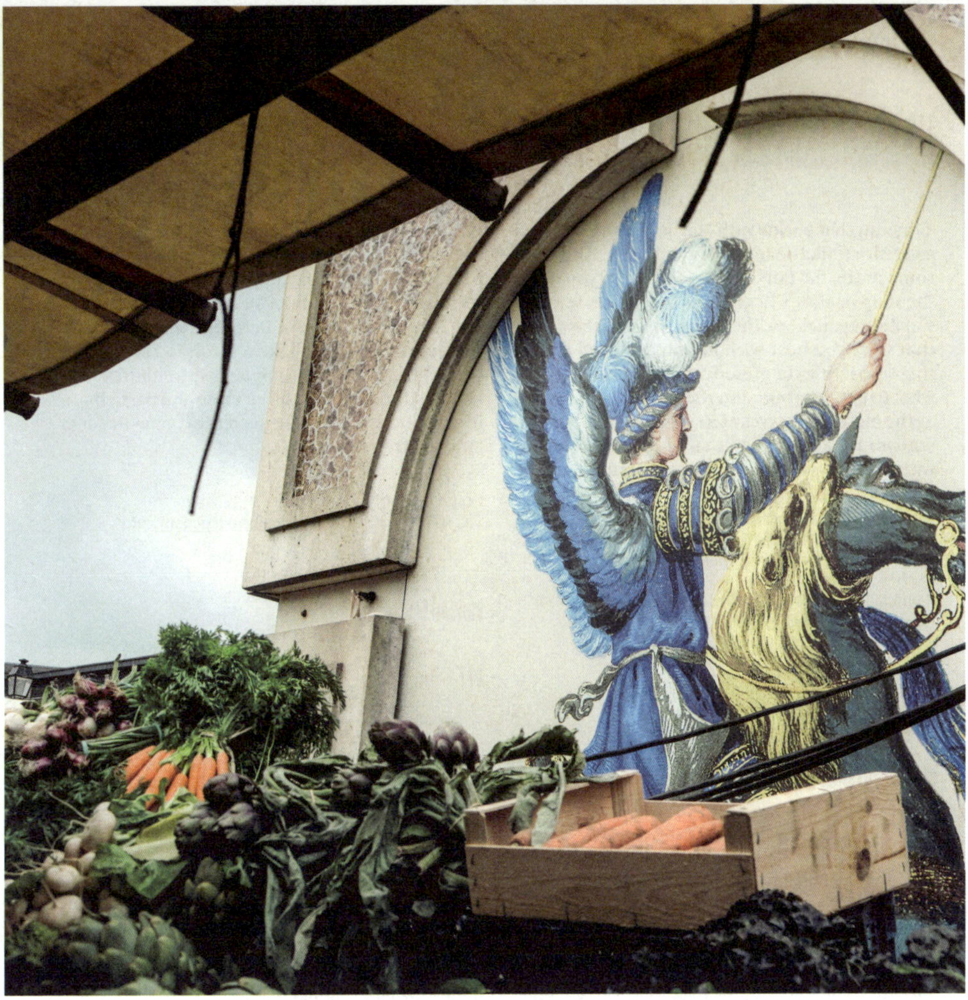

His Highness the Carrot | *Marché Notre-Dame, Versailles.*

CHEVREUSE

114 L'ALCHIMISTE

#FRUITBASKET #NOARTIFICALCOLOURING #ONEOFAKIND

Corsican clementine with Mayotte flavours, greengage with tonka beans, apple and curry... these are some of the flavours to discover when you enter the shop of Marc Chenue, one of France's few artisanal syrup makers. There, you will find the nectar that suits you best without any artificial flavourings, colourings or preservatives. If you're not sure what to get, step out onto the terrace for a tasting as the place also serves as a syrup bar. You can also register for a workshop to make your own elixir with the master. Floral, spicy or aromatic?

Price: Gourmet tasting: €9 per person / €7 per person for groups of 10 to 20 people / Free for under-6s. Gourmet workshop: €35 per person / €22 for under-12s. Thematic syrup-making workshops and guided tours can be booked ahead. Boutique opening hours: Wednesday to Sunday, 10am to 12.30pm and 2–7pm.

9, rue Joseph Jérôme Lalande, 78460 Chevreuse
Tel: +33 (0)1 30 45 18 87
lalchimiste-artisan-siropier.com

CLAIREFONTAINE-EN-YVELINES

115 BOULANGERIE LE HÉRISSON

#BREADWINNER #DELUXECHOUQUETTES #HIGHLYADDICTIVE

Clairefontaine was already renowned for being home to France's National Football Centre. Now, this village in the upper Chevreuse valley, whose residents include a certain Bernard Arnault (the richest man in the world at the time of writing), is also known for its bakery-patisserie Le Hérisson (which is also a tearoom and a grocery shop selling local produce). As well as its excellent breads (we recommend the pumpkin seed bread as well as the "atypical" bread and the charcoal baguette, both black), the stars here are the Hérichoux, chouquettes filled with the airiest of mousses. A word of warning: their creations are highly addictive.

Tuesday to Saturday 7am to 1.30pm and 3.30–7.30pm, Sunday 7am to 1pm.

Place de la Mairie, 78120 Clairefontaine-en-Yvelines
Tel: +33(0)1 34 87 60 20
Facebook @boulangerieleherisson

- Transilien — Line N or TER: Rambouillet then bus 4 to Clairefontaine

SAINT-CYR-L'ÉCOLE

116 LES FERMES DE GALLY

#FRUITANDVEGPICKING #CAFERESTAURANT #MULTIFUNCTIONALFARM

When you're not sure what to do, there is always the Fermes de Gally. In addition to self-service fruit-and-vegetable picking in 60 hectares of fields from April to November, you can shop in a grocery stocked with local produce, dine in a cosy café-restaurant and then take a stroll in the garden centre. The place is also popular with children who can see the farm animals up close and participate in workshops to learn the secrets of bread-making, among other things.

Open daily.

Route de Bailly, 78210 Saint-Cyr-l'École
Tel: +33 (0)1 30 14 60 60 / lesfermesdegally.com

VERSAILLES

117 LES BADAUDS

#UNBEATABLEVIEW #WINEBAR #LOCAVORE

With its wonderful terrace and château view, this bar is a must for a *versaillais* night out. If you are lucky enough to find a table, it is difficult to leave. The menu includes fine plates of cheese and charcuterie but also a préfou from the Vendée – a bread topped with finely chopped fresh garlic and butter – that shouldn't be missed. As for drinks, you can choose from a selection of beers from local microbreweries and wines from independent, mainly organic winemakers.

Draught beers from €5. Closed Monday.

1, avenue de Saint-Cloud, 78000 Versailles
Tel: +33 (0)1 72 78 72 96 / lesbadauds.fr

- RER — C: Versailles Château – Rive Gauche
- Bus — 171: Château de Versailles

118 LONG STORY

#AMONGSTFRIENDS
#COCKTAILS #BRUNCH

Opened by three friends, Long Story is a successful blend of cocktail bar and coffee shop. It's a great place to hang out on the terrace or to take in the cosy atmosphere of the first floor to enjoy pancakes, gourmet sandwiches or the signature cocktails such as the Marionnettiste or the Bergamot Spritz, depending on the time of day. And, because there's more to life than Sundays, you can brunch every day of the week.

Open daily from 9am to 1am.

23, rue du Maréchal Foch, 78000 Versailles
Tel: +33 (0)1 75 45 66 36 / long-story.fr

- Transilien — Line L: Versailles - Rive Droite

outdoors

RAMBOUILLET

119 FORÊT DE RAMBOUILLET AND ÉTANGS DE HOLLANDE

#BIGGERTHANPARIS #HIKE
#SWIMMING

Much like the human being, Greater Paris has two lungs, the Fontainebleau forest (see p. 149) and the smaller Rambouillet forest. With 14,000 hectares – 4,000 more than the capital – it is popular with walkers and cyclists alike thanks to its network of cycle paths (see the next entry). It is also appreciated by equestrians who have made it their backyard, and even by beach-goers, many of whom head to the outdoor leisure park at the Étangs de Hollande when the sun really starts to hit.

Price: €5.70 (full price), €4 (reduced price).
The leisure centre is open from June to 31 August.

Tel: +33 (0)1 34 86 30 50 / onf.fr/enforet/rambouillet and rt78.fr/base-de-loisirs-des-etangs-de-hollande

- Transilien — Line N: Rambouillet

120 THE CYCLING TRAILS OF THE RAMBOUILLET FOREST

#CYCLINGTRAILS #BIKERENTAL
#EASYBIKER

With its 70 kilometres of paved cycle paths, the Rambouillet forest is an ideal setting for cycling. If you don't have a bicycle, no matter: you can find them on site at Loca Cycles , Les Vélos d'Emily (1.7 km on foot from Rambouillet station) or Toc-Toc Location de vélos (900 metres on foot from Rambouillet station). Now imagine yourself happily pedalling your way through this green jungle. And don't worry about getting lost, everything is signposted.

Loca Cycles:
Price: €14 for 4 hours.
Tel: +33 (0)6 07 64 15 87 / rambouillet-location-velos.fr

Les Vélos d'Emily:
Price: €15 for a half-day.
Tel: +33 (0)1 85 77 10 62 / rambouillet.club

Toc-Toc Location de vélos:
Price: €17 for a half-day.
Tel: +33 (0)1 84 60 19 57 / toctoclocationdevelos.com

- You can also take your bicycle on board Transilien trains free of charge.
- Transilien — Line N: Rambouillet

ROCQUENCOURT

121 ARBORETUM OF VERSAILLES-CHÈVRELOUP

#BOTANICALGARDEN #2500TREESPECIES
#AWAYFROMTHECROWDS

The Chèvreloup arboretum borders the Château de Versailles domain. Even if it is less extensive than its prestigious neighbour – 200 hectares versus 815 – you will still need at least half a day to fully enjoy this landscaped botanical garden and its many worlds including the Japanese grove, the circle of giants, the glade of conifers, the cedar circle and the Patagonian grove. In total, the arboretum boasts 2,500 species of tree which you can discover far from the crowds rushing to the Château.

Price: €7 (full price), €5 (discounted price).
Open from 10am–6pm from 1 March to 31 October and from 10am to 5pm from 1 November to late February.

30, route de Versailles, 78150 Rocquencourt
Tel: +33 (0)1 39 55 53 80
arboretumdeversailleschevreloup.fr

- Accessible by bus from the three train stations in Versailles.

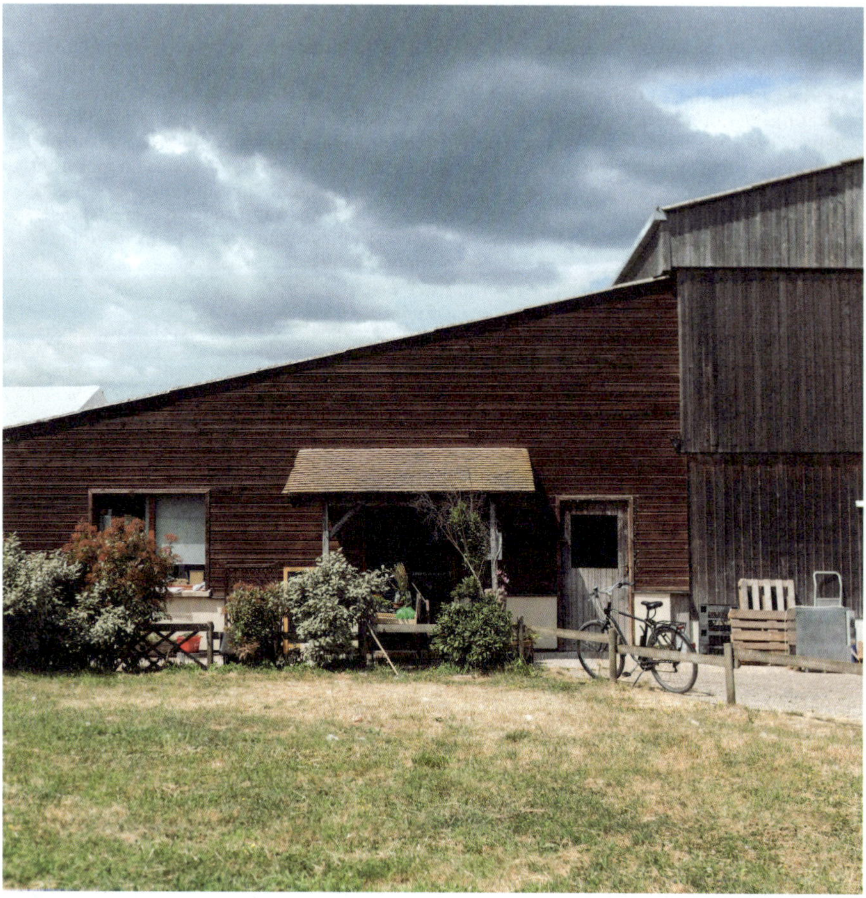

The farm to be | *Ferme des 4 étoiles, Auffargis.*

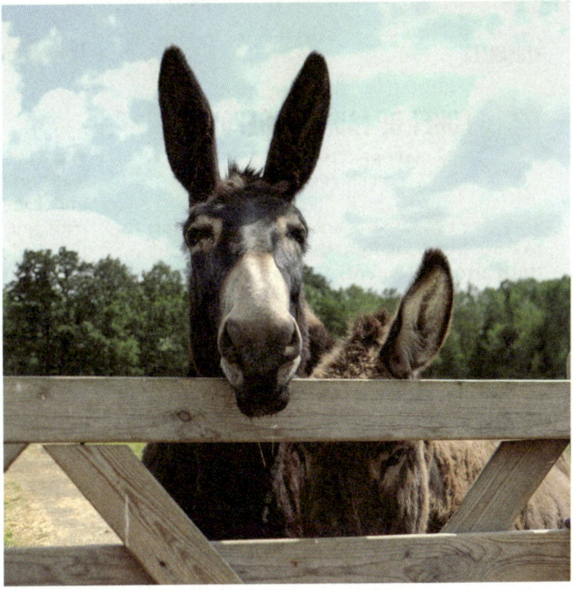

Doing the donkey work | *Ferme des 4 étoiles, Auffargis.*

4-star boss | *Ferme des 4 étoiles, Auffargis.*

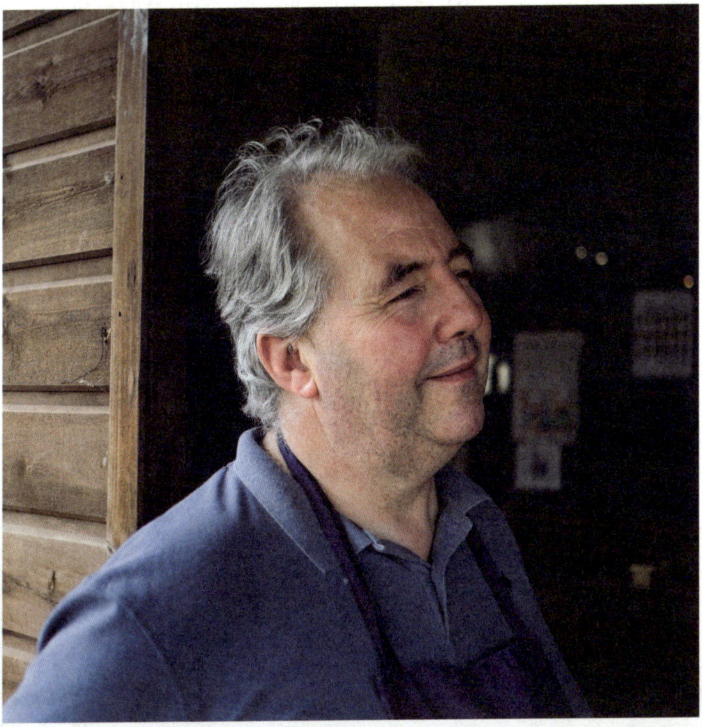

VERSAILLES

122 FORÊT DE FAUSSES-REPOSES

#FORESTINTHECITY
#ZEN #PONDS

This green expanse is one of the closest forests to Paris. Just 6 km from the Porte de Saint-Cloud (16th arrondissement), Fausses-Reposes offers strollers 69 km of walking paths, twice the length of the Paris *périphérique*. It also boasts two further gems: the Haras de Jardy, the over-100-year-old equestrian centre, and the famous ponds of Ville-d'Avray, immortalized by the impressionist painter Jean-Baptiste Camille Corot and on the edge of which is a highly recommended hotel (see p. 84).

146, avenue des États-Unis, 78000 Versailles
onf.fr/enforet/fausses-reposes

- Transilien — Line L: Montreuil, Chaville - Rive Droite
- Bus — 471: Gauthier de Clagny

123 PARC DU CHÂTEAU DE VERSAILLES

#NOWTHATISAGARDEN
#FREE #ENDLESSLAWNS

Over twice as big as Central Park, the Château de Versailles park is an endless source of exploration. Its 815 hectares hide many wonders, including the crown jewels that are the gardens created by Le Nôtre (fee-paying on certain days during the musical fountains show), the Queen's hamlet and the Trianon (fee-paying all year round). When you are ready to get away from the crowds, venture to the end of the two-kilometre-long Grand Canal. If you are in a bucolic mood, you will find refuge in the clearing located near the sailors gate. Away from the hustle and bustle, you can take a nap under a tree. Just as unmissable is the Lake of the Swiss Guard, around which it is pleasant just to walk in circles. And for the rest, plan to come back. Again and again.

Free entry.
Open daily from 7am to 8.30pm.

Grille de la Reine, boulevard de la Reine,
78000 Versailles
chateauversailles.fr

- Transilien — Line L: Versailles Rive Droite
- Bus — 171: Château de Versailles

124 POTAGER DU ROI

#HERITAGE #INNOVATION
#ORGANICAGRICULTURE

The King's kitchen garden (Potager du Roi) is a legacy of the past that looks to the future. Created under Louis XIV to provide the king's table with fruit and vegetables, it has become a laboratory and a showcase for organic farming where gardeners have eschewed any form of treatment, whether chemical and organic, and replaced them with insects and biocontrol methods. This makes the Potager du Roi unique throughout the seasons.

Price: €5 (full price), €3 (discounted price).
Open year round (opening hours vary according to the season).

10, rue du Maréchal-Joffre, 78000 Versailles
ecole-paysage.fr

- RER — C: Versailles Château - Rive Gauche
- Transilien — Line N: Versailles Chantiers
- Transilien — Line L: Versailles Rive Droite

YVELINES

125 PARC NATUREL DE LA HAUTE VALLÉE DE CHEVREUSE

#ONHORSEBACK
#ONABIKE #ONFOOT

Hiking trails, cycle routes, horseback riding – the Haute Vallée de Chevreuse has so much to offer, which makes sense for an area of 630 km², or six times the size of Paris. You can choose to take one of the routes listed on parc-naturel-chevreuse.fr and rando.pnr-idf.fr, cycle along the Véloscénie trails (veloscenie.com), take the wheel of a 2CV (4roues-sous-1-parapluie.com) or enjoy the many horse trails (to be found on yvelines.fr). If you don't have your own set of wheels, L'Aiguillage (laiguillage-tourisme-mobilite.fr), located opposite the RER B station in Saint-Rémy-lès-Chevreuse, offers half-day or full-day bicycle rental (electric or not) and Twizy electric cars.

parc-naturel-chevreuse.fr

where to eat

LE CHESNAY-ROCQUENCOURT

126 LA CUILLER EN BOIS

#LOCALPRODUCE
#WOODENTABLES #GARDEN

Once you make your way through the curtains at the entrance, you will be seated around wooden tables on comfortable leather sofas, to sip a beer from the Ile-de-France region before moving on to a saffron risotto with octopus and supreme of chicken. The produce is bought from local suppliers and portions are reasonable, so you'll be sure to have room for dessert. The restaurant even has a view over a charming little garden. A tasty and meditative interlude.

Price: from €50 per person (starter, main course, dessert).
Tuesday to Saturday, 12–3pm and 7.30–11.30pm

43, rue de Versailles, 78150 Le Chesnay-Rocquencourt
Tel: +33 (0)1 75 45 50 72 / lacuillerenbois.com
- RER — C: Versailles - Rive Droite

MONTFORT-L'AMAURY

127 FILOMENA

#NEAPOLITANSTYLE #VILLAGESQUARE
#BESTPIZZAINGREATERPARIS

In Montfort-l'Amaury, a chic and charming village in the Parc Naturel de la Haute Vallée de Chevreuse (see p. 80), you can enjoy one of the best pizzas Greater Paris has to offer on the Place de l'Église, a stone's throw from Maurice Ravel's former home (see p. 73) where he composed his famous *Boléro*. Here, at Yann Marteau's, the dough rises for 24 hours and is not degassed, as is the Neapolitan tradition, making it easier to digest. Try the Tartufa (stracciatella, truffle spread, olive oil), the Pancetta (yellow tomatoes, pancetta, provolone, mozzarella, basil) or the Capricciosa (tomato sauce, mushrooms, white ham, spianata, artichoke, mozzarella, basil, Grana Padano, olives). Washed down with a glass of Italian wine, of course.

Pizzas from €11.50.
Closed Monday.

6, place de la Libération, 78490 Montfort-l'Amaury
Tel: +33 (0)1 34 86 49 41 (booking recommended)
ristorantefilomena.fr
- Transilien — Line N: Montfort-L'Amaury-Méré

VERSAILLES

128 LA TABLE DU 11

#EXCEPTIONALCUISINE
#YOUNGCHEF #MICHELINSTAR

Don't waste any time before you book because you will have to wait at least two months before having dinner at the Table du 11, one of the hottest gastronomic experiences in Greater Paris. At the helm is a young chef who is under thirty years old, Jean-Baptiste Lavergne-Morazzani, who trained with Gordon Ramsay, the star chef of the Trianon, the local luxury hotel. Although the student has not yet surpassed his master's Michelin® star tally, he did receive a star in 2016. The cuisine revolves around seasonal, preferably local produce prepared with infinite finesse for a truly stunning gourmet experience.

Price: Tasting menu for €125.
Closed Sunday and Monday.

La Cour des Senteurs, 8, rue de la Chancellerie, 78000 Versailles
Tel: +33 (0)9 83 34 76 00 / latabledu11.com
- RER — C: Versailles Rive Gauche
- Transilien — Lines N, U: Versailles Rive Gauche
- Bus — 171: Château de Versailles

family

ÉLANCOURT

129 FRANCE MINIATURE

#HONEYISHRUNKTHECOUNTRY
#2000MODELS #GEOGRAPHYLESSON

Although no one has managed to bottle Paris yet, France Miniature has successfully shrunk France to the size of an amusement park shaped like a map of the country. Here, 2,000 models make it possible to go from the Eiffel Tower® to the Arena of Nîmes by way of the Mont Saint-Michel, all in a few minutes. A good way to brush up on your French geography. As a bonus, there are activities for children aged 4 and up, like the Ronde des Zotos, where kids travel across a comic-book version of France in an electric car.

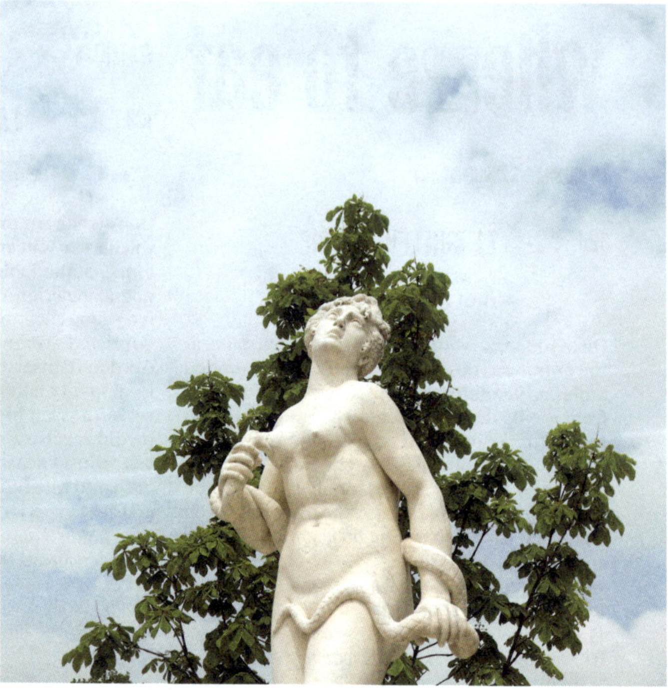

Green screen | *Jardin de Versailles, Versailles.*

Wooden GPS | *Forêt de Rambouillet.*

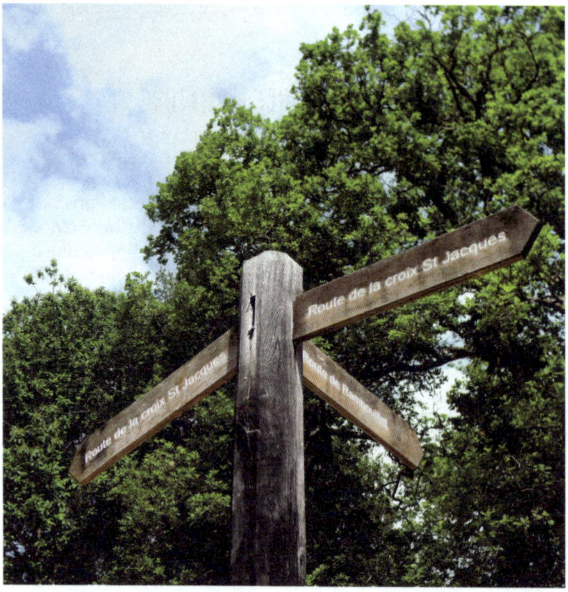

Price: from €20.
Open from April to November.
Opening hours and days vary according to the season.

Boulevard André Malraux, 78990 Élancourt
Tel: +33 (0)8 26 30 20 40 (€0.15/min) / francеminiature.fr
- Transilien — Lines N, U: La Verrière then bus 420, 422, 459: France Miniature

JOUY-EN-JOSAS

130 FERME DE VILTAIN

#GOODPRODUCE #PICKYOUROWN #COUNTRYLIVING

If you're tired of pushing a shopping trolley down a supermarket aisle, then head to the Ferme de Viltain where, since 1980, people have been shopping in 50 hectares of fields from April to November. Obviously, you have to resist the urge of eating the strawberries before you go to the checkout. In addition to fruit and vegetables, you can also pick yourself a bouquet of flowers. And if you prefer the comfort of a store to stock up on supplies, the "Marché de la Ferme" shop is open all year round. During your visit, take the opportunity to visit the cows that inhabit the kingdom of Viltain. The milking parlour and the stable are open to visitors.

"Marché de la Ferme" shop open Monday to Saturday from 9am–7pm and Sunday from 10am–7pm.
Fruit and vegetable picking from April to November every day from 9am–7pm.

Chemin de Viltain, 78350 Jouy-en-Josas
Tel: +33 (0)1 69 41 22 23 (picking)
and + 33 (0)1 39 56 38 14 (shop)
cueillettedeviltain.fr and viltain.fr

LA QUEUE-LEZ-YVELINES

131 LA SERRE AUX PAPILLONS

#FAIRYTALE #MINIJUNGLE #EDUCATIONALTOUR

In France's largest butterfly aviary, hundreds of butterflies fly around you, sometimes landing on your head and shoulders. Over 700 of them dance through the air with their colourful wings in the middle of an equatorial mini-jungle with temperatures to match. The specimens come from Malaysia, Amazonia, Madagascar and more. To explore further, the aviary offers an educational tour of the world of these multicoloured insects and the different stages of their short lives.

Price: €11 (full price), €8 (3–14 year-olds).
Open daily from 9.30am to 6pm, from February to December.

1, avenue des Platanes, 78940 La Queue-lez-Yvelines
Tel: +33 (0)1 34 86 67 55 / serreauxpapillons.com
- Transilien — Line N: Garancières - La Queue

RAMBOUILLET

132 BERGERIE NATIONALE

#EDUCATIONALTOUR #LOCALPRODUCE #LOUISXVI

Created by Louis XVI in 1783 with the aim of making it a model farm, the Bergerie nationale de Rambouillet is a must for family outings. The farm, with its 300 sheep and 60 dairy cows, includes a trail to visit the animals. You can also make a few purchases as the Bergerie sells its locally made products in its own shop.

Price: €8 (adults), €6 (3–12 year-olds) / Free for under-3s.
Open Wednesday, Saturday, Sunday, public holidays and during school holidays in Zone C from 2–5pm in winter, and from 2–5.30pm in summer.

Parc du Château, 78120 Rambouillet
Tel: +33 (0)1 61 08 68 70 / bergerie-nationale.educagri.fr
- Transilien — Line N: Rambouillet

133 MUSÉE RAMBOLITRAIN

#MODELTRAINS #GIANTMAQUETTE #AMAZEMENT

The Rambolitrain museum brings together the work of a lifetime: nearly 4,000 miniature trains, dating from the 19th to the 20th century, brought together by the passionate collector, Jacques Visbecq. In addition to the displays which recount the history of the toy train, the highlight of the show awaits on the top floor of this millstone house; a model with surprising details which occupies the entire space and where the trains of the Compagnie Internationale des Wagons-Lits run in front of your awe-struck eyes.

Price: €4.50 (full price), €3.50 (under-18s) / Free for under-3s.
Open Wednesday to Sunday and on public holidays from 10am–12pm and from 2–5.30pm.

4, place Jeanne d'Arc, 78120 Rambouillet
Tel: +33 (0)1 75 03 44 60 / rambolitrain.com
- Transilien — Line N: Rambouillet

SONCHAMP

134 ESPACE RAMBOUILLET

#WILDLIFEPARK #BELLOWINGDEER
#FORESTTRAIL

Better than a zoo, a forest and wildlife park. Deer, stags and wild boars roam freely across the 250 hectares of the Espace Rambouillet but you will have to be discreet to see them. The spectacle of the forest of the eagles, where birds of prey fly low above your head, is just as stunning. Finally, from mid-September to mid-October, visits are organized in the evening and early morning to listen to the deer bellowing at the top of their lungs.

Price: €16 (full price) and €13 (3–11 years old).
Open from early February to late November.

Route du Coin du Bois, 78120 Sonchamp
- Transilien — Line N and TER: Rambouillet, then bike or prearranged pickup (bookings on espacerambouillet.fr)

where to sleep

RAMBOUILLET

135 CAMPING HUTTOPIA®

#CAMPINGPARADISE #INTHEWOODS
#NATURALSWIMMINGPOOL

Leave the N10 road, drive past the L'Oréal® factory, drive another kilometre through the woods and you will find yourself in paradise, at Camping Huttopia®. Set up in the heart of the Rambouillet forest (see p. 77), it is the perfect place to escape if you're experiencing an urban overdose. You can pitch your own tent or choose from different types of accommodation: cabins, trailers, trapper tents or airstream caravans. As you won't want to leave unless it's to go for a hike in the forest, a grocery shop and a restaurant with its terrace overlooking a pond are there to keep you going.

Price: from €18/night for a pitch up to €165/night for a chalet.
Open from April to November.

Route du Château d'Eau, 78120 Rambouillet
Tel: +33 (0)1 30 41 07 34
europe.huttopia.com/site/camping-rambouillet
- Transilien — Line N: Rambouillet then 3 km on foot or by bicycle.

VILLE-D'AVRAY

136 ÉTANGS DE COROT

#NATURE #SPA
#STAYCATION

The painter Jean-Baptiste Corot gave his name to the lakes of Ville-d'Avray, as well as to the hotel that rests quietly on their shores. At Les Étangs de Corot, which has been awarded the Relais & Châteaux label, everything is conducive to relaxation. The bar looks like a speakeasy; one of the restaurants (the hotel has a restaurant, a bistro, and a café) is Michelin-starred; the rooms pay homage to the atmosphere of artists' studios and will win you over with their elegant vintage charm; as for the Kos and Phytomer spa, it will take you to the nirvana of well-being. The little secret: the jacuzzi can be privatized.

Price: from €179/night (excluding breakfast).

55, rue de Versailles, 92410 Ville-d'Avray
Tel: +33 (0)1 41 15 37 00 / etangs-corot.com
- Transilien — Line L: Sèvres - Ville-d'Avray, then buses 469 or 471: Les Étangs

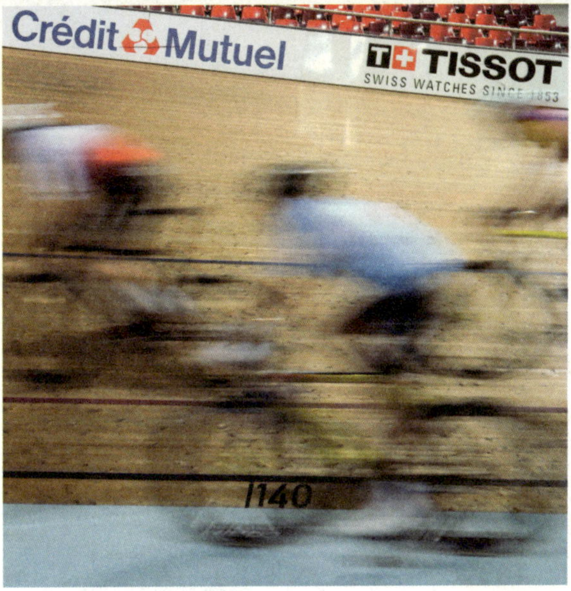

...the need for speed | *Vélodrome National, Montigny-le-Bretonneux.*

I feel the need... | *Vélodrome National, Montigny-le-Bretonneux.*

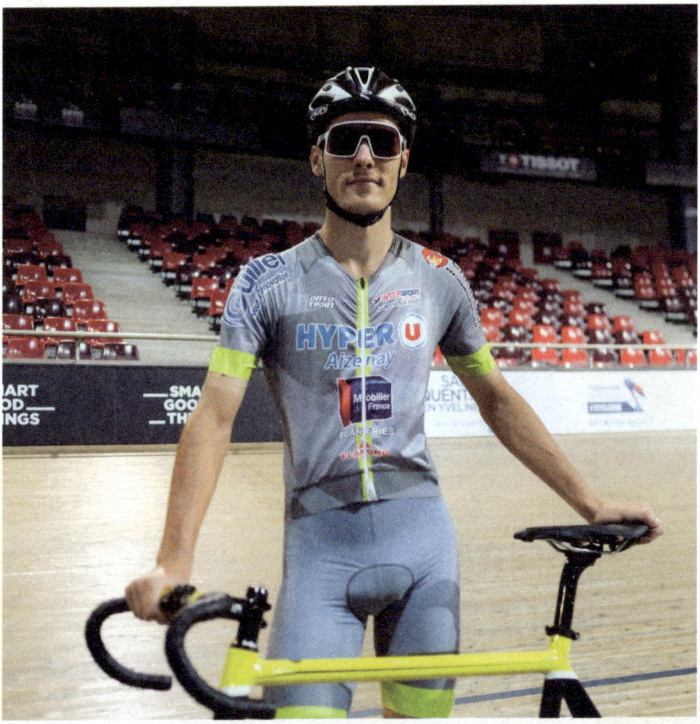

TH

R@

ARGENTEUIL
CORMEILLES-EN-PARISIS
SANNOIS

E
OF
TOP

Auvergne has the Massif Central, Burgundy has the Morvan and Greater Paris has the Buttes du Parisis. With their breathtaking views of both inner and outer Paris, the Butte d'Orgemont and the Butte des Châtaigniers allow you to jump from La Défense to Montmartre in the blink of an eye. Picnics and football matches can be improvised on their grass-covered high plateaus. Provided that the wind that sometimes blows there doesn't get out of hand.

THE ROOF TOP

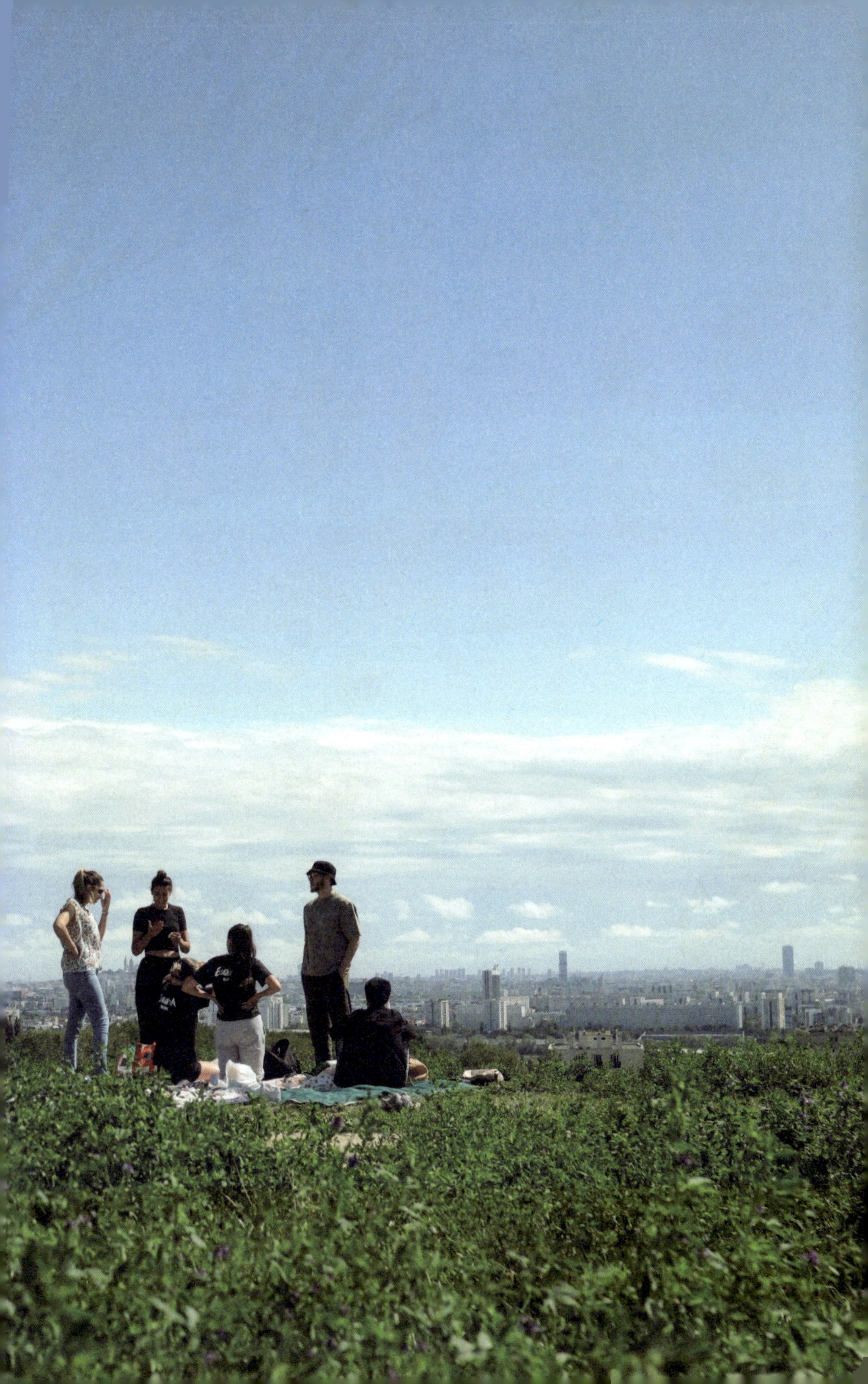

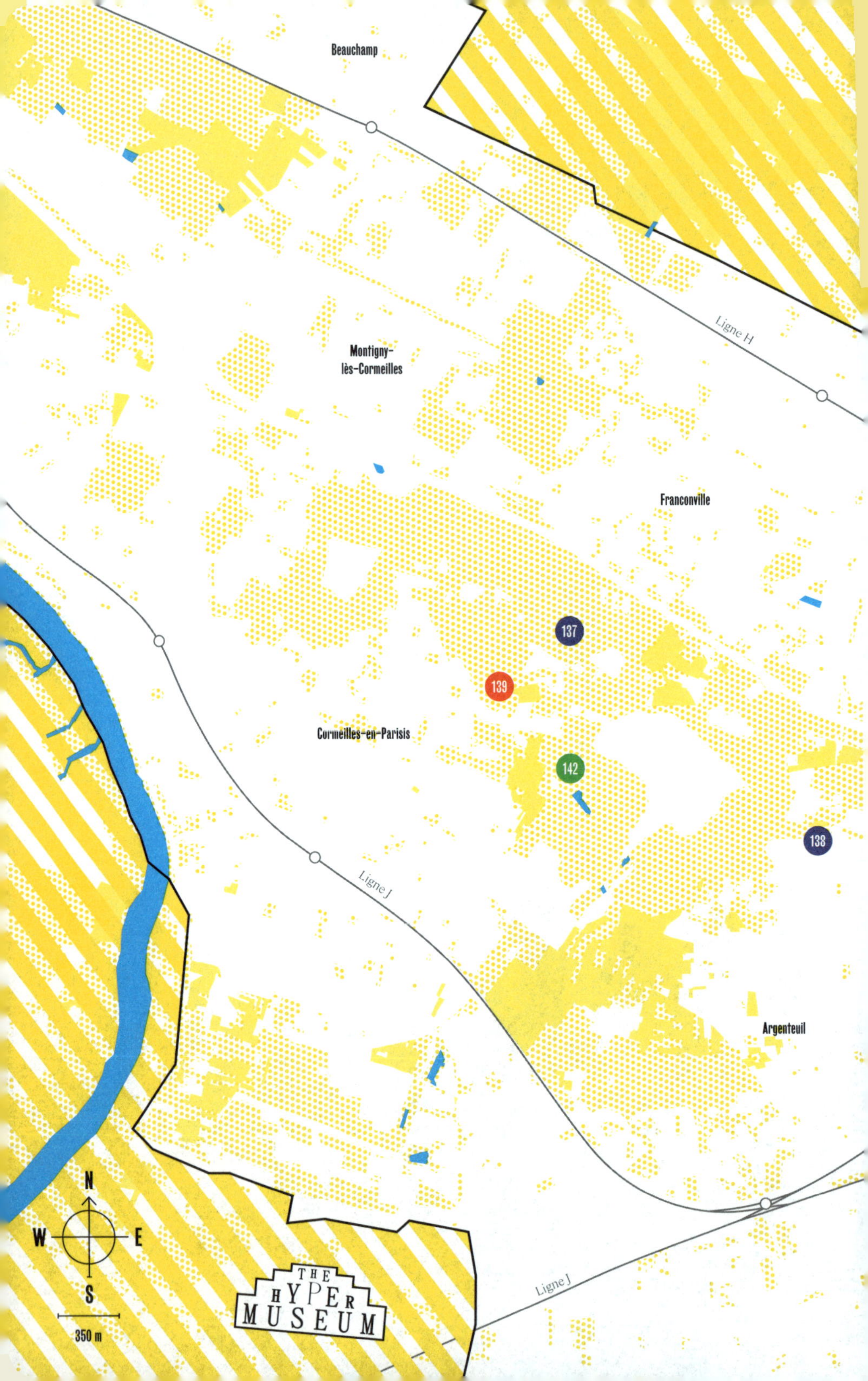
Beauchamp
Ligne H
Montigny-
lès-Cormeilles
Franconville
137
139
Cormeilles-en-Parisis
142
138
Ligne J
Argenteuil
N
W
E
S
350 m
Ligne J
THE HYPER MUSEUM

THE ROOFTOP

SPORT

137 TRAIL DES CHÂTAIGNES
138 ECOPARK MOULIN DE SANNOIS

CULTURE

139 FORT DE CORMEILLES-EN-PARISIS

OUTDOORS

140 BUTTE D'ORGEMONT
141 BUTTE DES CHÂTAIGNIERS
142 FORÊT RÉGIONALE DES BUTTES DU PARISIS

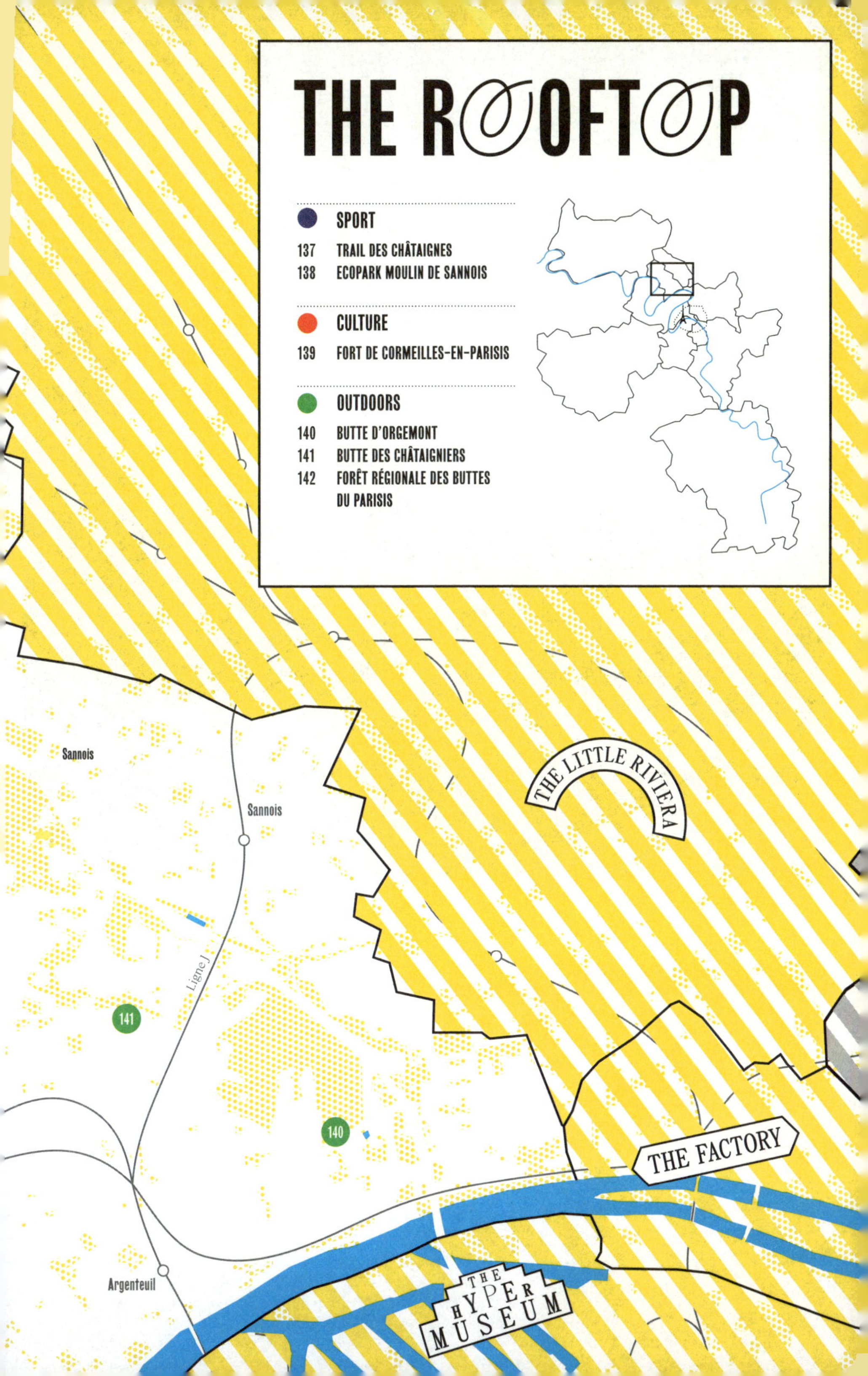

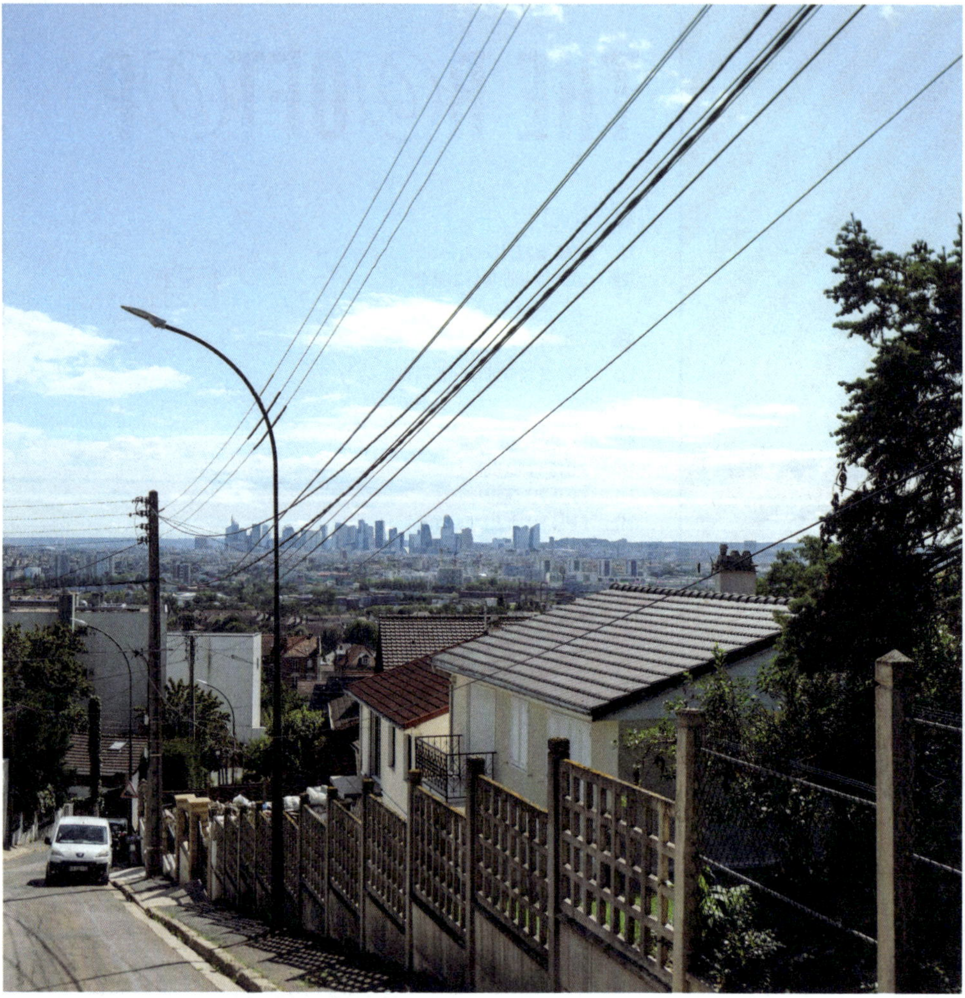

All downhill from here | *Rue d'Orgemont, Argenteuil.*

sport

CORMEILLES-EN-PARISIS

137 TRAIL DES CHÂTAIGNES

#YOURLOCALALPS #CHESTNUTTRAIL
#MILITARYFORT

No need to go as far as the Alps or the Pyrenees to enjoy a trail run worthy of the name. As winter approaches, sports enthusiasts from all over Ile-de-France meet up in Cormeilles-en-Parisis for the Trail des Châtaignes. The race begins at the town's military fort (see below), built at the end of the 19th century to defend Paris. You can choose between four races, including a night race, through the Buttes du Parisis (see p. 94), with ascents of of up to 1,900 metres. Who says Greater Paris is flat?

From €19.
Mid-November.

trail-des-chataignes.com
- Transilien — Line J: Cormeilles-en-Parisis

SANNOIS

138 ECOPARK MOULIN DE SANNOIS

#TREETOPS #13ROUTES
#2ANDUP

The city, the road, and the concrete fade away as you set off along a sandy path alongside an old football pitch. Then you start to hear the whoops of those darting through the treetops. In the Sannois forest, less than 20 kilometres from the *périphérique*, the canopy is criss-crossed by a network of zip lines and rope bridges. Whether you're a beginner or an experienced squirrel, the Sannois Ecopark offers 13 courses for adventurers from the age of 2, with no less than 2,000 metres of routes. Something for everyone!

From €8.
Open from mid-February to mid-November.

Rue de l'Ermitage (Tour du mail roundabout),
95110 Sannois
Tel: +33 (0)7 62 82 12 12
sannois@ecopark-adventures.com
- Transilien — Line J: Argenteuil, then Bus line 2, Le Moulin stop

culture

CORMEILLES-EN-PARISIS

139 FORT DE CORMEILLES-EN-PARISIS

#MILITARYBASTION #DEFENCEOFPARIS
#IMPRESSIVE

Inherited from the fortification plans drawn up in the second half of the 19t century by General Raymond Adolphe Séré de Rivières, the fort of Cormeilles-en-Parisis is an impressive military bastion built in the middle of the forest which remains magnificently preserved, even if nature has taken over in parts. Guided tours take place every first Sunday of the month (except for January and August). If that's too long a wait, you are still able to walk around the impressive structure. A great way to immerse yourself in the history of the defence of Paris.

Price: free participation.
Guided tours every first Sunday of the month (except for January and August).

Route Stratégique, 95240 Cormeilles-en-Parisis
fortdecormeilles.fr
- Transilien — Line J: Cormeilles-en-Parisis

Outdoors

ARGENTEUIL

140 BUTTE D'ORGEMONT

#PANORAMA #SPRAWLINGLAWNS #WOWFACTOR

To enjoy one of the most beautiful views of Greater Paris, climb the 250 steps of the hilltop of Orgemont or take the path that winds up to the summit. From the top of its 124 metres, this hill topped by a mill is the ultimate viewpoint, offering an exceptional and unrivalled view of Montmartre, the Eiffel Tower®, La Défense and the port of Gennevilliers. At the top, a gigantic lawn serves as a green balcony, ideal for picnics, sunbathing, kicking a ball around or flying a kite. The only downside is the proximity to the A15 motorway. The Butte, which was transformed into a park in 2017, is accessible 7 days a week and 24 hours a day. A classic Greater Paris pilgrimage.

176, avenue de Stalingrad, 95100 Argenteuil
iledefrance-nature.fr

- Transilien — Line J: Argenteuil
- Bus — 7: Vaucelle
- Vélib' — Gare d'Argenteuil

141 BUTTE DES CHÂTAIGNIERS

#PANORAMA #SPRAWLINGLAWNS #WOWFACTORPART2

From the top of the Butte des Châtaigniers, you can look out over more than twenty centuries. Like its neighbour, the Butte d'Orgemont, the Butte des Châtaigniers offers a 24-hour panoramic view of Paris: Mont Valérien, La Défense skyline, Eiffel and Montparnasse towers, you can see it all. To reach the summit, you will have to climb even more steps than at Orgemont: 360 versus 250. Here again, it's possible to bypass them by opting for a path that winds its way to this natural roof terrace. Halfway up, a large lawn is used as a picnic area as well as a playground. And if you are a glutton for punishment, the Trail des châtaignes (see p.93) will make you see the hill in an entirely different light, with a 1,900-metre ascent.

15, boulevard Youri Gagarine, 95100 Argenteuil
iledefrance-nature.fr

- Transilien — Line J: Argenteuil
- Bus — 18: Châtaigniers
- Vélib' — Gare d'Argenteuil

SANNOIS

142 FORÊT RÉGIONALE DES BUTTES DU PARISIS

#TREK #ADVENTURECOURSE #MILITARYFORT

For those who know how to explore it, this forest hides unsuspected treasures like the incredibly well-preserved military fort of Cormeilles-en-Parisis (see p. 93). In a much more contemporary genre, a treetop adventure course located in the city of Sannois offers 10 routes, one of which is open to toddlers (see p. 93). Finally, the prize for the most unexpected experience goes to the Chemin des Crêtes, which winds its way 170 metres up with some beautiful panoramic views from the Butte d'Orgemont to the Butte des Châtaigniers (see above).

iledefrance-nature.fr

- Transilien — Line J: La Frette Montigny

CHAMPS-SUR-MARNE
CHELLES
CRÉTEIL
ÉVRY-COURCOURONNES
JUVISY-SUR-ORGE
MAISONS-ALFORT

D

MARNE-LA-VALLÉE
MOISSY-CRAMAYEL

NOISIEL
ORLY
PARIS
PÉRIGNY

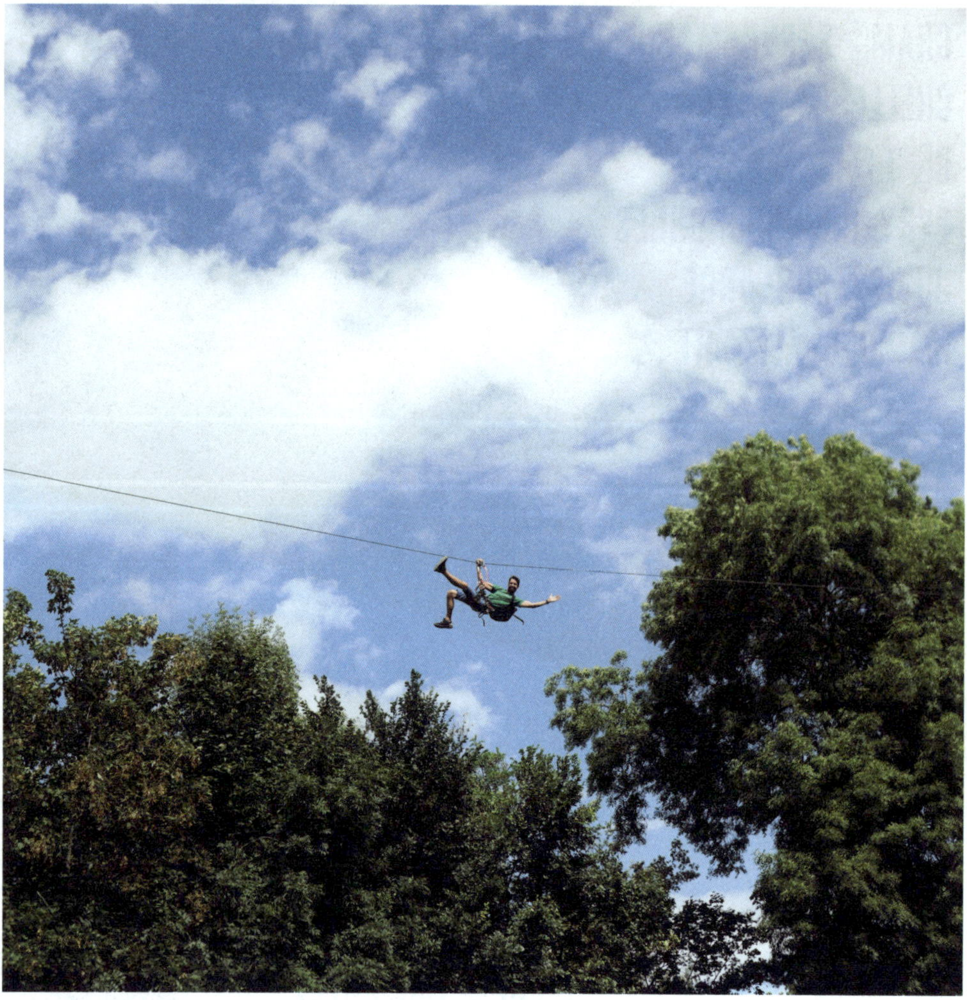

Zip-a-Dee-Doo-Dah | *Ecopark Adventures, Sannois.*

THE ELTA

VAIRES-SUR-MARNE
VINCENNES
YERRES

RIS-ORANGIS
SAINT-MAUR-DES-FOSSÉS
SUCY-EN-BRIE

In 1990, the then mayor of Paris, Jacques Chirac, announced on television: "In three years, I'll go swimming in the Seine in front of witnesses." While this promise remained unfulfilled it is now more relevant than ever, since two 2024 Olympic swimming events will take place in the river before three public swimming areas are opened in 2025. On the banks of the Marne, too, there is a campaign to have the river reopened to wild swimming. Meanwhile, throughout The Delta, pedestrians are taking over riverbanks while barges keep them entertained.

THE DELTA

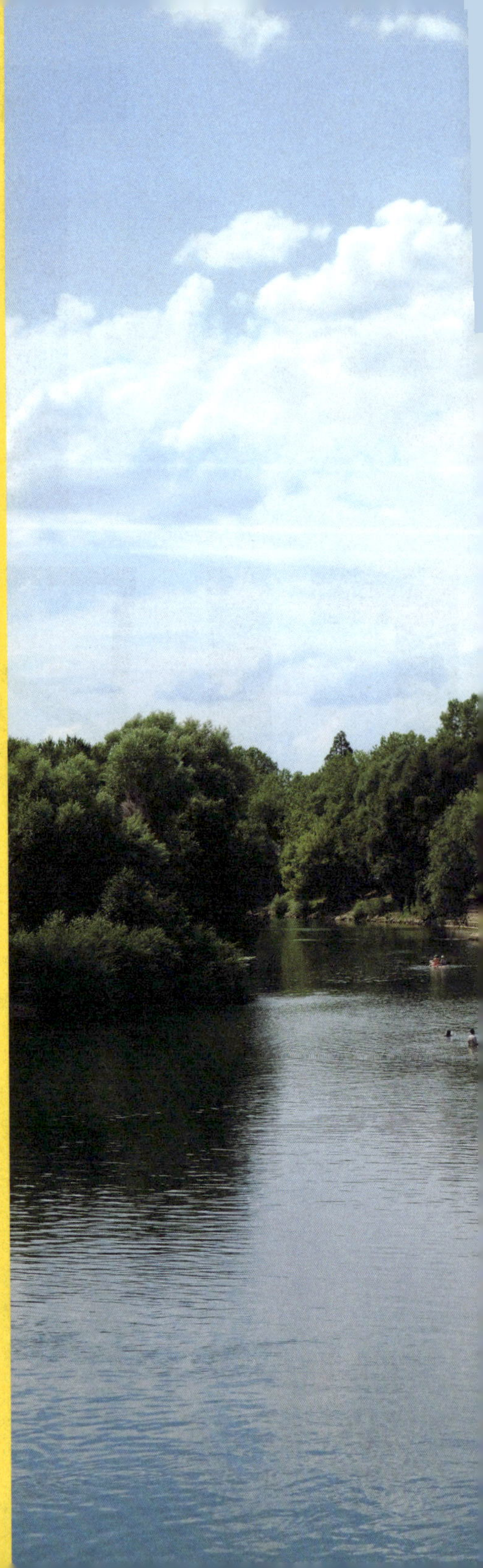

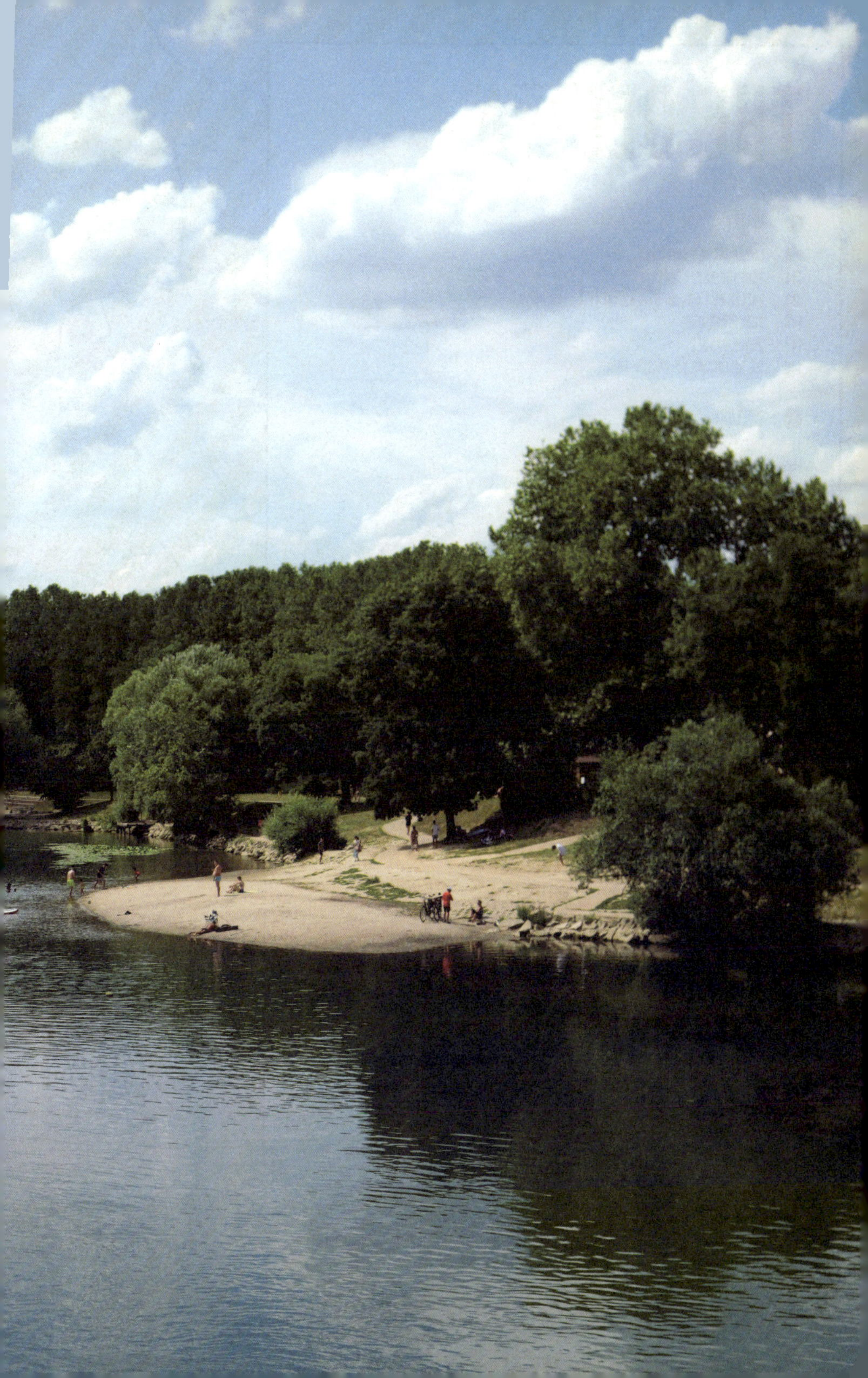

THE DELTA

SPORT

143 COSANOSTRA SKATEPARK
144 ECOPARK ADVENTURES
145 VALLÉE DE L'ART DU DÉPLACEMENT
146 SCANDIBÉRIQUE
147 BEACH PADDLE
148 ÎLE DE LOISIRS DE VAIRES-TORCY

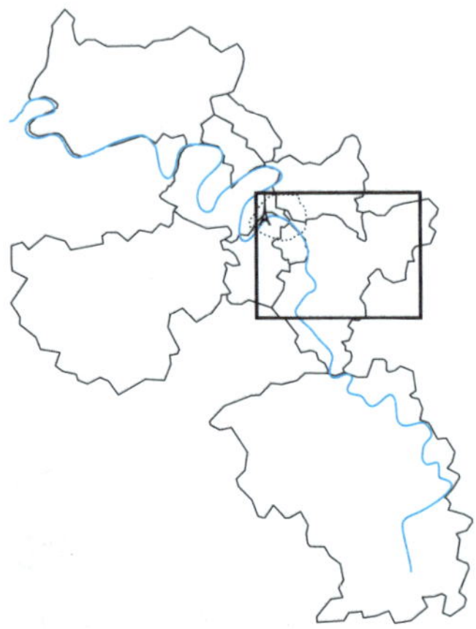

CULTURE

149 CHÂTEAU DE CHAMPS-SUR-MARNE
150 KHÁNH-ANH PAGODA
151 MUSÉE FRAGONARD
152 LA FERME DU BUISSON
153 CARTOUCHERIE DE VINCENNES
154 MUSÉE PICASSO
155 PAVILLON DE L'ARSENAL
156 FONDATION DUBUFFET – CLOSERIE FALBALA
157 LE PLAN
158 MAISON CAILLEBOTTE

LIFESTYLE

159 PARIS-ORLY AIRPORT
160 ROSA BONHEUR À L'EST
161 PETIT-BAIN
162 LA GRIFFE NOIRE

OUTDOORS

163 STROLL ALONG THE MARNE
164 LAC DE CRÉTEIL
165 PARC DE NOISIEL
166 BOIS DE VINCENNES
167 JARDIN D'AGRONOMIE TROPICALE RENÉ-DUMONT
168 PARC DES RIVES DE SEINE RIVE DROITE
169 THE MARNE LOOP
170 FORÊT DE NOTRE-DAME

WHERE TO EAT

171 LE MONTOROS
172 WAT THAMMAPATHIP PAGODA
173 MAMA JACKSON SOUL FOOD
174 L'ATELIER 28
175 L'OURS
176 TITAN ARTISAN KEBABIER

FAMILY

177 DISNEYLAND PARIS
178 MUSÉE NATIONAL DE L'HISTOIRE DE L'IMMIGRATION
179 CHÂTEAU DE VINCENNES

WHERE TO SLEEP

180 PÉNICHE CANALA
181 HÔTEL PARADISO
182 OFF PARIS SEINE

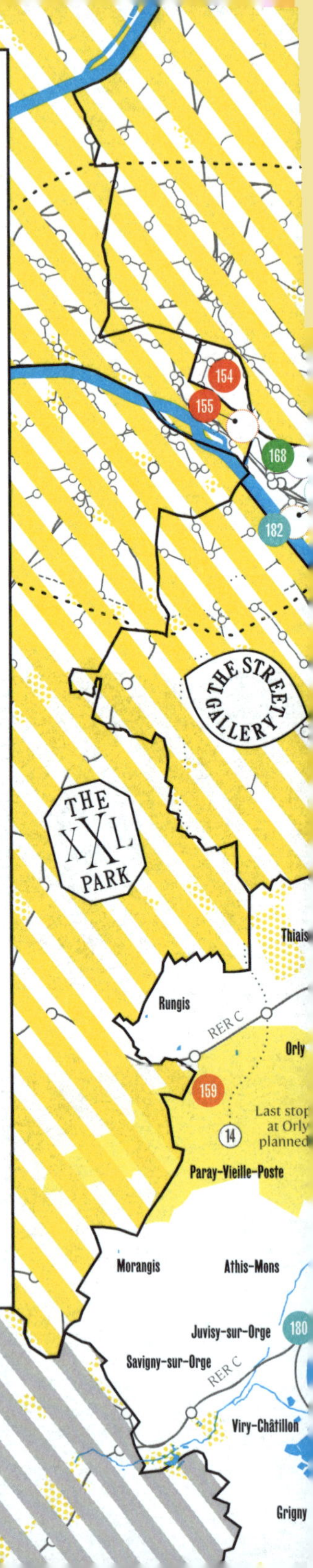

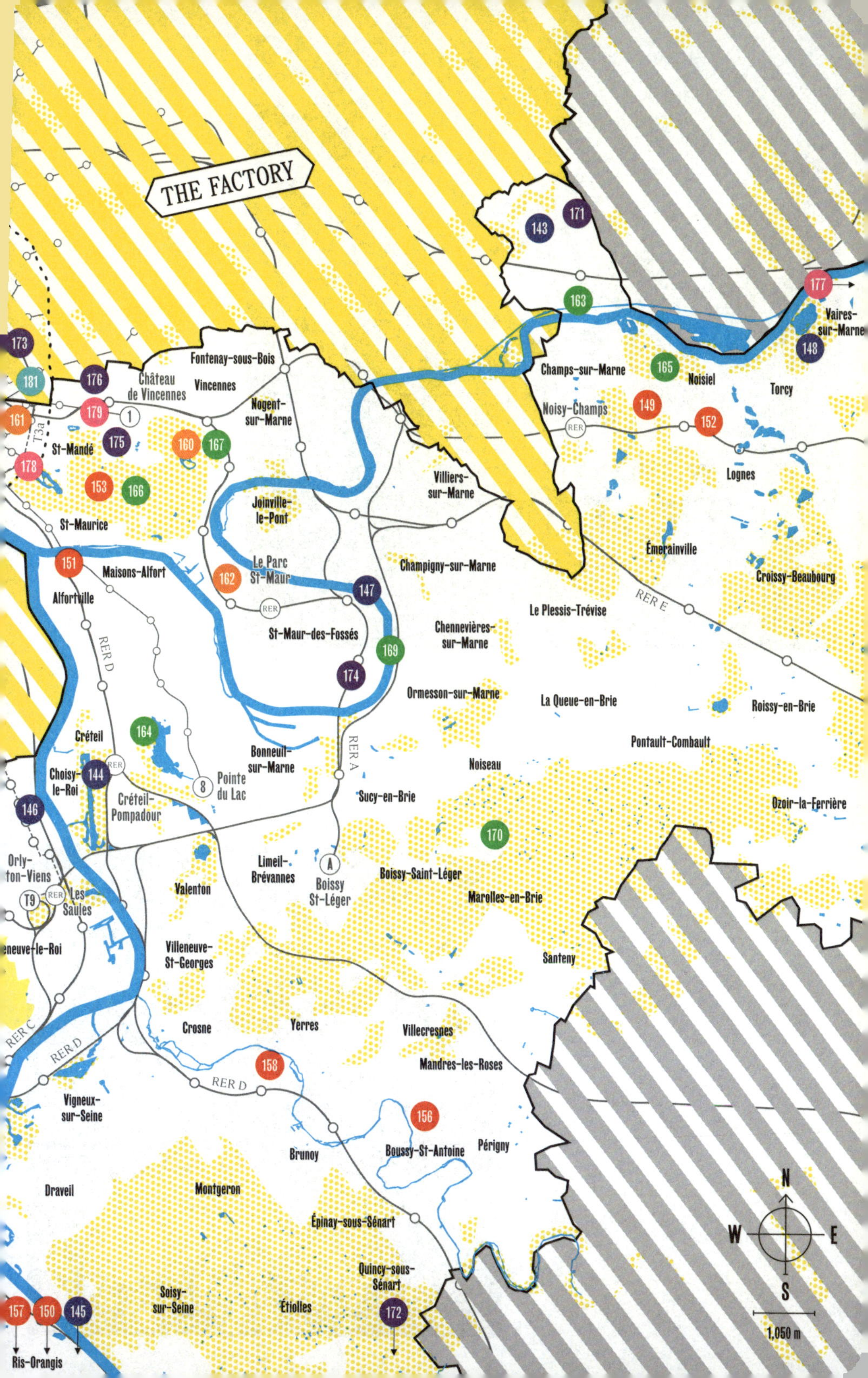

THE FACTORY
Fontenay-sous-Bois
Château de Vincennes
Vincennes
Nogent-sur-Marne
St-Mandé
St-Maurice
Joinville-le-Pont
Le Parc St-Maur
Maisons-Alfort
Alfortville
St-Maur-des-Fossés
Villiers-sur-Marne
Champigny-sur-Marne
Champs-sur-Marne
Noisiel
Torcy
Vaires-sur-Marne
Noisy-Champs
Lognes
Émerainville
Croissy-Beaubourg
Le Plessis-Trévise
Chennevières-sur-Marne
Ormesson-sur-Marne
La Queue-en-Brie
Roissy-en-Brie
Pontault-Combault
Créteil
Choisy-le-Roi
Créteil-Pompadour
Pointe du Lac
Bonneuil-sur-Marne
Noiseau
Sucy-en-Brie
Ozoir-la-Ferrière
Orly-ton-Viens
Les Saules
Limeil-Brévannes
Boissy St-Léger
Boissy-Saint-Léger
Marolles-en-Brie
Valenton
Villeneuve-St-Georges
Santeny
eneuve-le-Roi
Crosne
Yerres
Villecresnes
Mandres-les-Roses
Vigneux-sur-Seine
Brunoy
Boussy-St-Antoine
Périgny
Draveil
Montgeron
Épinay-sous-Sénart
Quincy-sous-Sénart
Soisy-sur-Seine
Étiolles
Ris-Orangis
RER A
RER C
RER D
RER E
T3a
T9
N
S
E
W
1,050 m

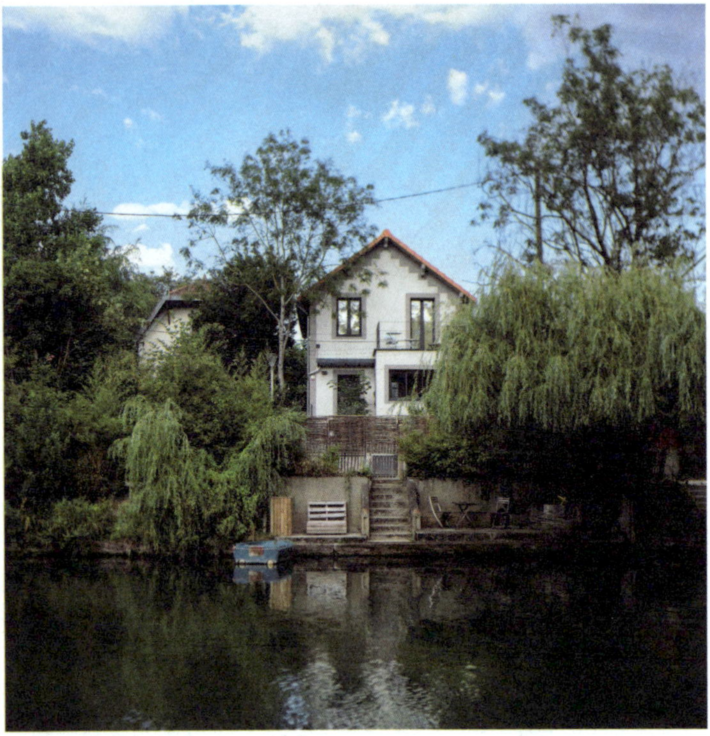

Riverside life | *Quai de la Marne, Joinville-le-Pont.*

Green, green, and more green | *Canal de Chelles, Neuilly-sur-Marne.*

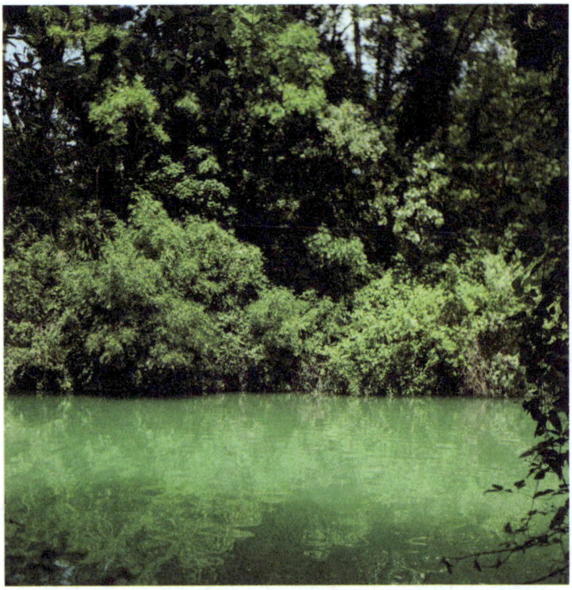

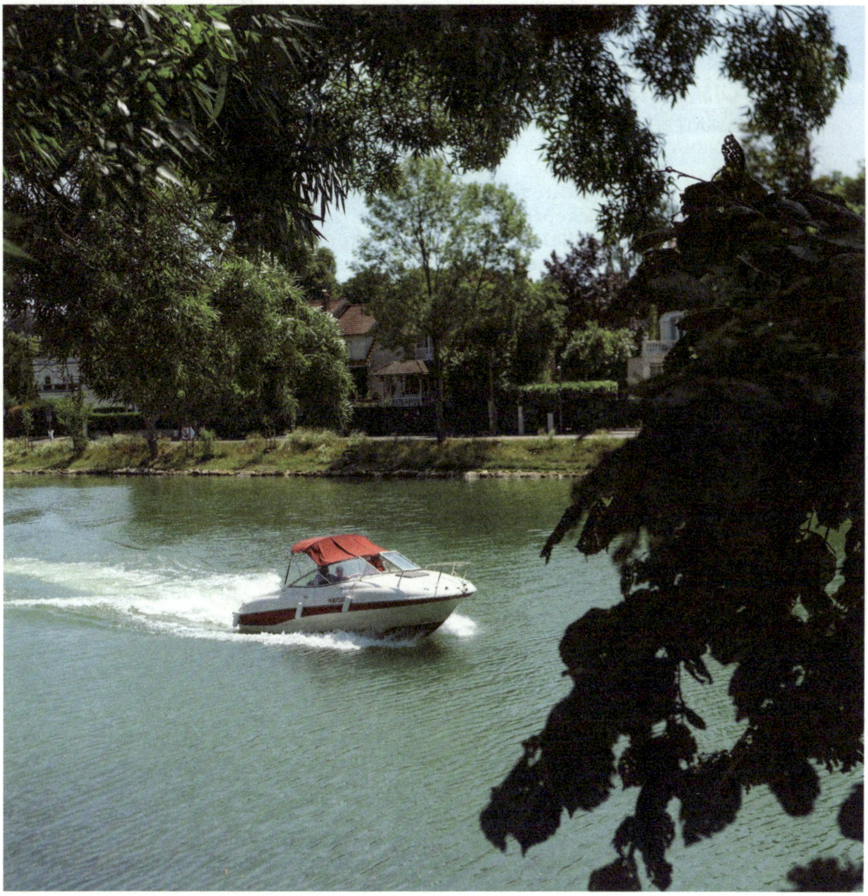

Miami on Marne | *Quai de Marne, Thorigny-sur-Marne.*

Sport

CHELLES

143 COSANOSTRA SKATEPARK

#SKATEBOARDINGSCHOOL
#INDOOROUTDOOR #PARISOLYMPICS

As the official preparation centre for the Paris Olympics, the Cosanostra skatepark is not only open to elite riders. Thanks to the local skateboarding school, which offers introductory lessons over three sessions with a qualified instructor, as well as courses during the school holidays, anyone can jump aboard. A great way to take advantage of the top-of-the-range facilities, from the large indoor space with its array of different modules (pyramids, rails, etc.) to the outdoor bowl set among the pine trees.

Price: €7 admission.
Open to the public from Thursday to Sunday.

18, rue du Tir, 77500 Chelles
Tel: +33 (0)1 64 72 14 04 / cosanostraskatepark.com

- RER — E: Chelles-Gournay then bus 7 and 9s, Skatepark stop
- Transilien — Line P: Chelles-Gournay then bus 17 and 9s, Skatepark stop
- Bus — 613: Quatre Routes

CRÉTEIL

144 ECOPARK ADVENTURES

#TREECLIMBING #ZIPLINE
#AERIALADVENTURES

If swinging from tree to tree like Spiderman is what you're after, then get yourself down to Créteil. Over eleven tree climbing courses (from age five upwards) you will be able to explore the tree canopy across suspension bridges, nets, zip lines and swings. The main attraction (and the first of its kind in France) is the 11 zip-lines running over the Lac de Créteil which amount to 1,200 metres of thrills above the water.

Price: from €20 per person (booking is strongly recommended).
Open from mid-February to mid-November.

Parc interdépartemental des sports (plaine Nord), Chemin des Marais, 94000 Créteil
Tel: +33 (0)7 69 94 69 65 / ecopark-adventures.com

- RER — D: Créteil Pompadour
- Bus — 393: Pompadour

ÉVRY

145 VALLÉE DE L'ART DU DÉPLACEMENT

#PARKOUR #THEARTOFMOVEMENT
#URBANADVENTURE

Imagine a forest of metal bars of different heights running over a distance of some twenty metres. This is the setting for the poetically entitled "valley of the art of movement" in Évry-Courcouronnes. The aim here is not just a few chin-ups, but to complete the course by running, jumping and acrobatics, all without any equipment whatsoever. This is a parkour or freerunning course, a discipline invented some twenty years ago by young people in Essonne and made popular in France by the film *Yamakasi*. To help you become a master of the art, the Add Academy association, run by experts, offers courses and workshops, on site as well as in Paris and Choisy-le-Roi.

Open daily.

Place Pierre-Mendès-France, 91000 Évry-Courcouronnes
Courses with the Add Academy association:
addacademy.evry@gmail.com / add-academy.com

- RER — D: Evry-Courcouronnes
- Bus — 401, 402, 403, 404, 405, 407, 414, 415, 416, 453: Évry-Courcouronnes

PARIS

146 SCANDIBÉRIQUE

#LONGESTCYCLEROUTEINFRANCE
#SEINEGONEWILD #MAJESTICVILLAS

Running across 1,700 km, the Scandibérique is the longest cycle route in France. And yet, the French portion only represents a third of the overall route, which covers over 5,000 km from Trondheim (Norway) to Santiago de Compostela (Spain). In the Greater Paris region, which it crosses from north to south, it follows the Seine from Paris onwards, allowing you to discover the river's wild landscapes and its majestic villas known as the Affolantes from Le Coudray-Montceaux onwards. You can access the route at multiple points thanks to the many train stations along the way (you and your bike can board a Transilien or RER train outside rush hour on weekdays and without any restrictions on weekends and public holidays).

scandiberique.fr

SAINT-MAUR-DES-FOSSÉS

147 BEACH PADDLE

#ARCHIPELAGO #PADDLEFOR10
#GUIDEDTOUR

Beach Paddle is a little corner of paradise where you can gently slalom on your paddle board between four islands in the Marne. For large families, ten people can climb aboard an XXL board. Boards can be rented independently or you can also book a guided tour. And when back on dry land, take the opportunity to walk the Marne loop (see p. 115).

Price: €10/30 minutes, €17/hour and €30/2 hours.
Open Monday to Friday from 2–7pm,
Saturday and Sunday from 10am–7pm.

At the corner of Quai du Mesnil and Rue Sainte-Catherine, 94100 Saint-Maur-des-Fossés
Book online or on +33 (0)6 10 81 49 98 / beachpaddle.fr

- RER — A: Champigny
- Bus — 111: Gustave Goublier

VAIRES-SUR-MARNE

148 ÎLE DE LOISIRS DE VAIRES-TORCY

#WATERSPORTS #OLYMPICGAMES
#RAFTINGADVENTURES

The Île de Loisirs will host the canoe, kayak and rowing events of the 2024 Olympic Games. Until then, you have time to quietly enjoy the island of Vaires-Torcy and its 2km-long lake for water sports (rowing, paddle board, catamaran, windsurfing). For the more adventurous, it's even possible to head out on a rafting adventure on the whitewater river that was inaugurated in 2019 for the Paris Olympics by Tony Estanguet himself, a three-time single canoe Olympic champion.

Open year round.

Rue du parc de loisirs de Torcy, 77360 Vaires-sur-Marne
Tel: +33 (0)1 60 20 02 04 / vaires-torcy.iledeloisirs.fr

- RER — A: Torcy, then bus 211, 421 Les Cantines stop

culture

CHAMPS-SUR-MARNE

149 CHÂTEAU DE CHAMPS-SUR-MARNE

#ÉLYSÉELOOKALIKE #COPPOLA
#REMARKABLEGARDEN

You might get a feeling of déjà vu, because the Château de Champs-sur-Marne looks just like the Élysée palace. This former family residence inhabited by the Marquise de Pompadour, among others, houses no less than 900 collectible pieces of furniture by the great cabinet makers of the 18th century. In 1935, the owner Charles Cahen of Antwerp gave it to the French State in exchange for maintaining the posts of gardeners, servants, gamekeepers and about fifty other employees. Since then, many directors have made it their home, including Stephen Frears in *Dangerous Liaisons* (1987), Patrice Leconte in *Ridicule* (1995) and Sofia Coppola in *Marie-Antoinette* (2005). Champs-sur-Marne also has an 85-hectare park with the Jardin remarquable (Remarkable Garden) government label with both English and French-style gardens (free entry).

Price: €8 (full price) / Free for under-26s. Closed Tuesday.

31, rue de Paris, 77420 Champs-sur-Marne
Tel: +33 (0)1 64 62 74 42 / chateau-champs-sur-marne.fr

- RER — A: Noisiel
- Bus — 220, 312, 421: Mairie de Champs

ÉVRY

150 KHÁNH-ANH PAGODA

#LARGESTPAGODAINEUROPE
#COLLECTIVEWORK #BUDDHISM

Évry is home to the largest pagoda in Europe, the Khánh-Anh pagoda. Built on the banks of the mythical Nationale 7 holiday route, its construction called upon many volunteers and the generosity of Buddhists from all over the world until it was completed in 2017 after more than thirty years of work.

Visits by appointment from Monday to Saturday between 10am and 4pm.

Parc aux Lièvres, 8, rue François Mauriac, 91000 Évry-Courcouronnes
Tel: +33 (0)1 64 93 55 56
Facebook @PagodeKhanhAnhEvry

- RER — D: Le Bras-de-Fer
- Bus — 401, 404: Saint-Exupéry

MAISONS-ALFORT

151 MUSÉE FRAGONARD

#ANATOMICALCURIOSITIES #EIGHTLEGGEDCALF #MUMMIES

You better have a strong stomach, because the anatomical oddities awaiting you at the Fragonard Museum are not for the squeamish: calves with eight legs or two heads, mule fetuses, infections of all kinds but also animal skeletons – including a magnificent pink python specimen. The highlights of the show are the skinned anatomical figures of the anatomist Honoré Fragonard (1732–1799), mummies that seem to have come straight from a zombie film. Astonishing, like the premises that serve as the decor for this cabinet of curiosities: the national veterinary school, created in 1766 and which extends over 12 hectares, 70 percent of which is green space.

Price: €8 / Free for under-26s.
Closed Monday, Tuesday, Friday and public holidays.

7, avenue du Général de Gaulle, 94700 Maisons-Alfort
Tel: +33 (0)1 43 96 71 72
vet-alfort.fr/domaine-d-alfort/musee-fragonard

- M — Line 8: École Vétérinaire de Maisons-Alfort
- Bus — 104, 181: Bouley - École Vétérinaire
- Vélib' — Rue de la Marne

NOISIEL

152 LA FERME DU BUISSON

#NATIONALSTAGE #CULTURALMULTIPLEX #NOTANORDINARYFARM

This is the story of a farm that has perfectly succeeded in its conversion. Over some 30 years, the Ferme du Buisson has become a stronghold of culture in the suburbs, with 100,000 people flocking there each year to enjoy its programming as well as its magnificent setting. Once you enter the gates, the charm of this place immediately becomes apparent. In the middle of the courtyard stands a huge brick building that has become a stage. All around, the water trough, the stables and the attic have kept their name but have also changed vocation, making the Ferme du Buisson a cultural multiplex with a theatre, art centre, cinema and musical space and restaurant, le Relais du Buisson.

Open year round.

Allée de la Ferme, 77186 Noisiel
Tel: +33 (0)1 64 62 77 00 / lafermedubuisson.com

- RER — A: Noisiel
- Bus — 211: Ferme du Buisson

PARIS

153 CARTOUCHERIE DE VINCENNES

#FORMERFACTORY #SUNTHEATRE #INTHEWOODS

Make love, not war – the famous saying comes alive at the Cartoucherie de Vincennes. A former weapons and gunpowder factory, the Cartoucherie changed its focus in the early 1970s under the guidance of director Ariane Mnouchkine and her company, the Théâtre du Soleil, joined by the Théâtre de la Tempête, the Théâtre de l'Epée de bois and the Théâtre de l'Aquarium. Installed in these former abandoned barracks, these theatres form an explosive ensemble in the heart of the Bois de Vincennes and immerse you in an unexpected setting. As for the programming, it includes both great classics and more contemporary creations.

4, route du Champ de manœuvre, 75012 Paris
cartoucherie.fr

- M — Line 1: Château de Vincennes (on the evenings of performances, shuttles connect the metro station to the Cartoucherie before and after the show)
- Bus — 112: Cartoucherie
- Vélib' — Avenue du Tremblay

154 MUSÉE PICASSO

#HOTELPARTICULIER #TAKEYOURTIME #FROMCOCTEAUTOBRASSAI

Upon arrival at the ticket counter, the audioguide assistant will inform you right away with a first-class air steward's manner that experiencing the Picasso Museum takes time. The sarcophagus formed by the marble and woodwork of the Salé hôtel particulier opens onto a maze of thematic rooms where Pablo's artistic lives unfold. The audience moves from work to work in a contemplative silence. Smartphones are drawn sparingly to capture the emotion of being confronted with a masterpiece, a photograph by Brassaï or a postcard by Jean Cocteau, as this museum has successfully combined Picasso's works with photographs, souvenirs and slices of life. There is no right way to visit the Picasso Museum, but go too fast and you

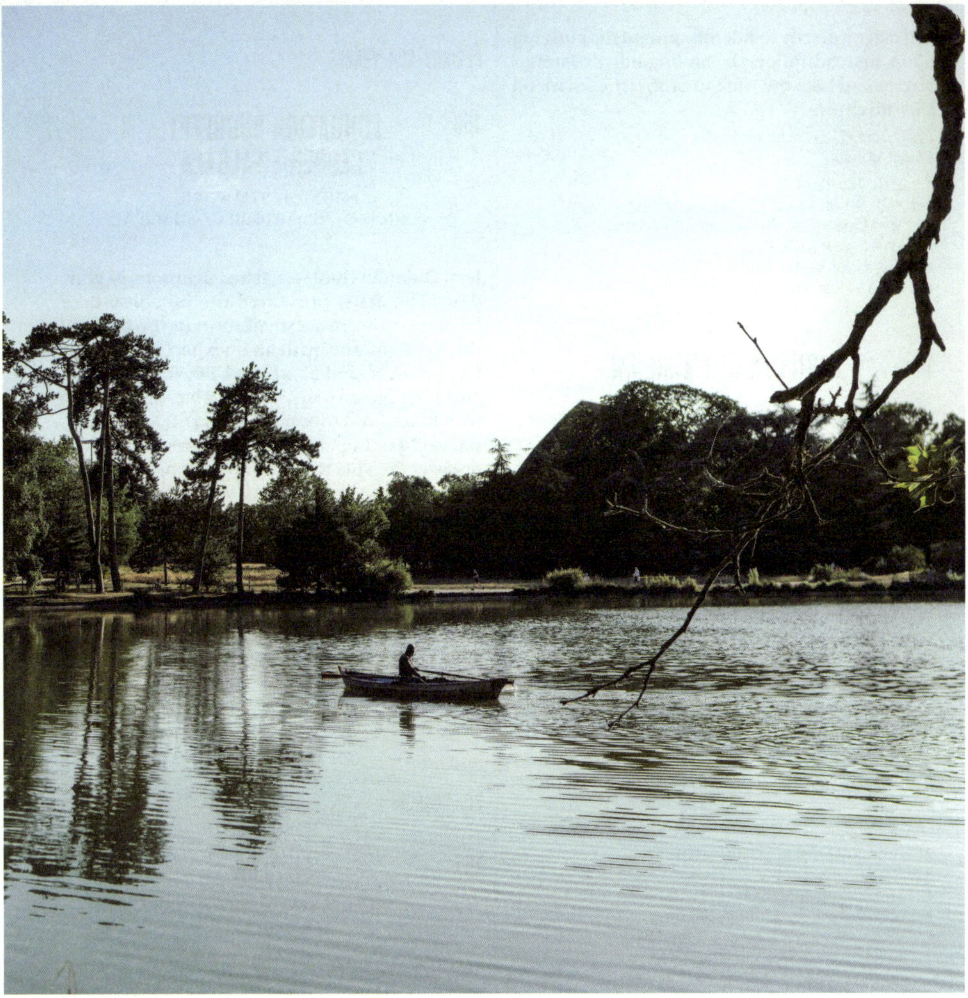

On the banks of the Amazon | *Lac Daumesnil, Paris.*

will end up dizzily wandering around the museum shop. Instead, follow the audioguide assistant's advice and take the time to properly embark on this adventure.

Price: from €11 / Free for under-26s.
Closed Monday.

5, rue de Thorigny, 75003 Paris
Tel: +33 (0)1 85 56 00 36 / museepicassoparis.fr

- M — Line 8: Saint-Sébastien - Froissart, M — Line 1: Saint-Paul
- Bus — 96: Saint Claude
- Vélib' — Rue Vieille du Temple, Paris 3rd

155 PAVILLON DE L'ARSENAL

#ARCHITECTURE
#STORYOFGREATERPARIS #FREE

The story of Paris, from the great to the small, is told at the Pavillon de l'Arsenal. This beautiful space topped by a glass roof is a must for anyone interested in architecture and the city. Recent exhibitions have explored Haussmann's world, the *périphérique* and agriculture in the Île-de-France region as well as the forecourt of Notre-Dame Cathedral. For experts and neophytes alike, you will always discover something new about the City of Light. Children are also welcome and invited to participate in activities specially designed for them. In addition to the temporary exhibitions, an 800-m² space is dedicated to the city and its projects, with a 3D digital map as the centrepiece.

Free entry.
Closed Monday.

21, boulevard Morland, 75004 Paris
pavillon-arsenal.com

- M — 7: Sully-Morland
- Bus — 67, 72, 86, 87: Sully-Morland
- Vélib' — 2, quai des Célestins, Paris 4th

PÉRIGNY-SUR-YERRES

156 FONDATION DUBUFFET - CLOSERIE FALBALA

#MONUMENTALWORK
#UNIDENTIFIEDARTOBJECT #MAGICAL

Jean Dubuffet (1901–1985) had delusions of grandeur. The artist presented the inhabitants of Périgny-sur-Yerres, a small town in the heart of the Val-de-Marne, with an unexpected architectural work, a kind of artistic UFO. To begin, imagine high curved walls, painted white and covered with black lines over more than 1,600 m². This is the world of the Closerie Falbala. Inside, you will discover the Villa Falbala, a mysterious room covered with strange writing. All you have to do is let yourself be carried away by the magic of the place. Remember, this monumental work can only be visited by appointment.

Price: €8 (full price), €4.5 (reduced price) / Free for under-10s.
Open year round. Closed Monday, Tuesday and public holidays. Visits by appointment only (by phone).

Rue du Moulin Neuf, Sente des Vaux,
Ruelle aux Chevaux, 94520 Périgny-sur-Yerres
Tel: +33 (0)1 47 34 12 63 / dubuffetfondation.com

RIS-ORANGIS

157 LE PLAN

#CONCERTS #FROMROCKTOHIPHOP
#TRAILBLAZER

Two brand new rooms, a trailblazing programme and unbeatable prices: Le Plan is one of the temples of music of Greater Paris. Since 1984, this pure rock venue has evolved to make way for other sounds. Bertrand Belin, Christophe, Marianne Faithfull, Tiken Jah Fakoly, Maceo Parker, IAM and Lou Doillon are some of the headliners that have already featured here.

1, avenue Louis Aragon, 91130 Ris-Orangis
Tel: +33 (0)1 69 02 09 19 / leplan.com

- RER — D: Orangis-Bois-de-L'Epine
- Bus — 404, 405, 406, 418: Ris-Orangis - Bois de l'Épine

YERRES

158 MAISON CAILLEBOTTE

#IMPRESSIONISM #GARDEN #MUSEUM

Entering the Caillebotte estate in Yerres is like stepping back in time into the daily life of a wealthy family in the late 19th century. This recently restored residence, a former farmhouse from the 16th century, was inhabited by the painter Gustave Caillebotte (1848–1894) and his family. Between original furniture and pieces bequeathed by the Mobilier National, the visit is stunning. From the women's lounge with its beautiful sewing table to the flashy billiards room and the bedroom with multiple views of the park, colours and ornaments immerse visitors in the atmosphere of this bourgeois house. All around, a splendid garden extends over 11 hectares with six follies, small temples typical of English-style gardens, a vegetable garden maintained by local volunteers, and even a restaurant, the Table du Parc.

Price: €8 / Free for under-16s.
Visits of the residence from Tuesday to Sunday from 2–6.30pm.
Garden open daily. Free entry.

8, rue de Concy, 91330 Yerres
Tel: +33 (0)1 80 37 20 61 / maisoncaillebotte.com
- RER — D: Yerres

lifestyle

ORLY

159 PARIS-ORLY AIRPORT

#PANORAMICTERRACE #BEHINDTHESCENES #FLIGHTSIMULATOR

Orly airport is not just a place of transit, it is also a destination in and of itself. In 1961, Gilbert Bécaud even made a song about it, "Dimanche à Orly". Just as the French singer did some sixty years earlier, you can still enjoy the panoramic terrace on the fourth floor of the South terminal to watch the ballet of the aeroplanes. And that's not all – it's now possible to go behind the scenes with Explore Paris (exploreparis.com) for just €5 and even to pilot an Airbus A320 in the AviaSim Paris Orly Belle Epine simulator (aviasim.com).

Aérogare d'Orly, 94390 Orly
parisaeroport.fr/en
- M — Lines 14, 18 (planned 2024/2026): Aéroport d'Orly
- RER — B: Antony + Orlyval
- Tram — T7: Aéroport d'Orly

PARIS

160 ROSA BONHEUR À L'EST

#SWITZERLANDINPARIS #CHALET #INTHEWOODS

Like a corner of Switzerland on the edge of Paris... In the heart of the Bois de Vincennes (12th arrondissement), on the banks of the Lac des Minimes, the Chalet de la Porte Jaune is an unusual red and white building nestled among century-old trees. Run by the Rosa Bonheur team since 2021 (hence its new name), who also operate in the Buttes-Chaumont (19th arrondissement), on the Seine at Les Invalides (7th arrondissement) and in Asnières (HyperMuseum), it has become a destination as fun as it is bucolic, where you can dance to a playlist that is always carefully curated. Breathe in the woodland air, surrounded by ducks and rowers, while enjoying tapas and pizzas with a glass of Chablis. With the added bonus of a sunset right over the lake.

Closed Monday, Tuesday and Wednesday.

Avenue de Nogent, 75012 Paris
rosabonheur.fr/rosa-est
- RER — A: Fontenay-sous-Bois
- Bus — 114, 210: Porte Jaune
- Vélib' — Avenue de Nogent, Paris 12th

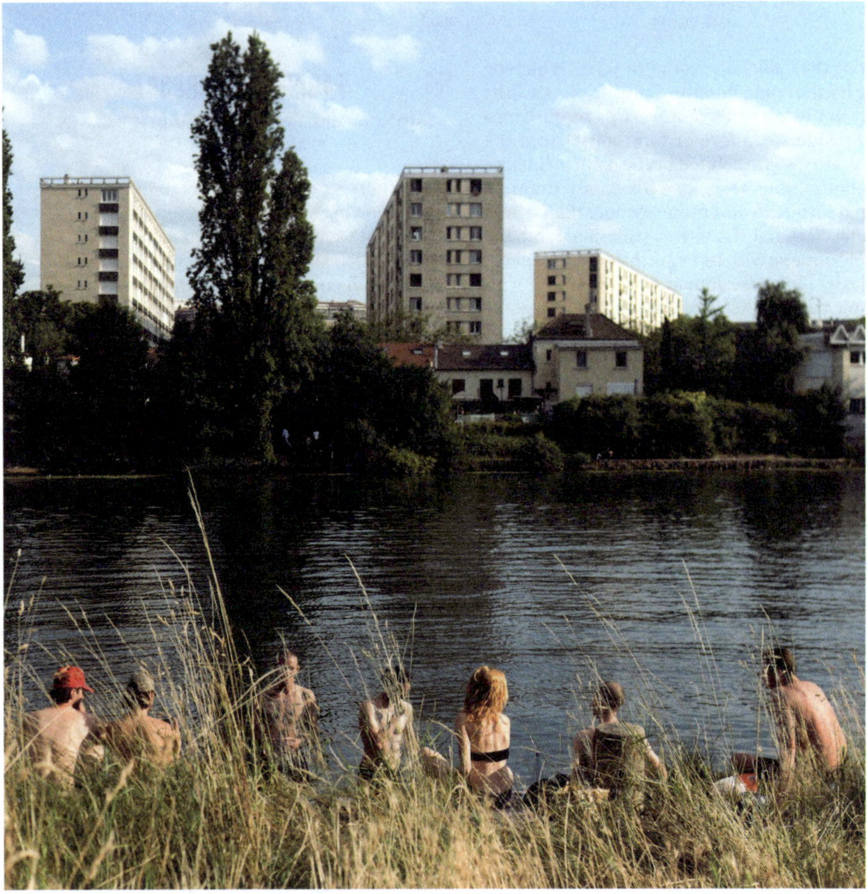

Local beach | *Towpath, Saint-Maurice.*

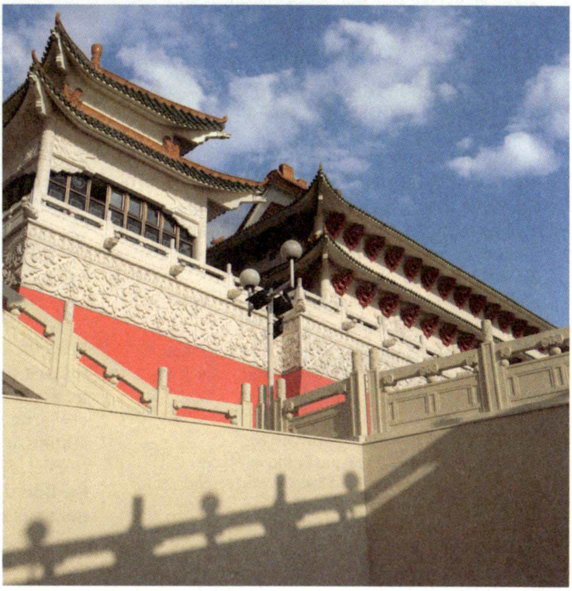

Unforbidden city | *Chinagora, Alfortville.*

Goooooooooal ! | *Chemin de halage, Saint-Maurice.*

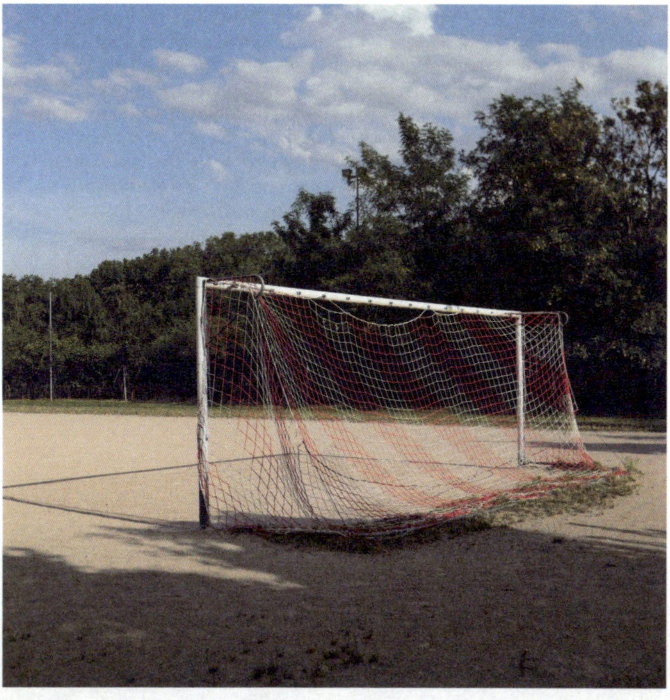

161 PETIT BAIN

#CABINONTHEWATER #CONCERTS #ROOFTOPTERRACE

Next to the Josephine Baker floating pool, the Petit Bain barge is one of the symbols of the renewal of the Paris riverbanks. Easily recognizable for its contemporary-cabin-set-on-the-water look, it has one of the most intimate concert halls in Paris. Another appeal of the Petit Bain is its roof terrace where you can toast and enjoy yourself while watching the Seine go by.

Open on performance nights from 6pm and until 2am from Monday to Thursday / Friday and Saturday from 6pm to 6am.

7, port de la Gare, 75013 Paris
Tel: +33 (0)1 43 49 68 92 / petitbain.org

- M — Line 14: Bibliothèque François Mitterrand
- RER — C: Bibliothèque François Mitterrand
- Bus — 71 : Pont de Tolbiac
- Vélib' — Quai François Mauriac

SAINT-MAUR-DES-FOSSÉS

162 LA GRIFFE NOIRE

#BOOKSTORE #GÉRARDCOLLARD #LITERARYADVICE

You will never see so many handwritten book review cards in one place. Yellow, pink, green, orange, blue, they line this bookstore where the most famous bookseller in France, Gérard Collard, officiates with his signature quiff and dark glasses. In the window, the famous cards and their flashy colours attract the eye and draw you in. They are not always kind, sometimes even scathing, as with Michel Houellebecq: "If this man is the greatest contemporary French writer, I am a dancer at the Folies Bergères!" The opposite is true for the American author Marcia Davenport and her book *My Brother's Keeper*, "One of the discoveries that made us proud to be a bookseller". If you are in need of sound literary advice, the Griffe Noire is the place for you.

Closed Sunday.

2, rue de la Varenne, 94100 Saint-Maur-des-Fossés
Tel: +33 (0)1 48 83 67 47 / lagriffenoire.com

- M — Line 15 (planned 2025/2026): Saint-Maur - Créteil
- RER — A: Saint-Maur - Créteil
- Bus — 111, 112, 306: Croix Souris

Outdoors

CHELLES

163 STROLL ALONG THE MARNE

#LONGESTIVERINFRANCE #STATIONTOSTATION #THESEBOOTSAREMADEFORWALKING

With its 514 kilometres, the Marne is one of the longest rivers in France. To catch a glimpse of it, head for the Chelles - Gournay station in Seine-et-Marne for a 16-km walk to Pontault-Combault station, which will take you through the Parc de Noisiel, a little-known green oasis (see p. 113), and the Bois de la Grange. More information on this itinerary is available on enlargeyourparis.fr.

enlargeyourparis.fr: "Balade le long de la Marne, de la gare de Chelles à la gare de Pontault-Combault".

- RER — E and Transilien — Line P: Chelles - Gournay

CRÉTEIL

164 LAC DE CRÉTEIL

#SPRAWLINGLAWNS #SAILAWAY #INLANDSEA

To hoist the mainsail, all you need is a Navigo pass. Take a seat on metro line 8 and head to the Créteil - Pointe du Lac station. There, on the shores of Lake Créteil - an inland sea of sorts - a nautical base allows you to set sail on the vessel of your choice: from catamarans, dinghies, Optimists and windsurfers to kayaks. If needed, you can train at the sailing school from the age of 8. And in case you get seasick, you can settle for the lakefront, especially the "West Coast", which is particularly green with its large lawns and its view of the very seventies Créteil skyline on the opposite bank.

9, rue Jean Gabin, 94000 Créteil
Tel: +33 (0)1 48 98 44 56 / creteil.iledeloisirs.fr

- M — Line 8: Créteil Université, Créteil Préfecture or Pointe du Lac depending on the desired access point
- RER — D: Créteil Pompadour
- Bus — TVM: Base de Loisirs de Créteil

NOISIEL

165 PARC DE NOISIEL

#OFFTHEBEATENPATH #HIDDENTREASURE #BANKSOFTHEMARNE

While some well-trodden paths have a certain aura, the lesser-known trails sometimes harbour unsuspected treasures. That is the case of the paths of the Parc de Noisiel, next door to the Château de Champs-sur-Marne, which, although a little better known, still stands in the shadow of the giants of the Paris region like Versailles (see p. 80) and Fontainebleau (see p. 149). In total, the Parc de Noisiel stretches out over 90 hectares of greenery (more than four times the size of the Luxembourg Gardens in Paris) along the banks of the Marne, where those in need of shade can discover a remarkable 34-metre tall chestnut tree with a 28-metre spread.

Free entry.
Open daily. (opening hours vary according to the season)

Parc de Noisiel, cours du Château, 77186 Noisiel
agglo-pvm.fr

- RER — A: Noisiel (then 1 km on foot)
- Bus — 220, 421: Maison de Retraite

PARIS

166 BOIS DE VINCENNES

#LARGESTGREENSPACEINPARIS #WOODS #WILDPLANTS

With its 995 hectares, the Bois de Vincennes is the largest green space in Paris. It includes: the Parc Floral, a 35-hectare botanical garden (as big as the Luxembourg Gardens and the Parc Montsouris combined) that serves as a setting for several festivals such as the Paris Jazz Festival or Classique au vert; the Hippodrome de Paris-Vincennes; the Ferme de Paris, an educational farm open to all; the Paris zoo and its monumental tropical greenhouse; as well as Lake Daumesnil, where you can go rowing. The Bois de Vincennes' 500 species of wild plants make it a herbalist hotspot on the nature trail (lechemindelanature.com), who organize group pick-your-own trips there. Since 2017, it has also been a popular destination for naturists who have their own dedicated area from April to October. Finally, hidden away a few hundred metres from the racecourse, the Butte aux Canons provides a surprising, unobstructed view of the woods and Vincennes itself.

Accessible 24/7.

Avenue Daumesnil, 75012 Paris
More information on paris.fr

- M — Line 8: Porte Dorée
- RER — A: Nogent-sur-Marne
- Tram — T3a: Porte Dorée
- Bus — 46, 201: Porte Dorée
- Vélib' — Avenue Daumesnil, Paris 12th

167 JARDIN D'AGRONOMIE TROPICALE RENÉ-DUMONT

#SURPRISINGSTROLLS #MICROFARM #LOSTOASIS

Created at the end of the 19th century to increase agricultural production in the French colonies, the Jardin d'agronomie tropicale is a hidden treasure in the heart of the Bois de Vincennes, on the border with Nogent-sur-Marne. You can stroll around its nearly five hectares which are dotted with buildings, most of which were inherited from the colonial exhibition of 1907. The garden also houses V'Île Fertile, a micro-farm open from 2.30–6pm on weekends and public holidays that sells its vegetables from 3–5pm every first Sunday of the month during the months of May to October, and is constantly on the lookout for volunteers.

Free entry. Open daily
(opening hours vary according to the season).

45, avenue de la Belle Gabrielle, 75012 Paris
More info on paris.fr

- RER — A: Nogent-sur-Marne
- Bus — 113, 114, 120, 210: Nogent-sur-Marne RER
- Vélib' — Avenue Georges-Clémenceau, Nogent-sur-Marne

168 PARC DES RIVES DE SEINE RIVE DROITE

#UNESCOWORLDHERITAGE #PEDESTRIANPARADISE #GOINGGREEN

Paris only has one entry on the UNESCO World Heritage list and this honour belongs to the banks of the Seine, which, since 2013, have gradually been returned to pedestrians after being the preserve of motorists for many years. The setting is enchanting, from the Grand Palais to Notre-Dame and the Île Saint-Louis. Now that the former urban highway has gained in greenery what it has lost in cars, playgrounds, sports facilities, bars and restaurants have emerged. Is the Seine stealing the title of the most beautiful avenue in the world from the Champs-Elysées? Especially as it will become swimmable in 2025.

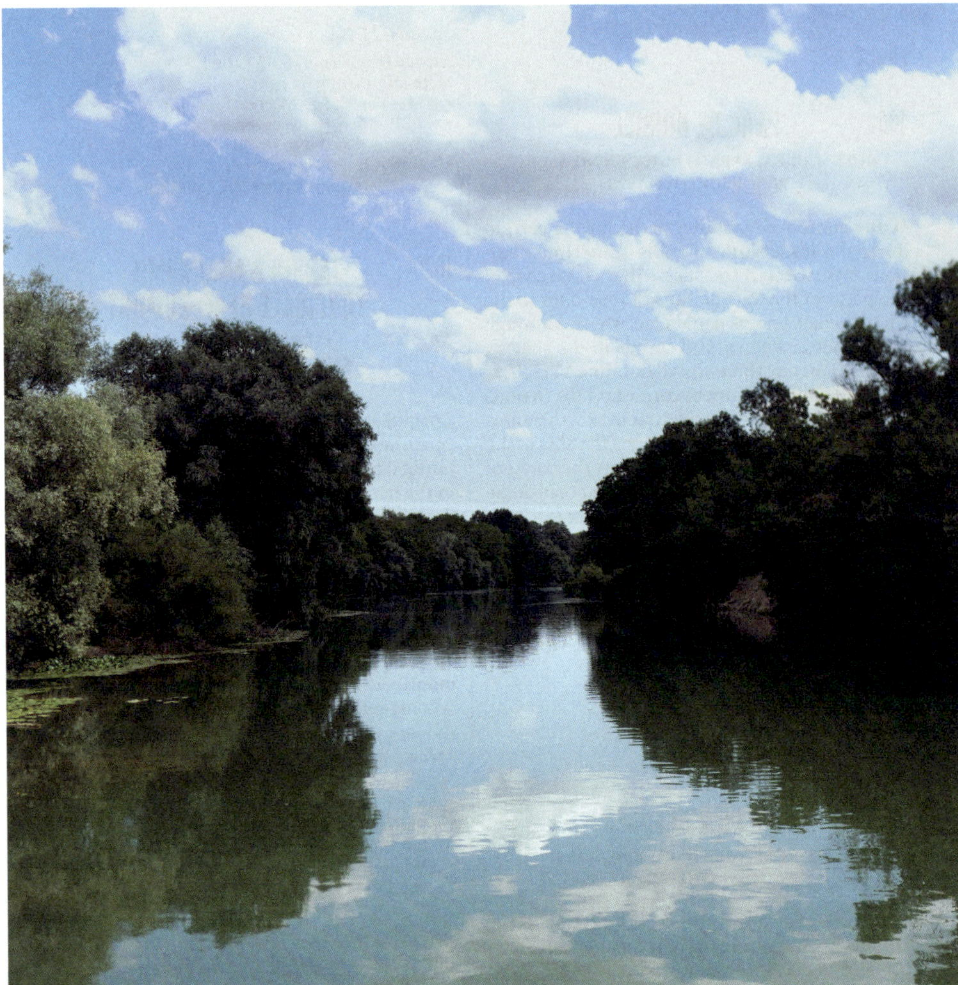

The river is always greener... | *Footbridge, Vaires-sur-Marne.*

Voie George-Pompidou, between the Pont-Neuf, the Pont de Sully and the Bassin de l'Arsenal, 75004 and 75011 Paris
paris.fr
- M — Lines 1, 11: Hôtel de Ville
- Bus — 67, 69, 72, 75, 76, 96: Hôtel de Ville
- Vélib' — Rue de Lobau, Paris 4th

SAINT-MAUR-DES-FOSSÉS

169 THE MARNE LOOP

#STROLL #RIVERSIDE
#TERRACES

Of all the walks to be done in Greater Paris, that from the Marne loop to Saint-Maur is one of the most beautiful, especially the section stretching from the Promenade des Anglais to the Quai de Champignol. These four kilometres of landscaped riverbanks provide a view of an archipelago of small islands with lush vegetation and luxurious villas. The Marne flows peacefully between the two. You can either get right up close by taking the narrow path along the water or get a little more perspective and enjoy the wide bike trails at street level. On your way, you will probably be tempted by one of the many terraces, such as the Riad Salam restaurant located at 101 Quai Winston Churchill, or the Beach Garden snack bar at number 27. And if you need a compass to guide you, go to enlargeyourparis.fr/balade-boucle-marne.

Promenade des Anglais, 94210 Saint-Maur-des-Fossés
- RER — A: La Varenne - Chennevières
- Bus — 111, 112: La Varenne Chennevières RER

SUCY-EN-BRIE

170 FORÊT DE NOTRE-DAME

#LARGESTFORESTINVALDEMARNE
#GREENOASIS #GETWALKING

If you ask Google® to take you to the edge of the Fôret de Notre-Dame and you find yourself on the parking lot of a council estate in Lésigny, don't worry, this is one of the access points. Notre-Dame is particularly suitable for family outings, with its network of alleys and wide paths. Although it is the largest forest in the Val-de-Marne, it is impossible to get lost here. The flora and fauna have preserved their wild character, which gives the area a real charm.

Carrefour de la Patte d'Oie, 94370 Sucy-en-Brie
onf.fr
- RER — A: Boissy-Saint-Léger

where to eat

CHELLES

171 LE MONTOROS

#TURKISHFOOD #HOMESTYLE
#WOODFIREGRILL

If you think you've had your fill of gyros, why not try some of the lesser-known Turkish specialities at Montoros in Chelles. Hasan and Céline, a young couple originally from Anatolia in southern Turkey, opened this restaurant where they serve homemade family-style cuisine. Starters include hot and cold mezes, such as the fresh *havuç tarator* with cheese and grated carrots. Then you can fill up on grilled meats or hearty portions of homestyle dishes like *beyti* or *alti ezmeli* with spicy flavours.

Open Tuesday to Sunday, 12–3pm and 7–11pm.

20, avenue de la Résistance, 77500 Chelles
Tel: +33 (0)1 64 26 43 48
Facebook @RestaurantMontoros
- RER — E and Transilien — Line P: Chelles-Gournay
- Bus — 9: La Poste

MOISSY-CRAMAYEL

172 WAT THAMMAPATHIP PAGODA

#STREETFOOD #ZEN
#BETWEENTHEBUDDHAS

Transformed into a pagoda by the International Thai Buddhist Association in France, the Château de Lugny in Moissy-Cramayel is also a temple of Asian street food. At weekends, the place comes alive with stalls serving *pad thai*, *bò bún*, beef *phô* and sticky rice. In fine weather, you can eat in the large park, surrounded by Buddhas. If it's too wet or cold, take shelter around the large tables. Not to be missed.

Price: dishes are €6 (cash only).
Open on Saturday, Sunday and public holidays.

Château de Lugny, 243, rue des Marronniers, 77550 Moissy-Cramayel
Tel: +33 (0)7 71 02 91 19 / Facebook @thammapathip
- RER — D: Lieusaint - Moissy
  then bus 22, La Ferme stop

PARIS

173 MAMA JACKSON SOUL FOOD

#SOULFOOD #FRIEDCHICKEN
#FINGERFOOD

Born in Harlem in the 1920s, soul food has finally made its mark in Paris. The chicken waffle is one of its iconic dishes: a waffle covered with fried chicken, often drizzled with maple syrup. Just head to Mama Jackson Soul Food to get a taste in a cosy room with a few seats and a TV showing R'n'B music videos, where you can watch Lauryn Hill or Destiny's Child while you eat your chicken with your fingers (of course). In this soul food den, deep-frying is de rigueur, Cajun spices are everywhere and the portions are ultra-generous. A place made for chicken lovers with a serious appetite.

Dishes from €14.5 to €16.5.
Closed Monday.

147, rue de Charenton, 75012 Paris
Tel: +33 (0)9 83 51 25 47
Facebook @mamajacksonsoulfood

- M — Lines 1, 8: Reuilly-Diderot
- Bus — 57, 215: Reuilly-Diderot
- Vélib' — Boulevard Diderot, Paris

SAINT-MAUR-DES-FOSSÉS

174 L'ATELIER 28

#JOANA&PAUL #INTIMATE
#LOSTBRICK

In this intimate restaurant with no more than eight tables, Joana and Paul give free rein to their imagination while carefully selecting their suppliers. No freezers here, only fresh produce from handpicked producers which is used in daily specials that change for lunch and dinnerDeliciousness is always on the menu, from the caramelized apple tatin, the crème diplomate, the speculaas streusel, the salted butter caramel and the vanilla mascarpone Chantilly cream. Before you get to dessert, you may have had the pleasure of trying the tacos with kebab-style slow-cooked lamb, smoked barbecue sauce and fresh herb tzatziki or the crispy teriyaki-marinated tuna, smoked mashed potatoes, with a crying tiger and sriracha condiment. Whatever your order, you're sure to exchange smiles with Joana, whose warm welcome is always a joy.

Price: €45 (2 courses) / €55 (3 courses).
Closed Monday and Sunday.

28, rue Saint-Hilaire, 94210 Saint-Maur-des-Fossés
Tel: +33 (0)1 48 86 55 76 / latelier28.com

- RER — A: Champigny
- Bus — 111: Église de la Varenne

VINCENNES

175 L'OURS

#MICHELINSTAR #LOCAVORE
#IMPROVISATION

L'Ours is the Michelin-starred gastronomic lair opened by chef Jacky Ribault. Elegantly worn rugs, large bay windows, touches of greenery – this is a bear with a sense of decor, but above all with a lot of ideas when it comes to garnishing your plate with local produce. Every day, the menu is an improvisation: eel risotto, beetroot, ground cacao; dashi, duck foie gras, Pontoise cabbage. The only constant is the level of creativity on display.

Price: €70 (3-course lunch menu from Tuesday to Friday), €110 (5 courses), €150 (6 courses).
Open from Tuesday to Saturday.

10, rue de l'Église, 94300 Vincennes
Tel: +33 (0)1 46 81 50 34 / loursrestaurant.com

- M — Line 1: Château de Vincennes
- RER — A: Vincennes
- Bus — 118, 124: Vincennes RER
- Vélib' — Avenue de Vorges

176 TITAN ARTISAN KÉBABIER

#GOURMETKEBAB
#EVERYTHINGISHOMEMADE #LOVESTORY

When they opened Titan in 2021, Mehmet and Hatun Goksungur have set themselves the challenge of making the residents of Vincennes fall in love with the kebab. With Turkish roots, the couple are no novices in this discipline as they had been delighting the people of Alfortville for ten years. Their shop front reads "artisan kebabier" (artisanal kebab-maker), because everything here is homemade, down to Mehmet's own secret marinade. Enhanced with homemade sauces, fried vegetables, raw vegetables, Turkish cheese, crispy onions and homemade bread (from a choice of three types), the kebabs they serve stand out from the crowd. And to further set themselves apart, Mehmet and Hatun have opted for 100% authentic decor, with objects brought in from Turkey.

Price: kebabs from €8.
Closed Sunday.

184, rue de Fontenay, 94300 Vincennes
- M — Line 1: Château de Vincennes
- RER — A: Vincennes
- Bus — 115, 318: Fraternité
- Vélib' — Rue de Lagny, Vincennes

family

MARNE-LA-VALLÉE

177 DISNEYLAND PARIS®

#MICKEYDONALDANDME
#400MILLIONVISITORS #STARWARS

Since it opened in 1992, Disneyland Paris has become nothing less than Europe's leading tourist destination, with over 375 million visitors in 30 years. Among the must-see attractions in the two parks – Disneyland and Walt Disney Studios – are the "Sleeping Beauty Castle", inspired by the Mont-Saint-Michel, the Marvel Avengers Campus. A wide variety of shows are organized throughout the year, all included in the price of a ticket. With or without a ticket, you can also wander the aisles of Disney Village®, with its restaurants, bars, and shops and even take a ride in a hot-air balloon. Finally, to keep the fun going, you can choose from seven themed hotels, including Davy Crockett Ranch where your nights are guaranteed to be as beautiful as your days.

From €56 for a child day pass.
Open year round.

Boulevard du Parc, 77777 Marne-la-Vallée
09 69 32 60 61 / disneylandparis.com
- RER A — Marne-la-Vallée - Chessy

PARIS

178 MUSÉE NATIONAL DE L'HISTOIRE DE L'IMMIGRATION

#EDUCATIONAL #ARTDECOPALACE
#TROPICALAQUARIUM

An art deco gem, the Palais de la Porte-Dorée was originally built for the Paris Colonial Exposition in 1931. In its new life, since 2007, it has retraced two centuries of immigration history in France through unique exhibitions as well as a permanent display, which mixes personal accounts, archives and contemporary art in a highly educational way. Don't miss the tropical aquarium in the basement, with its multicoloured fish, piranhas, pig-nosed turtles and its famous albino alligators.

Price: €10 (museum) / €10 (aquarium) / €14 (museum + aquarium) / Free for under-26s.
Closed Monday.

Palais de la Porte-Dorée, 293, avenue Daumesnil, 75012 Paris
Tel: +33 (0)1 53 59 58 60 / histoire-immigration.fr
- M — Line 8: Porte Dorée
- Tram — T3a: Porte Dorée
- Bus — 46: Porte Dorée
- Vélib' — Place Édouard Renard, Paris

VINCENNES

179 CHÂTEAU DE VINCENNES

#DUNGEON #PANORAMA #ESCAPEGAME

Built between the 14th and 17th centuries, the Château de Vincennes is one of the largest surviving fortified castles and its 52-metre high keep is the highest in Europe. From King Saint Louis (who dispensed justice there under his oak tree) to the Marquis de Sade (who was imprisoned there) to Mazarin (who died there), the Château de Vincennes is home to so many historical secrets. Above all, don't miss out on the Sainte Chapelle, the jewel of the fortress, which is at its most beautiful when the rays of the sun stream in.

Price: €9.50 (full price) / Free for under-26s.
Open daily.

Avenue de Paris, 94300 Vincennes
Tel: +33 (0)1 48 08 31 20 / chateau-de-vincennes.fr
- M — Line 1: Château de Vincennes
- Bus — 56, 115, 118, 124, 318, 325: Avenue du Château
- Vélib' — Cour des Maréchaux, Vincennes

where to sleep

JUVISY-SUR-ORGE

180 PÉNICHE CANALA

#FLOATINGLOFT #KICKBACKANDRELAX #CHANGEOFSCENE

A few hundred metres can sometimes change everything. When you set off along the banks of the Seine in Juvisy-sur-Orge, it's hard to imagine that you're going to be spending in a haven of tranquillity. But the further you go along the Quai Jean-Pierre Timbaud, the more the scenery changes. When you reach the Canala, an authentic Freycinet barge, the atmosphere is suddenly less urban. On the opposite bank, the Port aux Cerises leisure island, with its 200 hectares of greenery, stretches out in all its glory. Once you board the barge, the change of scenery is complete. Welcomed by the host Benoît, who has lived here for 15 years and with whom it's easy to imagine heading off on a long-distance crossing, you will be able to kick back in a 100 m² duplex where even the bed and the bath have a view of the Seine. Total relaxation.

Price: €130 per night for 2 (up to 6 passengers)

Quai Jean-Pierre Timbaud, 91260 Juvisy-sur-Orge
Bookings on airbnb.fr

- RER — C: Juvisy

PARIS

181 HÔTEL PARADISO

#MYOWNPRIVATECINEMA #MIDDAYCHECKOUT #ROOFTOP

The big screen experience from the comfort of your own room: that's the idea behind Hôtel Paradiso, launched by the mk2 cinemas in Nation. Each room is equipped with an overhead projector so you can enjoy a private movie session with access to a huge catalogue of films (mk2 Curiosity, MyCanal, Mubi, Netflix, Amazon Prime Video, Arte, Vidéo Club Carlotta Films, Shadows and LaCinetek). And as a bonus, you don't have to check-out until midday, so you may even have time for a matinee. There's also a karaoke room for the more musically inclined, and access to a rooftop where you can get a breathtaking travelling shot of Paris. In short, all the ingredients you need for a silver-screen experience.

Price: rooms from €143.

135, boulevard Diderot, 75012 Paris
Tel: +33 (0)1 88 59 20 01 / mk2hotelparadiso.com

- M — 1, 2, 6, 9: Nation
- RER — A: Nation
- Bus — 26, 56, 57, 71, 86, 215, 351: Nation
- Vélib' — Boulevard Diderot, Paris 12th

182 OFF PARIS SEINE

#FLOATINGHOTEL #UNBEATABLEVIEW #BARRESTAURANT

A couple of swans frolicking, a police boat at full speed, a barge drifting slowly by – these are just some of the things you can expect to see from the window of your room at OFF Paris Seine, a floating hotel moored on the Quai d'Austerlitz. Although the atmosphere is reminiscent of a boat, this is not a converted barge. Designed with two hulls topped by a wooden, zinc, copper and glass structure, OFF has fifty-eight rooms arranged like cabins around a magnificent central glass roof. And to enliven your experience, the hotel also houses a bar-restaurant with a two-storey terrace, a mini swimming pool and even a marina from where you can go for a "breakfast cruise" or an "aperitif cruise".

Price: from €124/night.

86, quai d'Austerlitz, 75013 Paris
Tel: +33 (0)1 44 06 62 65 / offparisseine.com

- M — Lines 5, 10: Austerlitz
- RER — C: Austerlitz
- Bus — 24, 57, 61, 63, 89, 215: Austerlitz
- Vélib' — Place Valhubert, Paris 13th

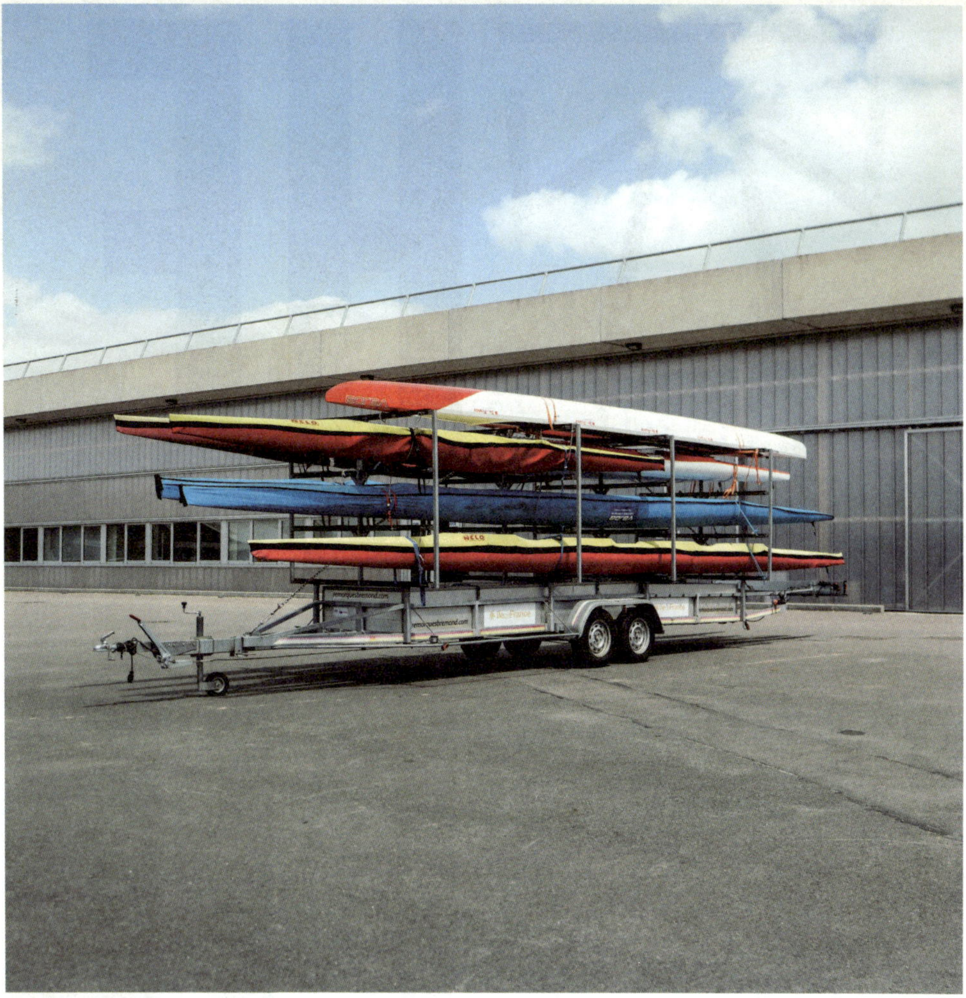

Lying in wait | *Olympic Nautical Stadium, Vaires-sur-Marne.*

THE
FIE

AUVERS-SUR-OISE
BONNIÈRES-SUR-SEINE

CERGY-PONTOISE
CONFLANS-SAINTE-HONORINE

LA ROCHE-GUYON
MAGNY-EN-VEXIN
MONTGEROULT

NEUVILLE-SUR-OISE
PONTOISE

LDS

SAINT-CLAIR-SUR-EPTE
SAINT-OUEN-L'AUMÔNE
THÉMÉRICOURT
VÉTHEUIL

White cliffs overlooking the Seine, fields as far as the eye can see, charming villages, oak and chestnut trees – the landscapes of the Parc naturel du Vexin Français recall those of neighbouring Normandy. They also echo the canvases of the landscape and impressionist painters who explored this region to create some of their masterpieces. Masters like Monet in Vétheuil, Pissarro in Pontoise and Van Gogh in Auvers-sur-Oise, where he spent the last months of his life and created over seventy paintings, including the celebrated *Wheatfield with Crows* and *The Church at Auvers*. Follow in their footsteps and dive into these beautiful landscapes.

THE FIELDS

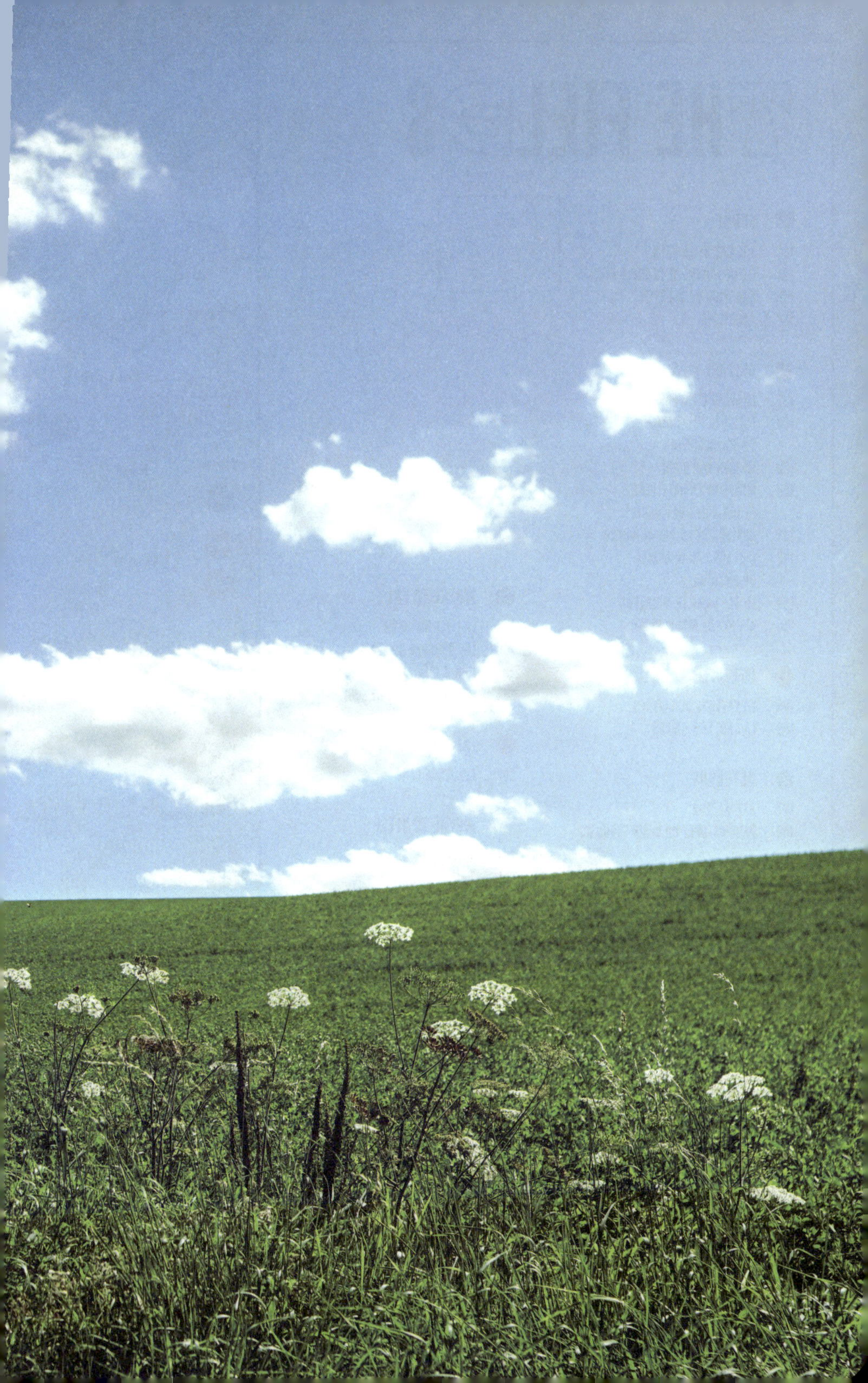

THE FIELDS

SPORT

183 THE GR2 SEINE PATH
184 ÎLE DE LOISIRS DE CERGY-PONTOISE
185 CANOEING ON THE EPTE
186 CANOSEINE

CULTURE

187 CHÂTEAU D'AUVERS-SUR-OISE
188 ÉGLISE NOTRE-DAME-DE-L'ASSOMPTION
189 MAISON VAN GOGH
190 MUSÉE DE LA BATELLERIE ET DES VOIES NAVIGABLES
191 CHÂTEAU DE LA ROCHE-GUYON
192 CELLARS AND QUARRIES OF PONTOISE
193 MUSÉE CAMILLE-PISSARRO
194 ABBAYE DE MAUBUISSON

LIFESTYLE

195 LA CAVERNE AUX LIVRES
196 LA GROTTE À BIÈRES

OUTDOORS

197 AXE MAJEUR
198 PARC NATUREL DU VEXIN FRANÇAIS

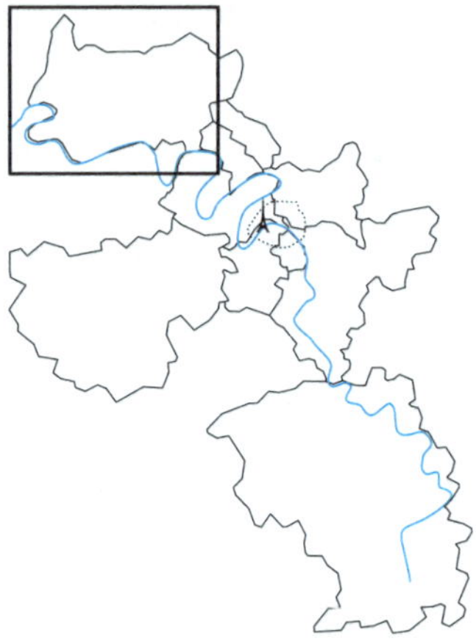

WHERE TO EAT

199 LE P'TIT BOUCHON
200 LES BROCHES DU VEXIN
201 L'OR Q'IDÉE
202 LE PETIT BISTROT DE LUCY

FAMILY

203 AVENTURE LAND

WHERE TO SLEEP

204 HÔTEL DES IRIS

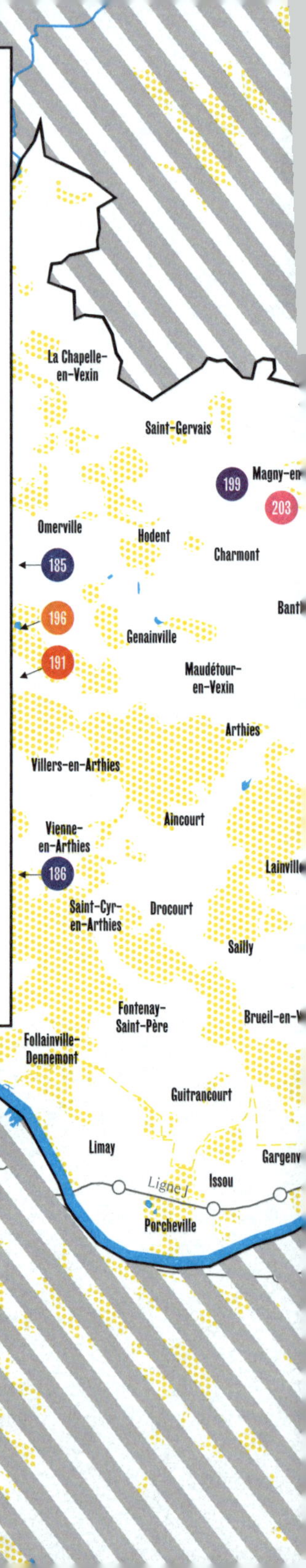

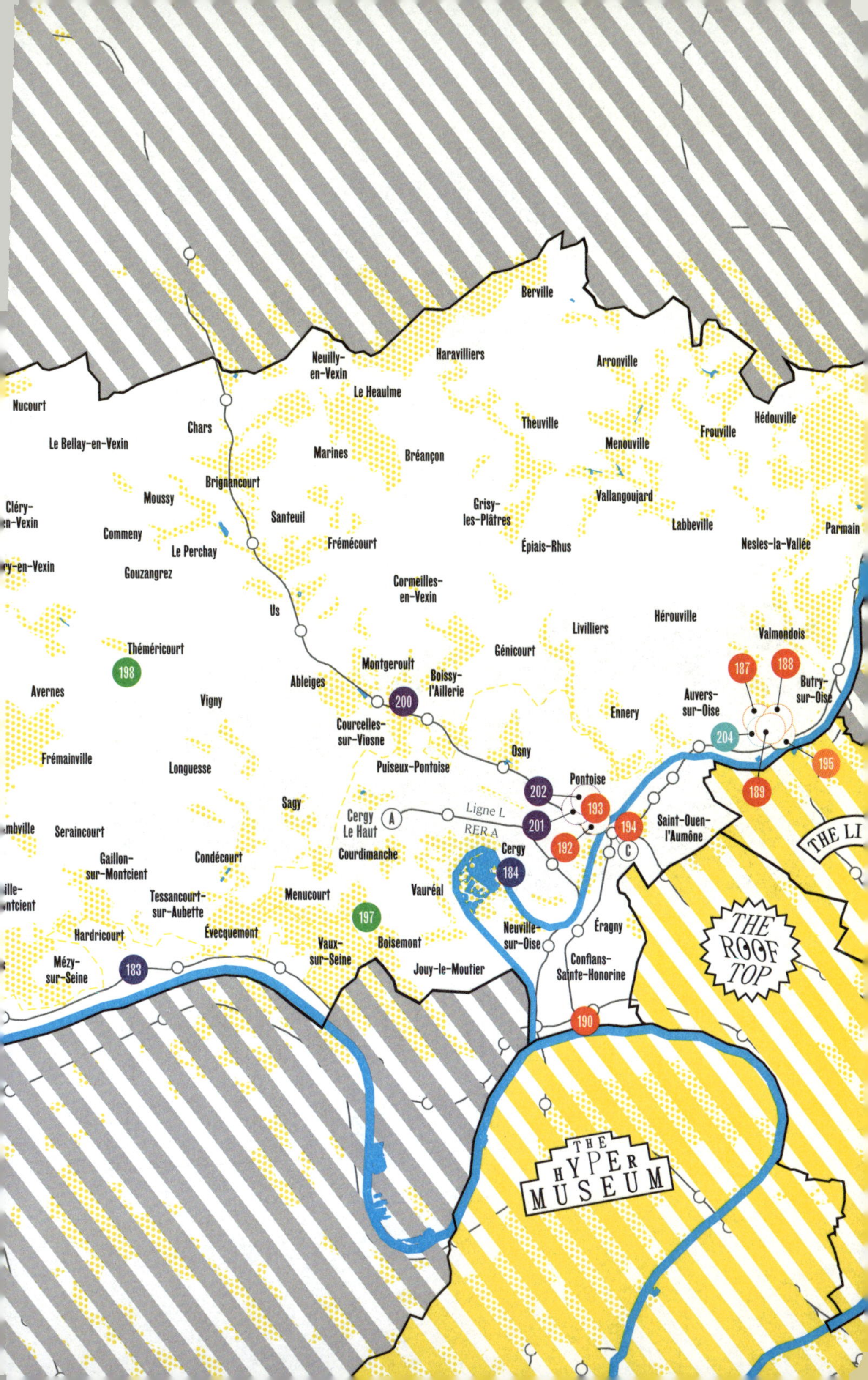

Berville
Neuilly-en-Vexin
Haravilliers
Arronville
Le Heaulme
Nucourt
Chars
Hédouville
Theuville
Frouville
Le Bellay-en-Vexin
Menouville
Marines
Bréançon
Brignancourt
Moussy
Vallangoujard
Clery-en-Vexin
Grisy-les-Plâtres
Santeuil
Labbeville
Parmain
Commeny
Frémécourt
Épiais-Rhus
Nesles-la-Vallée
Le Perchay
Gouzangrez
Cormeilles-en-Vexin
Us
Hérouville
Livilliers
Valmondois
Théméricourt
198
Génicourt
187
188
Montgeroult
Boissy-l'Aillerie
Butry-sur-Oise
Ableiges
Avernes
Vigny
200
Auvers-sur-Oise
Ennery
Courcelles-sur-Viosne
204
Osny
195
Frémainville
Longuesse
Puiseux-Pontoise
Pontoise
202
189
Sagy
193
Cergy Le Haut
A
Ligne L
RER A
201
194
Saint-Ouen-l'Aumône
THE LI
Seraincourt
Cergy
192
C
Courdimanche
Gaillon-sur-Montcient
Condécourt
184
Vauréal
Tessancourt-sur-Aubette
Menucourt
THE ROOF TOP
197
Éragny
Hardricourt
Évecquemont
Neuville-sur-Oise
Vaux-sur-Seine
Boisemont
Conflans-Sainte-Honorine
Mézy-sur-Seine
183
Jouy-le-Moutier
190
THE HYPER MUSEUM

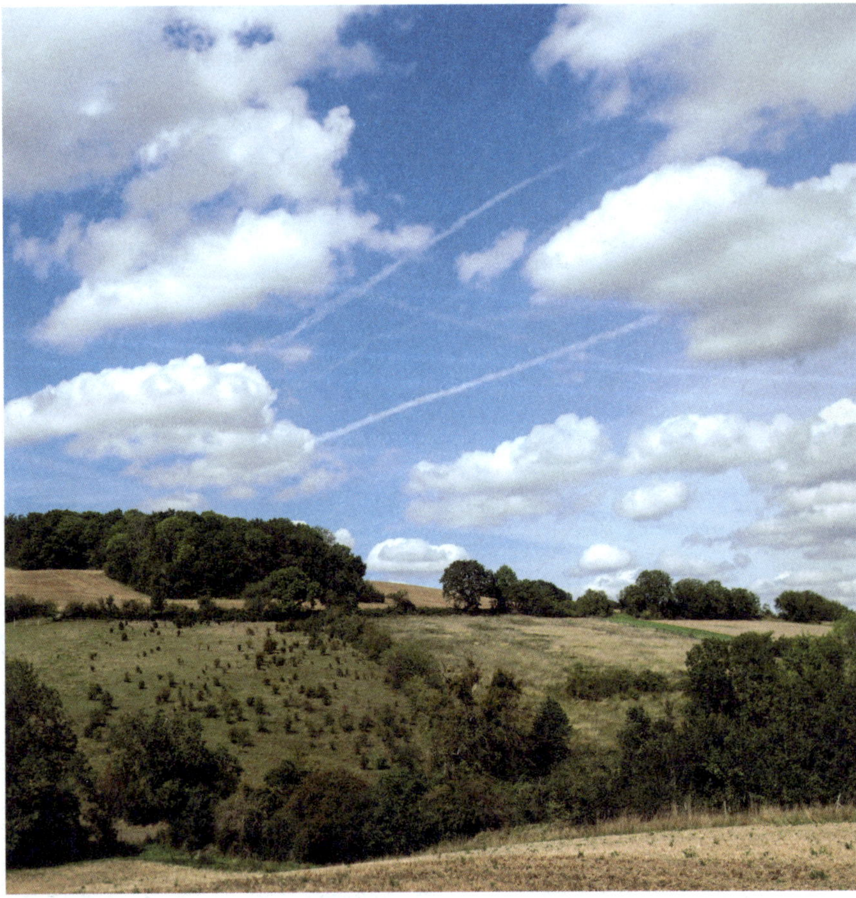

Field of clouds | *Route de la Mairie, Vienne-en-Arthies.*

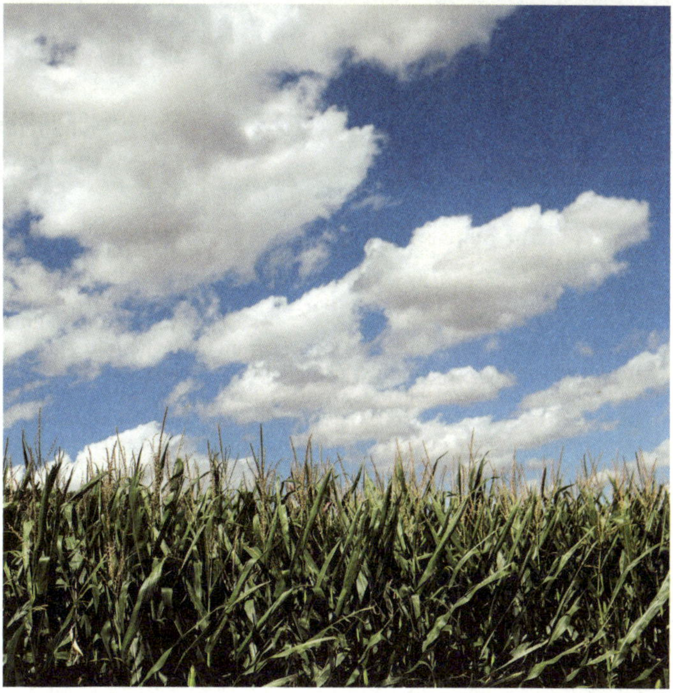

Baby popcorn | *Rue des Vaux Bouillons, Vexin-sur-Epte.*

Egyptian agriculture | *Grande Rue, Avernes.*

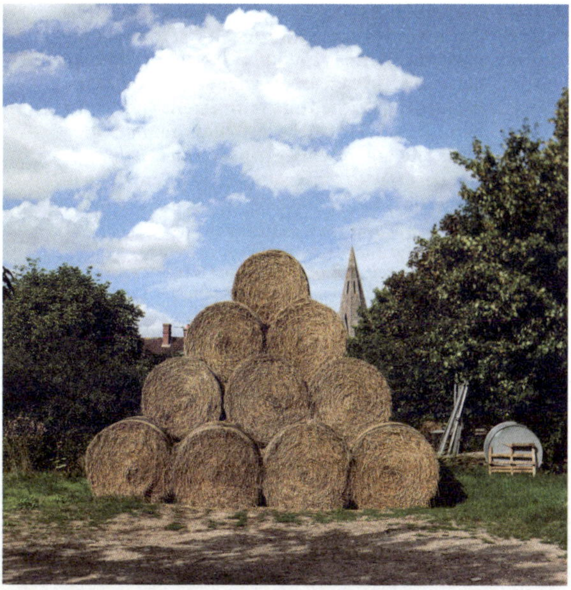

Sport

BONNIÈRES-SUR-SEINE

183 THE GR2© SEINE PATH

#SPECTACULARSCENERY #ALONGTHESEINE
#NOTREDAMETWIN

You won't believe your eyes. Starting from Bonnières-sur-Seine station, this thirty-kilometre walk follows a section of the GR2 (which connects Dijon to the Seine estuary at Le Havre) and takes you up to the heights of the Seine amidst the unsuspected scenery of the Parc naturel du Vexin Français (see p. 133). You'll pass through the magnificent villages of La Roche-Guyon (see p. 130) and Vétheuil, and your journey will end in Mantes-la-Jolie where, before catching the train again, you can take the opportunity to admire the Collégiale Notre-Dame church, a kind of twin to Notre-Dame de Paris.

Download the "Sur les balcons de la Seine" trail free of charge from helloways.com.

- Transilien — Line J: Bonnières-sur-Seine

NEUVILLE-SUR-OISE

184 ÎLE DE LOISIRS DE CERGY-PONTOISE

#SURFING #RAFTING
#WAKEBOARDING

Against all odds, Europe's largest outdoor standing surf wave is found on the shores of the leisure island of Cergy. You can try to tame it, standing or lying on your board, during one-hour sessions. And that is not the only pleasant surprise here: there is also an artificial river for rafting and a water ski lift for wakeboarding. You will leave with your sea legs.

Open year round.

Rue des Étangs, 95001 Neuville-sur-Oise
cergy-pontoise.iledeloisirs.fr

- RER — A: Cergy Préfecture
- Transilien — Line L: Cergy Préfecture then bus 48: Base de Loisirs

SAINT-CLAIR-SUR-EPTE

185 CANOEING ON THE EPTE

#NATURE #CALM
#PADDLEAWAY

On the right bank, a beaver hurries into his burrow at the surface of the water. On the left, ducks gather up their ducklings. All around, the lush green of the forest. And in the distance, a superb 14th century vaulted bridge spanning the Epte, the natural border between Île-de-France and Normandy. To enjoy this landscape, just take a seat in a canoe, which is what Fabienne Desheulles, founder of CanoEpte, has to offer. Three routes of 7, 9 and 17 km are available departing from the charming village of Saint-Clair-sur-Epte, to discover the river alone or with your family.

Price: €60 for a two-person canoe, €30 for a single canoe.

Rue de l'Ermitage, 95770 Saint-Clair-sur-Epte
Tel: +33 (0)6 19 57 52 53 / canoepte.com

- RER — A: Cergy-Saint-Christophe then bus 95-04: Église de Saint-Clair-sur-Epte

VÉTHEUIL

186 CANOSEINE

#LANDANDWATER #FOLLOWTHEGUIDE
#MINIADVENTURES

He knows the Vexin like the back of his hand. No wonder: he was born there and still lives there, exploring it by every possible means of transport. His name is Julien Masson. This seasoned sportsman offers rides for the whole family on the Seine between Vétheuil and the Château de La Roche-Guyon (see p. 130). And if you're after even more thrills, this adventurer has more tricks up his sleeve. He can also be your guide on the GR2 (see above), perched on the limestone cliffs of the natural park. Finally, he also hires out mountain bikes and organises day trips so you can do it all. The best way to make sure you miss anything of the Vexin.

*Price: from €40 for a boat for 2 adults /
From €60 for 2 adults and 2 children.
Combined canoe + mountain bike from €80 for 2 people /
Mountain bike hire from €20 / Hiking trips on request.*

Tel: +33 (0)6 81 09 49 82 / canoseine.com

- Transilien — Line J: Mantes-la-Jolie then bus 95-15 to Vétheuil

AUVERS-SUR-OISE

187 CHÂTEAU D'AUVERS-SUR-OISE

#HISTORYOFIMPRESSIONISM #IMMERSIVE
#LUNCHEONONTHEGRASS

The Château d'Auvers-sur-Oise takes visitors into the heart of the history of impressionism, with an immersive digital journey. Its walls are adorned with XXL projections of the masters' paintings. A sound system recounts the stories and juicy anecdotes of the artists of the time, while a beautiful collection of original works provides the final touch. As for the 8-hectare garden, it is the ideal place to replay Manet's *Luncheon on the Grass*, with slightly less nudity.

Price: €12 (full price), €7.50 (reduced price) / €10 for Navigo pass holders / Free for under-7s. Open Tuesday to Friday from 9am–6pm, Saturday and Sunday from 9am–7pm. Closed Monday.

Chemin des Berthelées, 95430 Auvers-sur-Oise
Tel: +33 (0)1 34 48 48 45 / chateau-auvers.fr
- Transilien — Line H: Auvers-sur-Oise

188 ÉGLISE NOTRE-DAME-DE-L'ASSOMPTION

#VANGOGH #GLOBALSTAR
#ROMANOGOTHICSTYLE

Stopping at this 11th-century church mixing Gothic and Romanesque styles is a rite of passage for anyone visiting Auvers-sur-Oise. Van Gogh's painting of the church, the reproduction of which faces the building, is now one of the main pieces in the Musée d'Orsay collection (see p. 56). The painter's melancholy and homesickness are evident: the church seems ready to crumble under the weight of a threatening sky and the only human presence is a woman walking away, wearing the Dutch headdress of the time. Van Gogh is buried alongside his brother in the village cemetery. Every year when the weather turns fine, the church hosts some of the concerts of the prestigious Auvers-sur-Oise classical music festival. Once you've visited this site, Van Gogh's paintings will never look quite the same.

Open daily.

Place de l'Église, 95430 Auvers-sur-Oise
paroisses-pontoise.fr
- Transilien — Line H: Auvers-sur-Oise

189 MAISON VAN GOGH

#GHOSTS #FINALBREATH
#MOVING

Also known as the Auberge Ravoux where Van Gogh's rooms have been preserved, it was here that the painter agonized for two days, with his brother Theo at his bedside. Although it is no longer furnished, the neighbouring room, where fellow Dutch painter Anton Hirschig lived, gives an idea of the artists' living conditions. There is little to see but everything to feel. A video presents excerpts from the 200 letters left behind by the artist as well as period photographs.

Price: €6 (full price), €4 (12 to 17 year-olds) / Free for under-12s. Open Wednesday to Sunday from 10am–6pm from March to November.

52-56, rue du Général de Gaulle, 95430 Auvers-sur-Oise
Tel: +33 (0)1 30 36 60 60 / maisondevangogh.fr
- Transilien — Line H: Auvers-sur-Oise

CONFLANS-SAINTE-HONORINE

190 MUSÉE DE LA BATELLERIE ET DES VOIES NAVIGABLES

#CHATEAUWITHAVIEW
#RIVERSTORY #PARK

Overlooking the Seine and the port of Saint-Nicolas, the Château du Prieuré is known for its elegance. Since the 1960s, boats have had pride of place in this 19th century gem. The boating museum displays the history of navigation on rivers and canals. From vaulted to ceremonial rooms, you can sail past the many boat models, artworks, photographs and engravings depicting a little-known world. Before you leave, spend some time in the park, whose magnificent greenhouses host exhibitions, events and even film shoots, such as Alain Chabat's *Marsupilami* in 2012.

Price: €5 (full price), €3 (reduced price) / Free for under-4s. From 10am–12pm and 2–5.30pm on Tuesday, Thursday, Saturday and Sunday. From 2–5.30pm on Wednesday and Friday. Closed Monday.

3, place Jules-Gévelot, 78700 Conflans-Sainte-Honorine
Tel: +33 (0)1 34 90 39 50 / musee-batellerie-conflans.fr
- Transilien — Line J: Conflans-Fin-d'Oise

LA ROCHE-GUYON

191 CHÂTEAU DE LA ROCHE-GUYON

#TROGLODYTIC #DUNGEON
#ORGANICKITCHENGARDEN

Perched at the top of a cliff overlooking the Seine, the keep of La Roche-Guyon is a must-see. To get there, you have to take a troglodytic staircase carved in limestone. This is one of the curiosities that make the Château de La Roche-Guyon so original, alongside the chapels and bunkers which are also troglodytic, as well as its vegetable garden, which converted to organic methods over ten years ago. Stunning.

Price: €9 (full price), €6 (13–18 year-olds, students and unemployed), €5.50 (6–12 year-olds) / Free for under-6s. Open Monday to Friday, from 10am–6pm, and 10am–7pm on weekends and public holidays (annual closure end of November to beginning of February).

1, rue de l'Audience, 95780 La Roche-Guyon
Tel: +33 (0)1 34 79 74 42 / chateaudelarocheguyon.fr
- Transilien — Line J: Mantes-la-Jolie then bus 95-11: Mairie de La Roche-Guyon

PONTOISE

192 CELLARS AND QUARRIES OF PONTOISE

#UNDERGROUND
#GUIDEDTOURS #KEEPCOOL

With some 1,100 underground passages dug in its limestone subsoils, Pontoise is a Gruyère cheese that the tourist office invites you to explore. Let yourself be guided through the maze of the old Pontoise before going down several dozen metres under the Place des Moineaux and the Pissarro Museum. Medieval castellans had stone blocks extracted in order to build their castles, while traders used the stone to keep their produce fresh. Throughout the visit, you will discover the tools used to carve the rock and the traces left over the centuries by visitors. A walk combining history, geology and sociology.

Price: €8 (full price), €6 (7–12 year-olds) / Free for under-7s. Open Sunday from 2.30–4.30pm

1, place de la Piscine, 95300 Pontoise
Tel: +33 (0)1 34 41 70 60 / ville-pontoise.fr
- Transilien — Lines J, H: Pontoise

193 MUSÉE CAMILLE-PISSARRO

#FATHEROFIMPRESSIONISM
#GARDEN #PANORAMA

Perched on the heights of Pontoise and offering a panoramic view of the Oise, the Musée Camille-Pissarro pays tribute to this father of impressionism, who stayed in the city from 1866 to 1883, with Cézanne and Gauguin following in his footsteps. While only two of Pissarro's works are exhibited here, there are beautiful paintings by his apprentices and the building and its "garden of the five senses" alone are reason enough for a visit.

Price: €5 (full price) / €4 (reduced price) / Free for under-12s. Cash only. Closed Monday and Tuesday.

17, rue du Château, 95300 Pontoise
Tel: +33 (0)1 30 38 02 40 / ville-pontoise.fr
- Transilien — Lines H, J: Pontoise RER C

SAINT-OUEN-L'AUMÔNE

194 ABBAYE DE MAUBUISSON

#CONTEMPORARYART
#FREE #PICNICSPOT

Founded by Blanche de Castille (the mother of Saint-Louis), Maubuisson Abbey first welcomed well-bred girls, before serving as a royal residence, and then as a necropolis. Today, nestled in the middle of century-old trees, it has become a centre for contemporary art and hosts free exhibitions year round. It also regularly offers artistic workshops open to all. And as if all this were not enough, the abbey is surrounded by a ten-hectare park that is ideal for extended picnics.

Free entry / Workshops from €5/person. Closed Tuesday.

Avenue Richard de Tour, 95310 Saint-Ouen-l'Aumône
Tel: +33 (0)1 34 33 85 00
valdoise.fr/163-l-abbaye-de-maubuisson.htm
- RER — C: Saint-Ouen-l'Aumône
- Transilien — Line H: Saint-Ouen-l'Aumône
- Bus — 56, 57, 58, 34 sud: Mairie de Saint-Ouen-l'Aumône

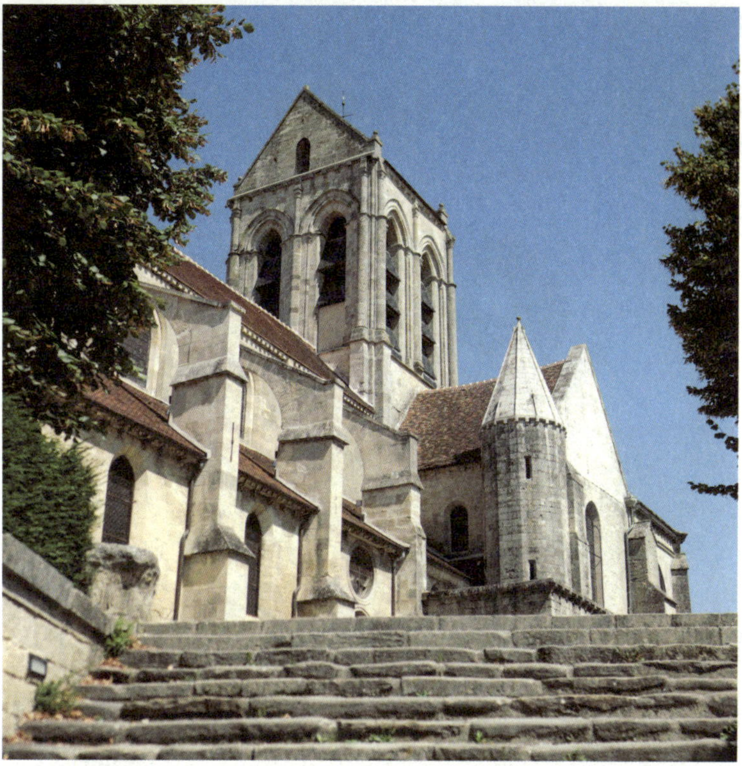

Vincent's favourite church | *Église d'Auvers-sur-Oise, Auvers-sur-Oise.*

Head in the clouds | *Route de Gasny, Fourges.*

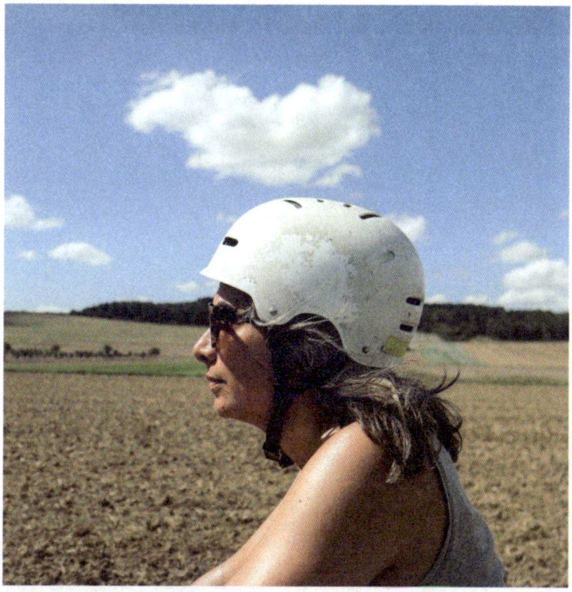

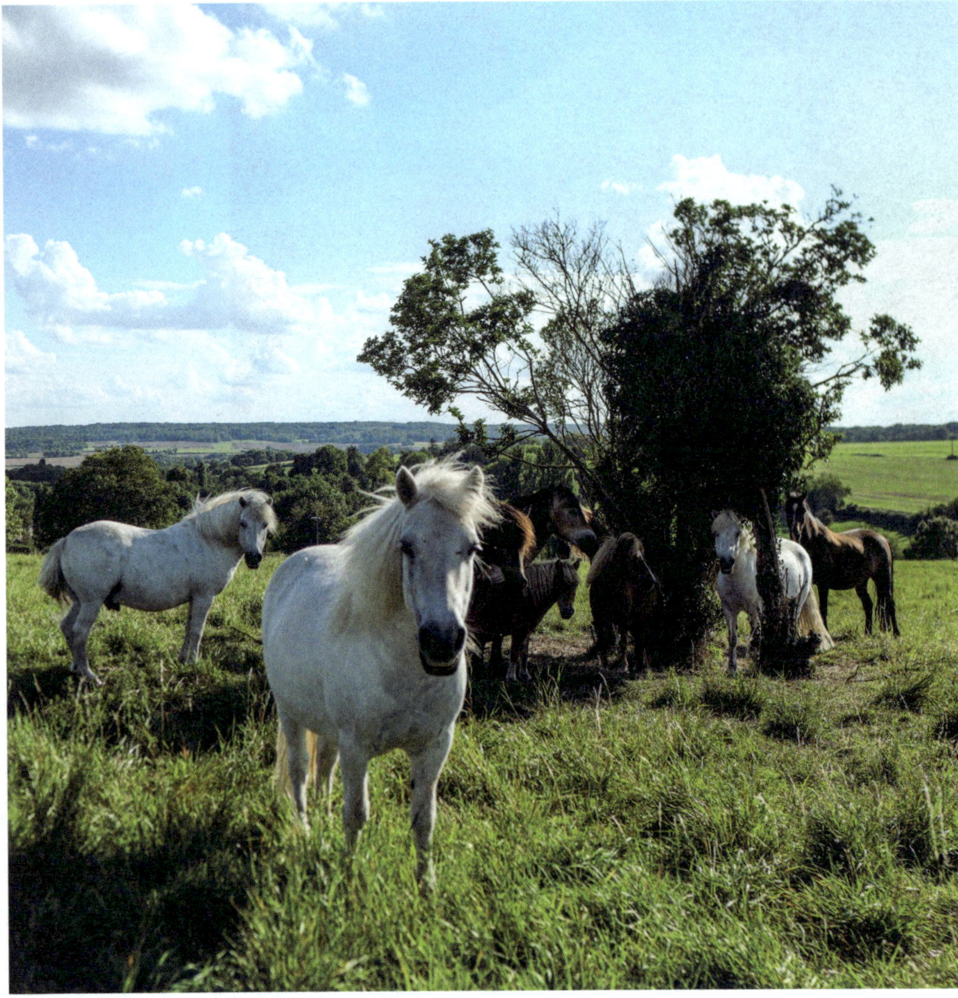

"You talking to me?" | *Rue de la Cavée, Seraincourt.*

lifestyle

AUVERS-SUR-OISE

195 LA CAVERNE AUX LIVRES

#BOOKSHOP #TRAINCARRIAGES
#LITERARYJOURNEY

You have probably never seen a bookshop like this one. Opened by a former journalist, Philippe Ferry, the Caverne aux Livres was set up in old postal train carriages next to Auvers-sur-Oise station, which are now home to thousands of second-hand books. A cargo that is now under the watchful eye of Philippe's son, Antoine. Prepare yourself for an unforgettable literary journey.

Open Thursday and Friday from 2–6pm and Saturday and Sunday from 11am–6pm. Closed, Monday, Tuesday and Wednesday.

1, place de la Gare, 95430 Auvers-sur-Oise
Tel: +33 (0)1 34 48 02 87
Facebook @lacaverneauxlivres
- Transilien — Line H: Auvers-sur-Oise

LA ROCHE-GUYON

196 LA GROTTE À BIÈRES

#TROGLODYTICCAVE #FORHOPLOVERS
#HIBISCUSBEER

Enjoying a fine beer in a troglodytic cave is worth a little effort. Allow a good 10 minutes to climb from the Château de La Roche-Guyon (see p. 130) before you settle into the Grotte à Bières, which is set into the chalky cliff. This spot for hop lovers serves as both a specialist shop – choose from a wide selection of beers including hibiscus beer – and a bar with a rocky atmosphere lit by discreet fairy lights. No menu. Tell Jean-Michel Kubler, the boss, what you like, he will take care of the rest, including a copious plate of charcuterie and cheese to accompany your tasting.

From €5 for a 33cl beer, €10 for a cheese and charcuterie plate. Closed Monday.

Rue de la Vieille Charrière de Gasny,
95780 La Roche-Guyon
Tel: +33 (0)6 09 40 83 18 / Facebook @LaGrotteABieres
- Transilien — Line J: Mantes-la-Jolie then bus 95-11: Route de Gasny

outdoors

CERGY-PONTOISE

197 AXE MAJEUR

#CURIOSITY #WALK
#UNBEATABLEVIEW

A leaning tower, a pyramid on the water and a succession of red arches that recall the Fushimi Inari shrine in Kyoto, Japan. A monumental work celebrating the new city of Cergy, the Axe Majeur is a landscape and architectural curiosity that may one day be a hot destination for Instagrammers. At 3 kilometres long, it connects the top of the city to the Neuville ponds across the Oise River. A square with columns designed by the Spanish architect Ricardo Bofill marks the starting point of the walk, with its breathtaking view of the towers of La Défense. This route is likely to become a highlight of Greater Paris in years to come, so make sure you enjoy it before the crowds arrive.

Free entry.
Open daily, year round.

Rue de l'Esplanade de Paris, 95000 Cergy-Pontoise
Tel: +33 (0)1 34 41 70 60 / ot-cergypontoise.fr
- RER — A: Cergy-Saint-Christophe then 5 minutes walk

THÉMÉRICOURT

198 PARC NATUREL DU VEXIN FRANÇAIS

#NATURALPARK #HIKING
#INTHESKYORONTHEWATER

The Parc naturel du Vexin Français is one of Greater Paris's four natural parks alongside the Haute Vallée de Chevreuse (see p. 80), the Gâtinais Français (see p. 150) and the Oise - Pays-de-France. On the border with Normandy, with which it shares common traits such as limestone cliffs, the Vexin Français extends over 710 km², which is seventy times the size of the Bois de Vincennes. Reason enough to explore its treasures in a canoe (see p. 128), a hot air balloon (vexinmontgolfiere.fr) or even in the company of a donkey if you prefer to take your time (anesenvexin.fr). It's also worth trying out the downloadable trails on helloways.com, a website specialising in hikes accessible by public transport, which includes a trail called "Sur les balcons de la Seine".

Maison du Parc, rue Achim d'Abos, 95450 Théméricourt
Tel: +33 (0)1 34 48 66 10
pnr-vexin-francais.fr and helloways.com

where to eat

MAGNY-EN-VEXIN

199 LE P'TIT BOUCHON

#CHECKEREDTABLECLOTHS
#HERBSANDSPICES #CAFÉTRÈSGOURMAND

A quintessential French bistro (exposed beams, checkered tablecloths and curtains) overlooking an old medieval-style square, which has inspired a number of period film shoots. In the heart of the old town of Magny-en-Vexin, Anne and her second-in-command César are a joyful duo. Their cuisine is certainly in tune with the *terroir* (Burgundy snails, rump steak fillet with Comté cheese mash), but with the extra twist of their passion for spices, herbs, and flavours from around the world. Their creativity shines through, especially in the evenings and on weekends. When they're in season, don't miss the scallops in Chardonnay broth served with ravioles de Royans. And if you can't decide between the cherry clafoutis, chestnut fondant, or revisited lemon tart, go for the aptly named café très gourmand, so you can try them all! Good wines, good advice, and a terrace to boot.

Menus from €17.90 / A la carte: dishes from €12–€24.
Closed Monday and Tuesday.

8, place du Marché aux fruits, 95420 Magny-en-Vexin
Tel: +33 (0)1 75 81 02 62 / lepetitbouchon-magny.fr

MONTGEROULT

200 LES BROCHES DU VEXIN

#RÔTISSERIE #REGIONALCHEESES
#ASTÉRIXANDOBÉLIX

Behind this pink facade with blue shutters hides one hell of an Auvergne rotisserie! They serve up a banquet worthy of Asterix and Obelix: roast ribs in a honey-mustard sauce; whole cockerel on the spit (and piglet leg on Sundays), all flanked with potatoes and market vegetables. There's also a game terrine from the Île-de-France region, frogs' legs or snails in parsley sauce, AAAAA andouillette with aligot, beef tomahawk steak, etc. For vegetarians or non-fanatical meat-eaters there is celeriac with hard-boiled egg and Espelette pepper mayo, market fresh fish, or king prawns in white wine. Don't forget to save room for regional cheeses and desserts, including the unmissable baba kouglof, washed down with old rum and homemade chantilly. Classic wines by the glass, *fillette*, or bottle and craft beers from the Vexin. There's even a south-facing terrace to enjoy the fine weather.

Lunch menu (weekdays) from €25 /
A la carte dishes from €7–34.
Closed Monday and Tuesday.

1, rue du Moulin, 95650 Montgeroult
Tel: +33 (0)1 34 42 71 28 / lesbrochesduvexin.fr
◆ Transilien — Line J: Montgeroult-Courcelles

PONTOISE

201 L'OR Q'IDÉE

#TOPCHEF #MICHELINSTAR
#BOOKAHEAD

L'Or Q'Idée is one of many restaurants that prove that you don't have to be in Paris to taste exceptional dishes. Run by Naöelle D'Hainaut, the winner of French Top Chef 2013 who has lived in the Val-d'Oise for over ten years, L'Or Q'Idée feels like a small private residence. Enter through a discreet door around the bend of an old Pontoise street to discover a huge dining space with a refined decor. The food is a delight for the taste buds with a six-course carte blanche menu, that the chef changes regularly. The Michelin made no mistake in awarding Naöelle her first star in 2019. The price of success: to get a table, better to book several weeks in advance.

A la carte dishes from €34 / Carte blanche menu for €95 Closed Monday and Sunday. Open for lunch only on Tuesday and Wednesday and only for dinner on Saturday.

14, rue Marcel Rousier, 95300 Pontoise
Tel: +33 (0)1 34 35 47 10 / lorqidee.fr

- RER — C: Pontoise
- Transilien — Lines H, J: Pontoise

202 LE PETIT BISTROT DE LUCY

#OLDTOWNBISTRO #ALLSMILES #JAZZSOUNDTRACK

Generous, comforting, and delicious: that is the spirit of Le Petit Bistrot de LuCy in a nutshell. Perched on the heights of Pontoise, a stone's throw from the Saint-Maclou cathedral, you can enjoy home-cooked dishes with subtle twists while listening to jazz. The gazpacho is spicy, the prawn risotto adorned with edible flowers, and the faces are all smiles.

Price: Bistrot menu (starter + main + dessert) €43 / Weekday lunch menu €24.

18, Rue de Gisors, 95300 Pontoise
Tel: +33 (0)1 30 75 07 74 / lepetitbistrotdelucy.fr

- Transilien — Lines H and J: Pontoise
- RER — C: Pontoise

family

MAGNY-EN-VEXIN

203 AVENTURE LAND

#GIANTZIPLINE #ECOPARK #TREETOPS

Surrounded by fields as far as the eye can see, Aventure Land is the opposite of an amusement park. No neon lights blinking frantically in this eco-park nestled in a small wood in the heart of the Parc naturel du Vexin Français. But while it may be quiet, there are thrills to be had. Take a ride on the Vir'Express, a giant 350-metre-long zip line, or jump from 5 metres high onto an air cushion with Vertig'haut. Aventure Land also has several treetop adventure courses, a labyrinth in the trees, as well as a bobsleigh track and inflatable bumpers, both on wheels. To enjoy all of this, all you have to do is to measure more than one metre tall.

Price: €25 (full price, visitors over 1.3m tall), €20 (visitors from 1–1.29m tall), €82 for the "pass tribu" (2 adults and 2 children) / Free for children under 1-metre tall. Open from early April to early November.

RD 14 – exit 19, 95420 Magny-en-Vexin
Tel: +33 (0)1 34 67 61 94 / aventureland.fr

- RER — A: Cergy – Préfecture then bus 9504 (except Sunday and public holidays): Dame Noire (Magny-en-Vexin)

where to sleep

AUVERS-SUR-OISE

204 HÔTEL DES IRIS

#OPPOSITEVANGOGH #INTIMATE #TEAROOM

For those who want to immerse themselves in Van Gogh's world for a weekend, Hôtel des Iris, situated in an old renovated post office opposite the Auberge Ravoux (see p. 129) where the painter used to live, is just the ticket. All eight rooms of this comfortable and intimate hotel are carefully decorated with an impressionist touch. Founders Julie Gambini and Sabrina Signori are great hosts, offering a delicious breakfast to residents. The hotel also has a tearoom which offers homemade organic pastries and fruit juices, as well as Nunshen® teas every day from 2pm to 6pm. On sunny days, grab an ice cream – made in the Alps – on the small patio.

Price: from €129/night.

21, rue du Général de Gaulle, 95430 Auvers-sur-Oise
Tel: +33 (0)1 30 37 79 18 / hoteldesiris.com

- Transilien — Line H: Auvers-sur-Oise

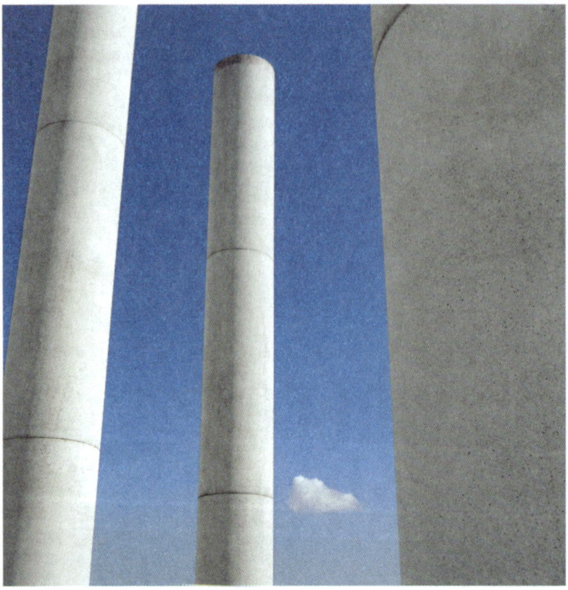

Stuck! | *Axe majeur, Cergy-Pontoise.*

The not-so-thin red line | *Axe majeur, Cergy-Pontoise.*

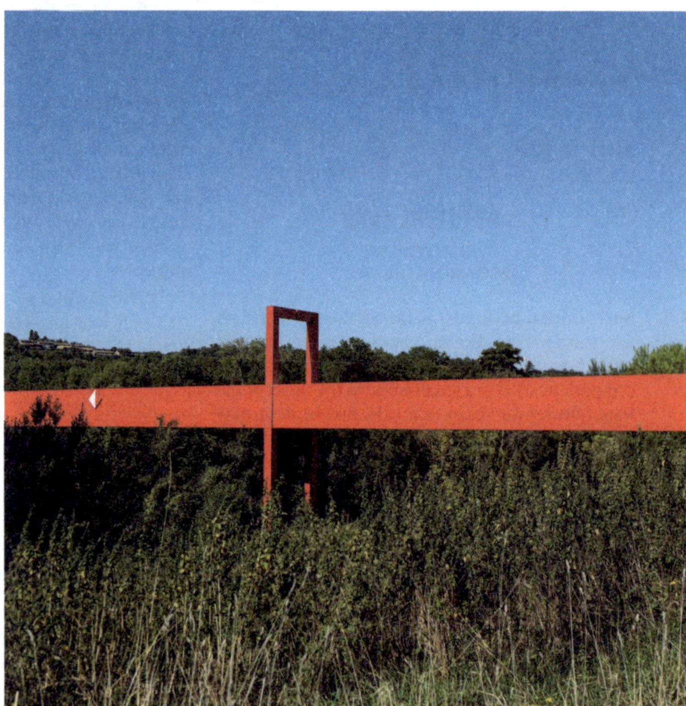

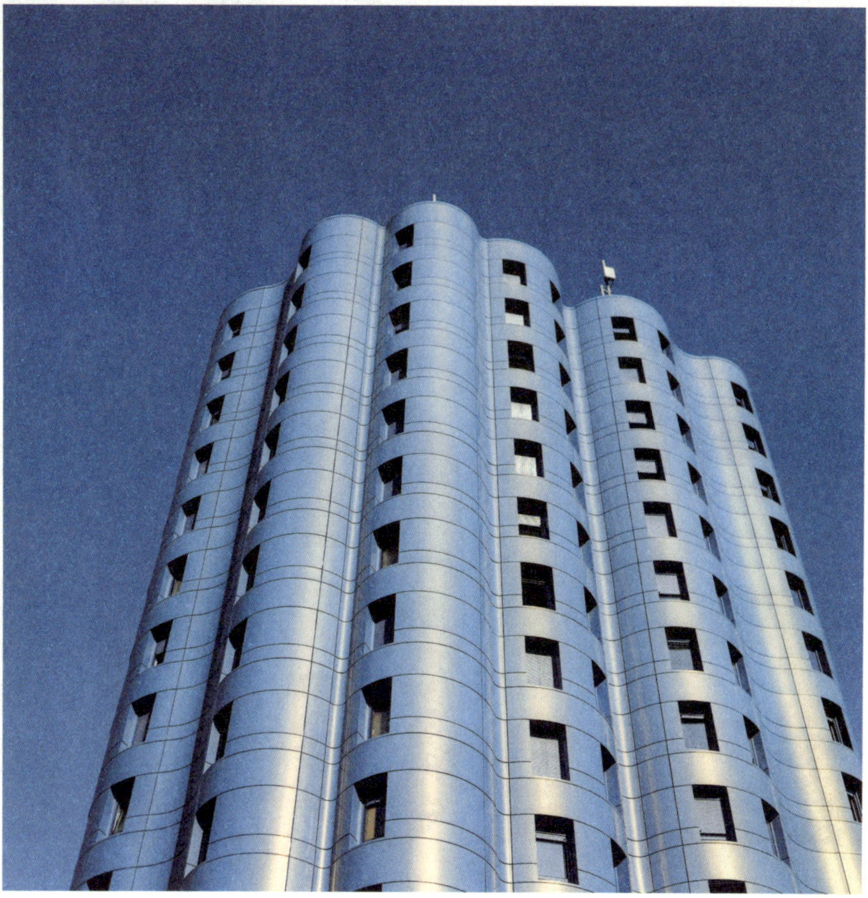

Kind of blue | *Chemin des Bourgognes, Cergy.*

THE ENCHA F

ACHÈRES-LA-FORÊT
ARBONNE-LA-FORÊT

BOIS-LE-ROI
FONTAINEBLEAU

LARCHANT

MAINCY

MILLY-LA-FORÊT

MONTIGNY-SUR-LOING

NEMOURS

NOISY-SUR-ÉCOLE

SAMOIS-SUR-SEINE

NTED REST

It has been home to the kings of France, inspired the landscape painters of the Barbizon school, delighted hikers and climbers from around the world, and may end up a UNESCO World Heritage site. The forest of Fontainebleau, with its surprising, unexpected landscapes, seems to come straight out of a fairy tale. To see for yourself, explore its 500 kilometres of signposted trails to discover the landlocked beach of Sables du Cul-du-Chien, the panoramic views from the hills of the Sentier des 25 bosses or the extra-ordinary boulders of the Franchard and Apremont gorges. Chances are you'll be delighted.

THE ENCHANTED FOREST

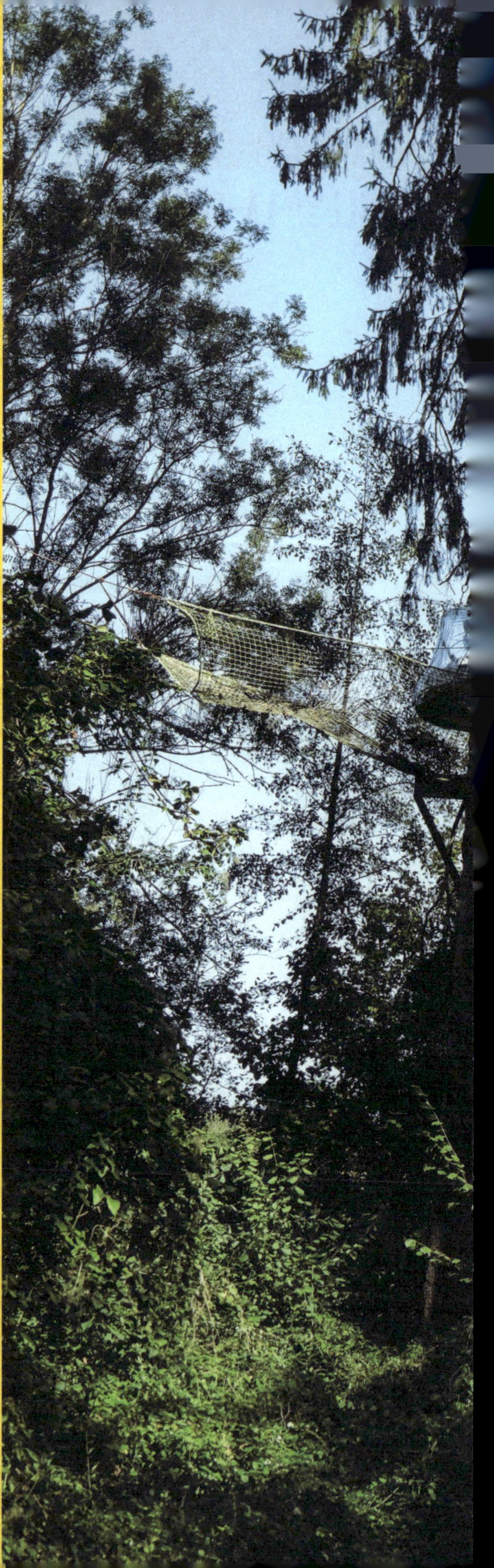

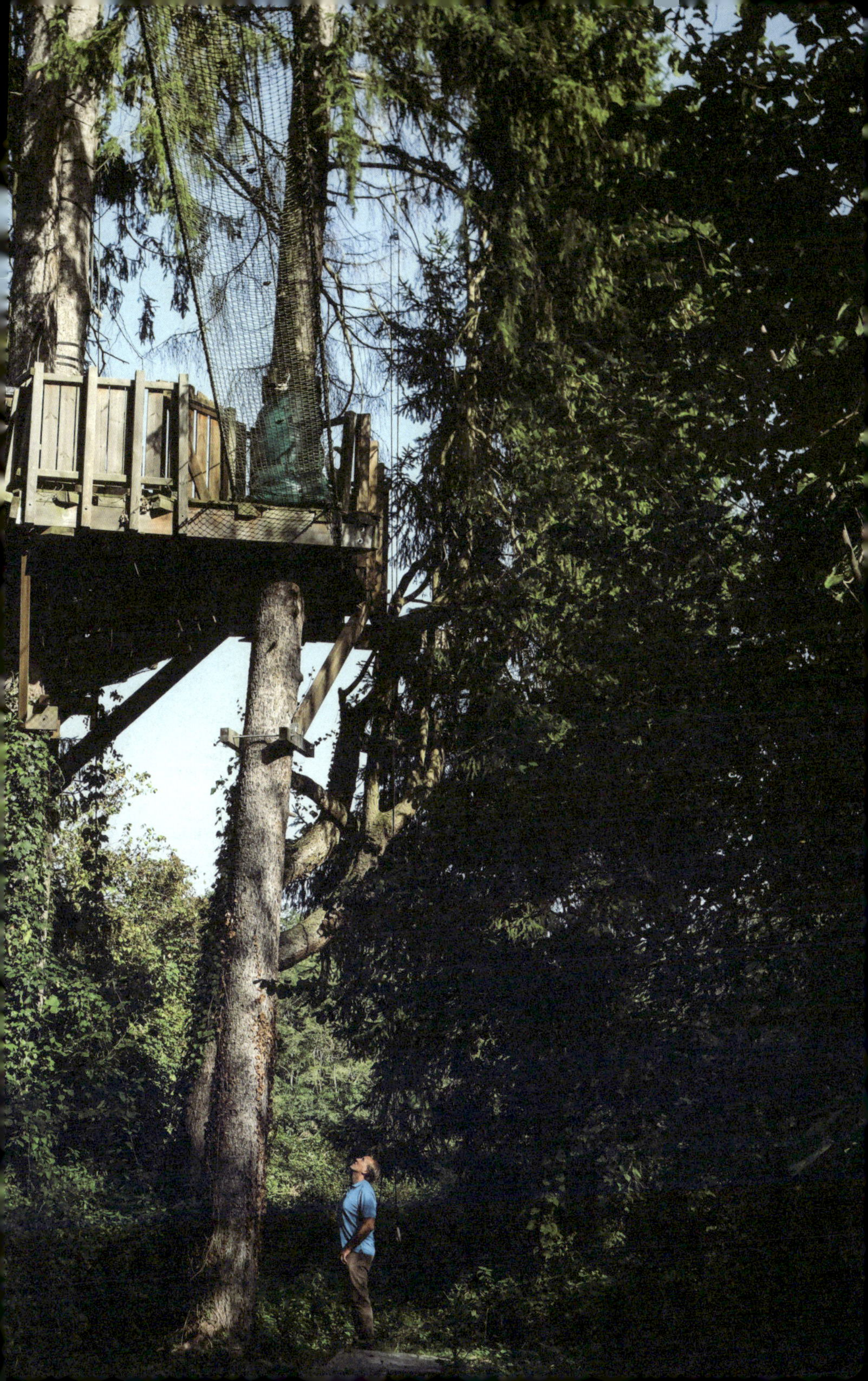

THE ENCHANTED FOREST

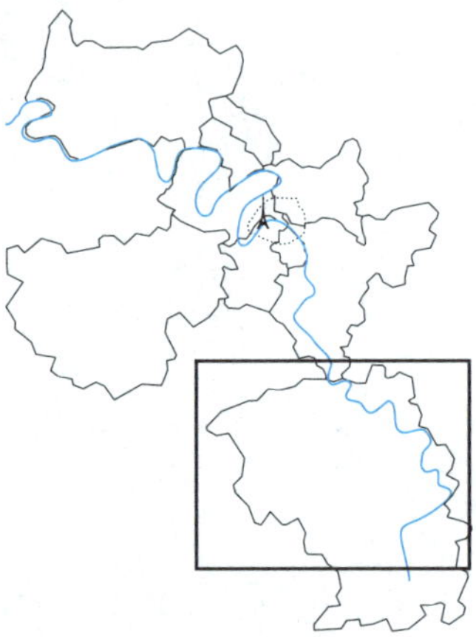

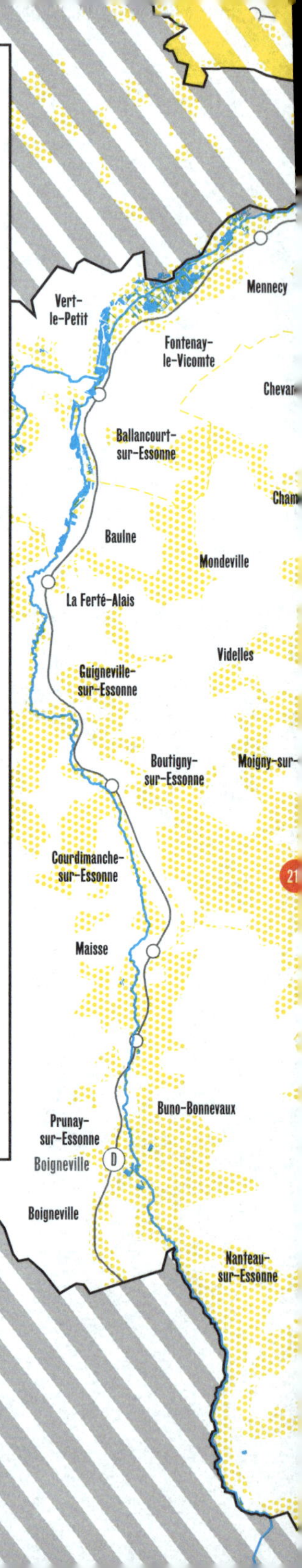

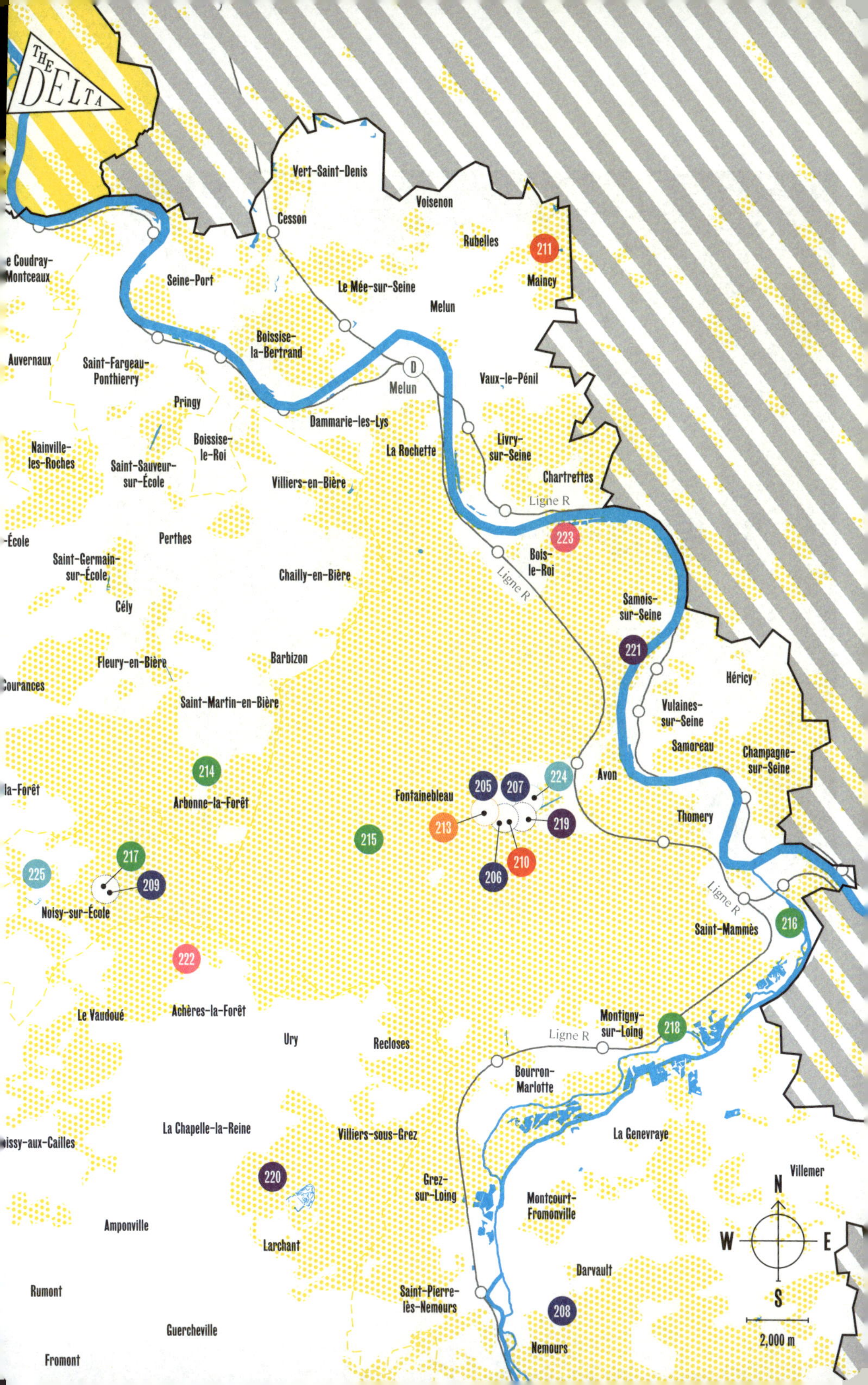

THE DELTA
Vert-Saint-Denis
Voisenon
Cesson
Rubelles
211
Maincy
e Coudray-
Montceaux
Seine-Port
Le Mée-sur-Seine
Melun
Boissise-
la-Bertrand
Auvernaux
Saint-Fargeau-
Ponthierry
D
Melun
Vaux-le-Pénil
Pringy
Dammarie-les-Lys
Nainville-
les-Roches
Boissise-
le-Roi
La Rochette
Livry-
sur-Seine
Saint-Sauveur-
sur-École
Villiers-en-Bière
Chartrettes
Ligne R
223
-École
Perthes
Bois-
le-Roi
Saint-Germain-
sur-École
Chailly-en-Bière
Ligne R
Samois-
sur-Seine
Cély
221
Fleury-en-Bière
Barbizon
Hérici
Courances
Saint-Martin-en-Bière
Vulaines-
sur-Seine
Samoreau
Champagne-
sur-Seine
214
224
Avon
205
207
la-Forêt
Arbonne-la-Forêt
Fontainebleau
Thomery
213
219
215
225
217
210
209
206
Ligne R
Noisy-sur-École
Saint-Mammès
216
222
Montigny-
sur-Loing
218
Le Vaudoué
Achères-la-Forêt
Ury
Recloses
Ligne R
Bourron-
Marlotte
La Chapelle-la-Reine
Villiers-sous-Grez
La Genevraye
issy-aux-Cailles
220
Grez-
sur-Loing
Villemer
Montcourt-
Fromonville
N
Amponville
W
E
Larchant
Darvault
S
Rumont
Saint-Pierre-
lès-Nemours
208
Guercheville
Nemours
2,000 m
Fromont

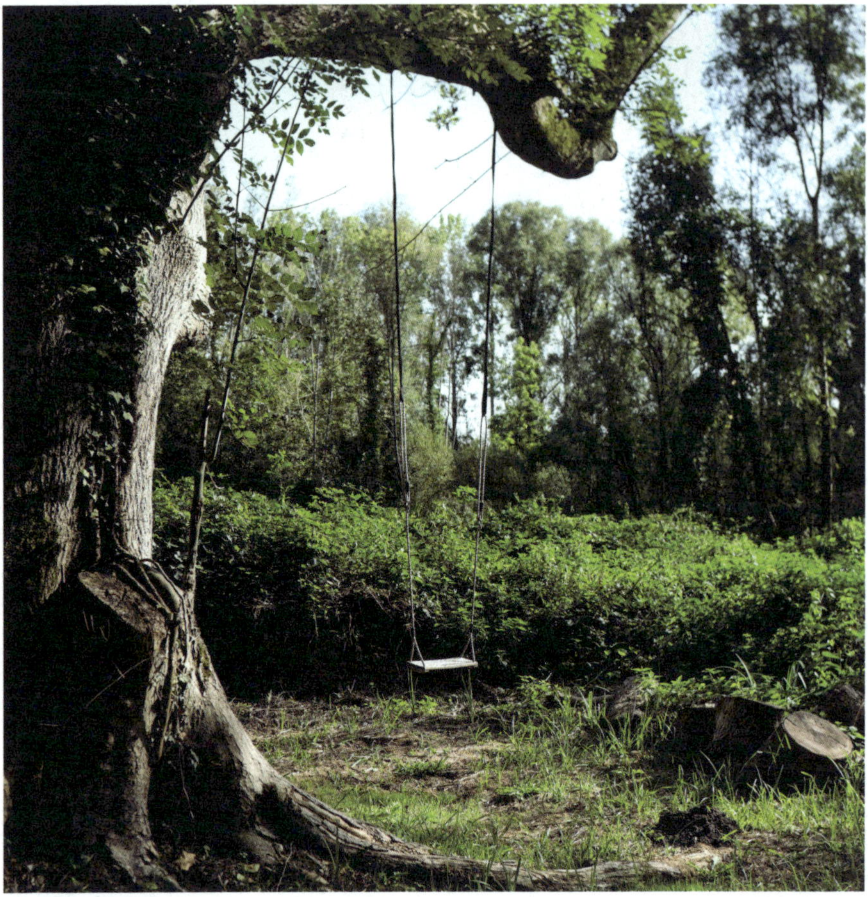

Organic roller coaster | *Maison du Rocher, Noisy-sur-École.*

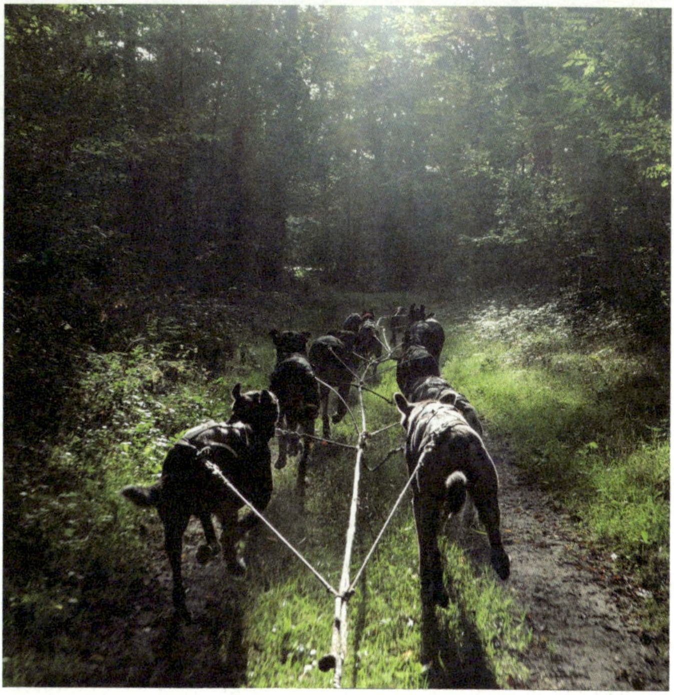

Dog day afternoon | *Forêt de Fontainebleau.*

The art of walking | *Forêt de Fontainebleau.*

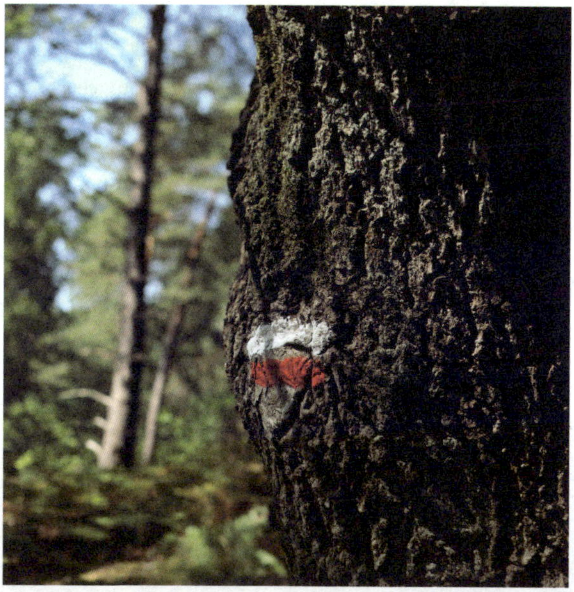

Sport

FONTAINEBLEAU

205 GLOBE CLIMBER

#SPIDERMANSTYLE
#BOULDERING #PROTIPS

If you have always dreamed of climbing walls like spider-man, then the Fontainebleau forest, one of the world's climbing hotspots, is the place to start. Here you can try out what is known in climbing jargon as bouldering, i.e. climbing on rocks without ropes or harnesses. A colour code informs you of the difficulty of the ascent: white for children, yellow for easy, blue for not easy at all and black for the boldest. Then all you have to do is choose from the many spots, some of which have fanciful names such as the Diplodocus, the Dog's Ass or the Elephant. To make things easier, you can be accompanied by an instructor from Globe Climber who will provide you with equipment (climbing shoes and mattresses) and give you the necessary advice to get to the top.

Price: €160 for a half-day for 3 people (from 7 years old) / €190 for 4 people / €215 for 5 people

3, rue Paul Tavernier, 77300 Fontainebleau
Tel: +33 (0)1 64 70 77 69 / globeclimber.com
◆ Transilien — Line R: Fontainebleau - Avon

206 INTRODUCTION TO THE JEU DE PAUME

#ANCESTOROFTENNIS #ROYALSPORT
#MYTHICALCOURT

An ancestor of tennis and the world's first racket sport, the jeu de paume has almost entirely disappeared. Played by kings, it reached its peak in the 17th century with close to 500 courts in France. Today, there are only two left, one in Paris and the other in the Château de Fontainebleau (see p. 147), built under Henri IV. The most incredible thing is that you can take part in introductory sessions organized by the jeu de paume circle. The perfect way to combine sport and history.

Price: 1h15 session for one or two people for €30 (and then €10 for the following sessions).

Château de Fontainebleau, boulevard Magenta, 77130 Fontainebleau
Tel: +33 (0)1 64 22 47 67 / chateaudefontainebleau.fr
◆ Transilien — Line R : Fontainebleau - Avon

207 TRANS'BLEAUSARDE

#MINIADVENTURE #SERIOUSHIKING
#BRANDNEW

With the Sentier des 25 bosses (see p. 147), the Fontainebleau forest already had an itinerary for experienced hikers. But this wasn't enough for the Helloways hikers, specialists in Greater Paris hikes accessible by public transport, who joined forces with the webzine *Les Others* in 2019 to create a brand new 52-km route with a 1,200-metre ascent: the Trans'Bleausarde. According to them, it is one of the most demanding hikes in the Île-de-France region. It took three months of work and scouting and requires 16 hours of walking, two to three days in total, with nights in a gîte or hotel. A mini-adventure, just a short train ride away.

Hiking trail from Fontainebleau - Avon station (Transilien line R) to Maisse station (RER D) through the forest of Fontainebleau.

helloways.com/randonnees/la-trans-bleausarde-avon

NEMOURS

208 NOLIMIT AVENTURE

#ADVENTURECOURSE #DONKEYKONG
#TREASUREHUNT

If you're looking for something different to the traditional forest walk, head for Nolimit Aventure in the Nemours forest where twelve adventure courses await among the treetops. A great way to enjoy the very beautiful scenery while swinging on ropes, climbing nets, and negotiating moving logs, barrels, vines, Himalayan bridges and even suspended surfing. A special course, perched 40 metres above the ground, offers a fabulous panorama with the longest zip line in Île-de-France flying some 200 metres over a valley. If you want more, Nolimit Aventure also has an escape game, a treasure hunt, paintball and canoeing on the Loing.

Price: from €10 for treetop courses.
Open daily year round.

Avenue de Stalingrad "Les Palis", 77140 Nemours
Tel: +33 (0)6 12 35 40 50 / nolimit-aventure.com
◆ Transilien — Line R: Nemours - Saint-Pierre

NOISY-SUR-ÉCOLE

209 SENTIER DES 25 BOSSES

#GR20TRAIL
#830METREASCENT #LOOP

Corsica has the GR20 trail, Greater Paris has the Sentier des 25 bosses in the Trois-Pignons forest, bordering the Fontainebleau forest. This 15-km circuit, created in the late 1960s by mountain hikers, boasts an ascent of 830 metres. In the Île-de-France region, where the highest peak reaches 216 metres (the hills of Rosnes in the Val-d'Oise), you have to see it to believe it. Allow six hours to complete the loop from the La Roche aux sabots car park in Noisy-sur-École. The itinerary, which is very well signposted, can be found on the IGN (Institut national de l'information géographique) website, ignrando.fr. Along the way, you will pass the Sables du Cul-du-Chien, a vast white sand beach in the middle of the forest (see p. 150).

Parking de la Roche aux sabots, Chemin de la Plaine de Jean des Vignes, 77123 Noisy-sur-École
ignrando.fr

culture

FONTAINEBLEAU

210 CHÂTEAU DE FONTAINEBLEAU

#WORLDHERITAGESITE #NAPOLEON
#NATIONALTREASURE

It is one of the forty-five UNESCO World Heritage Sites in France and has seen most of the French sovereigns go by, from Francis I to Napoleon III. The structure is a patchwork of styles, a synthesis of the arts from the 12th to the 19th century. Napoleon I held Pope Pius VII in captivity there from 1812 to 1814. It is surrounded by a 130-hectare park. If you haven't yet guessed which monument it is, it is high time for you to discover the Château de Fontainebleau. Among other things, it contains many relics that belonged to Napoleon I, such as his gabardine and his headgear, and you can visit the room where he signed his abdication in April 1814. You will be blown away by the view from the great library in the Galerie de Diane, pass through chapels and royal apartments, and open your eyes to the only remaining throne room in France. You just have to take your time.

Price: €14 / Free for under-26s.
Closed Tuesday.

Place Charles-de-Gaulle, 77130 Fontainebleau
chateaudefontainebleau.fr

- Transilien — Line R: Fontainebleau - Avon then bus 1 to the Château stop

MAINCY

211 CHÂTEAU DE VAUX-LE-VICOMTE

#LAVISH #CANDLELITEVENINGS
#WORTHTHETRIP

If you're going to build a castle, you might as well call upon the best. In choosing the architect Louis Le Vau, the gardener André Le Nôtre and the painter-decorator Charles Le Brun, who all left their mark on the Château de Versailles, Louis XIV's ambitious Superintendent of Finances Nicolas Fouquet had great ambitions for Vaux-le-Vicomte. This lavish heritage is still alive and well with multiple events throughout the year allowing visitors to appreciate all its facets, including candlelit evening visits from May to late September, the "Grand Siècle" costume day in June and Christmas light displays in November, December and January. Vaux-le-Vicomte is worth the trip.

Price: €17 (full price), €13.50 (6–17 year-olds) / Free for under-6s.
Open daily from 1 March to 5 November and mid-November to early January (except 25 December and 1 January).

77950 Maincy
Tel: +33 (0)1 64 14 41 90 / vaux-le-vicomte.com

- Transilien — Line R: Melun then Châteaubus shuttle (on weekends and public holidays from 1 April)

MILLY-LA-FORÊT

212 LE CYCLOP

#MONSTERINTHEFOREST #CONTEMPORARYART
#MONUMENTALWORK

Created in 1969 in the Bois des Pauvres in Milly-la-Forêt, the Cyclop by sculptor Jean Tinguely is one of the most fascinating works in Greater Paris. This huge steel head, standing 22 metres tall, houses a strange cabinet of curiosities where lovers of contemporary art can enjoy a shot of Dadaism, new realism, kinetic art and

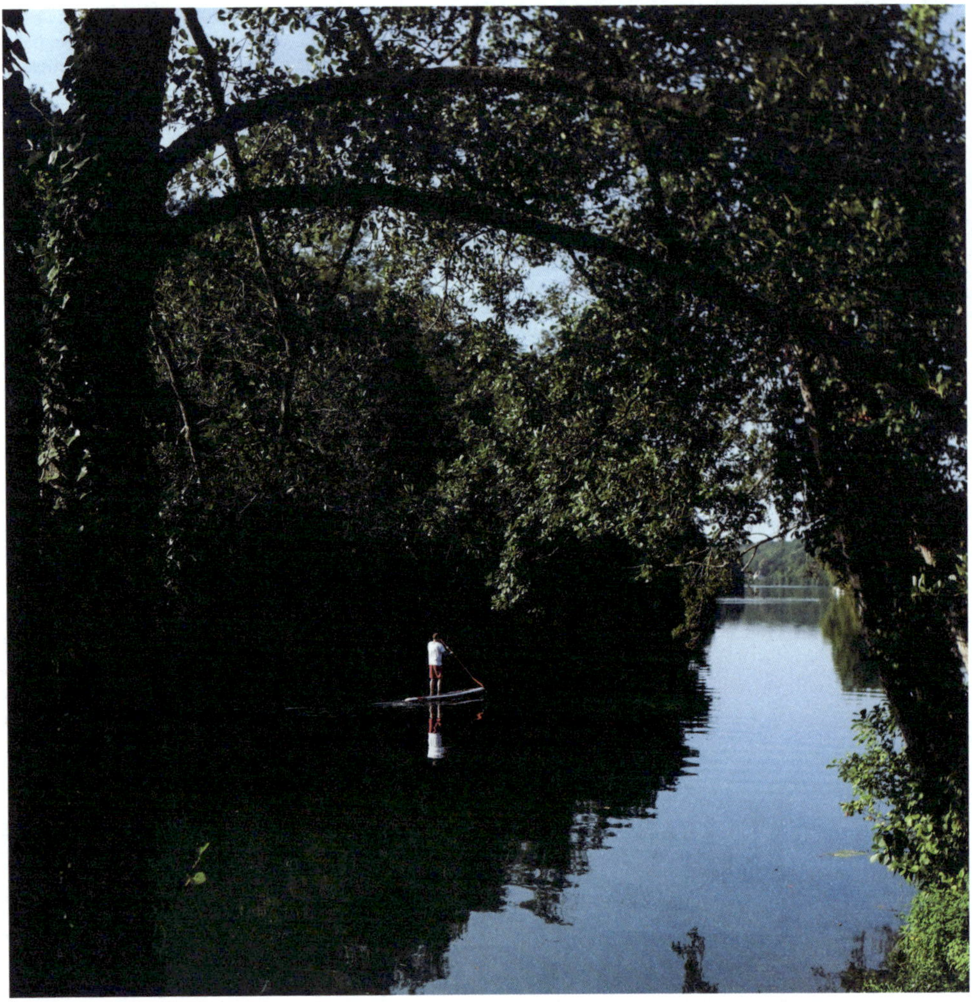

A day like any other | *On the Seine, Samois-sur-Seine.*

art brut. Some fifteen artists, including Niki de Saint Phalle, participated in the creation of this structure which is also known as "The Monster in the Forest", and which offers a new programme every year.

Price: €9 (full price), €6 (reduced price).
Open from April to October (Wednesday to Sunday in July-August from 2–6.30pm, Friday, Saturday and Sunday the rest of the year).
Tours of the Cyclop are guided and last for 45 minutes.

Rue Pasteur, 91490 Milly-la-Forêt
Tel: +33 (0)1 64 98 95 18 / lecyclop.com

lifestyle

FONTAINEBLEAU

213 BLEAUSARD

#EVERYTHINGCLIMBING
#MADEINFONTAINEBLEAU #ECOFRIENDLY

Climbing the boulders of Fontainebleau is great. Climbing them when dressed by a local brand is even better. Since 2017, Bleausard has been designing eco-friendly clothing and climbing equipment in Fontainebleau. Recycled or organic fibres for sweatshirts and t-shirts, pine resin for chalk (used by climbers to prevent their hands from slipping), recycled polyester crash-pads – at Bleausard, you can dress and equip yourself from head to toe. Don't forget to grab a climbing guidebook before setting off on your adventure.

Closed Sunday.

53, rue Saint-Merry, 77300 Fontainebleau
Tel: + 33(0)1 85 48 14 45 / bleausardclimbing.com
◆ Transilien — Line R: Fontainebleau – Avon

outdoors

ARBONNE-LA-FORÊT

214 SLED DOGS

#FORESTCIRCUIT #MUSHER
#WHITEFANG

Dog sledding isn't only for the Sami people. Since 2014, musher (the driver in dog-sledding) Christian Perlwitz (bronze medal at the 2017 world champsionships) has been importing the discipline into the Fontainebleau forest. Throughout the year, he organizes introductory tours aboard a kart on wheels pulled by his pack of huskies – Havane, Ice, Matika and the others – on a 4-km circuit in the heart of the forest. A way of making the practice accessible to as many as possible and to adapt it to climate change. Christian takes the time to share his passion with visitors, and if you get the sledding bug, he also offers introductions to kart-mushing.

Price: introduction to dog-sledding: €55 for adults and €40 for under-10s (sessions last around 1h30).
Open from early April to mid-December.

77630 Arbonne-la-Forêt
Tel: +33 (0)6 32 68 82 26
evasioncanine.e-monsite.com

FONTAINEBLEAU

215 FORÊT DE FONTAINEBLEAU

#CLIMBING #HIKING
#LOSEYOURSELF

With an area 2.5 times larger than Paris, the forest of Fontainebleau provides infinite opportunities for exploration and is surely one of the most beautiful sites in Greater Paris. The Barbizon School painters' muse in the 19th century, it is a playground for climbing enthusiasts from all over the world who come to practice on its many boulders with their convoluted shapes (see page 146). It is also particularly appreciated by hikers who enjoy its 1,600 km of forest roads and hiking trails, 300 km of which are signposted. You can also be dropped off by train in the heart of the forest, as the Transilien line R stops at the Fontainebleau-Forêt station on weekends. Make sure to bring an IGN map, because once you get off the train, you will be on your own. Remember, no trains in the direction of Fontainebleau-Paris stop here, so you will have

to make your way either to Fontainebleau – Avon (4 km) or Bois-le-Roi (5 km) stations.
onf.fr
◆ Transilien — Line R: Fontainebleau – Avon

MILLY-LA-FORÊT

216 PARC NATUREL DU GÂTINAIS FRANÇAIS

#ATHOUSANDCLEARINGS #ENDLESSWALKS #CHARMINGVILLAGES

Despite its relatively small size – 2 percent of the surface area of France – the Île-de-France region is home to four of the fifty-three regional natural parks: the Haute Vallée de Chevreuse (see page 80), the Vexin Français (see page 133), the Oise - Pays de France and the Gâtinais Français. The last of these parks, nicknamed "land of a thousand clearings and sandstone", covers 750 square kilometres, seven times the size of Paris. Pull on your hiking boots and explore the Trois-Pignons massif, crossed by the spectacular Sentier des 25 bosses (see page 147) or the charming villages of Barbizon or Milly-la-Forêt.

Maison du Parc, 20, boulevard du Maréchal Lyautey, 91490 Milly-la-Forêt
Tel: +33 (0)1 64 98 73 93 / parc-gatinais-francais.fr

NOISY-SUR-ÉCOLE

217 SABLES DU CUL-DU-CHIEN

#BEACHWITHOUTSEA #GEOLOGICALCURIOSITY #PICNICSPOT

You'd think you were on a beach in Bali, minus the sea. The Sables du Cul-du-Chien, in the Trois-Pignons forest, is a geological curiosity. Thirty million years ago, the area was covered by an ocean which deposited quartz, eventually disintegrating into sand. The vision that this white sandy beach surrounded by trees offers today is striking. It's the ideal place for a picnic and a post-prandial walk through the Sentier des 25 bosses, the Greater Paris GR20 hiking trail that passes alongside it (see page 147).

Parking de la Roche aux sabots, Chemin de la Plaine de Jean des Vignes, 77123 Noisy-sur-École
fontainebleau-tourisme.com

MONTIGNY-SUR-LOING

218 WALK ALONG THE LOING RIVER

#AQUATICBREADCRUMBTRAIL #20KMLOOP #MEDIEVALCITY

To escape along the Loing' start from Montigny-sur-Loing station. It's an opportunity to discover little-known landscapes such as the Basses Godernes nature reserve, the Épisy marsh, and the Sorques plain. These pearls are linked by an aquatic breadcrumb trail formed by the Canal du Loing, the Loing river, and the Seine, which you can follow easily (and without any difficulty in finding your way around). The twenty-kilometre loop will take you to the medieval town of Moret-sur-Loing (home of barley sugar, one of France's oldest confectionery products) before you return to your starting point, and therefore your destination.

◆ Transilien — Line R: Montigny-sur-Loing

where to eat

FONTAINEBLEAU

219 FUUMI

#MICHELINSTAR #BENTO #TRADITIONALCUISINE

He is quite simply one of the best Japanese chefs in Greater Paris. Having received a Michelin star for his restaurant L'Axel in Fontainebleau, Kunihisa Goto has now opened Fuumi. Don't miss the Kenta-san-style okonomiyaki (a traditional Japanese pancake made with cabbage, pork, and prawns, topped with sauce, nori seaweed, and dried bonito) and *age dori no negidare* (fried chicken breast with a sauce made from leeks, garlic, ginger, pepper, soy sauce, rice vinegar, and sesame oil).

Price: menus from €17 to €90 / Mains from €6.
Closed Monday and Sunday.

39, rue de France, 77300 Fontainebleau
Tel: +33 (0)1 60 72 10 32 / restaurant-fuumi.com
◆ Transilien — Line R: Fontainebleau – Avon then bus 1 to Château

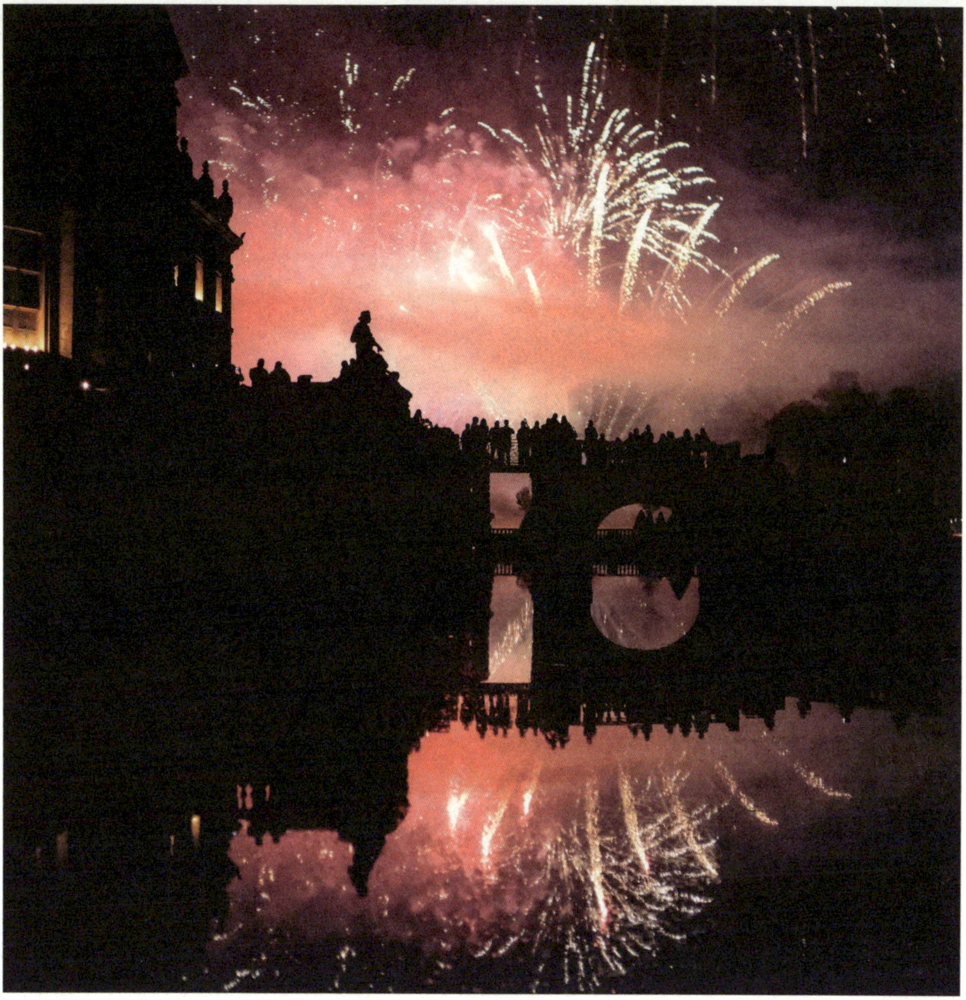

Let the show begin | *Château de Vaux-le-Vicomte, Maincy.*

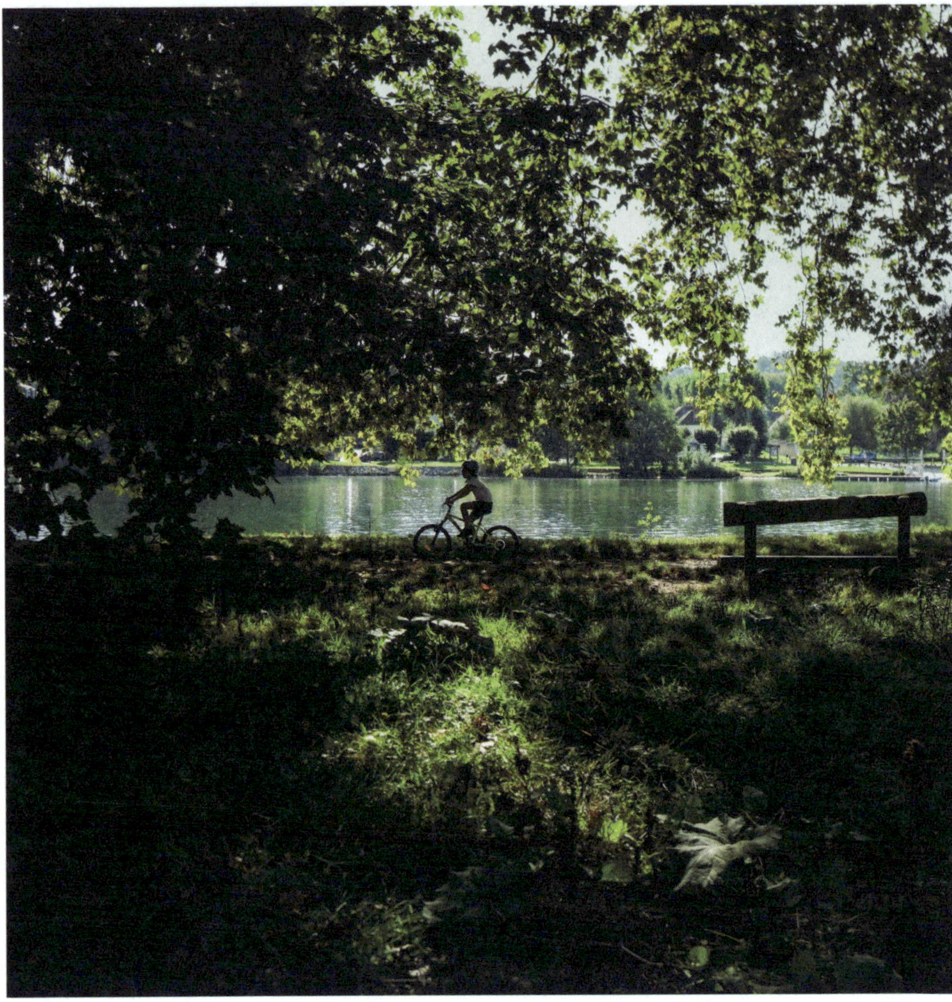

Morning bike ride | *Samois-sur-Seine.*

LARCHANT

220 LA DAME JOUANNE

#MOUNTAINSHELTER
#BIGTERRACE #FIREPLACE

If you're looking for a mountain shelter atmosphere but are nowhere near the Alps, head to the Auberge de la Dame Jouanne, whose name refers to the eponymous rock, the highest in the forest of Fontainebleau. This warm place in the heart of the forest is run by Laurence and Vincent Mével, who revive hikers by serving them generous cuisine such as Jobert terrine and its pickles, the pork chop with its homemade chips or the île flottante made with eggs from the Laveau farm (just 10km away). A restaurant for all seasons, with its large terrace in summer and its fireplace in winter.

Price: dishes from €9.50.
Open year round from Wednesday to Sunday at lunch and Friday and Saturday for dinner. Open Thursday for dinner in July and August.

Rocher de Dame Jouanne, 77760 Larchant
Tel: +33 (0)1 64 28 16 23 / ladamejouanne.fr

SAMOIS-SUR-SEINE

221 DÉMÉ

#PIZZA #SEINESIDE
#DJANGOREINHARDT

Démé is short for Demetrio Lavilla, an Italian pizzaiolo who arrived in France in 2016 and was runner-up in the French pizza championships in 2023. After opening his first restaurant in Fontainebleau, he set up shop (also in 2023) in the village of Samois on the banks of the Seine, with a terrace right on the river. Go with your eyes closed and your mouth wide open: try the Tartufata pizza with its exquisite toppings (black truffle cream, fior di latte mozzarella, mushrooms, baby spinach, truffle oil, roasted hazelnut slivers, fresh basil) all only for €18. To draw out the pleasure a little longer, take a stroll through the streets of Samois and pay a visit to the godfather of gypsy jazz, guitarist Django Reinhardt, who has been laid to rest on the Route du Cèpe.

Price: Pizzas from €11 / Mains from €7.50.
Closed Tuesday and Wednesday.

21, quai de la République, 77920 Samois-sur-Seine
Tel: +33 (0)1 60 70 42 45 / demefontainebleau.com

Family

ACHÈRES-LA-FORÊT

222 FONTÂNEBLEAU

#FONTAINEBLEAUFOREST
#DONKEYTRAIL #ENJOYTHERIDE

Venturing into a forest twice the size of Paris can be intimidating. To overcome any apprehension, Virginie Colboc set up Fontânebleau to offer walks with her donkeys, Marguerite, Hirondelle, and Laïos. Depending on the level, age and inclination of the participants, you can choose between the "Tour de la montagne blanche", a short walk with no change in altitude open to anyone from the age of 9, the "Tour du rocher Cailleau" (from the age of 12), which offers a beautiful panorama but also some more challenging sections, or the "Rocher cathédrale", a walk lasting at least 3 hours with a change in altitude (not recommended for under-14s). The principle is simple: donkeys carry picnics, water bottles, and any other belongings while you enjoy the scenery and the present moment.

Walks from 1h to 3h cost between €15 and €30 per person (maximum 6 people).

Fontânebleau, 77760 Achères-la-Forêt
Bookings with Virginie Colboc: +33 (0)6 12 93 52 67 or fontanebleau@gmail.com / fontanebleau.wixsite.com

BOIS-LE-ROI

223 ÎLE DE LOISIRS

#BETWEENRIVERANDFOREST
#OUTDOORACTIVITIES #CARAVANS

You couldn't ask for a more beautiful location. Located between the Seine and the forest of Fontainebleau, the Bois-le-Roi leisure island sits in an exceptional setting. In addition to its 8-hectare lake, which opens for swimming in the spring, many sporting activities are on offer, including a riding school, a skatepark, a treetop adventure course, basketball and beach volleyball courts, a water sports centre and even a golf course with a driving range on the water. To prolong the pleasure of being in nature, caravans are available for overnight stays.

Open year round.

Rue de Tournezy, 77590 Bois-le-Roi
Tel: +33 (0)1 64 81 33 00 / bois-le-roi.iledeloisirs.fr
- Transilien — Line R: Bois-le-Roi

where to sleep

FONTAINEBLEAU

224 HÔTEL DE CAVOYE

#CONTEMPORARYDESIGN
#JEANRACINE #RELAXEDCHIC

A former private home that saw writer Jean Racine and others pass through, the Hotel de Cavoye has become a charming hotel, the perfect blend of contemporary design and rustic touches. The owners created a refined decor while paying great attention to details such as the games room, in which you will find a giant Mikado set, backgammon and many other surprises. In addition to the twenty-seven rooms and suites, the Hôtel de Cavoye also has a bar with a glass roof, a huge terrace and a restaurant that looks like a modern hunting lodge. In this chic but relaxed atmosphere, the risk is that you may not want to leave.

Price: from €135/night.

36, rue Paul Séramy, 77130 Fontainebleau
Tel: +33 (0)1 60 70 20 00 / hoteldecavoye.com

- Transilien — Line R: Fontainebleau - Avon then bus 1 Hôtel de Ville stop

NOISY-SUR-ÉCOLE

225 LA MAISON DU ROCHER

#BULLESDANSLESARBRES
#PARALLELUNIVERSE #WILLYWONKA

There are some scenes you just wouldn't expect to see in Greater Paris. Like the one that you will witness at the Maison du Rocher, in the middle of the forest of Fontainebleau, at Noisy-sur-École. As soon as you arrive at the car park, you wonder what parallel universe you've stepped into as zip-lining Tarzans fly overhead, while on a football pitch two llamas graze serenely at the foot of a giant multicoloured elk. It's a world that Stéphane Durocher, the local Willy Wonka, has been tending to for many years now. It all began when he bought his house in this natural setting. A lover of the great outdoors, this native Quebecer gradually expanded his "garden" by buying up areas of forest all around. Rather than making it his own private domain, he decided to create an oasis for city dwellers in search of quiet and greenery, who hadn't given up on their childhood dream of sleeping in the trees. Stéphane is here to make these dreams come true in bubbles surrounded by vegetation up to twenty metres high. Ideal for gazing at the stars and letting your imagination wander.

Price: from €190 per night (including half-board)

11 bis, chemin des Prés, 77123 Noisy-sur-École
Tel: +33 (0)1 60 39 54 34 / maisondurocher.com

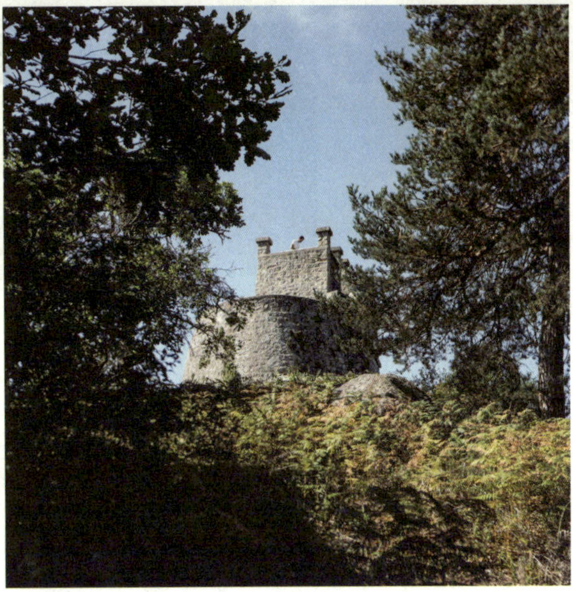

Pre-Eiffel tower | *Tour Denecourt, forêt de Fontainebleau.*

The floor is lava | *Rocher Canon, forêt de Fontainebleau.*

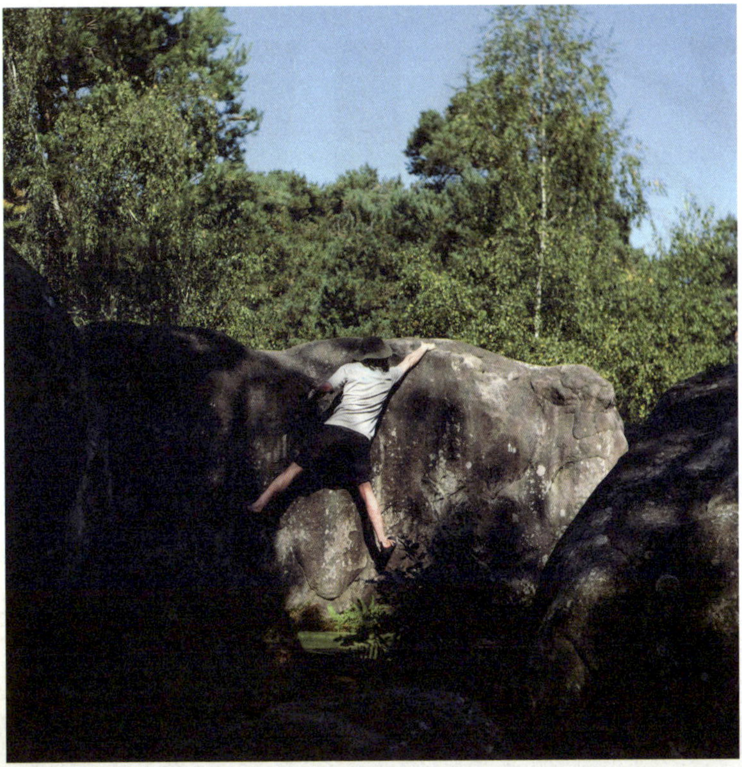

THE LI
ᗺIVI

ENGHIEN-LES-BAINS
ÉPINAY-SUR-SEINE

ERMONT
MONTMORENCY
SAINT-GRATIEN

TTLE
ERA

SOISY-SOUS-MONTMORENCY

With its palm trees, luxury villas, spa treatments and boats floating on the horizon, there is a Côte d'Azur feel to Enghien-les-Bains. The esplanade along the lake, a few steps away from the Casino and the Grand Hôtel – a scale model of the Majestic® in Cannes – could easily be mistaken for the famous Croisette boardwalk. This makes Enghien the ideal destination for a Riviera-style getaway without leaving Greater Paris, with the added bonus of travelling on the Francilien, the most beautiful suburban train that will get you there from the Gare du Nord in fifteen minutes.

THE LITTLE RIVIERA

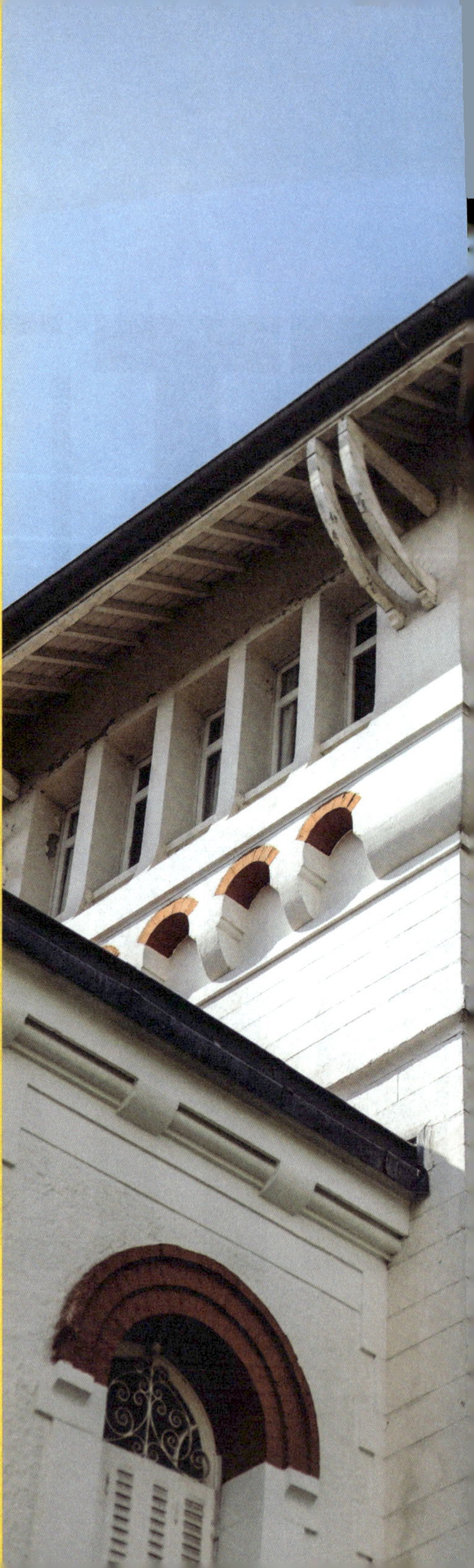

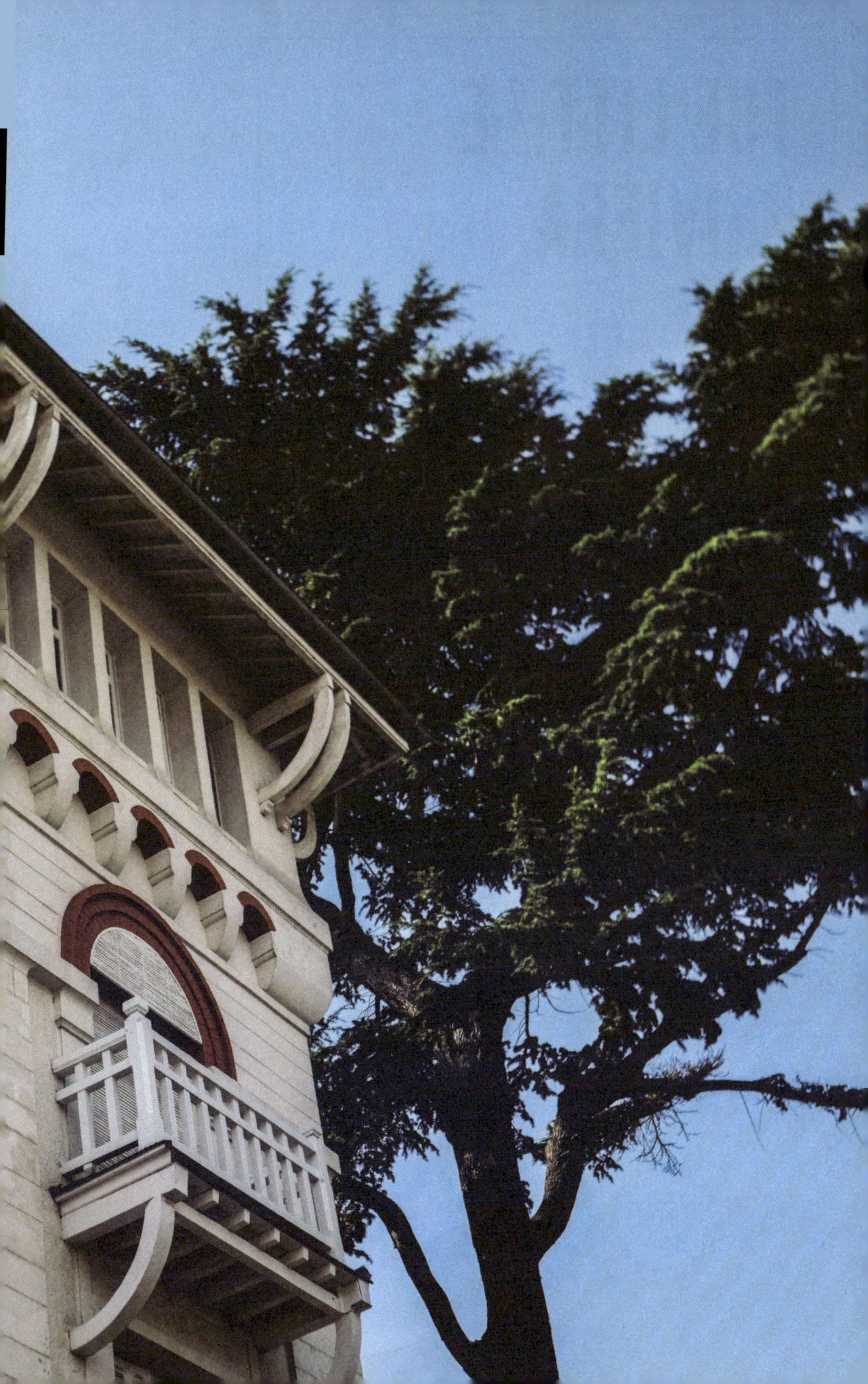

THE LITTLE RIVIERA

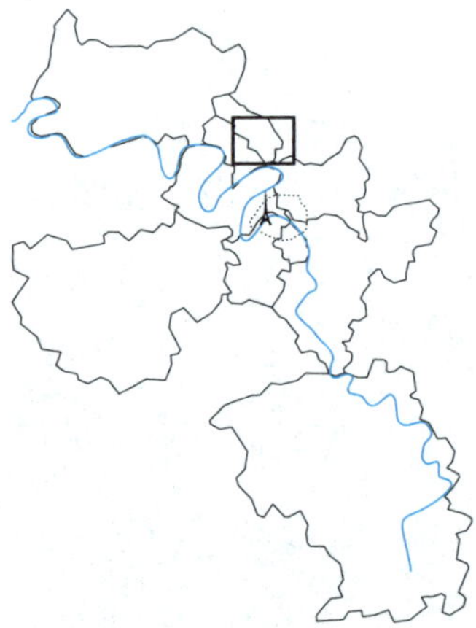

SPORT

226 LAC D'ENGHIEN-LES-BAINS

CULTURE

227 CENTRE DES ARTS
228 MUSÉE JEAN-JACQUES ROUSSEAU
229 CINÉMA LES TOILES

LIFESTYLE

230 CASINO BARRIÈRE
231 LIBRAIRIE IMPRESSIONS
232 SPA DIANE BARRIÈRE
233 L'ÉCLAIR
234 HIPPODROME D'ENGHIEN-SOISY

OUTDOORS

235 FORÊT DE MONTMORENCY

WHERE TO EAT

236 FOUQUET'S
237 VIN SUR VIN

FAMILY

238 PEDALO RIDE

WHERE TO SLEEP

239 GRAND HÔTEL BARRIÈRE

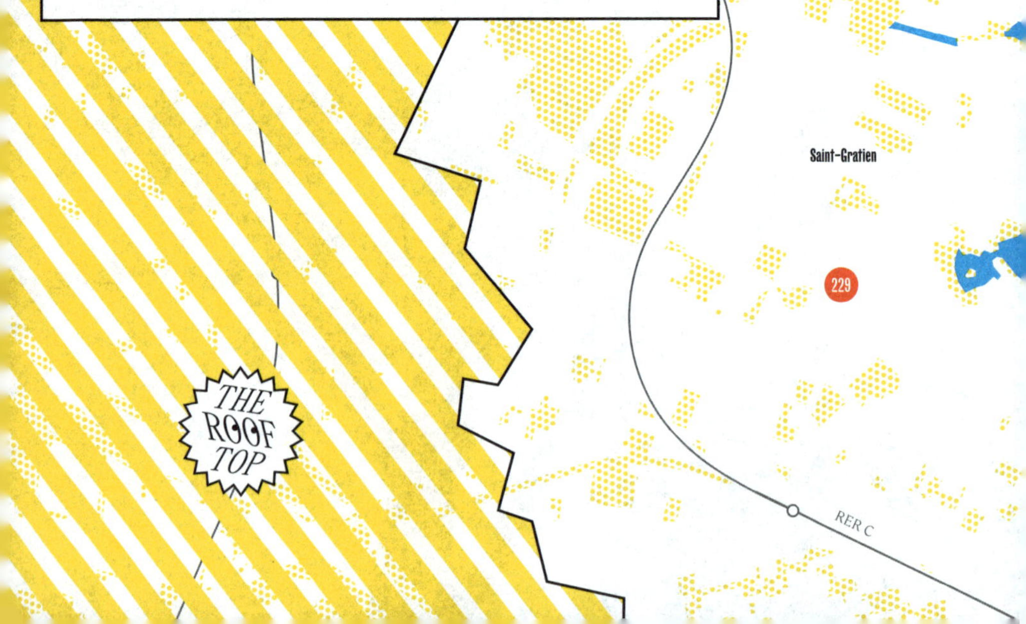

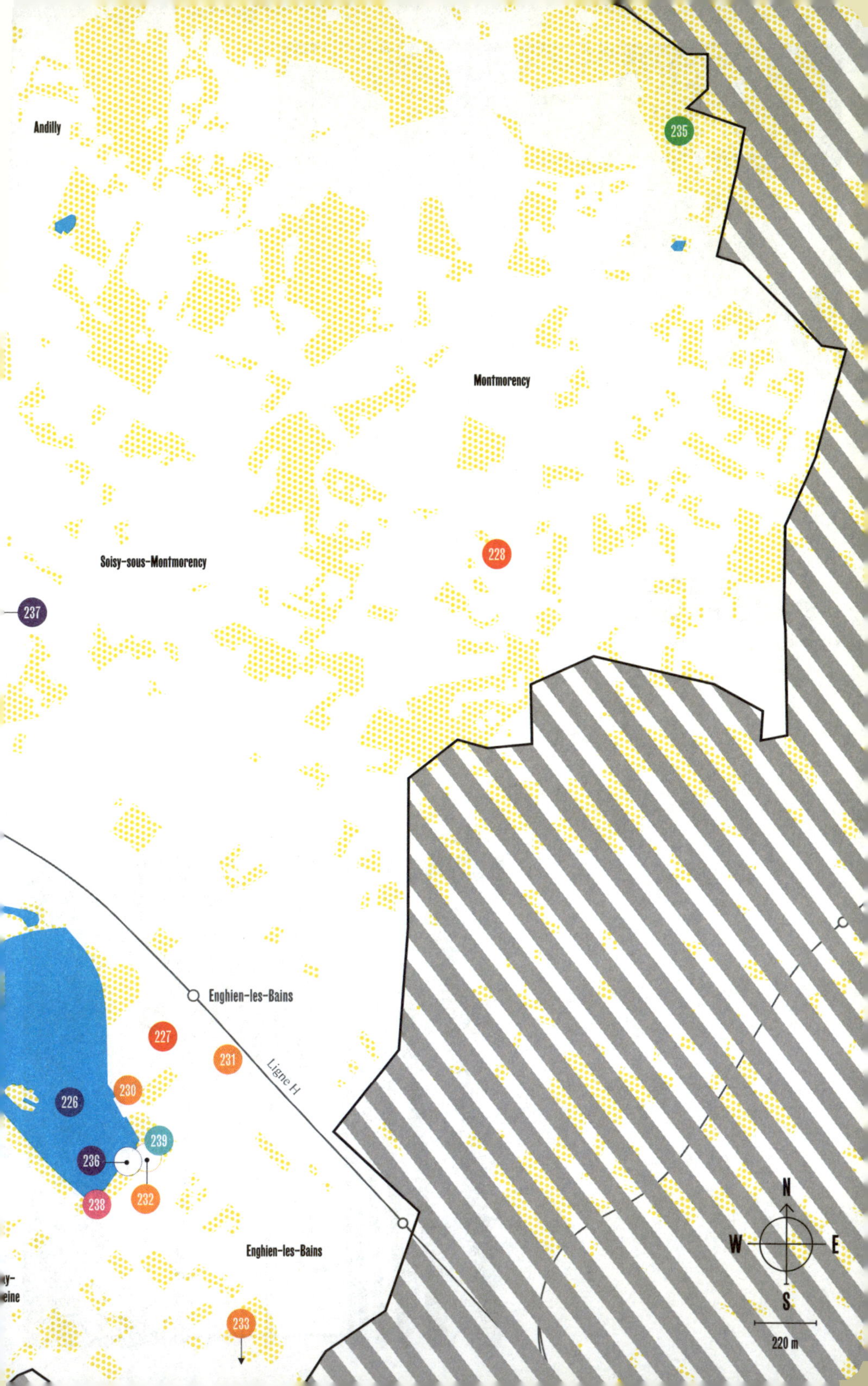

Andilly
235
Montmorency
Soisy-sous-Montmorency
228
237
Enghien-les-Bains
227
231
Ligne H
230
226
239
236
232
238
Enghien-les-Bains
233
N
W
E
S
220 m

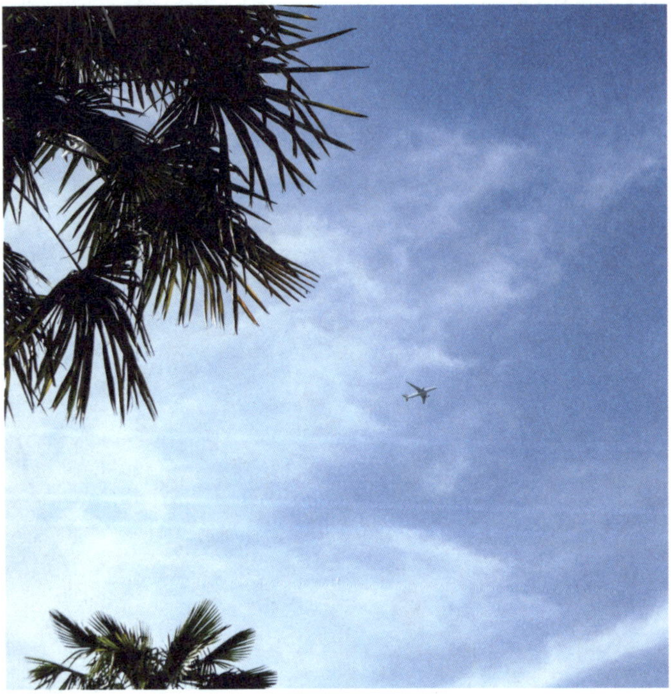

Welcome to LA | *Enghien-les-Bains.*

Jellyfish jackpot | *Casino Barrière, Enghien-les-Bains.*

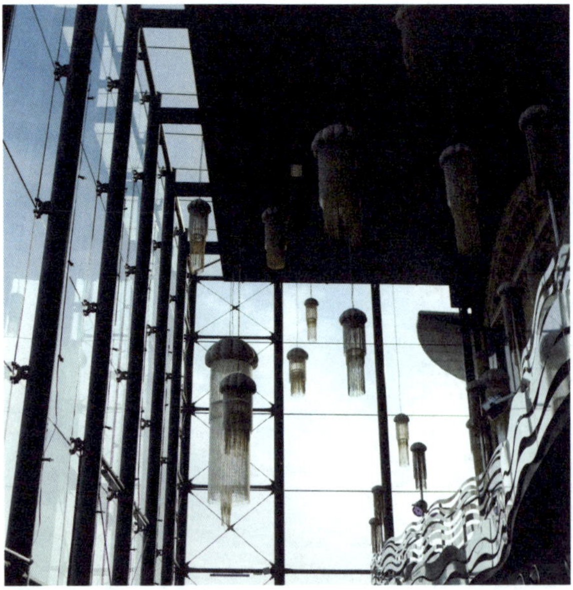

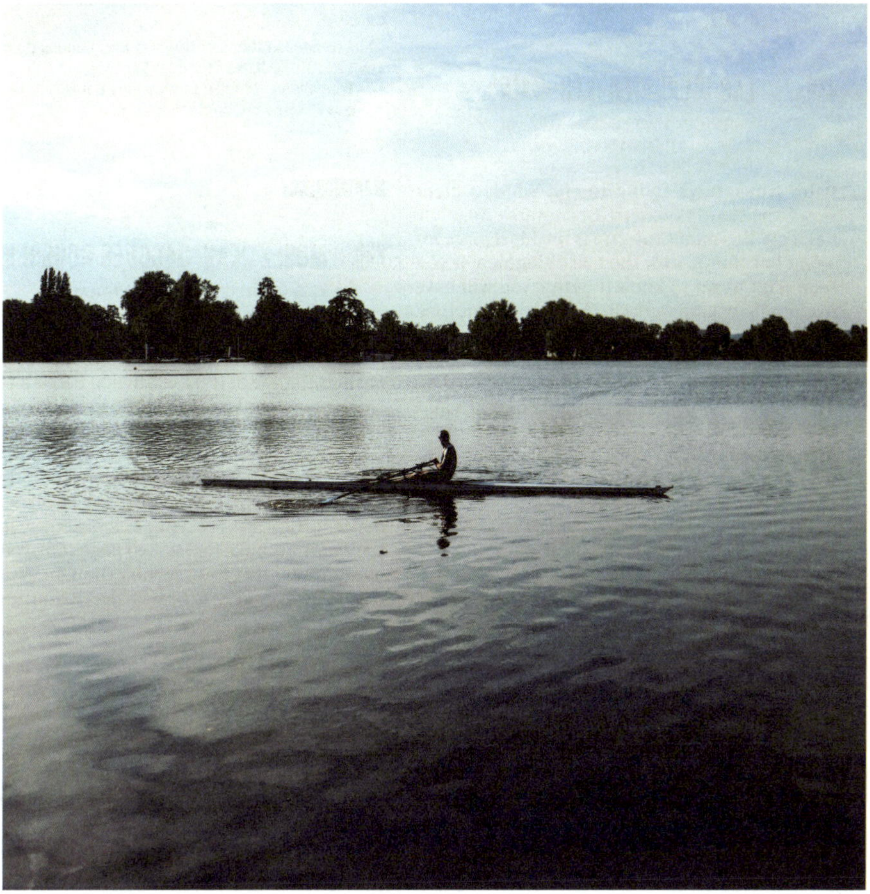

Row, row, row your boat... | *Enghien-les-Bains.*

sport

ENGHIEN-LES-BAINS

226 LAC D'ENGHIEN-LES-BAINS

#MINICROISETTE #PANORAMA
#PROMENADE

Palm trees, flags flying in the wind, a clear view – the Henri Patenôtre-Desnoyers esplanade has it all. This mini-Croisette is the ideal place for a first encounter with the Lac d'Enghien. If you then want to get to know it better, you will have to circumnavigate it on the Avenue de Ceinture. Although it doesn't perfectly follow its banks, this 3-km walk, which also attracts a lot of runners, has some beautiful views, especially from the park bordering the fishing school at number 81. You'll also be able to admire the plethora of villas or indulge in some cardio exercises facing the lake thanks to the fitness equipment installed in the square on the side of the Pont de la Muse.

Esplanade Henri Patenôtre-Desnoyers,
95880 Enghien-les-Bains

- Transilien — Line H: Enghien-les-Bains
- Bus — 254: Casino

culture

ENGHIEN-LES-BAINS

227 CENTRE DES ARTS

#DIGITALART #PERFORMANCES
#EXHIBITIONS

Of course, there are exhibitions, theatre, dance, cinema and concerts, but the Centre des arts (CDA) is also the first venue to receive the Ministry of Culture's "Écritures numériques" (digital culture) certification. A label that came about from Enghien being designated Creative City of Media Arts by UNESCO in 2013. The CDA's programming is therefore strongly influenced by digital culture with shows combining traditional disciplines, such as circus or dance, and digital technology. Each year, the CDA also hosts the Paris Images Digital Summit® dedicated to special effects in film, audiovisual production and video games.

Open Tuesday, Thursday, Friday and Saturday from 2–7pm, Wednesday from 10am–8pm, Sunday from 2–6pm.
Closed Monday.

12-16, rue de la Libération, 95880 Enghien-les-Bains
Tel: +33 (0)1 30 10 85 59 / cda95.fr

- Transilien — Line H: Enghien-les-Bains
- Bus — 254, 256: Enghien-les-Bains

MONTMORENCY

228 MUSÉE JEAN-JACQUES ROUSSEAU

#HOUSEMUSEUM #LIBRARY
#ENLIGHTENMENT

Nearly 300 years ago, the philosopher Jean-Jacques Rousseau (1712–1778) fled Paris, "a city of smoke, noise and mud", to settle in Montmorency. There, he wrote some of his major works such as *Emile, or On Education*. His residence now houses a museum dedicated to him as well as a library with some 30,000 documents (books, correspondence, critical studies). And as it is at the gates of the Montmorency forest (see page 166), you can meditate on this Rousseauist thought: "Nature never deceives us, it is we who deceive ourselves."

Price: €5.33 (full price), €2.72 (19–25 year-olds) / Free for under-19s.
Open Tuesday to Saturday from 2–6pm, from November to March, Tuesday to Sunday from April to October.

5, rue Jean-Jacques Rousseau, 95160 Montmorency
Tel: +33 (0)1 39 64 80 13

- Transilien — Line H: Enghien-les-Bains then walk 2 km
- Bus — 254, 256: Enghien-les-Bains then walk 2 km

SAINT-GRATIEN

229 CINÉMA LES TOILES

#ARTHOUSE #CINEMATICHERITAGE
#MULTIPLEXCOMPLEX

In case you are suffering from the multiplex complex, Les Toiles is the perfect cinema for you. Its programme directors share their love for arthouse films, in their original language of course, and champion the most delicate and singular works, with a mix of recent releases and films of yesteryear. It's a refuge for filmmakers, many of whom go there to meet the audience; the American documentary filmmaker Frederick Wiseman and the French writer-director Bruno Podalydès are regulars here. Les Toiles also has a fondness for short films and regularly screens them before features. This local cinema also has no qualms delving into cinematic history, so that today's releases rub shoulders with those of yesteryear. The perfect script.

Price: €7 (full price) / €6 (reduced price for students, under-16s, job seekers, over-60s, Navigo pass holders) / €4 (under-14s)
Open daily.

Place Francois-Truffaut, 95210 Saint-Gratien
Tel: +33 (0)1 34 28 27 96 / Facebook @cinemalestoiles

- RER — C: Saint-Gratien
- Bus — 138: Forum

lifestyle

ENGHIEN-LES-BAINS

230 CASINO BARRIÈRE®

#SLOTMACHINES #PLACEYOURBETS #MOSTPOPULARFRENCHCASINO

Enghien without its casino is like a poker game without an ace. The establishment is the glory of the city with more than 800,000 visitors per year, a record in France. The venue has come a long way from its spinning tops and bowling alleys in the 19th century. Today, the Casino has 500 slot machines and about 50 blackjack, roulette and punto banco tables. For those who don't have a gambling streak, the casino building with its immense glass facade and chandeliers in the form of multicoloured jellyfish is worth a visit in and of itself.

Price: €15 from Monday to Thursday, €16 from Friday to Sunday and on the eve of public holidays and public holidays / Free cloakroom (required for long coats)
Open daily from 3pm–4am on weekdays and from 3pm–5am on weekends.

3, avenue de Ceinture, 95880 Enghien-les-Bains
Tel: +33 (0)1 39 34 13 17 / casinosbarriere.com

- Transilien — Line H: Enghien-les-Bains
- Bus — 254: Casino

231 LIBRAIRIE IMPRESSIONS

#COMICBOOKS #22000TITLES #PIONEERS

This comic book shop, one of the oldest in France, contains some 22,000 titles from graphic novels to manga. Don't hesitate to ask for advice from Sylvain Insergueix and his team, all of whom are passionate about the art of the comic book and with whom discussions can go very far. You get the picture.

Open Monday to Saturday from 10am–7pm.

10, rue Jean Monnet, 95880 Enghien-les-Bains
Tel: +33 (0)1 34 12 32 06
canalbd.net/librairie-impressions

- Transilien — Line H: Enghien-les-Bains
- Bus — 254, 256: Enghien-les-Bains

232 SPA DIANE BARRIÈRE®

#RELAXATION #FITNESS #PANORAMICVIEW

Stretching and crunches have never felt so good. In the fitness centre of Spa Diane Barrière®, the view over the Lac d'Enghien makes all the effort that much more pleasant. Above all, once your session is over, you can enjoy the joys of winding down in a mosaic setting flooded with natural light. Infinity pool, waterfalls, geysers, sauna, hammam: water is here in all its forms. You can even see the Eiffel Tower® from this paradise, a reminder that you are still on Earth. Once you have finished relaxing, you can go back and try out an aqua bike class. The sports sessions take place throughout the day and are included in the price of admission. And if you really want to do yourself some good, treat yourself to a green tea facial or a Hawaiian massage.

Price: €62 for access to the spa / No access for under-16s.
Open Monday to Saturday from 8.30am–9pm and Sunday from 9am to 8.30pm.

87, rue du Général de Gaulle, 95880 Enghien-les-Bains
Tel: +33 (0)1 39 34 10 50
spadianebarriere-enghien.com

- Transilien — Line H: Enghien-les-Bains
- Bus — 254: Casino

ÉPINAY-SUR-SEINE

233 L'ÉCLAIR

#FORMERDREAMFACTORY
#GIANTPARK #GOODVIBES

What do cinema, the circus, the forest, and Épinay-sur-Seine have in common? The Éclair laboratories. Half of the 4 hectares of this former dream factory devoted to cinema have been turned into a giant park right in the centre of town. Youngsters can't wait to see the giant Connect 4, while the older generation heads to the dancefloor, beer in hand. The joyous atmosphere, provided by reggae, groove, or electro, spreads to the big top and the temporary stage set up on the edge of the woods. Concerts, shows, circus performances... Amidst the concrete, the one-of-a-kind Soukmachines collective has created a venue full of good vibes and colour.

Open on weekends from June to October.

8, avenue du Maréchal de Lattre de Tassigny, 93800 Épinay-sur-Seine
Tel: +33 (0)1 84 21 04 94 / leclair-epinay.com

- Transilien — Line H: Épinay-Villetaneuse
- RER — C: Épinay-sur-Seine
- Tramway — Line T8: Lacépède
- Bus — 37, 254: Lacépède

SOISY-SOUS-MONTMORENCY

234 HIPPODROME D'ENGHIEN-SOISY ®

#ATTHERACES #TAKEAPUNT
#PANORAMICRESTAURANT

A pilgrimage for horse gamblers, the Enghien racecourse saw the birth of the very first three-way bet in 1954. Not as well-known as Auteuil, Longchamp or Vincennes, this old racecourse specialized in trotting extends over forty hectares in Soisy-sous-Montmorency. Admire the scenery in a panoramic restaurant by spending the money you haven't lost at the races yet. Two highlights: the Prix de l'Atlantique in April and the Estivales ® in July, where the whole family can take a punt.

Price: €3, €1.5 for 18–25 year-olds / Free for under-18s.

Place André Foulon, 95230 Soisy-sous-Montmorency
Tel: +33 (0)1 34 17 87 00 / hippodrome-enghien.com

- Transilien — Line H: Champ de Courses d'Enghien

outdoors

MONTMORENCY

235 FORÊT DE MONTMORENCY

#2000HECTARES #HILLY
#CHÂTEAU

With its 2,000 hectares of hilly land, the Montmorency forest is the largest in northwest Greater Paris. You can choose from beautiful, wide forest roads, ideal for first bike rides without training wheels, or more winding trails. If you are fond of old stones, don't miss the Château de la Chasse, surrounded by the forest and standing on the edge of a pond. To find it, a map can be downloaded free of charge from the national forestry authority website.

onf.fr

- Transilien — Line H: Taverny

where to eat

ENGHIEN-LES-BAINS

236 FOUQUET'S

#MYTHICAL #PIERREGAGNAIRE
#LAKESIDEVIEW

The name has become legendary. But if you have never dared to cross the threshold of 99 avenue des Champs-Elysées, you may be less intimidated by its replica in Enghien. A faithful extension of the Parisian address, the Enghien Fouquet's reprises the brand's signature dishes, such as beef tartare or millefeuille, with the added bonus of an open view over the Lac d'Enghien. After dinner, go down a floor and slip into one of the armchairs of L'Escadrille cocktail bar, which organizes live concerts on Thursday evenings with an unrivalled view of the lake.

Price: 2-course menu for €39 at lunch and dinner from Monday to Friday / Menus from €54 on Saturday and Sunday.
Open daily.

66, rue du Général de Gaulle, 95880 Enghien-les-Bains
Tel: +33 (0)1 34 12 11 22 / casinosbarriere.com
- Transilien — Line H: Enghien-les-Bains
- Bus — 254: Casino

ERMONT

237 VIN SUR VIN

#SPECIALPLACE #RELAXEDATMOSPHERE
#EXCEPTIONALCUISINE

Vin sur Vin has something special. It is not only a place where you can eat (very) well, it has its own atmosphere. This is a place to burst out laughing and let everyone know that "you have never eaten fish so beautifully cooked in your entire life". At Vin sur Vin, even the palate cleansers make people groan with joy, like the celery soup with fried croutons. This all comes down to the talent and restless imagination of chef Hervé Horne, whose menu changes every day, and who has made his restaurant a warm place where you want to escape and forget everything for an evening.

Price: 3-course lunch menu for €43 / 5-course + appetizer for €74 / Wine pairing for €40.
Closed Monday and Sunday.

122, rue de Sannois, 95120 Ermont
Tel: +33 (0)1 34 14 64 19 / vinsurvin-ermont.fr
- RER — C: Cernay
- Transilien — Line H: Cernay

family

ENGHIEN-LES-BAINS

238 PEDALO RIDE

#PANORAMAS #FRESHWATER
#STARTPEDALLING

Even if the pedalo might be the most ridiculous floating object ever invented, it would be a shame to miss out on this lake crossing. Two particular lookout points are worth a visit: the Île des Cygnes with its magnificent view of the Villa du Lac and the collegiate church of Montmorency; and the pier where you can embrace the feeling of being surrounded by a huge body of water. Start pedalling ... unless you go for the electric boat option.

Price: €15/30 minutes, €25/hour (2-seater pedalo).
Open daily from April to the end of September from 1–7pm.

Esplanade Patenôtre-Desnoyers,
95880 Enghien-les-Bains
Tel: +33 (0)6 15 90 08 33 / ot-enghienlesbains.fr
- Transilien — Line H: Enghien-les-Bains
- Bus — 254: Casino

where to sleep

ENGHIEN-LES-BAINS

239 GRAND HÔTEL BARRIÈRE®

#ARTDECO #SPA
#ROOMWITHAVIEW

With its art deco facade and view over the water, the Grand Hôtel Barrière® has an air of the famous Majestic® in Cannes. But with only 43 rooms, rather than 300 for its Cannes counterpart, it has a cosier atmosphere. It's a peaceful retreat where the French football team stays the day before their matches at the Stade de France. You can also relax and unwind at the Spa Diane Barrière® (see page 165) which is directly connected to the hotel by a footbridge (access to the spa is included in the price of the rooms). While the hotel rooms are understated, they all have a balcony with a view of the lake or the Eiffel Tower®. All you have to do is choose your side.

Price: from €139/night.

85, rue du Général de Gaulle, 95880 Enghien-les-Bains
Tel: +33 (0)1 39 34 10 00 / hotelsbarriere.com
- Transilien — Line H: Enghien-les-Bains
- Bus — 254: Casino

THE & GALLE

ARCUEIL
GENTILLY

VILLEJUIF
VITRY-SUR-SEINE

IVRY-SUR-SEINE
PARIS

TREET
RY

It has become a cliché to reminisce about the golden era of Montparnasse with Picasso, Gauguin, Bourdelle and Modigliani. But what if Montparnasse had just moved to another district? Take a trip to the 13th arrondissement and you will see that art is everywhere, especially kerbside where street art murals – like those along the aerial metro line 6 – have blossomed. In Vitry, too – since 2008, the city has been transformed into an open-air gallery and has become recognized internationally. In the Street Gallery, former industrial sites have become places of artistic expression. Art is alive and well in Greater Paris.

THE STREET GALLERY

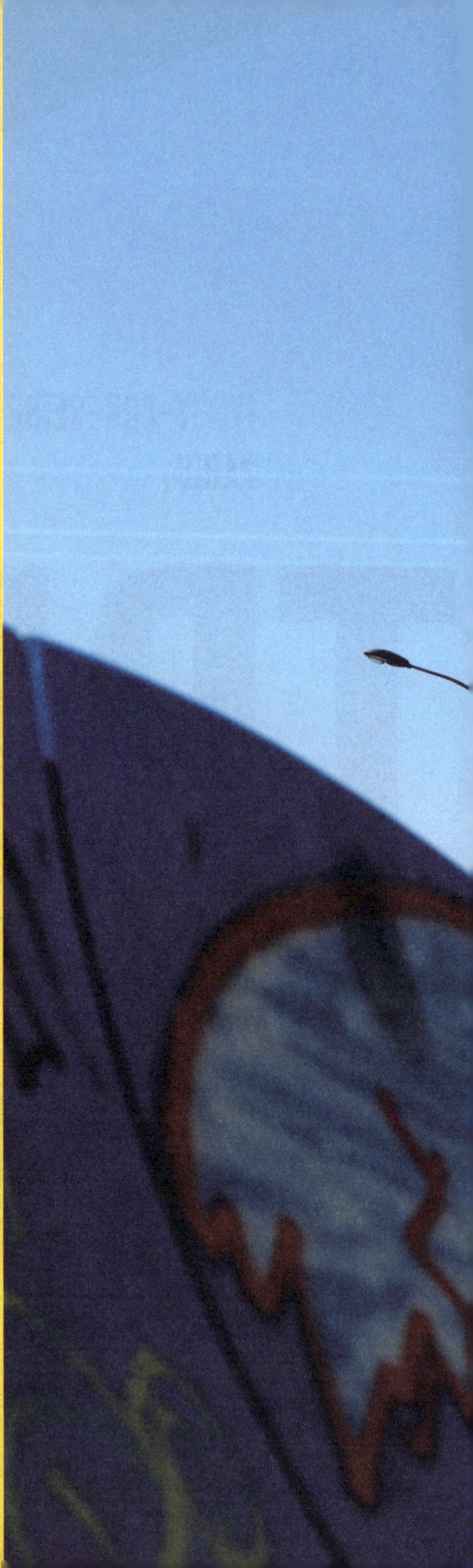

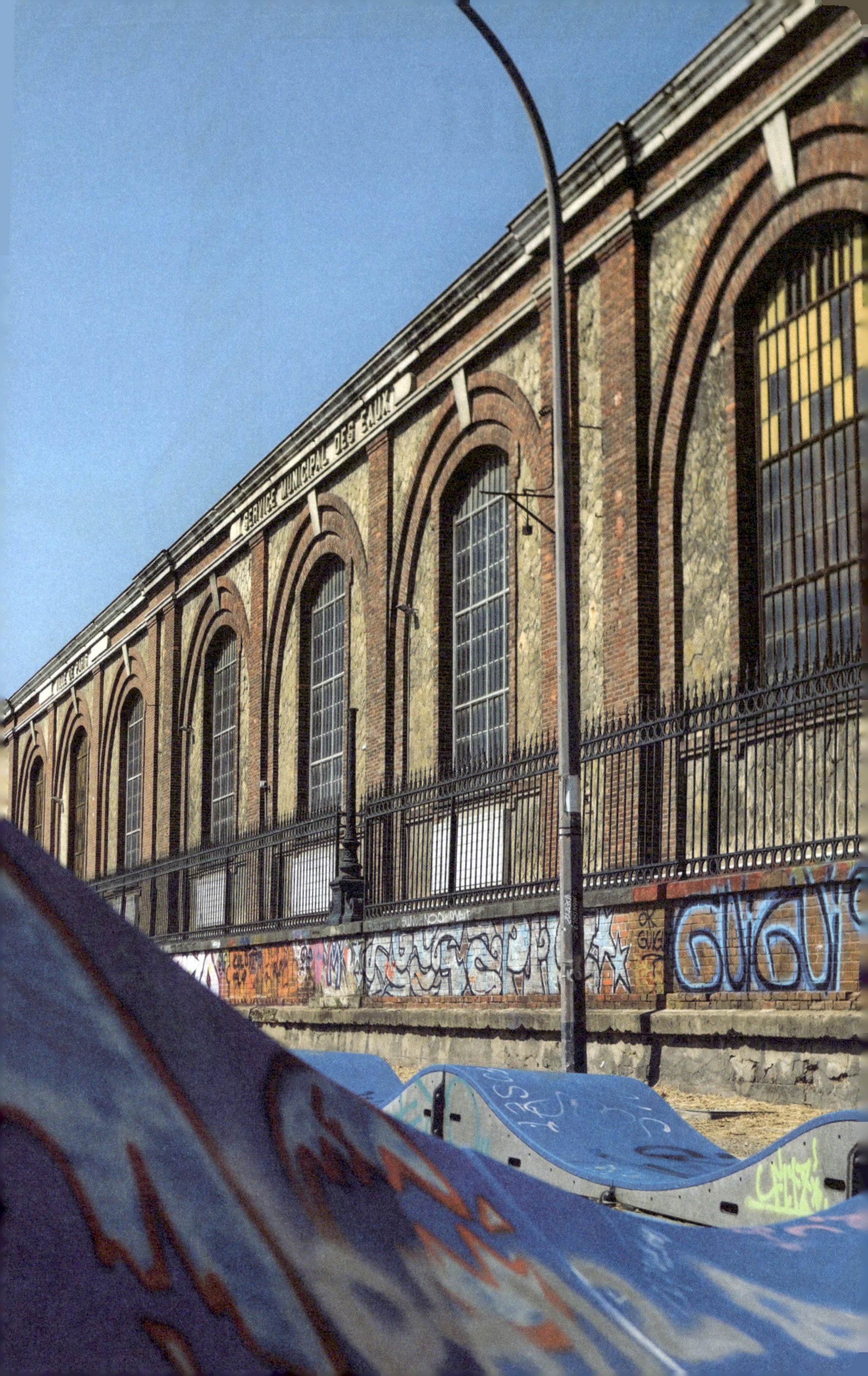
SERVICE MUNICIPAL DES EAUX

THE STREET GALLERY

SPORT

240 ARCUEIL SKATEPARK
241 GR75 "AROUND PARIS"
242 ANTREBLOC

CULTURE

243 MAISON DE LA PHOTOGRAPHIE ROBERT DOISNEAU
244 CREDAC
245 BOULEVARD PARIS 13
246 GALERIE ITINERRANCE
247 MAC VAL – MUSÉE D'ART CONTEMPORAIN DU VAL-DE-MARNE
248 NOUVEAU GARE AU THÉÂTRE
249 VITRY, STREET ART SHOWCASE

LIFESTYLE

250 LA MIROITERIE
251 LA PAGAILLE RECYCLERIE
252 LE LAVO//MATIK
253 LES FRIGOS
254 CHAKCHOUKA
255 LE KILOWATT
256 LE TOME 47

WHERE TO EAT

257 LA BRETELLE
258 UNE FRITERIE À VITRY FOOD TRUCK
259 LES PIEDS DANS LE PLAT

FAMILY

260 TIME TRIPPER

WHERE TO SLEEP

261 JO&JOE

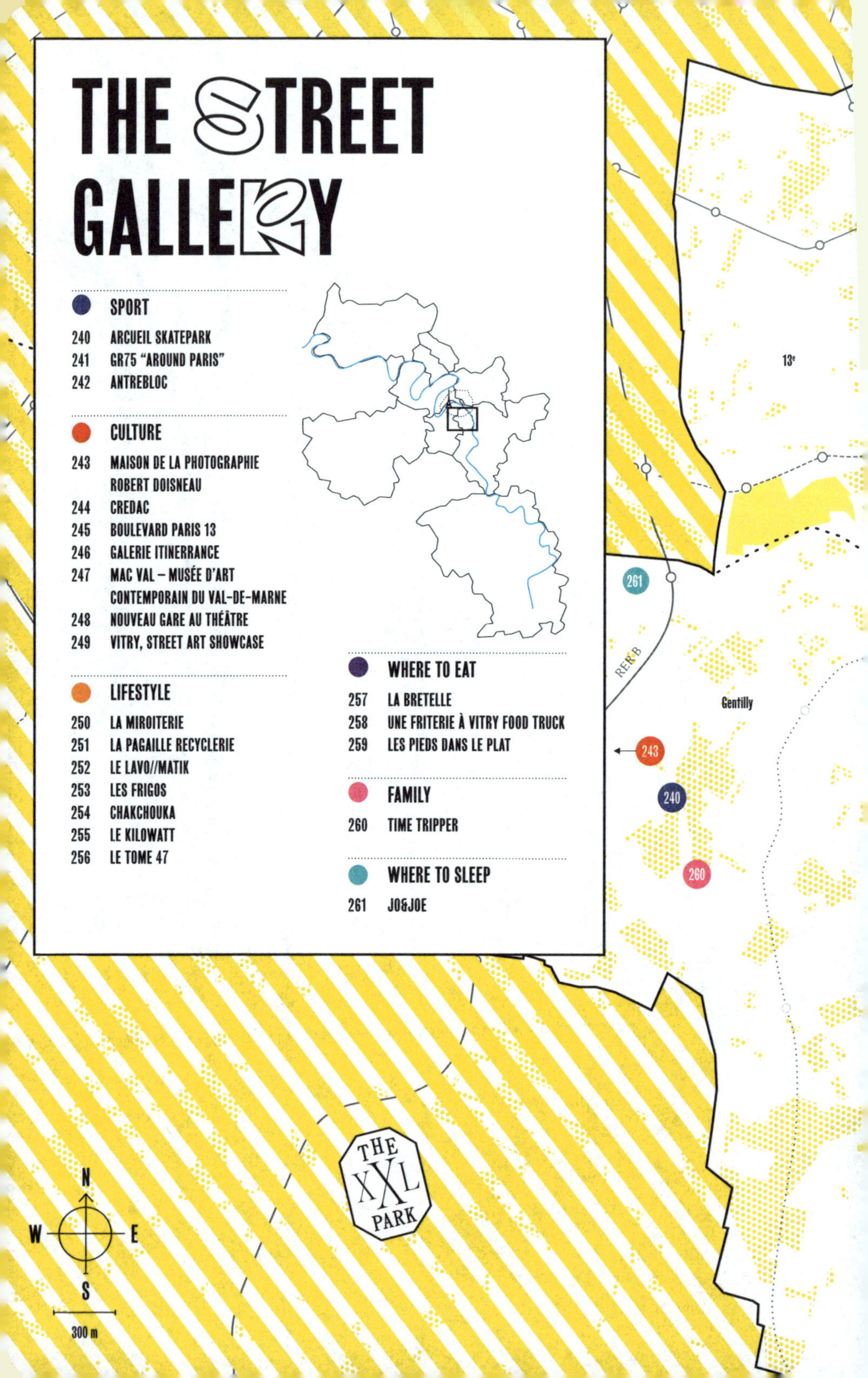

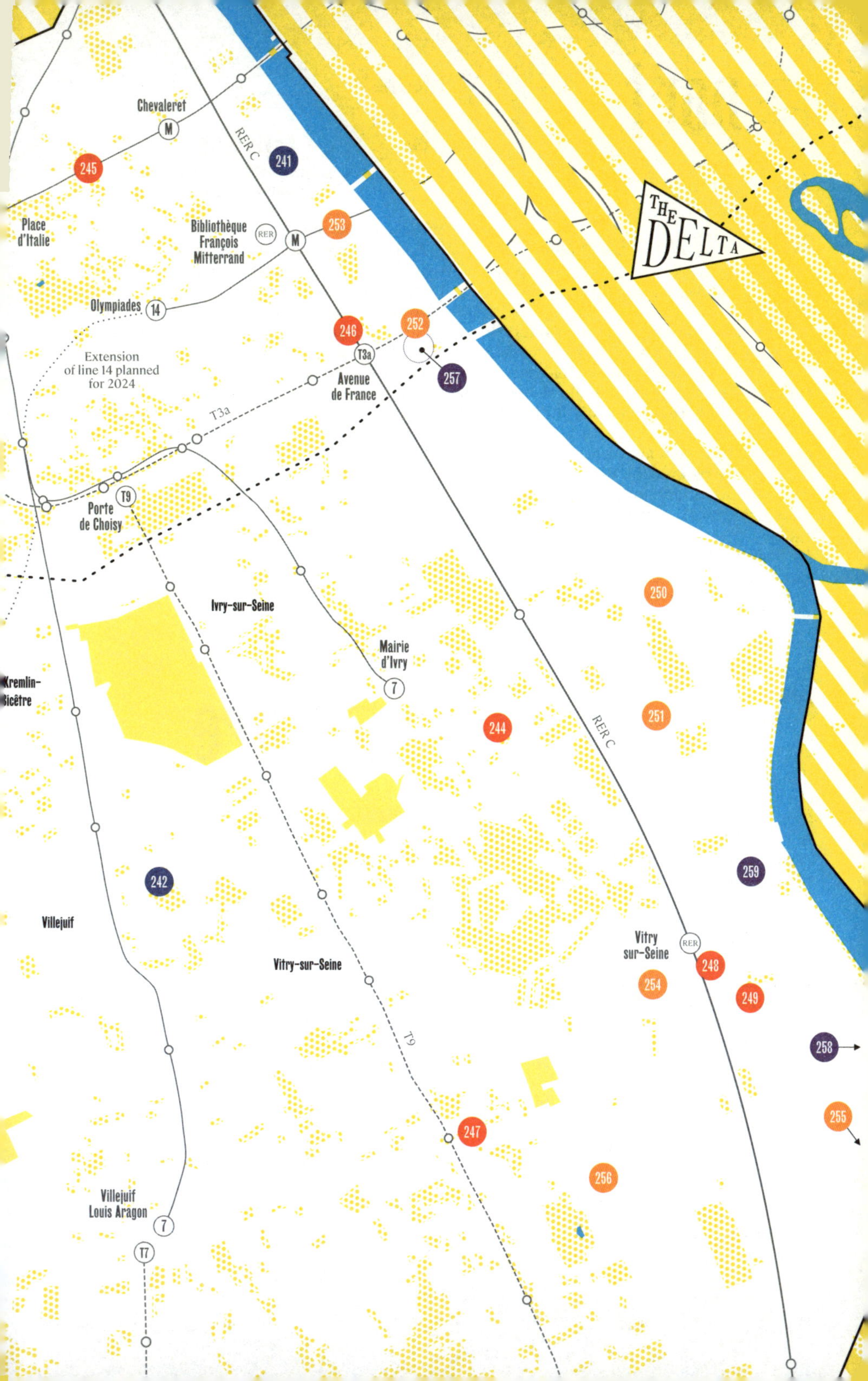
Chevaleret
RER C
241
245
Place d'Italie
Bibliothèque François Mitterrand
RER
M
253
THE DELTA
Olympiades
14
246
252
T3a
257
Extension of line 14 planned for 2024
Avenue de France
T3a
Porte de Choisy
T9
Ivry-sur-Seine
250
Mairie d'Ivry
7
Kremlin-Bicêtre
244
RER C
251
259
242
Villejuif
Vitry-sur-Seine
Vitry sur-Seine
RER
248
254
249
T9
258
255
247
256
Villejuif Louis Aragon
7
T7

sport

ARCUEIL

240 ARCUEIL SKATEPARK

#DÉCORDECINÉMA #SOUSLAUTOROUTE
#SKATESCOOTERROLLERBLADE

The setting is worthy of a film. Under the A6 motorway bridge, the Arcueil skatepark is a real eye-catcher, attracting young and old riders alike. On the ramps, rails, and low walls, skaters, scooterists, and rollerbladers jostle for position. A reminder that skateboarding has been an Olympic discipline since the Tokyo Games in 2021, and that it will be taking over the Place de la Concorde (8th arrondissement) for the Paris 2024 Games – a completely different setting than Arcueil.

Free entry.
Open daily from 8.30am–11pm (10pm on Sunday).

Parc départemental du Coteau de Bièvre,
58, avenue François-Vincent-Raspail, 94110 Arcueil

- RER — B: Laplace
- Bus — 184: Paul-Doumer
- Vélib'— Avenue Paul-Doumer, Arcueil

PARIS

241 GR75 "AROUND PARIS"

#HIKING #50KM
#FUTURESTAR

In the opinion of the President of the Comité départemental de la randonnée pédestre de Paris, there's no doubt about it: "One day, the GR75 will become even more famous than the GR20 trail". Created in 2017 in the context of the campaign for the 2024 Olympic Games, this trail around Paris does indeed have plenty of assets to become a star. It is 50 km long and offers a complete tour of the capital, running along the *périphérique* ring road, the Maréchaux (the former fortifications of Paris) and the former Petite Ceinture railway (see page 34), which is now partly planted with trees. In the 13th arrondissement, it can be reached from the Bibliothèque François-Mitterrand. Then you'll be able to read Paris like an open book.

GR75 "Around Paris", a 50km trail around Paris.
ffrandonnee-idf.fr/randonner/itinéraires/gr-75/

- M — Line 14: Bibliothèque François Mitterrand
- RER — C: Bibliothèque François Mitterrand
- Bus 62, 89, 132, 325: Bibliothèque François Mitterrand
- Vélib'— Rue Pau Casals, Paris 13th

VILLEJUIF

242 ANTREBLOC

#CLIMBING #BARANDTERRACE
#COMFYCOUCHES

Tucked away in an old restored industrial building in a small alleyway, the Antrebloc climbing gym is one of the oldest in Greater Paris. People come here for bouldering, of course – with around fifty routes with a maximum height of 11 metres – but also for the atmosphere, with its cosy bar and a cool terrace with comfortable sofas. Before or after your climbing session, you can lift weights in the gym upstairs.

Price: from €15.
Open Monday to Friday from 11am–11.30pm, Saturday and Sunday from 9am–9pm.

5, rue Henri-Barbusse, 94800 Villejuif
Tel: +33 (0)1 47 26 52 44 / antrebloc.com

- M — Line 7: Léo-Lagrange
- Bus — 185: Henri Barbusse
- Vélib'— Avenue de Paris, Villejuif

culture

GENTILLY

243 MAISON DE LA PHOTOGRAPHIE ROBERT DOISNEAU

#HUMANISTPHOTOGRAPHY
#EXHIBITIONS #FREE

Have you heard of humanist photography? If you're not quite sure what that means, just head down to the Maison de la photographie Robert-Doisneau. Located in a beautiful freestone building, this institution is not a sanctuary dedicated to the great French photographer who was born and lived in Gentilly. Rather, since it first opened in 1996, the Maison has championed humanist photography which has something to say about the world around us, from committed reportage to more intimate subjects, but never purely formal or aesthetic work. All the exhibitions in its programme are shown for the first time in France.

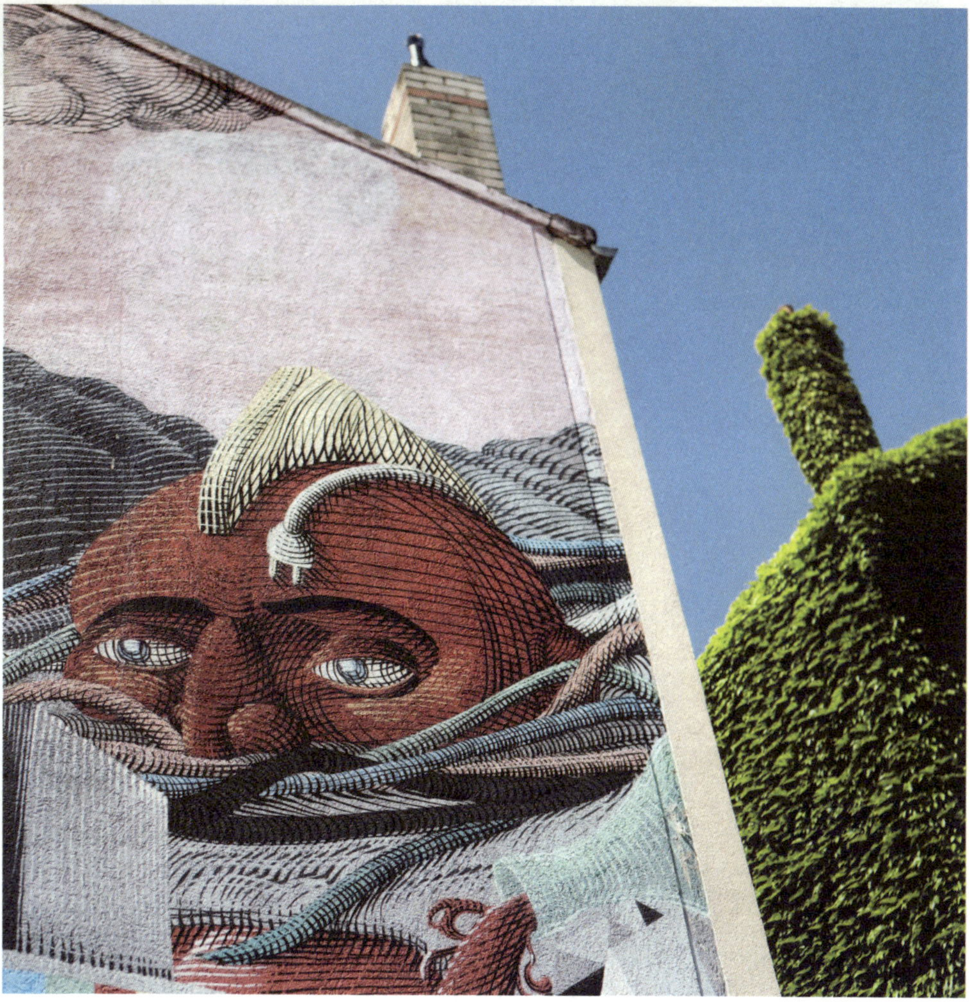

Plugged in | *Passage Irène et Frédéric Joliot-Curie, Vitry-sur-Seine.*

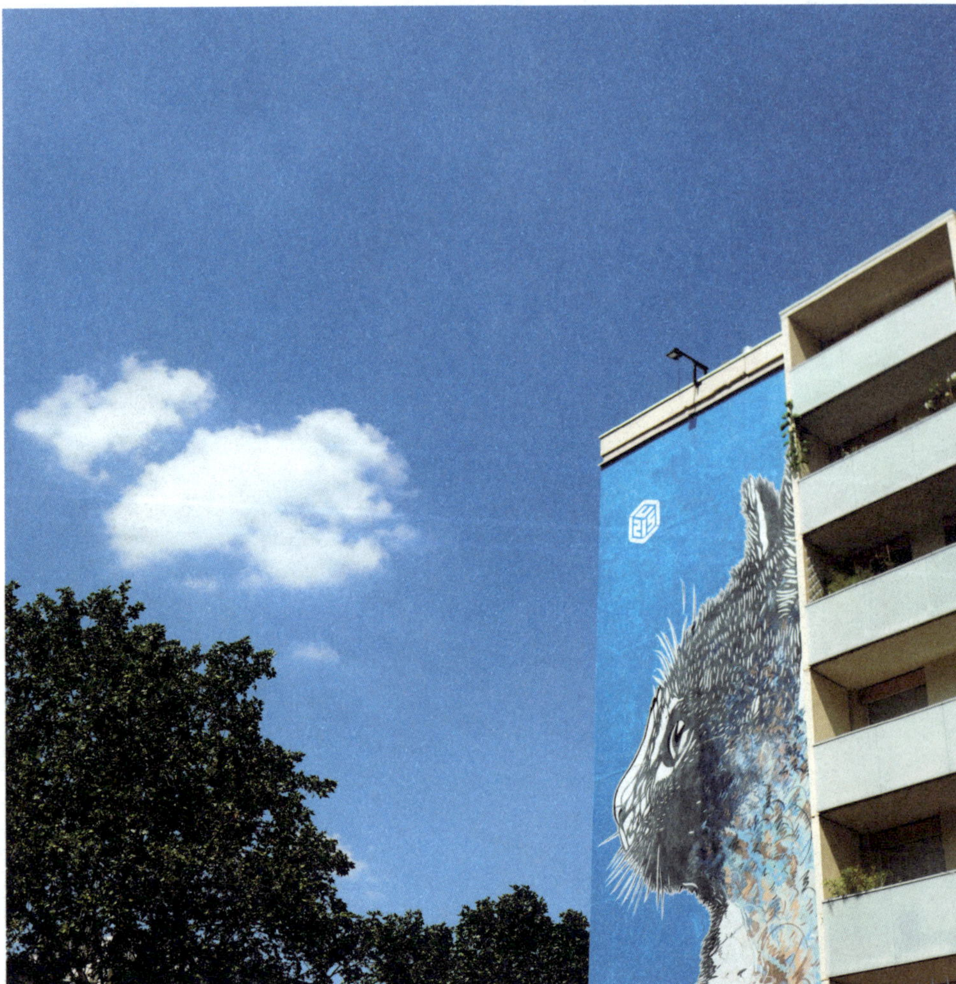

Cloud hunter | *Boulevard Vincent Auriol, Paris.*

Free entry.
Closed Monday and Tuesday.

1, rue de la Division du Général Leclerc, 94250 Gentilly
Tel: +33 (0)1 55 01 04 86
maisondoisneau.grandorlyseinebievre.fr

- RER — B: Gare de Gentilly
- Bus — 57: Division Leclerc / Médiathèque
- Vélib' — Rue Charles Frérot, Gentilly

IVRY-SUR-SEINE

244 CREDAC

#FORMERFACTORY #FREE
#CONTEMPORARYART

The CREDAC has been bringing contemporary art to life in Greater Paris for over thirty years. Before venturing inside, take the time to admire this superb building from another era, an old factory designed to allow as much light as possible to enter its workshops. This is what makes the large spaces that host the CREDAC's three annual exhibitions so attractive, with artists even being invited to adapt their creations to the characteristics of the site. Because the CREDAC is not a museum but a space dedicated to living art. The centre also organizes many activities, particularly for young people. A place to be experienced as much as to be seen.

Free entry.
Closed Monday and Tuesday.

25-29, rue Raspail, 94200 Ivry-sur-Seine
Tel: +33 (0)1 49 60 25 06 / credac.fr

- M — Line 7: Mairie d'Ivry
- RER — C: Ivry-sur-Seine
- Bus — 182: Saint-Just
- Vélib' — Rue Raspail - Manufacture des Oeillets

PARIS

245 BOULEVARD PARIS 13

#GIANTMURALS #BREATHTAKING
#BOULEVARD

For several years, Galerie Itinerrance (see next entry) and the town hall of the 13th arrondissement have been working to transform the line 6 aerial metro into an open-air art gallery. Launched in 2009, the Boulevard Paris 13 project has created numerous large-format murals along Boulevard Vincent Auriol, between the Seine and Place d'Italie, like the Marianne painted near the Nationale metro station. This contemporary interpretation of France's national symbol was painted by Shepard Fairey, the American artist, better known as Obey, who is celebrated for his iconic image for Barack Obama's 2008 campaign, in which the former US president appears on a blue and red background. As for the Marianne, in addition to this wall in the 13th arrondissement, there's even a smaller version hanging in Emmanuel Macron's office. Among the other big players who joined the project are the stencil maker C215, who has become one of the leading figures in street art in France, as well as Invader, whose *Space Invader* mosaics have taken over cities all over the world.

Boulevard Vincent Auriol between Place d'Italie
and the Quai de la Gare metro station, 75013 Paris
boulevardparis13.com

- M — Lines 5, 6, 7: Place d'Italie
- Bus — 27, 47, 57, 59, 61, 64, 67, 83: Place d'Italie
- Vélib' — Place d'Italie, Paris 13th

246 GALERIE ITINERRANCE

#STREETART #FREE
#GIANTMURALS

It is thanks to Mehdi Ben Cheikh, the owner of Galerie Itinerrance, that entire sections of buildings in the 13th arrondissement are covered with gigantic street art murals (see previous entry). In 2004, he opened his first space just a stone's throw from the Bibliothèque Nationale. He soon decided to exhibit his artists on the walls of the area, a logical move given that he sells street art. In search of spaces to be painted, he approached Jérôme Coumet, the mayor of the arrondissement. Together they canvased social housing landlords, of which there are many in this working-class district, to convince them to support the gallery. The first murals were soon commissioned and within a few years the 13th became the reference for street art in Paris. Today, the gallery has a huge space, in keeping with the large format work it exhibits.

Free entry.
Open Tuesday to Saturday from 12–7pm (during exhibitions).

24bis, boulevard du Général Jean Simon, 75013 Paris
Tel: +33 (0)1 44 06 45 39 / itinerrance.fr

- M — Line 14: Bibliothèque François Mitterrand
- RER — C: Bibliothèque François Mitterrand
- Tram — T3a: Avenue de France
- Bus — 89: Porte de France
- Vélib' — Rue de Patay, Paris 13th

VITRY-SUR-SEINE

247 MAC VAL – MUSÉE D'ART CONTEMPORAIN DU VAL-DE-MARNE

#CONTEMPORARYART #EXHIBITIONS #RESTAURANT

The MAC VAL was the first contemporary art museum created in the suburbs. Its opening in Vitry in 2005, had been long prepared by the elected Val-de-Marne representatives of particularly those of the former "red belt" municipalities, where contemporary art has always been very popular. This is why the museum's permanent collection retraces the history of the relations between the Communist Party and the major artists who were often its travelling companions. The collection includes many works by Jean Dubuffet, Sabine Weiss, Robert Doisneau, César, Christian Boltanski and Jean Tinguely. The permanent installation, renewed every six months, showcases the richness of this heritage. In addition, the museum organizes four temporary exhibitions per year that provide an overview of contemporary art. The MAC VAL also has a restaurant, "Le Vert-Verre", open from Tuesday to Sunday which offers seasonal cuisine, to be enjoyed on the terrace when the weather is good.

Price: €5 (full price) / Free for under-26s.
Closed Monday.

Place de la Libération, 94400 Vitry-sur-Seine
Tel: +33 (0)1 43 91 64 20 / macval.fr

- M — Line 7: Villejuif - Louis Aragon then bus 180: Camélinat or bus 172: Musée MAC VAL
- Vélib' — Place Saint-Just, Vitry

248 NOUVEAU GARE AU THÉÂTRE

#SHOWS #OLDTRAINSTATION #BEYONDAVIGNON

The transformation of an old freight station built in 1860 into a thriving cultural centre is the story of the Nouveau Gare au Théâtre. The place has it all: large indoor and outdoor spaces as well as a RER C station to get spectators to their destination. Since 1998, the programming has been on the cutting edge. In 2020 the theatre even opened a dedicated space for authors to work on their writing projects. In 2023, the legendary DJ Laurent Garnier came to do an unforgettable set. All aboard the creativity train.

13, rue Pierre Semard, 94400 Vitry-sur-Seine
Tel: +33 (0)1 43 28 00 50 / nouveaugareautheatre.com

- RER — C: Vitry
- Bus — 180: Vitry-sur-Seine RER
- Vélib' — Gare de Vitry-sur-Seine RER

249 VITRY, STREET ART SHOWCASE

#OPENAIRGALLERY #VITRY&CO #MONUMENTALFRESCOES

Vitry is one of the most beautiful street art galleries in the world. It has hundreds of works on its walls, mailboxes and EDF® electrical cabinets, some of which were created by famous artists such as C215 and Pixel Pancho. The Vitry'n urbaine organisation puts on regular events to promote this extraordinary heritage. Enlarge your Paris followed one of its members and founders, Jean-Philippe Trigla, and produced an itinerary with some of the highlights which is available on enlargeyourparis.fr.

- RER — C: Vitry-sur-Seine
- Bus — 180, 217: Vitry-sur-Seine RER
- Vélib' — Gare de Vitry-sur-Seine RER

lifestyle

IVRY-SUR-SEINE

250 LA MIROITERIE

#URBANBAZAAR #CULTURALCAFE #HUSTLEANDBUSTLE

In the Ivry-port district, on the endless Boulevard Paul Vaillant-Couturier, La Miroiterie and its yellow and red colours really stand out. Opened in 2019 in the midst of all this hustle and bustle, La Miroiterie is a "POP studio", an urban bazaar and a cultural café that thrives on barroom conversation. Here you can meet artists, craftspeople, and local residents, and enjoy a programme of workshops, exhibitions, discussions, shows, drinks, thrift shops, book sales, and happenings of all kinds, all organised by Stéphane and his team. La Miroiterie is a true reflection of its times.

110, boulevard Paul Vaillant-Couturier, 94200 Ivry-sur-Seine
la-miroiterie.org

- RER — C: Ivry-sur-Seine
- Bus 125, 323, 325: Gambetta
- Vélib' — Place de l'Insurrection d'août 1944, Ivry

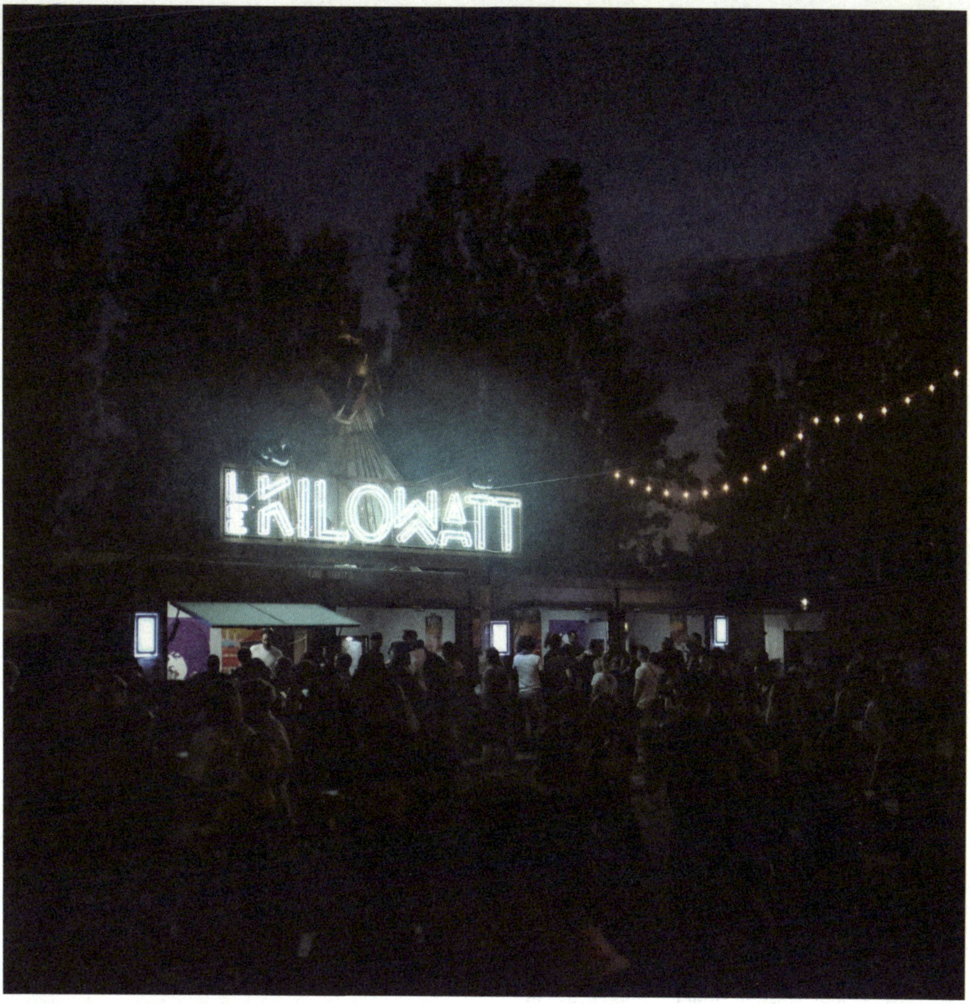

Powered up | *Le Kilowatt, Vitry-sur-Seine.*

251 LA PAGAILLE RECYCLERIE

#PARADISDESCHINEURS #CANTINEÀPRIXLIBRE #COMMESONNOMNELINDIQUEPAS

La Pagaille recycling centre is a treasure trove for bargain hunters. In the warehouse, second-hand items are carefully organized by category (clothes, crockery, furniture, toys, etc.) in clearly identified areas and shelves with finds for no more than a handful of euros. In 2023, La Pagaille launched a line of "Made in La Pagaille" accessories, designed entirely in-house, from conception to production by volunteers. Mini-collections made up of unique pieces combining bags, bumbags, snoods, bobs, hats and other ultra-trendy upcycled items. At lunchtime, you can also enjoy simple dishes at pay-what-you-want prices, shared on large tables so you can get to know your neighbours.

Open Tuesday to Saturday.
Shop open from 1–6pm, canteen from 12–2.30pm.

15, rue Ernest-Renan, 94200 Ivry-sur-Seine
Tel: +33 (0)9 80 53 86 90 / la-pagaille.org

- M — Line 7: Mairie d'Ivry
- RER — C: Ivry-sur-Seine
- Bus — 180: Maurice Gunsbourg
- Vélib' — Rue des lampes, Ivry-sur-Seine

PARIS

252 LE LAVO//MATIK

#BOUTIQUE #URBANARTS #STREETARTWALLS

Benoît, a former stencil artist and musician, opened the Lavo//Matik where he sells books, vinyl, streetwear and a range of artworks. Paintings, resin art, silkscreen prints, prints on paper and t-shirts – there is something for every price and every taste. This cheerful bazaar also serves as a gallery with solo and group exhibitions by emerging artists as well as established stars. In the neighbouring streets, the walls have gradually been taken over by street artists. To stop their work from being systematically scrubbed off by the road department, Benoît contacted the town hall, which appointed him as curator of this open-air gallery. A gem for lovers of urban art.

Closed Monday and Sunday.

20, boulevard du Général Jean Simon, 75013 Paris
Tel: +33 (0)1 45 83 69 92 / lelavomatik.com

- M — Line 14: Bibliothèque François Mitterrand
- RER — C: Bibliothèque François Mitterrand
- Tram — T3a: Avenue de France
- Bus — 89: Porte de France
- Vélib' — Rue de Patay, Paris 13th

253 LES FRIGOS

#MYTHICAL #ARTISTSTUDIOS #TABLEDHOTE

In the 1980s, the Frigos was a magnet for the trendy crowd and the best of the Parisian underground music scene. While those days are over, this former industrial warehouse now serves as an incubator for artists and craftsmen, all of whom pay rent to the city for their studio space. As a result, the building, a raw concrete block that looks like a fortress, is not quite as wild as it used to be, but it has not settled down completely. It includes two tables d'hôte: The Office, run by a graduate of the Ferrandi cooking school, and La Maison des Frigos, located in the studio of a Japanese artist. Another space open to the public, L'Aiguillage, is a small eclectic showroom (design, street art, photography, comics) with a bar and a micro-terrace.

19, rue des Frigos, 75013 Paris
les-frigos.fr

L'Aiguillage, gallery and bar
Tel: +33 (0)1 45 84 52 46

The Office, table d'hôtes
Reservations on theofficelatable.com

La Maison des Frigos, table d'hôtes
Tel: +33 (0)1 44 23 76 20

- M — Line 14: Bibliothèque François Mitterrand
- RER — C: Bibliothèque François Mitterrand
- Bus — 25, 64, 325: Pont de Tolbiac
- Vélib' — Rue Primo Levi, Paris 13th

VITRY-SUR-SEINE

254 CHAKCHOUKA

#DELICATESSEN #RESTAURANT #MIMIANDMOMO

There are many spots that you probably wouldn't have found without this guide, but Chakchouka is one of the best-kept secrets. It's run by Mimi (aka Myriam) and Momo (aka Mohamed), who have turned their delicatessen into a place that is all about sharing. People come here to enjoy their selection of Mediterranean produce, as well as their warm welcome. And let's not forget the cuisine, which Momo rustles up according to his mood. On weekends, the duo put on homemade pizza evenings using produce from the shop. On Sundays, their brunch is out of this world (no, really). The only question is whether you are any good at keeping secrets.

Closed Monday.

2, rue Franklin, 94400 Vitry-sur-Seine
Tel: +33 (0)1 43 91 82 98
Instagram @epiceriechakchouka

- RER — C: Vitry-sur-Seine
- Bus — 180, 182: Gabriel Péri
- Vélib' — Gare de Vitry-sur-Seine

255 LE KILOWATT

#BIGTOP #BEACH #ALTERNATIVE

Going through the Ardoines industrial estate in Vitry (Val-de-Marne) is a disconcerting experience, full of surprises, like this big red and yellow tent set up right next to a huge power station that has now been shut down. Le Kilowatt is the place to come for electro events, big rock concerts (or more intimate ones, like with Manu Chao Acoustic) or to test out your moves on the dancefloor of a small mobile seventies disco. Get plugged in, now you know.

18, rue des Fusillés, 94400 Vitry-sur-Seine
lekilowatt.fr

- RER — C: Les Ardoines
- Bus — 282: Rue des fusillés
- Vélib' — Rue Gabriel Péri, Vitry-sur-Seine

256 LE TOME 47

#COMICBOOKS #EVENTS #GRAPHICNOVELS

Grégoire Orsingher opened Le Tome 47 to have his own shop in which to showcase his favourite comics and graphic novels. Launched in 2013, it is based on a simple principle: in the era of Amazon®, there is no point for a bookshop to try to have everything. So, Grégoire takes his curation seriously with a selection ranging from children's comics to art books. There is also a programme of book-signing brunches and meet-the-author events which will keep you coming back.

Closed Monday.

47, avenue Guy Môquet, 94400 Vitry-sur-Seine
Tel: +33 (0)9 72 41 55 39 / Facebook @bdvitry

- RER — C: Les Ardoines
- Bus — 132, 180: Église de Vitry
- Vélib' — Place de l'Église, Vitry-sur-Seine

where to eat

PARIS

257 LA BRETELLE

#THIRDSPACE #ALLINONE #URBANOASIS

Opened between the 13th arrondissement and Ivry, on the so-called "noodle dish" formed by the ramps of the ring road, the restaurant La Bretelle is one of those third spaces, like Jardin21 (see page 37) or Kilomètre25 (see page 26), that are now springing up around the *périphérique* ring road, which celebrated its fiftieth anniversary in 2023. "The advantage of having the cars above your head is that you don't have your nose in the exhaust fumes like on all the other Parisian terraces," boasts Nicolas Spinola, co-founder of La Bretelle, who wanted to make the place "an oasis in a fairly barren district, with a festive restaurant that mixes simple food at lunchtime, afterwork in the evening, and a cultural programme on weekends". And he has succeeded, with dishes that are as creative as they are delicious, such as satay-fried broccoli with puffed rice, herb salad and confit peppers, or cauliflower cake with Parmesan cheese, pepper emulsion, Provençal herbs, and roasted sesame seeds.

Price: dishes from €6.
Closed Sunday.

9, rue Jean-Baptiste Berlier, 75013 Paris
Tel: +33 (0)7 49 72 23 66 / Instagram @labretelle.paris

- M — Line 14: Bibliothèque François Mitterrand
- RER — C: Bibliothèque François Mitterrand
- Bus — 89: Porte de France
- Tram — Line T3a: Avenue de France
- Vélib' — Rue Marie-Andrée Lagroua Weill-Hallé, Paris

VITRY-SUR-SEINE

258 UNE FRITERIE À VITRY FOOD TRUCK

#DOUBLEFRIEDFRIES #SMASHBURGERS #PERFECTCOMBO

Burger and fries: is there a better combo to win over the under-12s? Of course not, but it's still got to be good quality. And that is what you get from Samir Guédon's food truck in Vitry-sur-Seine. Smash burgers and double-fried beef tallow fries are on the menu, along with a range of sauces that would make any chip shop in the Hauts-de-France green with envy. To be enjoyed right off the truck, amongst the regulars who, of course, have all got the munchies.

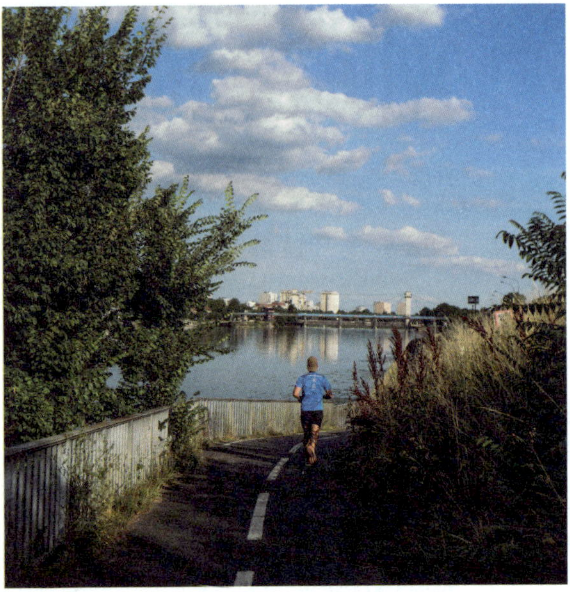

To infinity and beyond... | *Quai Jules Guesde, Vitry-sur-Seine.*

Brooklyn state of mind | *Pont du Port à l'Anglais, Alfortville.*

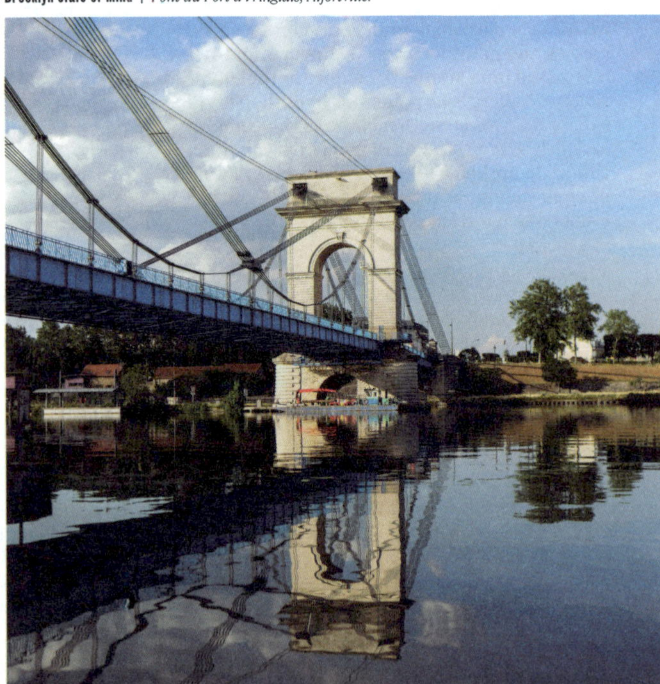

Price: from €3.50.
Wednesday and Thursday, 11am–2pm and 6–9pm

Place Jean-Vilar, 94400 Vitry-sur-Seine.

- Tram — Line T9: Mairie de Vitry
- Bus — 132, 180: Hôtel de Ville de Vitry
- Vélib' — Avenue du général Leclerc, Vitry-sur-Seine

Friday from 11am–2pm and 6–9pm,
Saturday from 11am–9pm non-stop

At the corner of rue Eugène-Hénaff and rue Edith-Cavell, 94400 Vitry-sur-Seine

- RER — C: Vitry-sur-Seine
- Bus — 182: Centre commercial Pont de Vitry
- Vélib' — Avenue du président Salvador-Allende, Vitry-sur-Seine

259 LES PIEDS DANS LE PLAT

#VILLAGESQUARE #LOCALPRODUCE
#RESTAURANTANDGROCERYSHOP

Vitry is not the smallest town in the Greater Paris region (93,000 inhabitants). Yet when you set foot in Les Pieds dans le Plat, you feel like you're in a village. Outside, children play football in the square, while on the pavement and on the terraces, the regulars chat quietly. People come here just as much to drink a coffee as to have a chat. As the place also serves as a restaurant (lunch and dinner) and grocery shop (with produce from local producers located less than 300 km away), there are plenty of reasons to come back.

Price: dishes from €4 to €12 (brunch on Sunday).
Closed Monday.

74, rue Pasteur, 94400 Vitry-sur-Seine
Tel: +33 (0)7 49 83 98 14

- RER — C: Vitry-sur-Seine
- Bus — 180, 217: Port à l'Anglais
- Vélib' — Gare de Vitry-sur-Seine

family

ARCUEIL

260 TIME TRIPPER

#ESCAPEGAME #PRISONBREAK #FORALLAGES

Escape from an Alcatraz prison cell, make your way forward without touching the ground, crawl through an air duct – these are the kinds of challenges worthy of an action movie that Time Tripper has in store. This new kind of escape game takes you through seven eras (Yucatan 850, Bunker 1944, Spaceship 3099, etc.) in which you must solve puzzles and take up team challenges in order to progress. Equal parts nail-biting and hilarious.

Price: from €20/hour, €15/hour for 8–15 year-olds.
Open Wednesday to Sunday during term time,
open daily during school holidays and on public holidays.

20, rue Marcel Vigneron, 94110 Arcueil
Tel: +33 (0)1 69 72 21 70 / timetripper.fr

- RER — B: Laplace
- Bus — 186: Ricardo
- Vélib' — Avenue Paul Doumer, Arcueil

where to sleep

GENTILLY

261 JO&JOE

#YOUTHHOSTEL
#DESIGN #TERRACE

On the edge of the *périphérique*, a stone's throw from the Sacré-Coeur de Gentilly church where the Portuguese community gathers every Sunday, JO&JOE provides a fresh take on the youth hostel. Although it has gone for a designer look, with walls covered in street art pieces by artists like Difus, Rik Lee, or Hazul, it keeps its prices very reasonable. You can cook, watch TV, or do your laundry in the shared space; or grab a burger or some tapas and quench your thirst with beers on tap in the self-service area. Unless you're more of a cocktail person in which case try the Dark & Stormy or some homemade creations like Lychee moi danser or Sex on periph'. JO&JOE also hosts a number of events, all good reasons to enjoy its superb terrace.

Price: from €26 in a dormitory.

93, avenue Paul Vaillant Couturier, 94250 Gentilly
Tel: +33 (0)1 84 23 37 60 / joandjoe.com

- RER — B: Gentilly
- Bus — 125: Gentilly RER
- Vélib' — Gare de Gentilly RER

THE

BAGNEUX
BIÈVRES
CHÂTENAY-MALABRY
CHÂTILLON

ISSY-LES-MOULINEAUX
LE PLESSIS-ROBINSON

ZA

L'HAŸ-LES-ROSES
MALAKOFF
MASSY

MASSY-PALAISEAU
MEUDON
MONTROUGE
PARIS

MXL
RK

SCEAUX
VERRIÈRES-LE-BUISSON

On sunny days, space in the Jardin du Luxembourg is at a premium. If you are after more than just a patch of grass, just hop on the RER B at Luxembourg station for a thirty-minute trip to a much larger Eden whose beauty makes all the other green spaces blush. This eighth wonder of the world is none other than the Parc de Sceaux, a masterpiece of landscaping that is one of the highlights of the XXL Park. With its many oases of greenery, you can explore this area of Greater Paris by riding your bike along the Coulée verte du Sud parisien from Paris to Massy.

THE XXL PARK

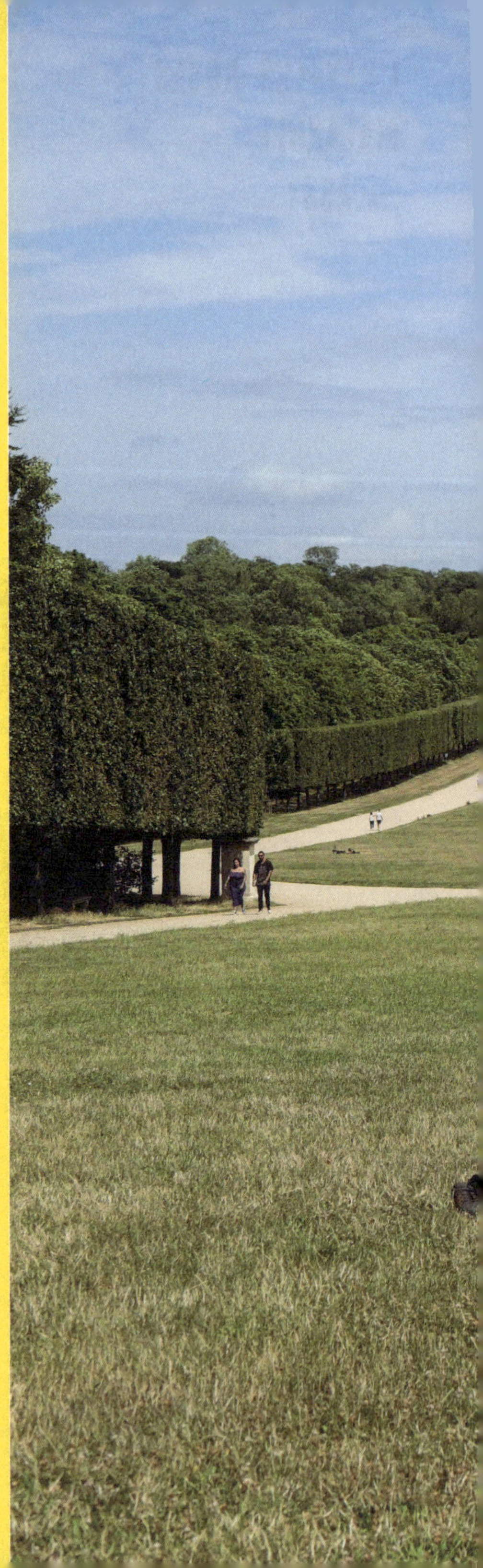

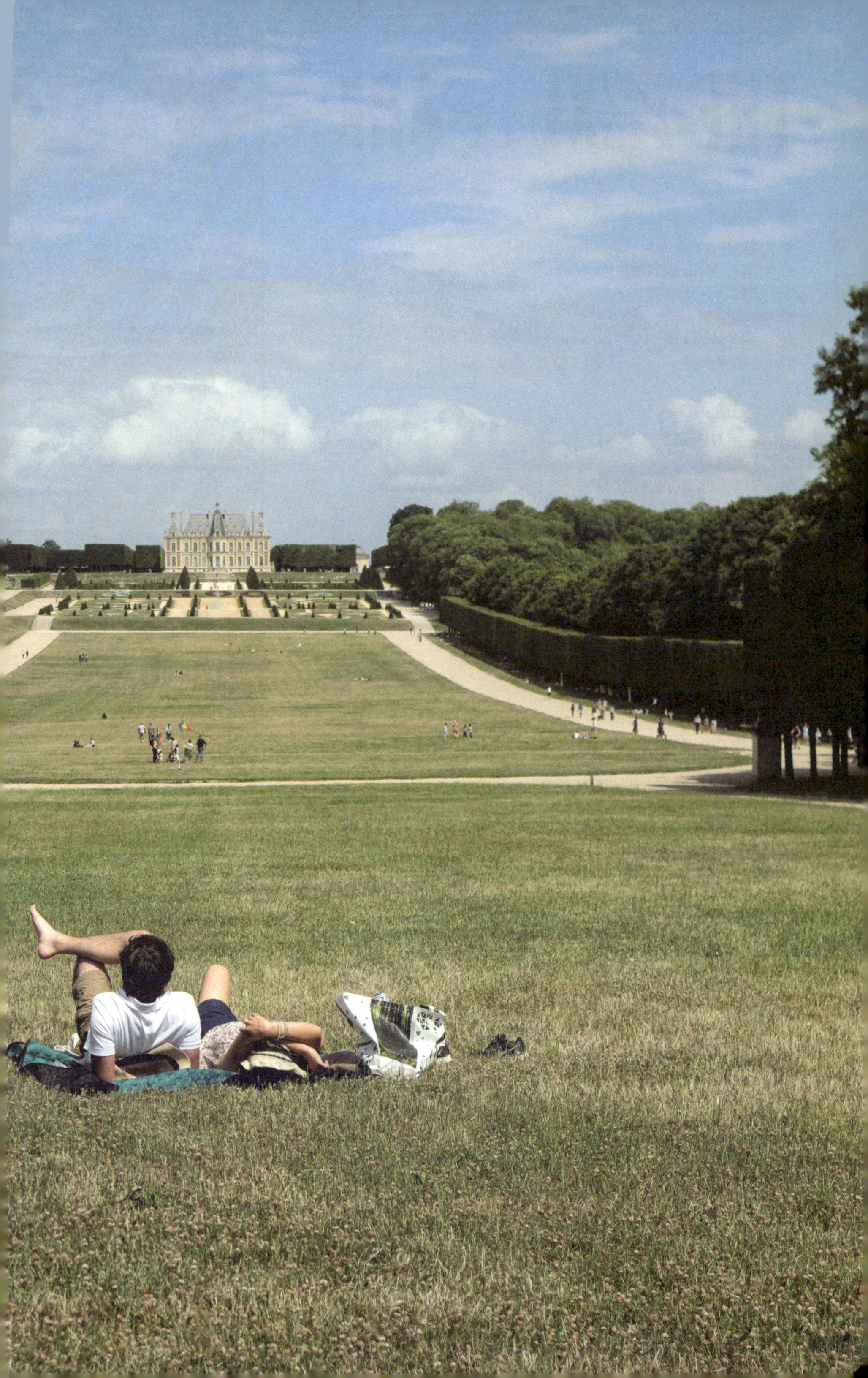

THE XXL PARK

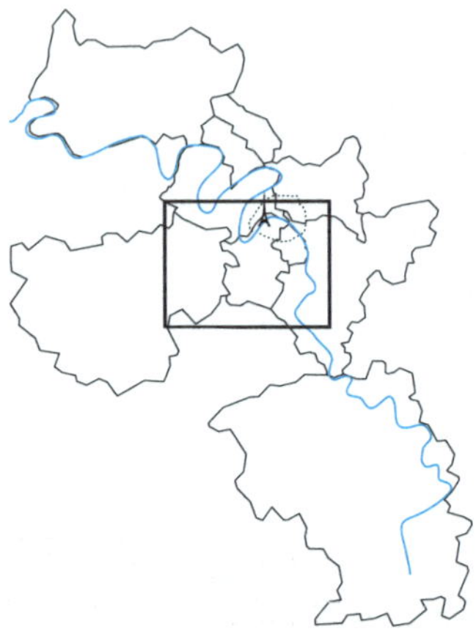

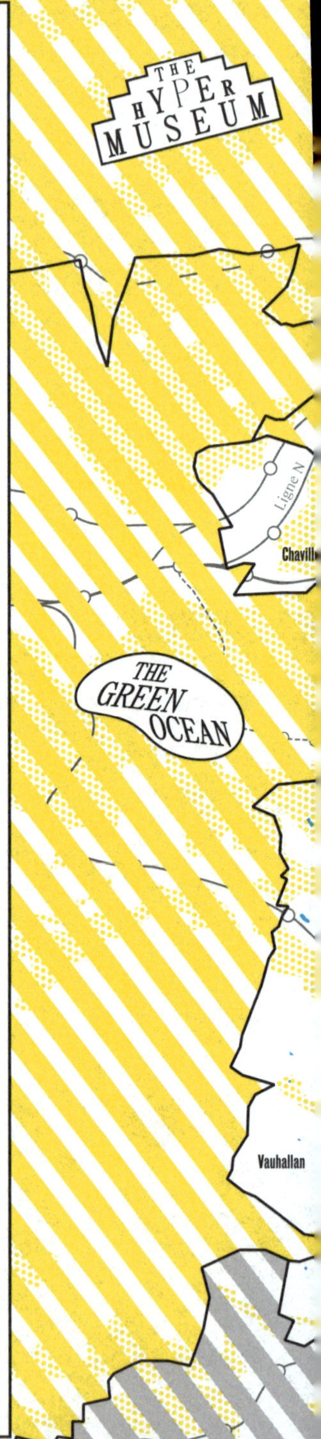

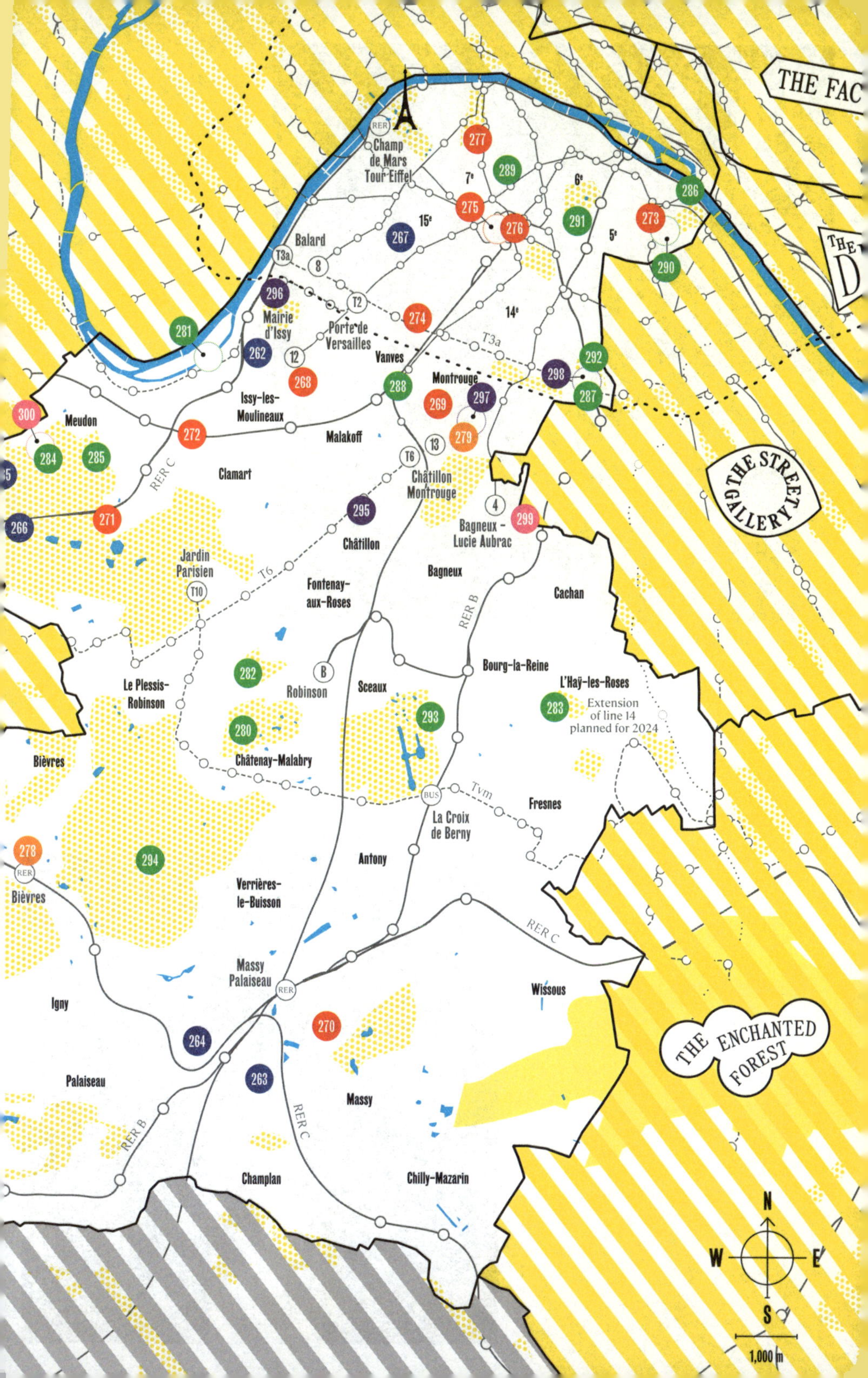
THE FAC
THE D
Champ de Mars Tour Eiffel
7e
6e
15e
5e
14e
Balard
T3a
T2
Mairie d'Issy
Porte de Versailles
Vanves
Montrouge
Issy-les-Moulineaux
Meudon
Malakoff
Clamart
RER C
T6
Châtillon Montrouge
Bagneux - Lucie Aubrac
THE STREET GALLERY
Châtillon
Jardin Parisien
T10
Fontenay-aux-Roses
Bagneux
Cachan
RER B
Bourg-la-Reine
L'Haÿ-les-Roses
Extension of line 14 planned for 2024
Le Plessis-Robinson
Robinson
Sceaux
Bièvres
Châtenay-Malabry
BUS
Tvm
La Croix de Berny
Fresnes
Antony
Verrières-le-Buisson
Bièvres
Massy Palaiseau
Igny
Wissous
THE ENCHANTED FOREST
Palaiseau
Massy
Champlan
Chilly-Mazarin
N
W
E
S
1,000 m

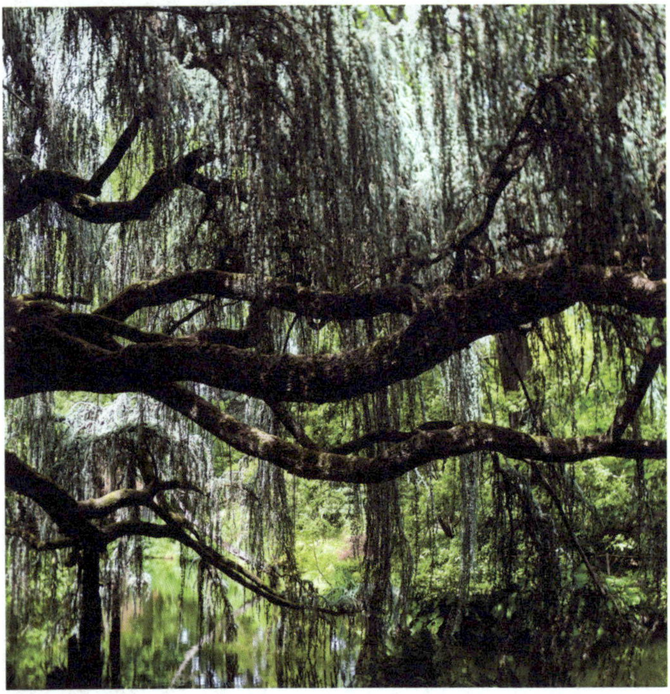

Louisiana, without the alligators | *Arboretum, Châtenay-Malabry.*

Wanted! | *Forêt de Meudon, Meudon.*

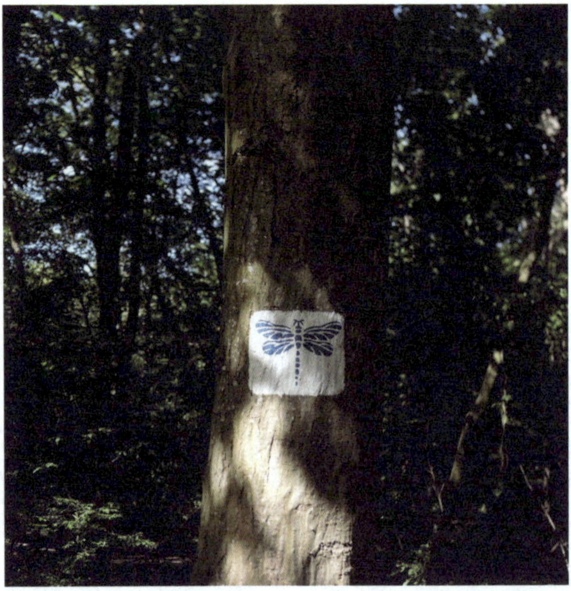

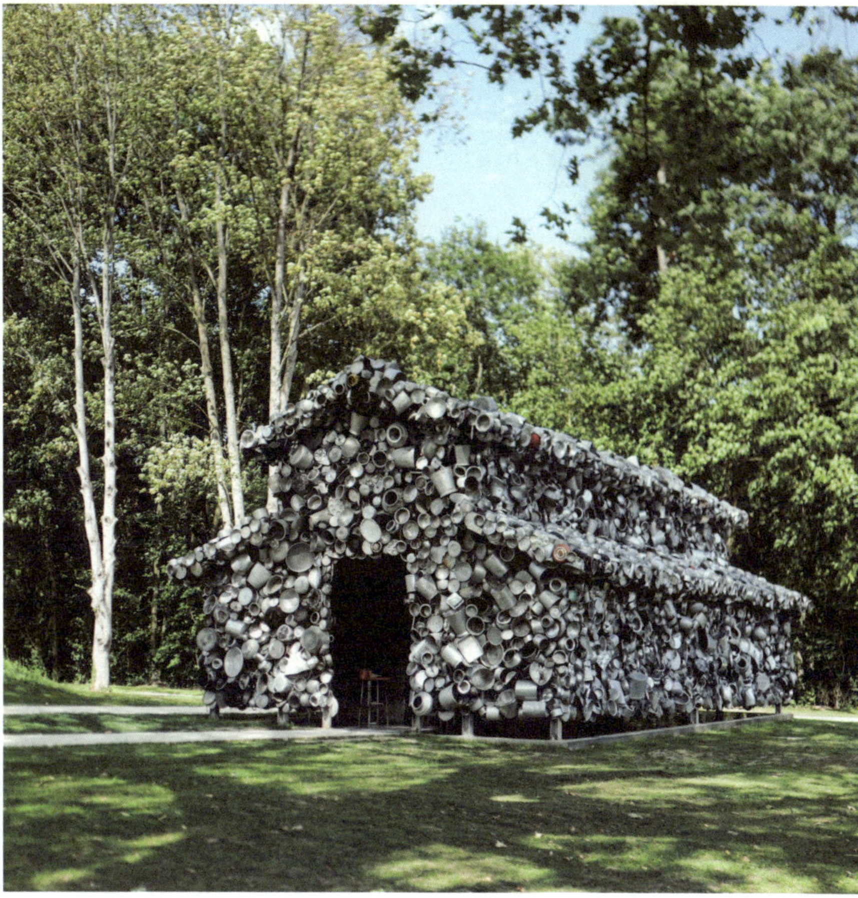

Whose turn is it to wash up? | *Hangar Y, Meudon.*

Sport

ISSY-LES-MOULINEAUX

262 ARKOSE CLIMBING GYM

#CLIMBINGGYM #DONTLOOKDOWN #BENEATHTHETRACKS

The arches of the Issy-les-Moulineaux railway viaduct hide a dizzying secret: a climbing gym hidden under the tracks! At Arkose, you can learn the art of indoor roped climbing across over 1,300 m². After trying out a few holds in the bouldering room to warm up, all you have to do is choose between a private lesson with an instructor or a solo climb, depending on your level. There are over 200 constantly changing routes to choose from.

Price: from €10.
Open daily from 7am to midnight (from age 4).

1-6 boulevard Garibaldi, 92130 Issy-les-Moulineaux
Tel: +33 (0)1 58 88 00 22
arkose.com/issy-les-moulineaux

- M — Line 12: Corentin Celton
- Bus — 123: Roger Salengro
- RER — C: Issy-Val-de-Seine
- Tram — Line T2: Jacques-Henri Lartigue
- Vélib' — Rue Jacques-Henri Lartigue, Issy-les-Moulineaux

MASSY

263 ARKOSE BOULDERING GYM

#CLIMBINGGYM #KIDS #BARRESTAURANT

One of France's biggest climbing gyms is hidden away in an industrial estate in Massy. Over an area of 1,500 m², walls with varying degrees of incline await, covered in multicoloured holds and graded into six levels of difficulty, from "not very difficult" to "abominable". On the ground, thick safety mats are ready to cushion your falls, while a special area is reserved for children, with climbing walls, a slide, and a rope bridge. If you're craving a homemade burger or a local beer after burning all those calories, you won't have to go far. A bar-restaurant with street art murals, wooden tables and club chairs can be found at the foot of these artificial cliffs. A special mention for the welcome, because at Arkose, even though this is climbing country, no one will look down on you.

Price: from €10.
Open daily from 7am to midnight.

4, rue Galvani, 91300 Massy
Tel: +33 (0)1 64 47 07 47 / arkose.com/massy

- M — Line 18 (planned 2025/2026): Massy Palaiseau
- RER — B, C: Massy – Palaiseau
- Bus — 319: Galvani NordSud

MASSY-PALAISEAU

264 RECYCLERIE SPORTIVE

#GOODDEALS #REPAIRWORKSHOP #CAFÉ

There are only a dozen or so in France. The Recyclerie sportive in Massy opened in 2020 in a former railway station. The idea is to offer sports equipment donated by individuals, shops and brands at low prices. And that's not all: there's also a bar, O'Massy Pale, run by two local microbrewers, a joint repair workshop for bikes, skates, scooters, and rollerblades, and a yoga room. What more could you ask for?

Open Wednesday to Saturday

7, place Pierre-Sémard, 91300 Massy
Tel: +33 (0)9 81 94 72 65 / recyclerie-sportive.org

- RER — B, C: Massy-Palaiseau
- Bus — 119, 196, 199, 319, 399: Massy – Palaiseau

MEUDON

265 ACCROCAMP

#TREETOPS #QUICKJUMP #CLOSESTFORESTTOPARIS

When you think of treetop confidence courses, you don't think of jumping from tree to tree a mere 7 km from the Paris *périphérique*. But that is just what you get in the Meudon forest (see page 198), the forest closest to Paris. This is where AccroCamp has opened seven courses, just 500 metres from Chaville – Rive Gauche station. And for thrill-seekers, there's the added bonus of a quickjump freefall from a 15-metre high diving board.

Price: €10 to €35 per person (online booking is recommended).
Open from February to November (from age 4).

Route des Huit Bouteilles, 92370 Chaville
Tel: +33 (0)1 84 19 94 68 / accrocamp.com

- Transilien — Line N: Chaville – Rive Gauche
- Bus — 171: Gare de Chaville – Rive Gauche
- Vélib' — Place Gaston Audonnet, Chaville

266 URBAN SOCCER

#FOOTBALLINTHEFOREST #15PITCHES #POSTMATCHBURGER

In the heart of the Meudon forest, this Urban Soccer centre is set up in an exceptional natural setting. It has a total of 15 pitches (13 outdoor pitches, one indoor pitch and a 7-a-side pitch) and a club house for the post-match debate on a Chesterfield sofa or to grab a bite to eat with a burger or a big salad.

Price: from €65 to €161, depending on the type of pitch, the time of day, and the day of the week.
Open daily.

50, route de la Mare Adam, 92360 Meudon la Forêt
Tel: +33 (0)1 78 16 43 90 / urbansoccer.fr

267 WAVE IN PARIS

#ARTIFICALWAVE #SURFORBODYBOARD #HANGTEN

Behind the golden facade and corrugated roof of the warehouse at 107 rue de la Croix-Nivert lies the capital's only artificial wave (16 metres long and 10 metres wide!). This high-tech facility uses a powerful water current to propel you along a sloping water surface for indoor surfing or body-boarding. Book your one-hour session and, thanks to the expert advice of the instructors, after a few minutes you'll be riding the wave like Kelly Slater on a Hawaiian breaker. At the end of the session, you can relax in the cosy bar, with a beautiful view of the artificial wave through a large bay window.

Price: from €25 an hour.
Open Monday to Friday 8.30am to 11pm, Saturday and Sunday 8.30am to 8pm.

107, rue de la Croix Nivert, 75015 Paris
Tel: +33 (0)6 66 07 49 75 / waveinparis.com

- M — Line 8: Commerce
- Bus — 39, 80: Abbé Groult
- Vélib' — Rue de la Croix-Nivert, Paris 15th

culture

ISSY-LES-MOULINEAUX

268 MUSÉE FRANÇAIS DE LA CARTE À JOUER

#ONEOFAKIND #POKERFACE #ESCAPEGAME

This museum of playing cards is unique in France: its impressive collection traces the history of card games around the world. In all, 11,000 sets of cards have been collected, highlighting the cultures and eras that gave birth to them. To attract a broad audience – this is not just a museum for card geeks – the museum also offers an escape game for players from the age of seven (teams of three to six players) in which you must find the Peace Cup and stop the Great Battle of Cards from starting up again.

Price: €6 (full price) / Free for under-26s.
Open Wednesday, Thursday and Friday from 11am–5pm, Saturday and Sunday from 2–6pm.
Annual closure from 15–31 August.
Escape game: €8 per person, sessions throughout the year on Sunday at 2.15pm and 3.45pm.

16, rue Auguste Gervais, 92130 Issy-les-Moulineaux
Tel: +33 (0)1 41 23 83 60 / museecarteajouer.com

- M — Line 12: Mairie d'Issy
- Bus — 169, 323: Musée
- Vélib' — Avenue Victor Cresson, Issy-les-Moulineaux

MALAKOFF

269 MAISON DES ARTS DE MALAKOFF

#CONTEMPORARYART #FREEENTRY #CHARACTERPROPERTY

The Maison des Arts de Malakoff illustrates the link that some cities in the former "red suburbs" (with communist mayors) established with contemporary art in order to make it accessible to as many people as possible. Opened in 1997 in a character property, it hosts four free exhibitions of a consistently high standard each year, all made accessible through a series of talks. The Maison belongs to the Tram network (tram-idf.fr), which includes some thirty venues dedicated to contemporary art on either side of the *périphérique*. For the record, this miniature palace once caught the

eye of André Malraux (1901–1976), then Minister of Culture, as he was travelling to the Chevreuse valley (see page 80).

Free entry.
Open Wednesday to Friday from noon to 6pm / Saturday and Sunday from 2–6pm / Monday and Tuesday by appointment.

105, avenue du 12 Février 1934, 92240 Malakoff
maisondesarts.malakoff.fr

- M — Line 13: Malakoff – Rue Étienne Dolet
- Bus — 194, 388: 12 Février 1934
- Vélib' — 102 avenue Pierre Brossolette, Malakoff

MASSY

270 PAUL B

#LIVEMUSIC #FESTIVAL
#SOUNDOFTOMORROW

Already rather proud of its opera, Massy can also boast of having one of the most beautiful concert halls in Greater Paris. With its two stages, one large and the other more intimate with a mezzanine floor, Paul B spares no effort in concocting a programme that combines headliners and emerging talents. A genuine melting pot of modern musical genres. The venue's expertise is highlighted each year in the autumn during the Primeurs de Massy, a festival that takes you off the beaten track and gives you the opportunity to work on your future playlists.

6, allée de Québec, 91300 Massy
Tel: +33 (0)1 69 75 12 80 / paul-b.fr

- M — Line 18 (planned 2025/2026): Massy Opéra
- RER — B, C: Massy-Verrières
- Bus — 119, 319: Hélène Boucher

MEUDON

271 HANGAR Y

#AIRSHIPHANGAR #ARTTRAIL
#INTHEFOREST

Having been abandoned for some forty years on the banks of the Etang de Chalais, this former airship hangar in the forêt de Meudon (see page 198) reopened to the public in 2023 after three years of work. A spectacular renovation for a venue that now hosts contemporary art exhibitions as well as cultural and scientific events, all surrounded by a park with an art trail, children's play areas, and its own café-restaurant.

Price: €3 admission to the park.
Park open daily / café-restaurant open daily (restaurant only Thursday to Sunday).

9, avenue de Trivaux, 92190 Meudon
Tel: +33 (0)1 84 74 45 50 / hangar-y.com

- Transilien — Line N: Meudon then bus 169, 289, or 389 to Cimetière de Trivaux stop

272 MUSÉE RODIN – VILLA DES BRILLANTS

#ARTISTRESIDENCE
#PARK #GRAVEOFRODIN

Beyond its Parisian location, the Rodin Museum also has a less well-known space in Meudon located in the Villa des Brillants. Overlooking the Seine, this beautiful residence was acquired at the end of the 19th century by Auguste Rodin. The villa provides an insight into the sculptor's inner world but also to his workshop where two literary monuments, Balzac and Hugo, appear in their birthday suits, carved from head to toe by the master's chisel. Other sculptures populate the place including plaster sketches of masterpieces such as *The Gates of Hell* or *The Burghers of Calais*. Not to mention a monumental *Thinker* in the grounds, under which the artist and his companion Rose Beuret lie surrounded by a park full of nooks and crannies conducive to meditation.

Free.
Open Saturday and Sunday from 10am–6pm (annual closure from October to spring).

19, avenue Auguste Rodin, 92190 Meudon
Tel: +33 (0)1 41 14 35 00 / musee-rodin.fr

- RER — C: Meudon Val Fleury then bus 169: Paul Bert

PARIS

273 ARÈNES DE LUTÈCE

#MINICOLISEUM #SQUARE
#MODERNGLADIATORS

Although more discreet than the Coliseum of Rome, the Arènes de Lutèce are a remarkable vestige of Paris's Gallo-Roman past. Incredibly well preserved, they are tucked away in Square Capitan, taking you back in time to the days of the gladiators, who have given up their place in the arena to pétanque players. Take a seat in the stands to enjoy the show and unfold your picnic tablecloth. And to see the place come alive even more, look out for the Nuits des Arènes festival which takes place every summer with a programme of concerts, theatre and talks.

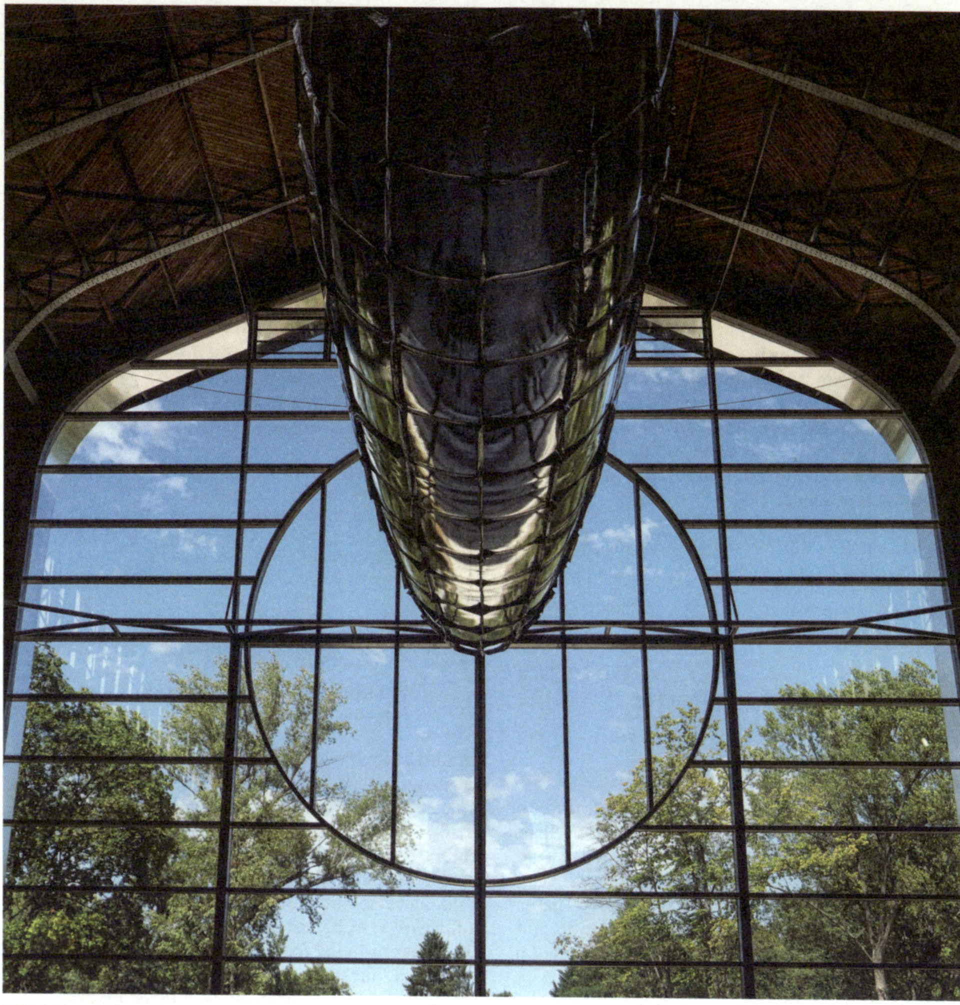

X files in Hangar Y | *Hangar Y, Meudon.*

49, rue Monge, 75005 Paris
Tel: +33 (0)1 45 35 02 56 / paris.fr
- M — Line 7: Jussieu
- Bus — 47: Cardinal-Lemoine
- Vélib' — Rue Lacépède, Paris

274 LE MONFORT

#THEATRE #ICONOCLASM
#SURPRISING

There is no way of knowing what will happen in the Monfort, so you have to enter with your eyes closed and play the game. As soon as you approach the theatre and its strange metallic tent, the show can begin at any time. You might be led to believe that the performance has been cancelled or stumble upon a play that seems to be ending. Theatre, circus, clowns, cabaret, puppets: at the Monfort, everything is possible.

106, rue Brancion, 75015 Paris
Tel: +33 (0)1 56 08 33 88 / theatresilviamonfort.eu
- M — Line 13: Porte de Vanves
- Tram — T3a: Brancion
- Bus — 95: Brancion
- Vélib' — Rue Brancion, Paris 15th

275 MUSÉE BOURDELLE

#ARTISTWORKSHOP
#GARDEN #SCULPTURES

In the work of the sculptor Antoine Bourdelle (1861–1929) the extraordinary begins in the garden where you will come face to face with an Adam hiding his face but little else. Here, everything conspires to a stroll along the flowered paths surrounding the artist's studio whose rooms and spaces have remained intact. It is less of a museum visit than an encounter with Gustave Eiffel, Beethoven, Anatole France or Rodin... Bourdelle welcomes you into his home for a quiet and intimate stroll through early twentieth-century Montparnasse, famous for its artist studios. Once you have filled up on art, grab a table at the Rhodia café-restaurant, one of Paris's best kept gastronomic secrets.

Price: exhibitions-talks €7 /
Free admission to the permanent collection.
Closed Monday.

18, rue Antoine Bourdelle, 75015 Paris
Tel: +33 (0)1 49 54 73 73 / bourdelle.paris.fr
- M — Line 4, 6, 12, 13: Montparnasse – Bienvenüe
- Bus — 28, 39, 58, 91, 92, 94, 95, 96: Gare Montparnasse
- Vélib' — Avenue du Maine, Paris 15th

276 MUSÉE DE LA POSTE ®

#6CENTURIESOFMAIL #FROMHORSESTODRONES
#FROMSTAMPSTOMAILART

After a six-year makeover, the Musée de La Poste ® reopened in 2019 to present the exciting history of mail distribution since the fifteenth century around three main themes: "Crossing the land", which presents an inventory of the means of postal transport, from horses to drones, trains, boats, and planes; "Men and trades", which looks behind the scenes of this great human chain and "La Poste, art and stamps", which dives into the world of philately. The museum also holds temporary exhibitions. A visit as easy as popping a letter in the post.

Price: €9 (full price) / Free for under-26s.
Closed Tuesday.

34, boulevard de Vaugirard, 75015 Paris
Tel: +33 (0)1 42 79 24 24 / museedelaposte.fr
- M — Lines 4, 6, 12 and 13: Montparnasse – Bienvenüe
- Transilien — Line N: Gare Montparnasse
- Bus — 39, 95: Armorique – Musée postal
- Vélib' — Boulevard de Vaugirard, Paris 15th

277 MUSÉE RODIN

#GARDEN #HÔTELPARTICULIER
#IMAGINARYCORRESPONDENCE

Paradoxically, it is not in the works presented in the museum that Auguste Rodin's (1840–1917) presence is felt most keenly but rather through wandering along the paths of the large garden of the Hôtel de Biron. There, in the shade of tall trees, Auguste speaks to you as if you were an old friend; of his successes and the scandals caused by some of his works; of Balzac, his companions and the sweetness of living in the countryside. Start by taking a detour through this magnificent garden, which overlooks both the Dôme des Invalides and the Eiffel Tower ®, and read Rodin's imaginary correspondence. They are judiciously placed, all along the way, in the form of small notes that provide a sensitive and essential introduction to better enjoy the museum visit afterwards.

Price: €13 (full price) / Free for under-26s.
Open Tuesday to Sunday from 10am–6.30pm.
Closed Monday.

79, rue de Varenne, 75007 Paris
Tel: +33 (0)1 44 18 61 10 / musee-rodin.fr
- M — Line 13: Varenne
- Bus — 69: Esplanade des Invalides
- Vélib' — Boulevard des Invalides, Paris 7th

lifestyle

BIÈVRES

278 MILLE FEUILLES

#BOOKSHOP #RESTAURANT #LOCALPRODUCE

Bookshops and the smell of food simmering on the stove do not usually go hand in hand. However, when you enter the Mille Feuilles at lunchtime, your attention won't be grabbed by the books, at least at first. That's because this bookshop is also a restaurant and a tea room with a panoramic view of the Verrières forest (see page 205). So, what does bookshop food look like? Actually, it depends. Véronique, the host, bases her menu on the seasons and what her producers have on offer, which might lead to a brandade of organic chicken from Bièvres or a tagine of organic lamb from the Ardennes. Another characteristic of the Mille Feuilles: there is always something going on. In addition to traditional book signings, there are regular exhibitions, concerts, talks and the space even acts as an art gallery. You could almost forget the books in all this. But they are there, and for all ages. In fact, you can even find them in the dining room to keep the children busy.

Dishes from €6 to €18.
Open Tuesday to Saturday from 10.30am–7pm.
Sunday from 10.30am–1pm / Closed Monday.

28, rue de l'Église, 91570 Bièvres
Tel: +33 (0)1 69 85 32 69 / millefeuilles.biz

- RER — C: Bièvres
- Bus — 15, 6133: Mairie de Bièvres

MONTROUGE

279 LA BOUTIQUE DU FUTUR

#CONCEPTSTORE #DESIGN #ONEOFAKINDGIFTS

Because finding an original gift never gets any easier, the Boutique du Futur is here to help. This one-of-a-kind concept store sells the inventions of its creator, Nicolas Trüb, a former telecoms engineer. And over the past twenty years, there have been dozens of them including Zébulon, the ingenious spring-shaped sock holder, Umbrelhat, the umbrella that you don't need to hold, and Savosec, a small tripod that clings to a bar of soap and stops it from melting on the sink. Some of these objects, such as the babyplane which will turn a baby spoon into an airplane, are sought after the world over. While the boutique's success is international, production is 100% local. No "made in China" here, but "made in France"; in fact, mostly made in Île-de-France. And that's not all. About fifteen years ago, this whimsical and talented engineer created the Cyclospace, a pedal- and solar-powered car that can transport up to eight people, depending on the version. You can hire it for a few hours a day, or a whole weekend.

Closed Monday and Sunday.

18, rue Périer, 92120 Montrouge
Tel: +33 (0)1 46 56 00 86 / laboutiquedufutur.fr

- M — Line 4: Mairie de Montrouge
- Bus — 128: Boileau
- Vélib' — Avenue Verdier, Montrouge

outdoors

CHÂTENAY-MALABRY

280 PARC DE LA VALLÉE-AUX-LOUPS

#GREENGEM #TREEOFTHEYEAR #CHATEAUBRIAND

Recognized as a Jardin remarquable (Remarkable Garden), the Parc de la Vallée-aux-Loups has something for everyone, starting with hikers who appreciate the ups and downs of its paths. Lovers of flora are also in for a treat. The area contains an arboretum with nearly 500 tree species, including a weeping blue Atlas cedar, named "Tree of the Year" in 2015. Lovers of literature won't be disappointed either: Chateaubriand, banned from the capital by Napoleon, bought the estate and settled there from 1807 to 1818. His residence, where he began writing his *Memoirs from Beyond the Grave*, is open to visitors, as is the Velleda tower, which served as his study for over a decade. You can even walk as far as the Île Verte (opposite the Vallée-aux-Loups), a wild garden with a small lake and an old vegetable garden.

Free admission.
Open daily (opening times vary according to the season / Maison de Chateaubriand closed on Monday).

87, rue Châteaubriand, 92290 Châtenay-Malabry
vallee-aux-loups.hauts-de-seine.fr

- RER — B: Robinson
- Bus — 14: Arboretum
- Vélib' — Gare de Robinson, Sceaux

ISSY-LES-MOULINEAUX

281 PARC DE L'ÎLE SAINT-GERMAIN

#ISLEOFBEAUTY #FIELDS #SPRAWLINGLAWNS

It is a pity that the title of "isle of beauty" has already been given to the island of Corsica, because the Île Saint-Germain is just as deserving of this honour. Once you arrive in this easily accessible Garden of Eden, you will instantly fall under the spell of its mosaic of rural-style gardens. All you have to do is choose one to serve as your reading room, nap area or dining room. You can also opt for the common room and enjoy the park's large, sun-filled lawns. On the east of the island there is an unusual 24-metre-high totem pole, the *Tower with Figures*, by Jean Dubuffet (1901–1985). Designed as a vertical labyrinth, it is scheduled to reopen in 2024.

Free admission.
Open daily (opening times vary according to the season).

170, quai de Stalingrad, 92130 Issy-les-Moulineaux
Tel: +33 (0)6 64 40 57 44 / hauts-de-seine.fr
and tourauxfigures.hauts-de-seine.fr

- RER — C: Issy-Val de Seine
- Tram — T2: Jacques-Henri Lartigue
- Bus — 260: Passerelle de l'Europe
- Vélib' — Rue Camille Desmoulins, Issy

LE PLESSIS-ROBINSON

282 PARC HENRI-SELLIER

#FORESTPARK #SPRAWLINGLAWNS #TERRACEWITHAVIEW

At the intersection of rue de l'Étang de l'Écoute-s'il-pleut and rue de Malabry, a few steps lead up to a large terrace. Once your ascent is complete, your eyes can wander across a panorama of southern Greater Paris to contemplate the Parc de la Vallée-aux-Loups (see page 197), the Parc de Sceaux and the Forêt de Verrières (see page 205) and the planes taking off from the Orly runways (see page 109). Once you have taken in the view, all you have to do is walk through this 27-hectare forest park, picnic on its lawns, take a seat in its theatre of green and try to find the giant California redwood that was planted here in the 19th century.

Free admission.
Open daily (opening times vary according to the season).

Rue de l'Étang de l'Écoute-s'il-pleut,
92350 Le Plessis-Robinson
Tel: +33 (0)6 64 40 57 52 / hauts-de-seine.fr

- RER — B: Robinson
- Bus — 179, 195, 390, 395, 415: Charles Pasqua
- Vélib' — Gare de Robinson, Sceaux

L'HAŸ-LES-ROSES

283 ROSERAIE DU VAL-DE-MARNE

#SUMMERTIME #11000ROSEBUSHES #ROSESARENTALWAYSRED

It's no surprise that the town of L'Haÿ-les-Roses has a rose garden, but this sublime garden is one of a kind, gathering one of the most important collections of old roses in the world. Created in the 19th century by Jules Gravereaux, who made his fortune by participating in the creation of Le Bon Marché® in Paris, it has 11,000 roses and nearly 3,000 different species. Open from May to September, it is located in the heart of a 13-hectare park with a picnic area, themed gardens and children's playgrounds.

Price: €4 (full price), €2 (reduced price) / Free for under-5s.
Open from June to September from 10am–7pm.

Rue Albert Watel, 94240 L'Haÿ-les-Roses
Tel: +33 (0)1 47 40 04 04 / roseraie.valdemarne.fr

- M — Line 14 (planned 2024/2026): L'Haÿ-les-Roses
- RER — B: Bourg-la-Reine then bus 172, 184, 192: Sous-préfecture – Roseraie

MEUDON

284 FORÊT DE MEUDON

#CLOSESTFORESTTOPARIS #OVER1000HECTARES #STEEPSLOPES

Only 5 km from the périphérique, the Fôret de Meudon is the closest forest to Paris. Covering over 1,000 hectares, 50 times the size of the Jardin du Luxembourg, with its sometimes-steep paths and many ponds, it has everything you need for an outdoor getaway. It also contains two archaeological curiosities: the menhir of the Pierre aux Moines, which is said to be over 4,000 years old, as well as the dolmens of the Missions oak tree, installed at

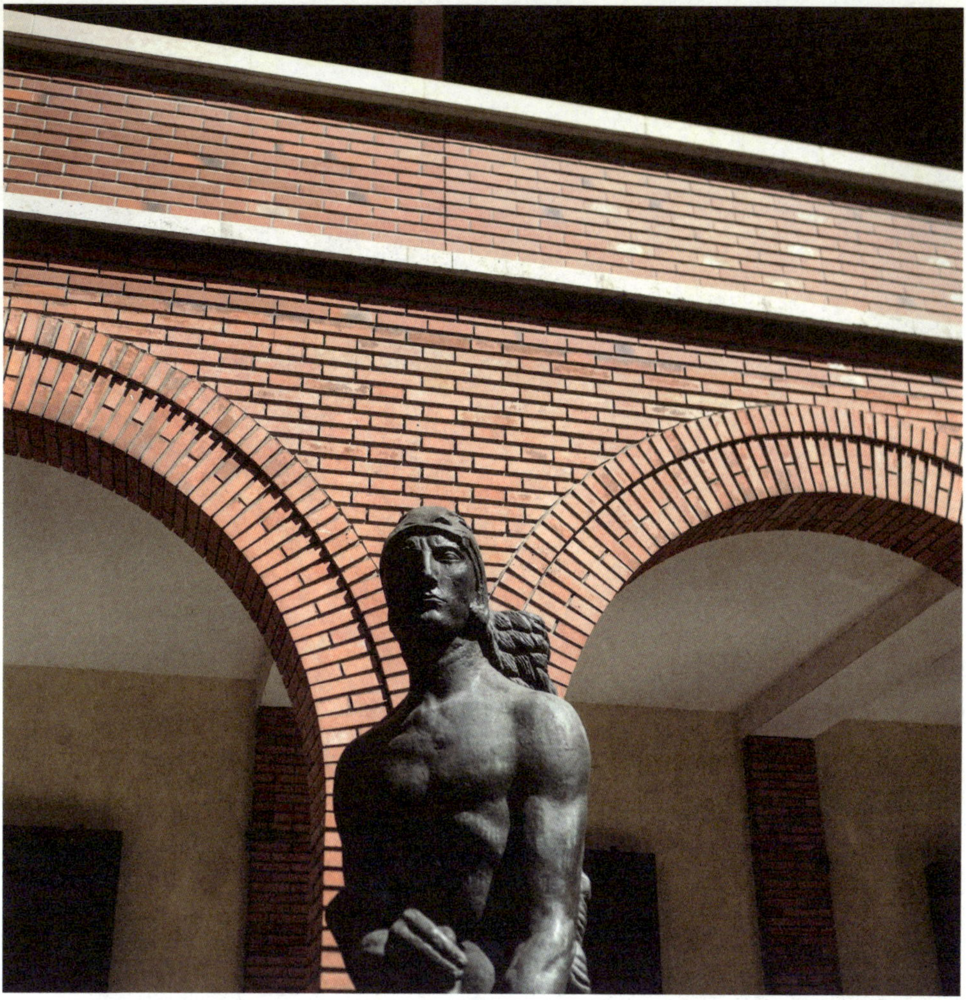

Of brick and bronze | *Musée Bourdelle, Paris.*

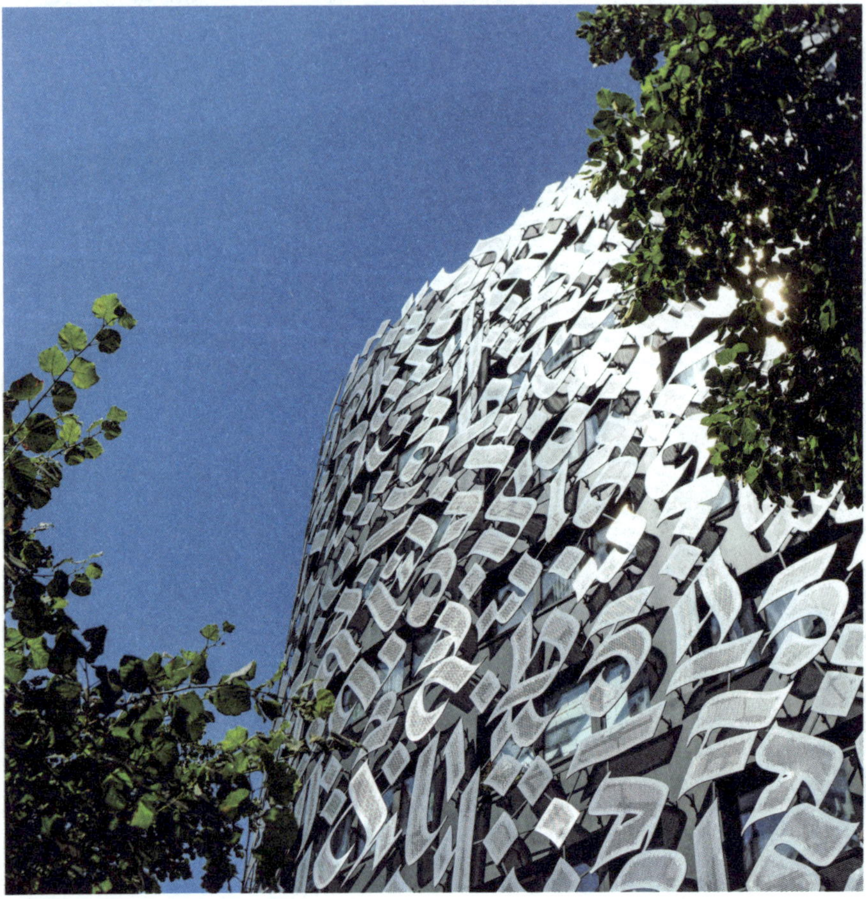

Literary graffiti | *Cité Universitaire internationale, Paris.*

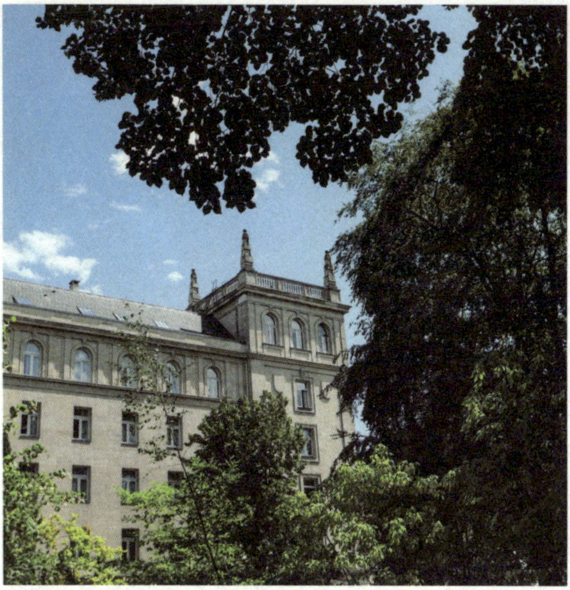

Hogwarts | *Cité Universitaire internationale, Paris.*

Student incubator | *Cité Universitaire internationale, Paris.*

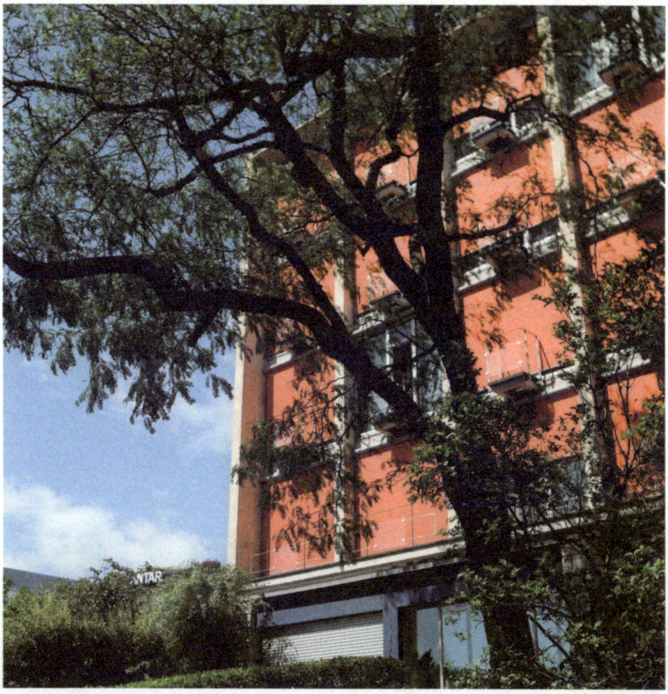

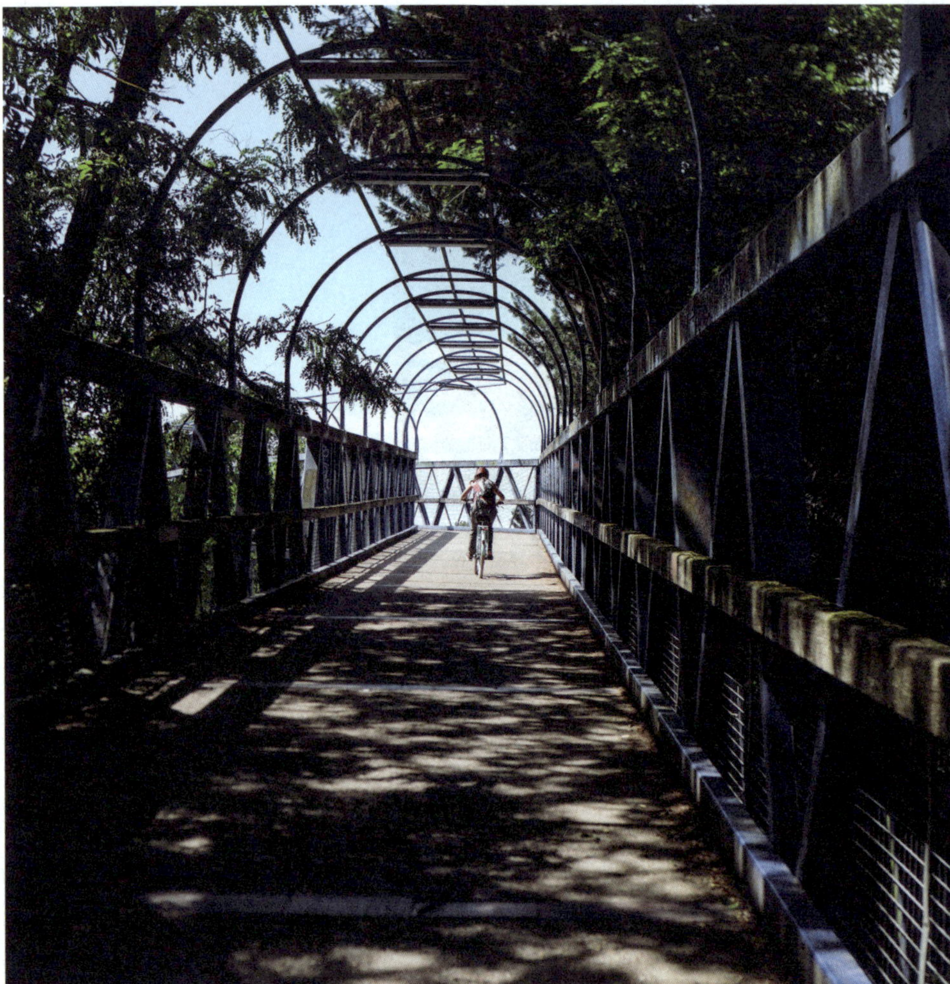

Sunshine at the end of the tunnel | *Coulée verte, Fontenay-aux-Roses.*

the end of the 19th century by Breton missionaries. It is also home to an architectural curiosity: Hangar Y, a former airship hangar that was transformed into an exhibition space in 2023 (see page 194).

Free admission.

92190 Meudon
onf.fr

- RER — C: Meudon - Val Fleury
- Transilien — Line N: Chaville - Rive Gauche
- Bus — 289, 389: Trivaux - Hangar Y
- Vélib' — Rue Audonnet, Chaville

285 TERRACE OF THE MEUDON OBSERVATORY

#TERRACEFORDAYS #PANORAMICVIEW
#SPRAWLINGLAWNS

What better way to admire Paris than on a 61,000-m² terrace? Perched above the city, the Domaine national de Meudon is one of Greater Paris's unique vantage points from which to contemplate the wonders of the capital away from the crowds. Once you have taken in the view, if the sun is shining, you will be able to enjoy the lawns lined with plane trees and take a closer look at the observatory built in 1876. You can also take a seat under the vaulted ceilings of the resident café, the Loggia de l'Observatoire (laloggiameudon.com).

Open daily (opening times vary according to the season)

5, place Janssen, 92190 Meudon
meudon.fr

- RER — C: Meudon Val Fleury
- Bus — 169, 289, 389: Église de Meudon
- Vélib' — Place Jean-Jaurès, Meudon

PARIS

286 BATOBUS

#SEINE #SILENTCRUISE
#MONUMENTS

If you are already an expert on the history of Parisian monuments, no need to board a bateau-mouche for a multilingual guided tour. But don't let that stop you from taking a cruise along the Seine. Board the Batobus boat shuttle that will take you along the river from the Jardin des Plantes (5th arrondissement) to Beaugrenelle (15th arrondissement). On the way, you'll see all the highlights, from the Eiffel Tower® to Notre-Dame, and the Musée d'Orsay. If one trip isn't enough, your ticket gives you access to unlimited cruises for 24 or 48 hours. And for the addicts, go for the year-round pass for €70, or just €50 if you have an Imagine R card or a full Navigo pass.

Price: one-day pass €19, €9 for children aged 3–15.
Open year round.

batobus.com

- M — Lines 5, 10: Gare d'Austerlitz
- RER — C: Gare d'Austerlitz
- Vélib' — Place Valhubert, Paris 5th

287 CITÉ UNIVERSITAIRE

#AROUNDTHEWORLDINAPARK
#ARCHITECTURE #SPRAWLINGLAWNS

Tree-lined paths connecting impressive student residences; this could be the Harvard campus. The Cité Universitaire houses 12,000 students and researchers from all over the world (as you'll find out from the noise levels). Built at the end of the First World War, the Cité U is a unique architectural monument as well as one of the largest parks in Paris, with thirty-four hectares in total. Free guided tours are organized regularly to explore its nooks and crannies. The programme can be found on citescope.fr. Another (very) good tip: several of the Cité U residences have restaurants where you can sample food from around the world (see page 207).

Free admission.

17, boulevard Jourdan, 75014 Paris
Tel: +33 (0)1 44 16 64 00 / www.ciup.fr

- RER — B: Cité Universitaire
- Tram — T3a: Cité Universitaire
- Bus — 21, 216: Cité Universitaire
- Vélib' — Boulevard Jourdan, Paris 14th

288 COULÉE VERTE DU SUD PARISIEN

#FROMPARISTOMASSY
#BIKETRAIL #NATURE

The Coulée verte du Sud Parisien is a landscaped and fully signposted bicycle trail where you can enjoy a long, peaceful bike ride for 12 km from Paris to Massy away from any traffic. The trail connects a string of parks and gardens, including the famous Parc de Sceaux (see page 205). It also passes near the Parc de la Vallée-aux-Loups (see page 197) in Châtenay-Malabry, which houses the former residence of Chateaubriand where he began writing his *Memoirs from Beyond the Grave*. And don't worry if you're not ready to compete in the Tour de France: the trail, while hilly, is accessible to all.

12 km bike trail between Paris and Massy.
In the Paris – Massy direction, departures from the Place de Catalogne in Paris (14th arrondissement) or the Malakoff-Plateau de Vanves metro station in Malakoff (92).

destination.hauts-de-seine.fr/coulee-verte.html

289 JARDIN CATHERINE LABOURÉE

#CLEARING #URBANTANNING #SPRAWLINGLAWNS

Pay attention or you just might walk right past it. The Jardin Catherine Labourée looks like a clearing in the middle of the city. Its large lawns lined with lime trees and poplars are a popular tanning spot. As a point of interest, the secret entrance to the Prime Minister's Hôtel de Matignon residence is just across the street, which explains the constant police presence on the footpath. While you're in the area, take the opportunity to visit the Chapelle Notre-Dame de la Médaille Miraculeuse. Located at 140 rue du Bac, it is one of the ten most visited cultural sites in Paris and houses the embalmed body of Catherine Labourée, to whom the Virgin appeared in 1830.

Open daily.

29, rue de Babylone, 75007 Paris
paris.fr

- M — Lines 10, 12: Sèvres-Babylone
- Bus — 86: Vaneau - Babylone
- Vélib' — Boulevard des Invalides, Paris 7th

290 JARDIN DES PLANTES

#MAJESTICFLORA #AMAZONJUNGLE #FREEGUIDEDTOURS

The Jardin des Plantes is probably the most beautiful location for a botany class. Along its paths, maintained by an army of passionate gardeners, you will get to know the flora while enjoying the beauty of the area. To complete your studies, thematic and free guided tours take place on Tuesdays in July and August (the full programme is available at jardindesplantesdeparis.fr/fr/le-savoir-faire-des-jardiniers), where you can get to know the flora while enjoying the beauty of the surroundings. Above all, do not miss a trip into the Amazon jungle by way of the lush forest of the large greenhouses.

Price: Greenhouses: €7 (full price), €5 (3–25 year-olds) / Menagerie: €13 (full price), €10 (3–25 year-olds) / Free for under-3s
Free entry to the rest of the garden.
Open daily (opening times vary according to the season).

57, rue Cuvier, 75005 Paris
Tel: +33 (0)1 40 79 56 01 / jardindesplantesdeparis.fr

- M — Lines 7, 10: Jussieu
- Bus — 67: Cuvier - Jardin des Plantes
- Vélib' — Place Valhubert, Paris 5th

291 JARDIN DU LUXEMBOURG

#NONSTOPSPECTACLE #PEOPLEWATCHING #FAMOUSGARDENSOFPARIS

There is always something worth watching in the Luxembourg Gardens: the grace of tai chi enthusiasts, the many strides of the joggers, the wake of miniature boats on the pond, tennis matches, the clicking of pétanque balls, the concentration of the chess players, photography exhibitions on the park's metal railings or the many flower beds. Impossible to be bored here. Especially since you can get involved in all these activities yourself and become the centre of attention.

Open daily (opening times vary according to the season).

2, rue Auguste Comte, 75006 Paris
Tel: +33 (0)1 42 34 20 00 / jardin.senat.fr

- M — Lines 4, 10: Odéon
- RER — B: Luxembourg
- Bus — 38, 82, 84, 89: Luxembourg
- Vélib' — Rue Guynemer, Paris 6th

292 PARC MONTSOURIS

#SPRAWLINGLAWNS #LAKE #PONYRIDES

Hilly, populated with remarkable trees with intriguing shapes, birds nesting near the lake and statues scattered on its wide lawns, the Parc Montsouris is a piece of nature touched by grace. Urban dwellers in search of a moment of tranquillity can lie down on the grass, study plant varieties, eat a waffle at the kiosk, take their children for a pony ride or follow in the footsteps of the many joggers. To prolong the pleasure, take a walk through the streets bordering the park with their magnificent houses.

Open daily (opening times vary according to the season)

2, rue Gazan, 75014 Paris
paris.fr

- RER — B: Cité Universitaire
- Tram — T3a: Cité Universitaire
- Bus — 21, 216: Parc Montsouris
- Vélib' — Boulevard Jourdan, Paris 14th

SCEAUX

293 PARC DE SCEAUX

#EIGHTHWONDEROFTHEWORLD #THREEINONE #SPRAWLINGLAWNS

With its 180 hectares, the Parc de Sceaux manages the feat of combining three great Parisian classics in one place: the estate of the Château de Versailles, the Bois de Boulogne and the Parc Montsouris. There are French-style gardens lined with alleys with views worthy of Versailles converging towards a castle, a wood covered with paths just like its Boulogne cousin, and large lawns where you can lounge in the Montsouris style, without ever being short of space. And that isn't all. In addition, there is a magnificent playground built entirely in wood and designed by children themselves, a large outdoor swimming pool (which is due to reopen in 2025), a canal where you can fish for carp and several cafes to keep hunger at bay.

Open daily (opening times vary according to the season).

Avenue Le Nôtre, 92330 Sceaux
Tel: +33 (0)1 41 87 29 50
domaine-de-sceaux.hauts-de-seine.fr

- RER — B: Parc de Sceaux, La Croix de Berny
- Bus — 6, 92: Parc de Sceaux
- Vélib'— Rue du Docteur Berger, Sceaux

VERRIÈRES-LE-BUISSON

294 FORÊT DE VERRIÈRES

#ONFOOT #CYCLING #WIDEPATHS

To really enjoy the Verrières forest as Henri IV did in his time, head for its centre. Located between the A86 and N118 motorways, you'll struggle to hear the birdsong along its edges. In order to escape the noise and discover its 575 hectares of oaks and chestnut trees, venture straight into its heart, on foot or by bike as its paths are wide, flat and some are even paved.

Route de Montauzin, 91370 Verrières-le-Buisson
onf.fr

- RER — C: Igny
- Tram — T6: Pavé Blanc
- Bus — 196, 294: Croix Belle Avoine or Les Antes
- Vélib'— Place Aimé Césaire, Meudon-la-Forêt

where to eat

CHÂTILLON

295 BARBEZINGUE

#ONEOFAKIND #TAPAS #MORETHANARESTAURANT

The Barbezingue is much more than a restaurant. It is also a barbershop, a jam session venue, a pétanque strip, a grocery shop and a wine bar. Chef Thierry Faucher, the commanding officer of this improbable mixture, worked in the Crillon® kitchens during the era of the three-starred Christian Constant. A devotee of bistronomy, this iconoclast has made his expertise accessible to everyone. At the bar, you can enjoy tapas including marrow bones in broth or veal bones to be gnawed on. On the first floor, you can sit on large wooden tables to enjoy an all-you-can-eat buffet for €31. For breakfast, you will be seated in the grocery shop and treated to homemade terrines and pastries for €16. Finally, for special occasions, you can enjoy a tasting menu for €60. It's just a shame the chef hasn't had the idea to open rooms yet.

All-you-can-eat buffet for €31 / tasting menu for €60.
Closed Sunday and Monday.

14, boulevard de la Liberté, 92320 Châtillon
Tel: +33 (0)1 49 85 83 50 / barbezingue.com

- M — Line 13: Châtillon-Montrouge
- Tram — T6: Centre de Châtillon
- Bus — 194, 394, 415: Centre de Châtillon
- Vélib'— Rue Gabriel Péri, Châtillon

ISSY-LES-MOULINEAUX

296 KOEDO

#STREETFOOD #JAPAN #VEGETARIANSUSHI

No, you're not going off the rails. There is indeed a bento shop on the platform of the Issy-Val de Seine tramway station. And you don't even need a Navigo pass to get your hands on the delicacies concocted by the chefs at Koedo, a tiny location with XXL flavours and a menu that changes daily. We tried an excellent aubergine stir-fry with tofu and curry, a kara age of Goma Amazu taro (a kind of fried chicken served with rice and vinegared raw vegetables), inari sushi (vegetarian sushi with caramelised tofu and vinegared rice) and a surprising vanilla waffle in the shape of a fish (a sure-fire hit with the younger palates). Everything is Japanese and fresh and the best part is that you can enjoy it all on a bench in the park on the nearby Île Saint-Germain (see page 198).

Price: dishes from €3.50 to €23.
Open Monday to Friday, 8.30am–8.30pm.

7, rue Rouget de Lisle, 92130 Issy-les-Moulineaux
Tel: +33 (0)1 46 42 08 74 / koedo.fr

- RER — C: Issy-Val de Seine
- Tram — Line T2: Issy-Val de Seine
- Buses — 126, 189, 260: Issy-Val de Seine
- Vélib' — Place Lafayette, Issy-les-Moulineaux

MONTROUGE

297 LA TABLE DE MAÏNA

#NIKKEICUISINE #TASTEBUDTRAVELS #SWISSCHALET

From France to Japan via Peru – a journey with an unforgiving carbon footprint. Except when you all these destinations are combined in one place. That's what the chef Maïna-Sophie Conil has done at La Table de Maïna. This restaurant specialises in Nikkei cuisine, a Japanese-Peruvian style of cooking that dates back to the period of Japanese immigration to Peru in the nineteenth century. A culinary art that the young woman learned in the kitchens of the great Japanese chef Nobu Matsuhisa. She reproduces it in her little restaurant, which looks like a Swiss chalet, with its wood-panelled walls. A word of advice: on your first visit, go for the "business" or "experience" menu, with several dishes to share so you can sample all of Maïna's influences: ceviche, kakiage (a kind of Japanese vegetable fritter), dry-aged beef... Your tastebuds will never have travelled so far.

Price: menu from €34.
Closed Monday and Sunday.

18, rue Périer, 92120 Montrouge
Tel: +33 (0)1 57 21 25 82 / latabledemaina.com

- M — Line 4: Mairie de Montrouge
- Bus — 128: République
- Vélib' — Avenue Verdier, Montrouge

PARIS

298 THE CITÉ UNIVERSITAIRE RESTAURANTS

#CULINARYVOYAGE #CURRYWURSTORBIBIMPAP #ENLARGEYOURPARISSELECTIONS

The Cité internationale universitaire de Paris is an astonishing campus on the edge of the Parc Montsouris in Paris, made up of 43 houses representing as many countries and regions, and home to 12,000 students, artists, and researchers (see page 203). The campus is home to several restaurants, three of which caught the eye (and the palate) of the Enlarge your Paris journalists: La Cafet' de la Maison Heinrich-Heine, where you can treat yourself to an authentic currywurst (open Monday to Saturday / maison-heinrich-heine.org), Café Zaïm, where you can enjoy Tunisian street food (open daily / cafezaim.fr), and Comptoir coréen, the place to be for a bibimbap (open daily / comptoircoreen.fr). But you can choose not to follow our advice and seek out other culinary journeys at the Cité U.

9C, boulevard Jourdan, 75014 Paris
Cité U: Tel: +33 (0)1 44 16 64 00 / www.ciup.fr

- RER — B: Cité Universitaire
- Tram — Line T3a: Cité Universitaire
- Bus — 21, 216: Cité Universitaire
- Vélib' — Boulevard Jourdan, Paris 14th

Family

BAGNEUX

299 LE PLUS PETIT CIRQUE DU MONDE

#JOINTHECIRCUS #SPECTACLE
#NOTALLTHATSMALL

Ladies and gentlemen, welcome to the smallest circus in the world! Despite its diminutive name, this circus arts centre has a lot to offer, with workshops and classes to learn circus techniques as well as other disciplines such as hip-hop, slackline or BMX. In addition to the workshops and training courses, the Plus Petit Cirque du monde also hosts shows and meet-ups. An ode to the beauty and singularity of Greater Paris!

Closed Sunday.

1, impasse de la Renardière, 92220 Bagneux
Tel: +33 (0)1 46 64 93 62 / lepluspetitcirquedumonde.fr

- RER — B: Fontenay-aux-Roses, Bourg-la-Reine then bus 390: Les Blagis
- Bus — 188: Rue des Brugnauts
- Vélib' — Avenue Jean Perrin, Fontenay-aux-Roses

MEUDON

300 ECOPARK LÉGENDES MEUDON

#NEVERLAND #TREETOPCABINS
#ADVENTURESINNATURE

It's a bit like Peter Pan's Neverland in the middle of the Meudon forest, just 6 km from the Paris *périphérique*. Designed to give children a chance to let off some steam in the middle of nature, Ecopark Légendes weaves its web between the trees with net mazes, trampolines, slides, treetop cabins and wooden games. There's every chance you'll be tempted back into childhood.

*Price: €12 for 1h30 (4 years and over) /
€5 (2–3 year olds with an accompanying adult).
Open from February to the Toussaint holidays inclusive /
Open Wednesdays, weekends, and public holidays
and open daily during zone C holidays.
For children aged 2 and over. Booking recommended.*

Route du Pavillon l'Abbé, Marcel Bec sports centre, 92190 Meudon
Tel: +33 (0)7 61 24 61 52 / ecopark-adventures.com

TO EXPLORE FURTHER

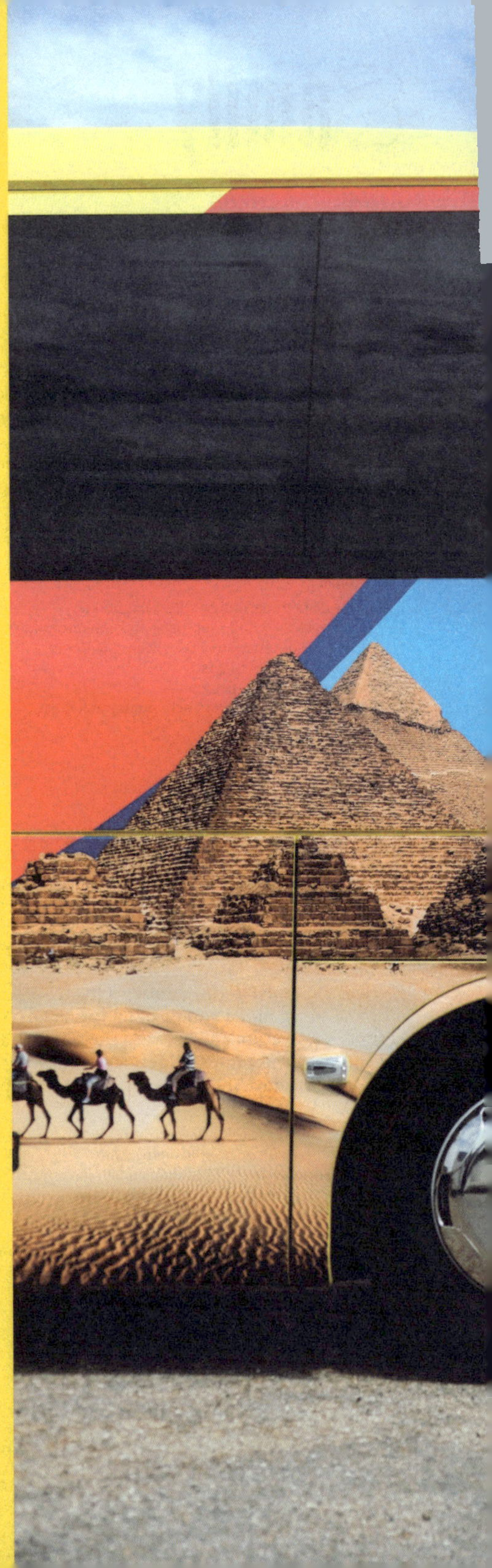

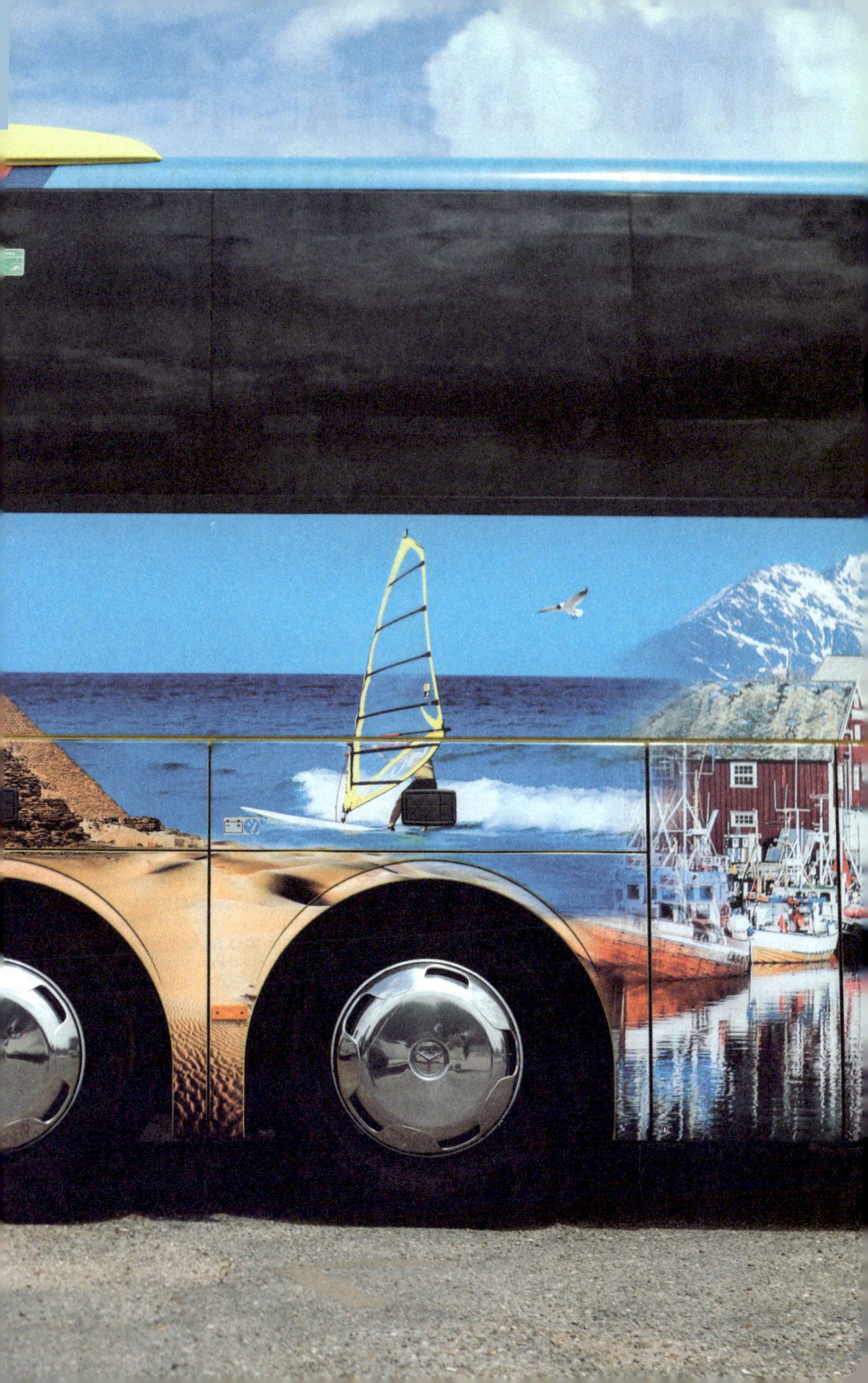

THE GREATER PARIS GUIDE CONTRIBUTORS

THE MAGASINS GÉNÉRAUX

Built in the early 1930s, the Magasins Généraux left their mark on industrial activity in Pantin for more than four decades. Abandoned and falling into disuse at the end of the 1990s before being converted by the architect Frédéric Jung, they began their second life in 2016 as the headquarters of the advertising agency BETC. They now house both workspaces on the upper floors and a cultural venue founded by the agency on the ground floor: the Magasins Généraux.

Open to all, the Magasins Généraux' year-round programme of exhibitions and events aims to seek out, support and showcase the emerging artistic and cultural talent of the moment. As a laboratory where different creative fields come together, the Magasins Généraux are a platform for unexpected encounters, a space for exchange and debate open to the city, where the art and ideas of tomorrow converge and come to life.

ENLARGE YOUR PARIS, THE LEADING MEDIA OUTLET FOR GREATER PARIS

While the suburbs of Paris are often portrayed through a multitude of clichés, Enlarge your Paris has been providing a different perspective on Greater Paris since 2013. An independent, free media outlet launched by a group of journalists, Enlarge your Paris reaches more than a million readers annually and has become the leading lifestyle media outlet for Greater Paris, with almost 4,000 articles available on enlargeyourparis.fr. Enlarge your Paris also regularly organizes hikes open to all, to help people discover the treasures of the outer suburbs, attracting a total of some 3,000 hikers of all ages and backgrounds.

THE JOURNALISTS
THREE HASHTAGS AND THREE SELECTIONS

RENAUD CHARLES
CO-FOUNDER OF ENLARGE YOUR PARIS AND GREATER PARISIAN FROM HERMERAY

#SUBURBANPRIDE #NOMORECLICHÉS #ENLARGEYOURPARIS!!!!!

- La Bretelle [-> 181]
- Parc naturel de la Haute Vallée de Chevreuse [-> 80]
- The Butte des Châtaigners [-> 94]

VIANNEY DELOURME
CO-FOUNDER OF ENLARGE YOUR PARIS AND A NATIVE PARISIAN

#FORESTSEVERYWHERE #ILOVEMYNAVIGO #WORLDSBIGGESTMUSEUM

- MAC VAL [-> 177]
- Parc Georges-Valbon [-> 31]
- Potager du Roi [-> 80]

OLIVIER PICARD
SUBEDITOR OF ENLARGE YOUR PARIS AND GREATER PARISIAN FROM CHARENTON-LE-PONT

#GETAWAY #HERITAGE #CUISINE

- The Parc de la Vallée-aux-Loups [-> 193]
- The Château de La Roche-Guyon [-> 130]
- L'Ours [-> 116]

RÉMI BELOT
JOURNALIST FOR ENLARGE YOUR PARIS AND GREATER PARISIAN FROM ROMAINVILLE

#DISCOVERY #ASTONISHMENT #UNDERGROUND

- Rosa Bonheur à l'Ouest [-> 59]
- Le Kilowatt [-> 180]
- Magasins Généraux [-> 22]

JOSÉPHINE LEBARD
JOURNALIST FOR ENLARGE YOUR PARIS AND GREATER PARISIAN FROM NOISY-LE-SEC

#GREATERPARISSTORIES #GENTRIFICATIONALERT #SEINESAINTDENISSTYLE

- Château de Champs-sur-Marne [-> 105]
- MC 93 [-> 18]
- Kebab Ev'et by Samy [-> 35]

MANON GAYET
JOURNALIST FOR ENLARGE YOUR PARIS AND GREATER PARISIAN FROM MAULE

#PLAYGROUND #CREATIVITY #DIVERSITY

- The château de La Roche-Guyon [-> 130]
- Canoeing on the Epte [-> 128]
- Le P'tit Bistrot de Lucy [-> 135]

VIRGINIE JANNIÈRE
JOURNALIST FOR ENLARGE YOUR PARIS AND GREATER PARISIAN FROM CACHAN

#SOUTHOFTHEPERIPH #SEINESIDE #ISSYCESTPARIS

- The Parc de Sceaux [-> 205]
- La Table de Maïna [-> 206]
- Hangar Y [-> 194]

TINA MEYER
JOURNALIST FOR ENLARGE YOUR PARIS, INSTAGRAMMER ON @AUBERVILOVE AND GREATER PARISIAN FROM AUBERVILLIERS

#GOODTIMES #SIZEMATTERS #OFFTHEBEATENTRACK

- Le Chinois [-> 25]
- La Station – Gare des Mines [-> 29]
- Le 19M [-> 38]

JULIE GOURHANT
JOURNALIST FOR ENLARGE YOUR PARIS, INSTAGRAMMER ON @LEGRANDPARISVUDEMAMINI AND GRAND PARISIAN FORM VITRY

#ILOVEMYSUBURBS #CYCLEGREATERPARIS #KUNDALINIYOGAVITRY

- Les Pieds dans le Plat [-> 183]
- Chakchouka [-> 180]
- Une friterie à Vitry [-> 181]

THE PHOTOGRAPHER
THREE HASHTAGS AND THREE SELECTIONS

VINCENT MIGRENNE
PHOTOGRAPHER, PHOTO-CAPTION-WRITER AND GREATER PARISIAN FROM THE 18TH ARRONDISSEMENT

#NOCLICHÉS #CLEARYOURMIND #CHILL

- Canoeing on the Epte [-> 128]
- Musée Bourdelle [-> 196]
- La Maison du Rocher [-> 154]

Eleven long-distance hiking trails criss-cross Greater Paris. To make them more accessible, the journalists at Enlarge your Paris have teamed up with data visualization specialists Wedodata to design a map inspired by the metro and the Transilien: the "Randopolitain". The map uses the routes of the Fédération française de la randonnée pédestre (French hiking federation) and the Comité régional d'Île-de-France de la randonnée pédestre (Île-de-France regional hiking committee), with the added bonus of the location of train stations and metro stops to access them. And since 2022, Enlarge your Paris, in partnership with Transilien SNCF and the Fédération française de la randonnée pédestre en Île-de-France, has been organizing a series of 100 hikes in the lead up to the Olympic Games.

More information on randopolitain.fr

MAP OF THE LONG-D

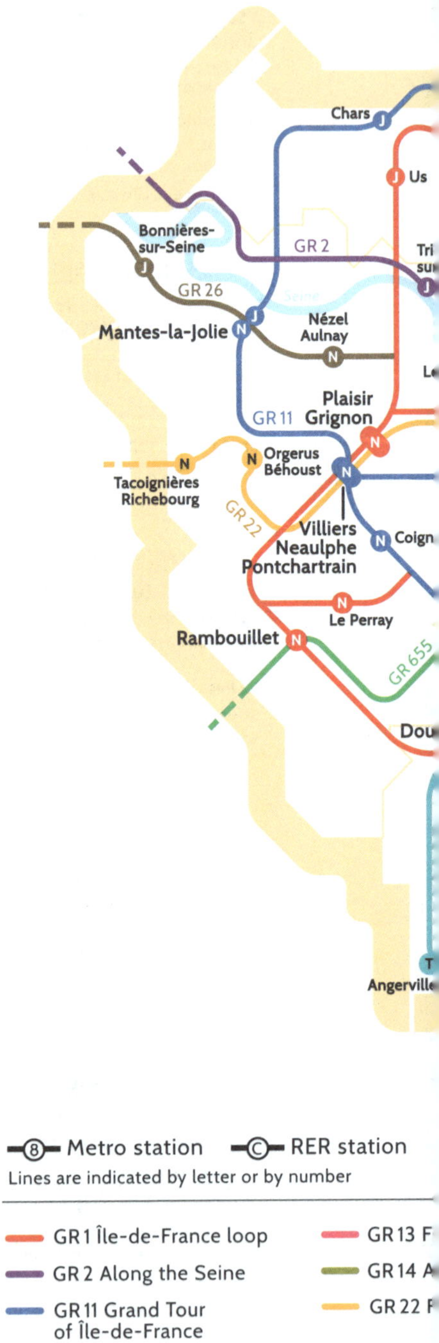

THE RANDOPOLITAIN

[cut off]CE HIKING TRAILS IN ÎLE-DE-FRANCE AND ACCESS POINTS BY TRAIN AND METRO

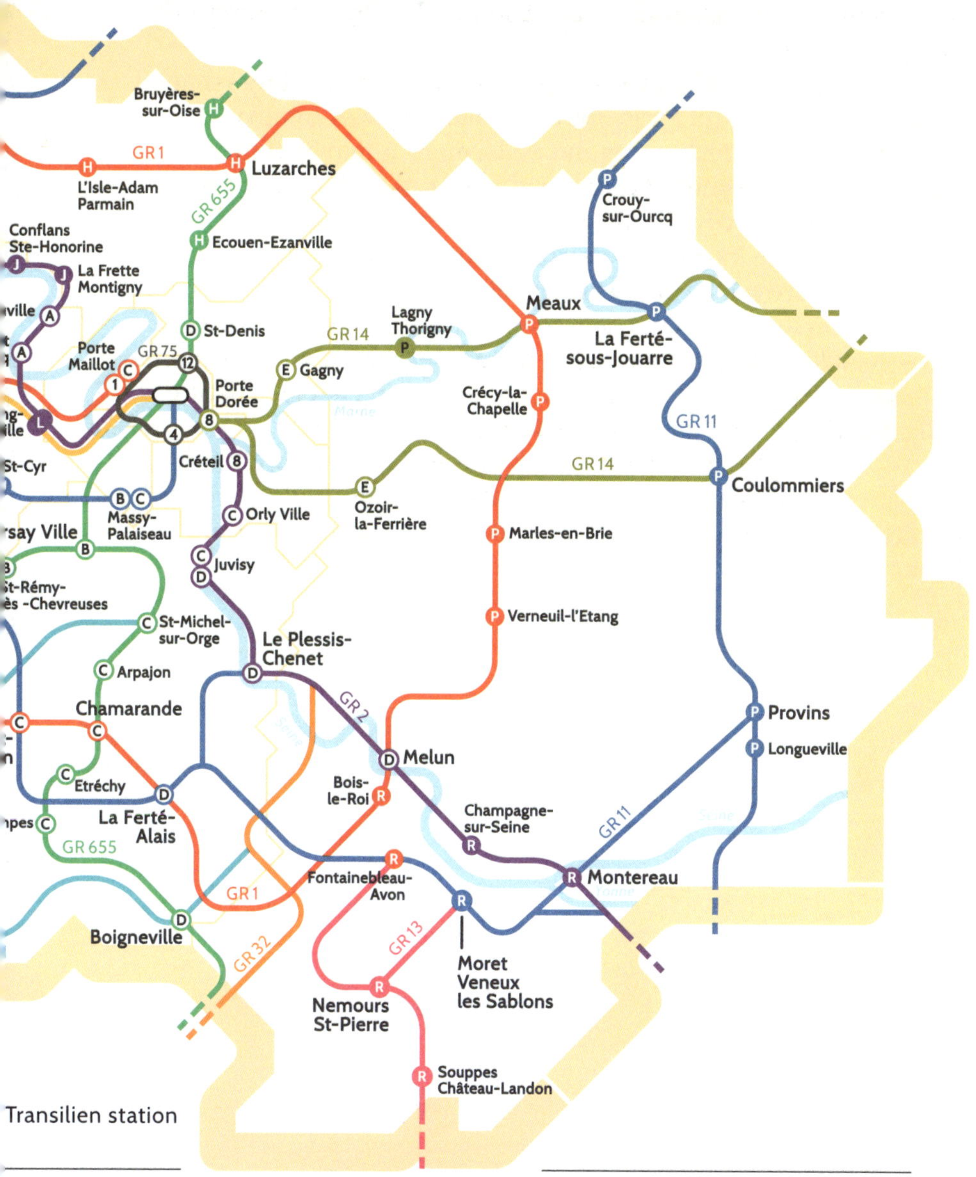

Transilien station

[…]ntainebleau to Burgundy

[…]e trail

[…]aris to the Mont-Saint-Michel

GR 26 From the Yvelines to the Calvados

GR 32 From the Seine to the Loire

GR 75 Inner Paris loop

GR 111 Essonne loop

GR 655 *Via Turonensis*, one of the Santiago de Compostela trails

with WEDODATA

#EXPLOREPARIS

Explore and rediscover Greater Paris.

Be inspired by our original tours, unusual experiences, walks through under-the-radar places, and come and enjoy adventures off the beaten track.

#ExploreParis is the leading platform for guided tours that reveal a different side of Paris, one that is buzzing with creativity, urban agriculture, third spaces and much more. A human dimension and conviviality are central to the exploration of each destination. Come along and discover a cosmopolitan, sustainable and festive Greater Paris with its parks, waterways and neighbourhoods, a place where adventure can be found around every corner.

Visits to unexpected heritage sites, street art tours, cruises and waterside activities, discovery of artisanal expertise, outdoor sports, culinary secrets – both local and from much further afield –, nature walks, workshops and unusual activities...

Discover Greater Paris as you've never seen it before, in the company of passionate people. Greater Paris will soon hold no more secrets for you! Dozens of tours are available online every day on ExploreParis.com

PARTNERS

THIS GUIDE WAS PUBLISHED WITH THE SUPPORT OF THE FOLLOWING MAJOR PARTNERS WHO ARE COMMITTED TO GREATER PARIS:

PARIS AÉROPORT
PARIS VOUS AIME

Société des Grands Projets

Plaine Commune GRAND PARIS

RATP

#ExploreParis
Les acteurs du tourisme métropolitain s'engagent

BETC

in Seine Saint-Denis

VILLE DE PARIS

eDF

LA POSTE

Métropole du Grand Paris

media transports
Pour une publicité utile

Disneyland PARIS

Région îledeFrance

GRAND PARIS EXPRESS

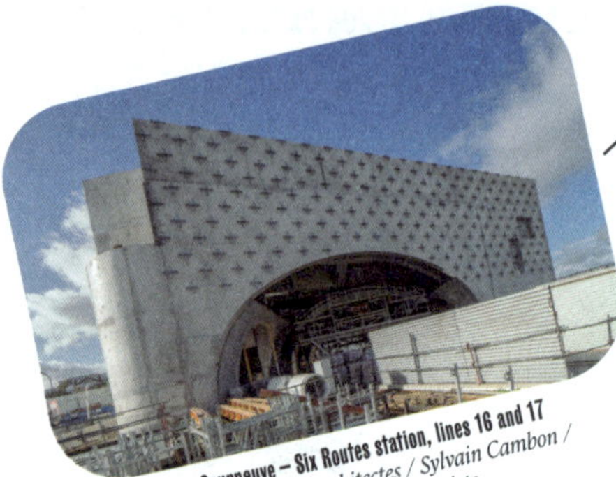

La Courneuve – Six Routes station, lines 16 and 17
©Chartier Dalix Architectes / Sylvain Cambon / Société des grands projets

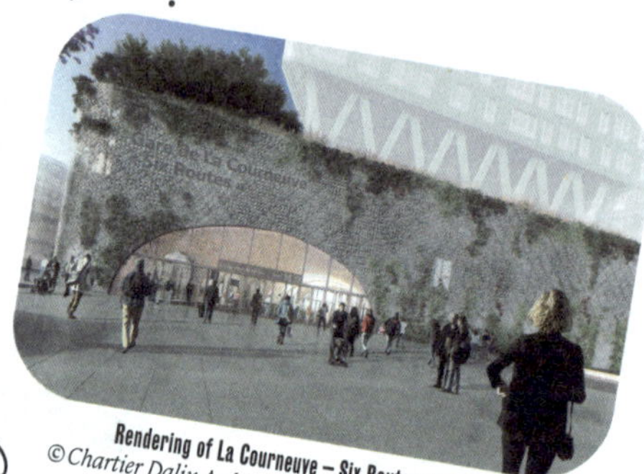

Rendering of La Courneuve – Six Routes station
©Chartier Dalix Architectes / Société des grands projets

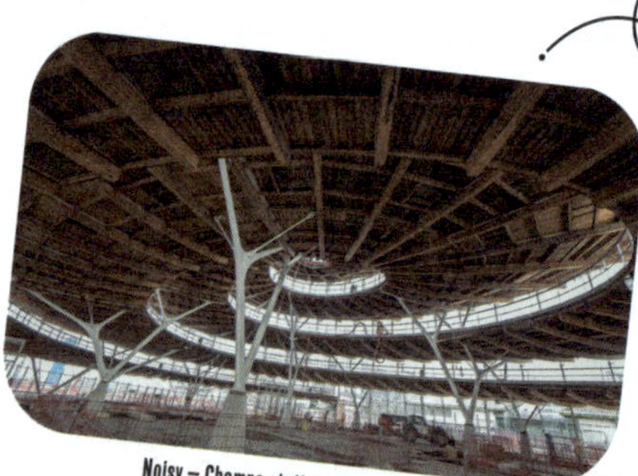

Noisy – Champs station, lines 15 and 16
©Agence Duthilleul / Gérard Rollando / Société des grands projets

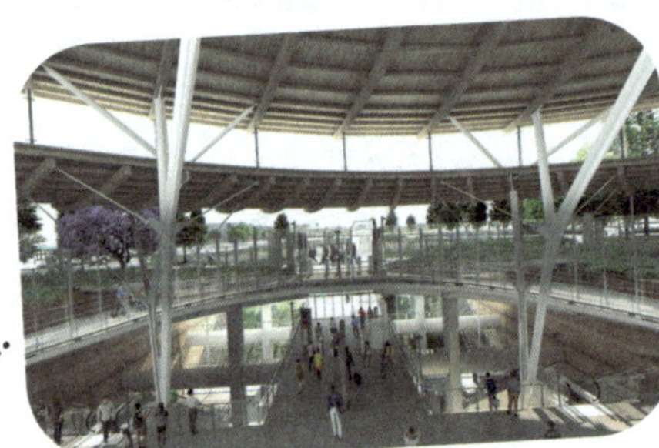

Rendering of Noisy – Champs station
©Agence Duthilleul / Société des grands projets

A NEW METRO: THE PROMISE OF A BETTER CITY

The Grand Paris Express is much more than a metro. Much more than a transport project. It is a promise of equality, made a decade ago and now becoming a reality, supported by Société des Grands Projets. In a metropolitan Paris defined by excessive centralisation, the new metro is turning the tables, breaking down boundaries, connecting communities, and bridging divides. It gives local authorities the opportunity to redesign entire neighbourhoods, with new homes and more social diversity. It means they can redefine the way people move around the city and rethink public spaces to reflect how they will be used in the future, putting pedestrians and cyclists first. The suburbs can take their rightful place in the city's fabric. Moreover, there is no intention of imposing an urban master plan on the 68 station districts. On the contrary, the new metro will open up a whole new world of possibilities, revealing a wonderful natural, urban, cultural, and sporting heritage. It will be a symbol of living together in a rapidly changing Greater Paris, and an invitation to travel and socialise.

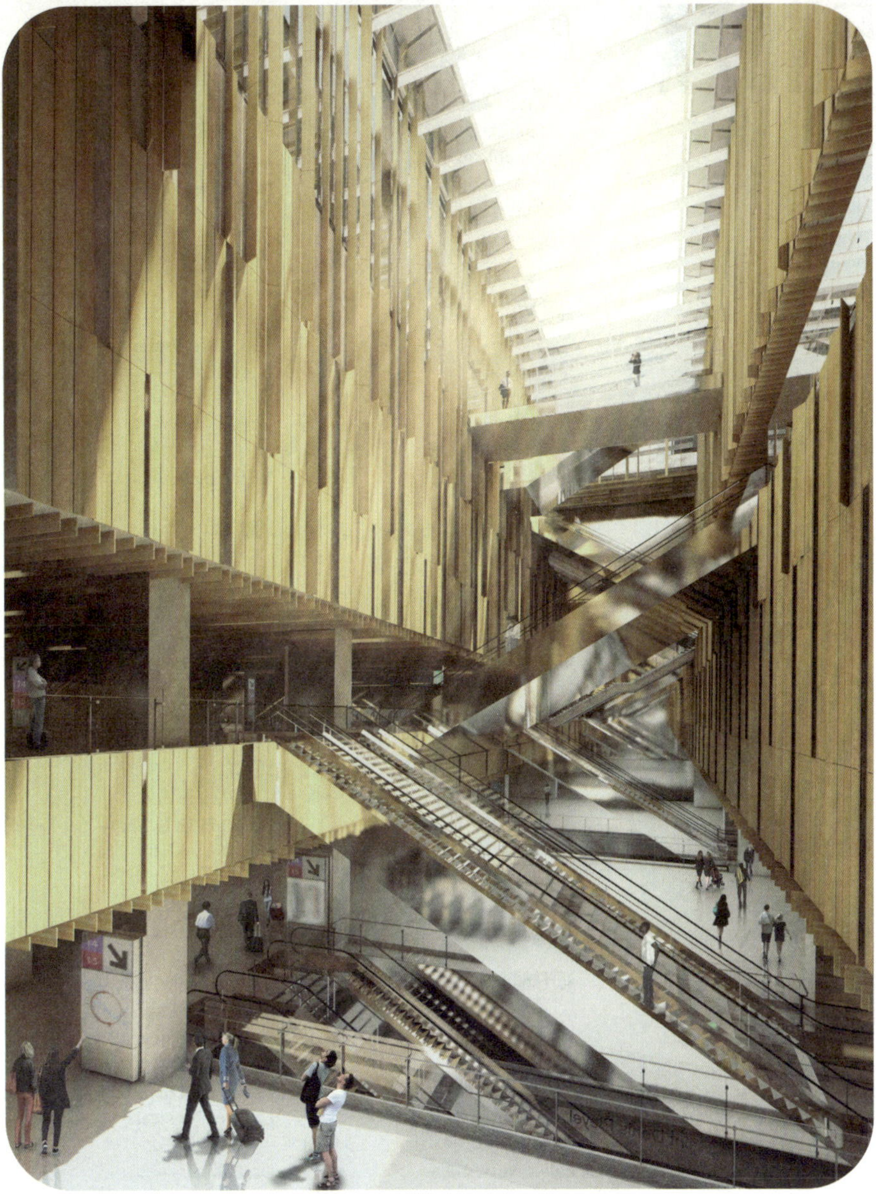

Rendering of Saint-Denis – Pleyel station | *© Kengo Kuma & Associates / Société des grands projets*

SAINT-DENIS – PLEYEL, THE BEATING HEART OF THE PARIS METROPOLITAN AREA

Saint-Denis – Pleyel station, designed by the world-renowned architect Kengo Kuma, will welcome its first passengers in time for the 2024 Olympic and Paralympic Games. The station will have a direct connection to Paris Orly Airport via the line 14 extension, and will gradually see the arrival of lines 15, 16, and 17 of the Grand Paris Express, making it one of the city's key interchanges. Eventually, 250,000 passengers will pass through the station every day, under the gaze of 108 Venus sculptures by the French artist Prune Nourry.

INDEX

D

E

F

G

I

N

O

P

President
Rémi Babinet

Publication director
Julia Dartois

Editorial directors
Renaud Charles
and Vianney Delourme

Publication managers
Caroline Arce Ross
and Émeric Descroix

Editorial manager
Prune Spire de Galard

Creative director
Aurélie Scalabre

Art direction, graphic design and production
Gr20paris

Photographs and captions
Vincent Migrenne

Translation from the French
Marc Feustel

Maps
Institut Paris Region and GR20paris

Printer
Musumeci
Loc. Amérique, 97
11020 Quart (AO)
Valle d'Aosta – Italy

ACKNOWLEDGEMENTS

Enlarge your Paris collaborated with the following people for this edition: Félix Barres, Karen Bastien, Rémi Belot, Audrey Bizet, Juliette Boisdormant, Alain Charles, Marianne Deula, Alicia Dorey, Malo Duquenne, Marc Feustel, Manon Gayet, Julie Gourhant, Virginie Jannière, Sophie Le Renard, Guillaume Le Roux, Joséphine Lebard, Jean-Fabien Leclanche, Anaïs Lerma, Corinne Martin-Rozès, Tina Meyer, Faustine Prévot, François Prosper, Virginie Senizergues, Lucinda Terreyre and Noé Termine.

The following people at BETC also contributed to this guide: Mercedes Erra, Chloé Bourdyot, Quentin Cordray, Benjamin Coton, Pierre-Charles Hegron, Saskia Millasseau, Lida Pour-Momen-Arabi, Marie-Caroline Pupin, Laurence Veyssière.

The Greater Paris Guide is produced by Enlarge your Paris and Magasins Généraux, created by BETC.

The Greater Paris Guide is published by Magasins Généraux,
7, rue de l'Ancien Canal 93500 Pantin.
magasinsgeneraux.com / lesgrandsparisiens@magasinsgeneraux.com

Registered as a single-shareholder €1000 simplified joint-stock company 808 293 823 RCS Bobigny

Legal Deposit: March 2024
Printed in May 2024

Portrait of Sarah Ourahmoune [p.11]: fresco by @Marko39 / Quai de l'Allier, Paris [p.14]: Florian Schneider Media ODV / Les Magasins Généraux [p.15 and p.19]: architect Frédéric Young / Playground Duperré [p.15]: basketball court Stéphane Ashpool and Ill Studio / Foreground building [p.19]: SOA architects / Background building [p.19]: Clément Vergély architects / Street Art, Montreuil [p.20]: SEYB art ©Adagp, Paris, 2024 / Rendez vous : Jade [p.20]: Mathieu Walter and Christophe Béesau / Passerelle de l'Hôtel de ville, Pantin [p.21] / 25 degrés Est bar, Paris 18th [p.24] / Restaurant Siseng [p.27]: 82 quai de Jemmapes, 75010 Paris / Nana bistrot thaï MK2 Quai de la Loire, Paris [p.28] / Papeterie Sill, Services commerciaux et show-room [p.32] : 146, quai de Jemmapes - BP 248 75464 Paris Cedex 10/ Les Grands Moulins BNP, Pantin [p.32] / Chanel Papyrus [p.33] : 8 rue du Cheval Blanc, Pantin , Quadri Fiore Architecture / Clim Up Aubervilliers [p.39]: 111, avenue Victor Hugo 93300 Aubervilliers / Jardin du Carroussel, Paris [p.43] / Les chevaux de Marly, Champs Elysées, Paris [p.46] / Passerelle Léopold-Sédar-Sanghor, Paris [p.47]: architect Marc Mimram / Luxor Obelisk, place de la Concorde, Paris [p.50] / Pont Alexandre III, Paris [p.50]: statues *La renommée des arts, La Renommée des sciences* – sculptor Emmanuel Frémiet; *La renommée au combat* - sculptor Pierre Granet; *Pégase tenu par la renommée de la Guerre* – sculptors Léopold Steiner and Eugène Gantzlin / Administrative building of the Parc de St Cloud estate [p.53] / Les Marches restaurant [p.58]: 5 rue de la Manutention, Paris / Rosa Bonheur sur Seine [p.58]: Port des Invalides, quai d'Orsay, Paris - architecture by Ronzatti / Seine, view of La Défense [p.63] / Gardens of Versailles [p.67]: Blue Fox Travel bicycles / Forest of Rambouillet [p.70 and p.82]_/ Parc du château de Rambouillet [p.71] / Marché Notre-Dame, Versailles [p.75] / Ferme des 4 étoiles, Auffargis [p.78 and p.79] / Jardins du parc de Versailles [p.82]: *Cléopâtre mourant* by Jean-Baptiste Goy / Vélodrome national de Saint Quentin en Yvelines [p.85]/ Butte d'Orgemont, Versailles [p.85]. Butte d'Orgemont, Argenteuil [p.89] / View of Argenteuil [p.92] / Ecopark Adventures, Sannois [p.95] / Parc du Vieux Moulin, Chelles [p.99] / Huatian Chinagora Hotel [p.111]: 1 place du Confluent France-Chine, Alforville / Football pitch in Saint-Maurice [p.111] / Hangar at the Olympic River, Vaires-Torcy [p.119] / Place de l'Église, Auvers-sur-Oise [p.131] / Major thoroughfare in Cergy-Pontoise [p.136] : ® work by Dani Karavan / "Tour des jeunes mariés", Cergy Pontoise [p.137]: AF Architectes / Maison du Rocher, Noisy-sur-École [p.141 and p.144]: Les bulles / Évasion Canine [p.145]: Forêt de Fontainebleau / Château de Vaux-le-Vicomte [p.151]: candlelit evenings / Tour Denecourt [p.155]: Pays de Fontainebleau tourist office, www.fontainebleau-tourisme.com / Casino Barrière, Enghien-les-Bains - architect Louis Soors [p.162] / Skatepark, Ivry-sur-Seine [p.171] / Passage Irène et Frédéric Joliot-Curie, Vitry-sur-Seine [p.175]: Nunca Art / Street art, boulevard Auriol, Paris [p.176]: C215 ©Adagp, Paris, 2024 / Le Kilowatt, Vitry-sur-Seine [p.179] / Pont du Port à l'Anglais, Vitry-sur-Seine - Alfortville [p.182] / Parc and château de Sceaux [p.187] / Jalsa, 2023 [p.191]: Subodh Gupta - collection Frédéric Jusset, Courtesy of Galleria Continua / Musée Bourdelle, Paris [p.199] / Tunisian pavilion of the Cité Universitaire, Paris [p.200] / German pavilion of the Cité Universitaire, Paris [p.201] / Spanish Pavilion of the Cité Universitaire, Paris [p.201] / Passerelle Pelnard, Fontenay-aux-Roses [p.202].

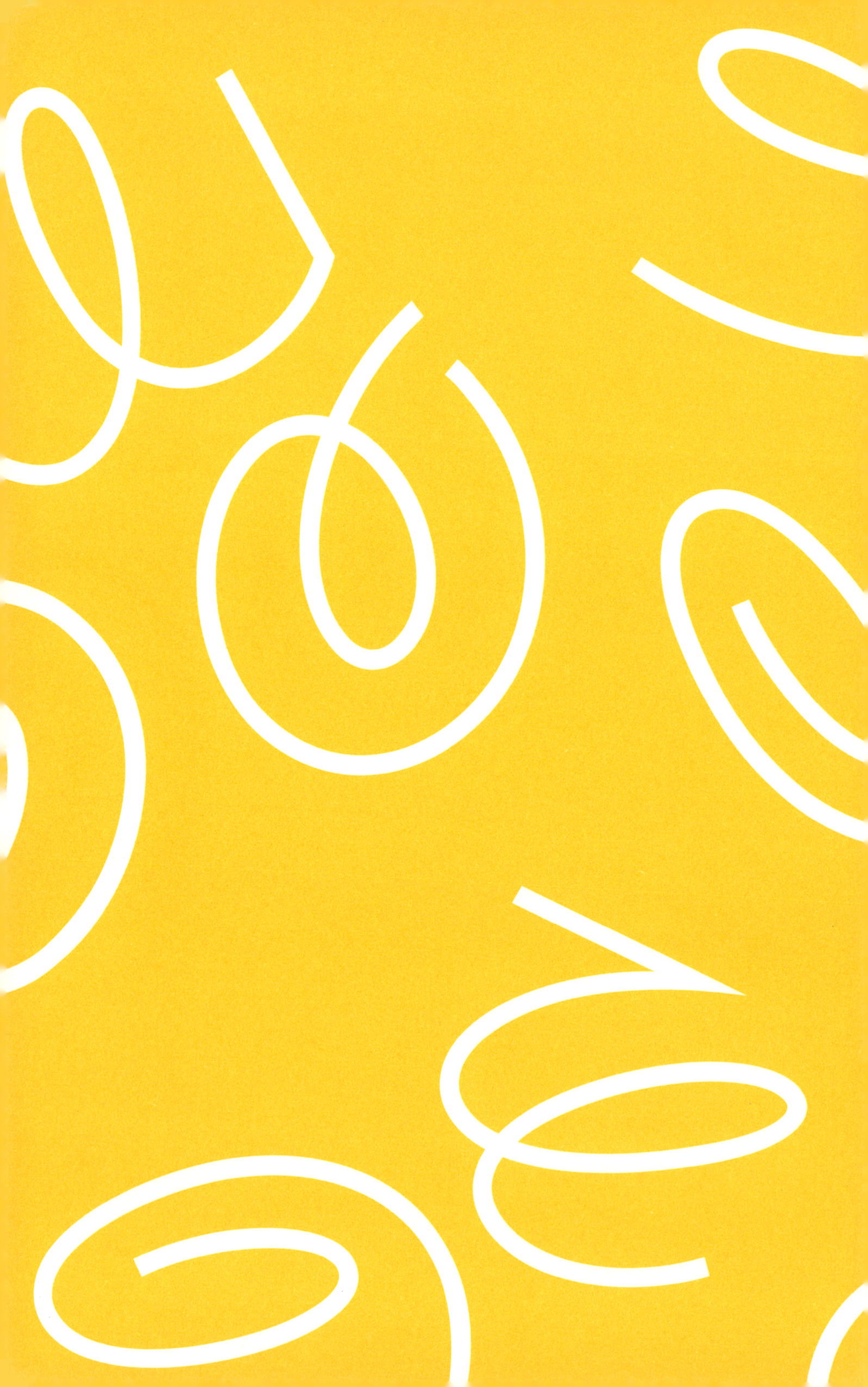